UNDER THE ABAYA

UNDER THE ABAYA

A Tapestry of Episodes from My 5-Year
Immersion into the Kingdom of Saudi Arabia

Dr. Elizabeth D. Taylor

WISDOM TO GO, INC.
San Francisco, California
Phoenix, Arizona. USA

UNDER THE ABAYA

Published in 2022 by Wisdom to Go, Inc.
San Francisco, California
Phoenix, Arizona. USA

Dr. Elizabeth D. Taylor, Publisher
Yvonne Rose/Quality Press, Book Packager
Cover Art - Nouf Ali Abdullah Al-Tallasy
Photography – Julian-Sebastian Taylor Gerdes

All Rights Reserved
All rights are reserved under the United States of America; therefore, no parts of this publication may be reproduced, stored in a retrieval system, or transmitted in any form or by any means—electronic, mechanical, digital, recording or any other without prior permission of the author or publisher—except for brief quotations in printed reviews.

This work depicts actual events in the life of the author as truthfully as recollection permits. While all persons within are actual individuals, names and identifying characteristics have been changed to respect their privacy.

The author may make any part of this book available to organizations that serve any of the following: youth organizations, educational organizations, training programs, cultural studies courses, or libraries upon written request to: etaylor@wisdomtogo.com

Copyright © 2022 by Dr. Elizabeth D. Taylor

Paperback ISBN #: 978-1-0878-9239-9

Hardcover ISBN #: 978-1-0879-7592-4

Ebook ISBN #: 978-1-0880-7819-8

Library of Congress Control Number: 2022913329

Appreciations

This book is written in appreciation of the women and men - Saudi nationals and ex-pats, close friends and acquaintances of Pakistani, Egyptian, Indian, and Sudanese descent, who witnessed me and showed me your stories and important things throughout this purposeful journey; and whose names are too numerous to list. You know who you are.

~ **Shukran**

UNDER THE ABAYA

A Fore Word
to Respected Readers

I do not purport to be an authority on the culture of Saudi Arabia. This book is an excursion into the fabric of life on the ground and the wonder of it all from my five-year immersion into the Kingdom of Saudi Arabia. It is the reality in the Kingdom as I saw and lived it. Saudi Arabia is an enigma to much of the world. Some would expect me to paint a rosy picture while some would expect a harsh and critical one. It is neither, but my firsthand exposé from living and working as a single professional woman at an acute transitional time in the Kingdom. This tapestry of episodes is culled from my best candid objective interpretations with no intent to give undo praise or to denigrate the culture of Saudi Arabia. Each episode is its own field of experience. These are stories and situations that stood out and made a lasting impression on me, and which I think are worth the telling.

This book is not a fiction. The episodes are not sequential, they did not occur that way, and are better expressed in themes that reflect their shared meaning. You can open and jump in at any episode that winks at you. It is my serene pleasure to share this journey with you and I thank you to step in and have a gander.

Alhamdulillah
Dr. Elizabeth D. Taylor

UNDER THE ABAYA

The Story Behind the Book Cover Art

Nouf, one of my university students invited me to an art gallery where her watercolor sketches were being showcased along with other Saudi artists' creations. I went without hesitation on a night in the middle of a hectic workweek. With bountiful Arabic coffee and deserts served in an elegant room adorned with cultural art and Saudi nationals ambling around, I was glad that I ventured out and sacrificed the few hours of sleep I would lose by going home and to bed late. There was a lot of interesting art on display, and one singular design that captivated me; I stood studying and appreciating it for a while. It was an odd depiction of an Arab woman, which pulled me in, and I found it hard to walk away. At that time, I was just getting situated into my newfound life in KSA and purchasing a painting was the last thing on my mind. Still, I was gripped by that imagery and took a photo of it so that it would live on my iPhone where I could view it at will.

Months later, it became ultra clear to me that because my unfolding experiences in KSA were so rich and compelling, I had to write a book. It was also then that the striking image of the Arabic woman in the art gallery piece kept coming back to me – her reticent sideways glance, her lively colors against the austere black and white background topped with a shimmering golden crown. It was altogether suggesting to me: *'That which you think you see is really something else, and a whole lot more'.* The image perfectly reflected the stories I was witnessing and living - they were the stories I wanted to tell. However, by that time, I had long forgotten the name of the art gallery that showcased the art piece. After making futile attempts to find the artist online or in social networks from what I could decipher from her signature on the piece, I resorted to having my driver spend an evening shuttling me to several notable galleries in town with me trying to recognize the building area and façade – going inside the galleries to see if they were familiar to me. I showed the photo of the art from my phone to several gallery proprietors in the hope that they would recognize the art piece or the artist. No luck. In frustration, after weeks of trying to find her, I let it all go.

Two years passed and my determination returned to find the artist and obtain the artwork if it was still available; because no other graphic image could match and capture what the book welling up inside me wanted to say and how it should be expressed. By that time, I really needed the artist's permission to use her artwork for the book. I had built a rapport with the Saudi artists' community by then and enlisted them to help me find the elusive artist of the enigmatic lady in the multi-colored abaya. In a short period of time a young female artist, also close to me, Aisha, found her and put me in touch with the artist whose name was Nouf Ali Abdullah Al-Tallasy, a Saudi national. In that moment of connecting with her I was elated and literally jumped up and down screaming in delight!

Nouf had already sold the artwork to a Kuwaiti Princess, and it was hanging on the wall in her palatial home far away. But Nouf readily contacted the Princess and secured her permission for me to use the art image as the book cover design for 'Under the Abaya'.

Nouf, I give my enduring respect and appreciation for your perfect artistic expression, and also for your gracious support, Princess Hessa Hamad Al-Khaled Al-Sabah.

The art piece is titled:
Al-Maliha with the Khimar.

Mashallah!

Contents

Appreciations V
A Fore Word to Respected Readers VII
The Story Behind the Book Cover Art IX
Contents XI
Prelude: A Mighty Door Had Opened XIII

Part One: CULTURE SHOCK, NATURALLY 1
   1. Walking Backwards Without a Plan – And God is Laughing 3
   2. The Frustration unto Hell 21
   3. The Bedouin on Friday 27
   4. Hating the Black – Loving the Black 31
   5. Crossing that Line – Close Encounter with a Saudi Gent 35
   6. See No Evil, Hear No Evil, Speak No Evil – It's Complicated 41
   7. The Missionary Meets the Muslim – More Questions than Answers 47
   8. Twice Dry 55
   9. An Inch Away from Thirty Lashes 62
   10. My Beautiful Cage 69
   11. Safe 75

Part Two: IN THE LIVES OF WOMEN AND MEN 79
   12. Womb Room 81
   13. Abiding the Abaya 86
   14. Beneath the Sparkling Chandeliers 93
   15. Reem – She Who Would Run with Wolves 101
   16. Dying To Be With One Another 107
   17. Tryst 113
   18. A Little Flirtation on the Way to Oud 118
   19. Planet of the Women – To Know Their Voices 122
   20. Graduation Night 127
   21. In the Men's Gathering Place – The Majlis 133
   22. Men Die Alone 139

Part Three: INTRIGUES OF THE ADVENTURE **145**
   23. Such Devotion 147
   24. The Surprising Things I Learned in the Grand Mosque 152
   25. Touching a Prince 157
   26. Magda's Meals 162
   27. His Robust Attention 166
   28. Next Oasis 171
   29. The Watch 175
   30. Yankee Doodle Dandy and Me 178
   31. Bacon, Lettuce and Tomato Sandwiches 181
   32. Why Stay? Because IT DOES Get Better 185

Part Four: JUST BELOW THE SURFACE **193**
   33. Dark Truths – Fear of Women 195
   34. "Miss, I Am Broken." 201
   35. Dowa's Tears 207
   36. Wegdan 217
   37. Sultan 222
   38. The Filipinos 226
   39. The Sad Prophets 235
   40. "Say, Bismillah!" 240
   41. The Jinn 243
   42. Runners 249
   43. Whatever Happened to Dr. Bonita? 258

Part Five: TOMORROW IS TODAY **265**
   44. God Save the Kingdom! 267
   45. Change and the Crown Prince 276
   46. "Woman, Drive!!" 288
   47. "Now Go Collect Your Driver's License." 293
   48. Riding in the Car with the 'Girls' – Things That Got Said 302
   49. Noura's Muhammad 310
In Closing 317
About the Author 318

Prelude:
A Mighty Door Had Opened

A convergence of factors led me to Saudi Arabia: professional calling, wanderlust, and race fatigue. In my truth, I went to Saudi Arabia to borrow some adventure, appreciate a change of scenery and to secure more meaningful and impactful work. That was also during a period when some sectors in the US economy were still regrouping from the latest financial crisis. In academia, full-time university teaching positions were in short supply in a vacillating and crowded market. I was in a state of ennui with it all, and it was daunting to even consider competing or pushing for the full-time professorial roles I had years prior; and I really did not care to try – for want of something fresh and new. Many of my academic colleagues in the US, both younger and older, were making a living teaching at several universities as adjuncts – taking on classes at different universities in order to fashion a full-time job and income. That seemed to be the norm, even for many seasoned professors. Some were driving miles on end and spending loads of time on the roads every day, going from one university to another, which made for a lot of long days and exhaustion. In fact, one of my dear colleagues suffered a stroke while driving the daily lengthy distances between the colleges where he was a professor.

That kind of professional life or reaching back for old stuff were not options for me. I was active in my part-time teaching and consulting and training business, but the work was becoming dull, dry, and too much of a hustle respectively, and I was more inspired to practice my trade on other horizons. Therefore, I sought a 'whole' assignment where I could plant my feet, focus, and work efficiently, while making a positive difference and some money at it, of course; and I was open to doing that anyplace in the world. Secondly, for much of my life, travel had been a strong value for me on which I spent 'boatloads' of cash over many years going to many places - touching five continents. Travel opened my eyes and heightened my perspectives; it grew me and was in my blood. The world was a wide and wondrous place - it was my playground. From that I entertained a lifelong desire to live for an extended time outside the United States. And then, one seeks relief where she can, away from inclement weather. As such, the racial climate in the United States had been a hazard throughout my life - replete in my experiences as a child, growing up, and as an adult. It was a long thrice-told tale that I had far outgrown, and in this mature phase of my existence, I needed a break from that.

I surprised myself by accepting the professional contract offer from Saudi Arabia. It was a heavy decision that also intimidated me, for up to then, I was hearing nothing good about the Kingdom of Saudi Arabia (KSA). A door had opened in answer to my desires and goals; however, I never imagined myself being transplanted to the Middle East, let alone Saudi Arabia. But as it would turn out, the Saudis needed me, and I needed them. My position would be Professor and Chair of the College of Business Administration on the female campus at Prince Mohammad bin Fahd University. It was a young and private university established in 2006 in the Eastern Province city of Khobar. My work activities would very soon extend into the business community and burgeoning campaigns to advance Saudi women into the workplace and as business leaders and entrepreneurs.

The hiring process was a breeze and fun, both on Skype and in person. I was flown to Washington DC and hosted in royal style by the Saudi university to meet its executive leadership team which had traveled from KSA to conduct interview sessions for select contract positions. Once hired, undergoing the rigorous process of getting medical examinations, lab tests and reports, security clearance and visa took almost two months - for the Saudis were very strict and particular about who they recruited into their country. Naturally, I did my research to better understand the 'lay of the land' where I was going. Key was that English was a common language in the Kingdom and in professional settings, which was good for me, as I was to later discover that Arabic was a difficult language to learn. But much of the country's information that I found online was too general; and it became evident that I would have a lot more to learn once I had boots on the ground. Some family and professional colleagues I had known for years were concerned and questioned my decision and even my frame of mind to venture so far away into the Middle East and particularly to Saudi Arabia, given the 911 history and all the negatives espoused about the country. But that had no effect on me. In my mind, since I had no direct experience with Saudi Arabia, I knew nothing; I trusted my decision, and was not going to allow other people's fears and phobias to interfere with my plans, however much they loved and cared about me, and vice versa. During the would-be five-year journey, it became clear to me that I was 'called' to the Kingdom by a higher hand.

A few days before my departure, I found a Middle Eastern shop in my home city of Phoenix, Arizona where I purchased two black abayas, or burkas as westerners called them, and scarves – which I knew I would be required to wear while in public, at all times in Saudi Arabia. Unbeknownst to me, ninety-five percent of the wardrobe in the four closets in my home which I had spent a small fortune on, would remain hanging untouched in those closets for the next five years. Moreover, I would be saying goodbye, for a long time to my habit of sporting leggings and tank tops outside in the hot weather in my home country. After spending hours in the shop trying on black abayas, I realized that the shape of my body did not agree with the abaya; in my opinion, it simply did not look right on me - more like a sack. I would later observe how flattering the abaya looked on the Saudi women and would wonder *'what was their secret?'* No worries, I would respect the custom, and wear the 'black', which was to be my first major hard adjustment to life in the Kingdom. The 'black' and the everyday feat of putting it on my body would be symbolic of my tenure in KSA – an immersive undertaking that was not just knee deep.

Here I Am, I AM Here

Traveling from the US to KSA was lengthy and depleting. After twenty cramped hours of coach in the air, I arrived dazed, drowsy, and bone-weary, at 2ish am on a Thursday in August. Not knowing where to go after deboarding the plane I followed the long sleepy drove of people, also disembarking, who did know where they were going and how to proceed. I tagged along behind them into an expansive assembly area where there were several designated stations for arriving people to go and line up: New Arrivals to the Kingdom in this line, Returning Ex-patriots (ex-pats) were in that line, Saudi Nationals in that one, and Migrants in another. There were hundreds of people in the area cueing up. The line for new arrivals was long and sluggish with travel-worn westerners in it, like me. As the line inched along, I slowly got my bearings realizing that I was there, in real time, in Saudi Arabia, the so-called 'strange, mysterious land'; and the next few moments as would the following days, presented unwonted trials for me.

My turn came to approach the counter where a youthful, and pleasantly stern Saudi man wearing the traditional white thobe and checkered red and white scarf (shemagh*) was to inspect my passport, visa, and flight tickets and take my index fingerprint. With no forewarning and something I did not expect, he quickly snapped a photo of me – exactly as I appeared at my worse from grueling travel - my face all puffed up with me looking ruffled and a bit glum, hair a mess, eyes droopy, etc. It was jarring – having the photo taken that way and the significance of it. "For your ID" he said. That upset me. The image of me that he captured in that photo was to be the official 'face' on my Iqama (Saudi Resident's ID) which would be stuck to me for the next five years. That moment of my arrival was forever imprinted in that awful snapshot. Sure, the diligent young man was just doing his job to process so many arrivals. But good grief! And woe was me! That dutiful sleight of hand certainly perked me up, right then and there. I would not know until later that the Iqama was the singular identification card that I was required to present for almost every essential privilege in the Kingdom: From making purchases, to banking and traveling, and to identify myself and verify my status - of who I was and why I was in KSA, whenever asked or required, which would be frequently. That 'face' would be lodged into the hardware of the Saudi public registry and information systems. I would come to detest that photo, which was so misrepresenting and could not be retaken. There was nothing more to it than that.

Once the young man checked me in and queried me, he lightened up when he noted that I was coming there under the classification as a 'teacher' – a professor at university. He smiled directly at me, giving me significant notice and welcome, and cheerfully waved me on. I would later come to know and appreciate the high value of my being in the Kingdom to 'teach'. I proceeded to collect my luggage from the baggage area, which was swarming with arriving people, and Pakistani and Indian men scurrying about them imploringly and trying to handle their bags, angling for needed tips. As I had no Saudi money to tip anyone and carrying the weight of exhaustion, I managed to lug my own heavy bags to customs. Customs was in no way frightful as I thought it might be. I had been warned not to bring 'this' and not to bring 'that' in case customs searched my bags and certain banned items would be confiscated or worse, I would be detained in some room and questioned. That did not happen. To my dreary delight there was a separate customs line for women which was shorter and faster. My bags rolled through the scanning conveyor with no incident, and I was whisked through with a gentle wave of the customs woman's hand. She was among the first Saudi women I would see wearing the black abaya in KSA. I too, was dressed modestly with loose-fitting dark clothes, which was acceptable at the airports upon arrival and departure.

After exiting customs, I looked for my name from the dozens of large white placards that drivers were holding outside in the partitioned area where travelers came through from customs. The university drivers were surely waiting for me amidst the thick late-night crowd, and I felt quietly relieved to see them there with my name, Dr. Elizabeth Taylor on the placard. I walked over to them and gave them my best tired smile. The two drivers were Pakistani men who handled my luggage and escorted me to a large black SUV in the airport parking lot. With few words they saw me into the vehicle and proceeded to steer the car through the darkest black flat night, for what felt like a very long time. They were taking me to a place I did not know and would not know until I got there, but where I could at last, lay my head - which was most immediately important to me. We arrived at the gated residential compound, passed through the security post and then to the door of my assigned villa. By then it was almost 4:00 am. Within ten minutes, once inside the modestly furnished and food stocked villa, I plopped into the king-sized bed to have three hours of anticipated luscious sleep before I was to get up and get ready in time to board the company transport bus at 7:15 am. It would take me to my office to begin my work assignment at 8:00 am.

After a few hours of light sleep which felt more like a catnap, I was wide-awake with a mix of anticipation and anxiety. In hindsight the tinge of fear I felt was from the stuff I had been told from others who questioned and warned me about venturing so far. But I was 'here' now, engaging the journey. Bathed and groomed, I unpacked the dreadful, ill-fitting black abaya that I bought in the US, put it on along with my game face, and stepped out of the villa with my rolling workbag in tow to board the bus, which was just about to leave. Although early, it was scorching hot outside, not much different from the Phoenix August weather. I had gone from one desert into another. But that much I could handle. It would be about a forty-minute ride to the university – and seeing the bus with its blue, orange, and tan company logo squatting on the road ahead as I approached was to be a most 'affective' sight for me from that first day on. I would either welcome or dread that sight at different times and from the hundreds of mornings and late afternoons I would spend on that bus to come. In my idiosyncratic mind, in that moment, I imagined that the bus was mockingly beckoning to me as if it were saying: *'I'm waiting for you Elizabeth, come on board. You don't want to miss this ride!'* Yes, the transport bus would play its part in the tour of the drama, intrigues, downfalls, and delights yet to unfold in the desert land of which I would be both, witness and subject.

I could not see it the night before, arriving in the dark, but now in broad daylight, there was so much sand! There was sand that was silky smooth and billowing through the air, sand that was rock coarse with jagged ridges fastened to the ground, and sand in between – sands going on forever - everywhere. Whoever made the comment that there were more stars in the universe than grains of sand upon the earth was surely exaggerating. Well, they had not been where I was standing, seeing what I see, I thought. Here, the sands ruled.

Upon entering the university halls, I was swiftly engulfed in a sea of young Saudi ladies in their late teens to early twenties, ranging from plain, pretty, to mostly drop-dead gorgeous in cream, honey, tan, tawny, and darker hued skin, and of all body types, wearing the black abayas, hijabs* and niqabs*. They were freshman, sophomore, junior and senior students, many pacing themselves to their classes and others camped out on the floors along the corridors with their coffees, snacking on za'atar* and meat breads, chocolates, chips, and pastries - visiting with friends between classes. Hundreds of pairs of precisely sculptured eyes were taking me in as I was taking them in. I was in amazement at the burst and discharge of exotic beauty, Arabic voices, intoxicating scents, youthful rush, and thousands of footsteps – all women, all wearing the 'black', hugging books and satchels, on their phones – the hustle bustle of going about the business of getting an education being played out there in that grand old desert, as it would be anyplace else on earth. It was at that juncture that I knew for sure that I was far from home, and that I was in for some next-level 'work' - both inside and outside myself in order to be 'here' and stay 'here'.

I did not know where to go standing there in the wide busy halls, as no instructions were given to me by the persons who handled my hiring process; just to report to the Human Resources (HR) office on said date – wherever that was. There I stood, among thousands of young Saudi women, feeling their energy buzzing around me. I just hung there feeling myself so foreign, yet, like a child in wonderment until a young woman approached me and drew me out of that spell – she was Jane, who was to be my secretary. I must have been conspicuous enough for her to recognize me. For one thing, my abaya was much too upscale compared to what the Saudi students were wearing. It had rhinestones on it; it left skin exposed at the neckline and was slightly tapered at the waist, making it a wee bit suggestive of my female form underneath. The abaya that I so painstakingly chose to buy was more like a modest evening gown. I probably overdid it while picking out something that was remotely suitable to my taste in the shop back in the US. But I fit right in for the most part because many of the Saudi students were my same skin tone.

Jane took me to the HR office where I registered my arrival and signed the two-year contract that would start me on my leadership assignment on the female campus and other associated roles. Jane was a petite Filipino woman who was 42 years-old and looked 25. She produced an amiable non-assuming waddle in her walk as she led and showed me around the campus halls, ending up at my office, which I found graciously large and well-appointed with a panoramic view of the vast sprawling desert outside. *"Wow, I must be really important"*, I thought. The office cabinets and desk were bare. While I had a specific program mandate to fulfill and faculty to supervise, there was no position description, no manuals, or basic files or notes to review. There was no one to greet me to show me the ropes, no one assigned to coach or provide guidance on my responsibilities, and no one coming; all were clear signs that the university was having growing pains. I was on my own - literally hitting the ground running; and I was going to take the newly-established position and make it my own, which was perfectly fine with me. Jane and I instantly liked and took to each other, and later that day on the bus ride home, another western woman offered to take me to a shop where I could buy a low-key abaya. That first day in KSA was an 'okay' start.

My full-on involvement with Saudi society and culture occurred during a novel transitional period in the Kingdom marked by the changeover of power from King Abdullah bin Abdulaziz Al Saud to that of King Salman Al Saud, and by extension, to the Crown Prince Mohammed bin Salman Al Saud - two rulers with strikingly different leadership styles and agendas for the Kingdom. But women 'by fate', would be at the center of both agendas. Many pivotal changes were on the horizon, even the possibility of women driving. The professional and leadership role I took on in the Kingdom was naturally a part of the rising course of action or campaign, to support the education and uplift of Saudi women. While Saudi women had been attending college since the

1970s, the period in which I was there was during a surge in their educational trajectory, whereby women were given greater access to education without boundaries. A western and Saudi collaboration generated and installed a western-based model of education at some universities, which had been in place for many years; now women would benefit from that same education.

The campaign would expand Saudi women's access into male-dominated fields, such as computer science, business and management, engineering, and medicine, and so on; and which were potent pathways for them to enter and advance in the business world that was gradually opening up to receive them. The westernization of education also generated more avenues for male and female Saudi students to attend universities in western countries. That bonus was extremely attractive for Saudi females and their families. The university enrollment of Saudi females rapidly surpassed that of males, with women comprising fifty-two percent of students in the Kingdom at that time, and that percentage was increasing. It was an extraordinary watershed juncture in time. The campaign was energizing and drew the brightest, most focused, and ambitious young Saudi women to campuses - many from wealthy families.

On any day, between classes the female campus was electric, filled with students in their abayas of mostly black, and of endless fashions. On a daily basis, I had to gingerly eke my way through the packed corridors going from and returning to my office for classes, meetings, and making rounds. And I was always awed by the apparent exuberance and promise on their faces as the army of young women entered and exited their classes in tennis shoes, sandals, flats, and heels, hair covered or hair flowing, jabbering aloud, or whispering among themselves, and the devotion with which some attended to their prayers in the secluded corners along the passageways. There was nothing like it. From my view, nowhere in the world was that kind of grand opening and stretch for women happening at that level. With expanded education and opportunities it seemed that their individual and group missions were to 'reap' and become the women they were meant to be. As professor and leader, I knew that I was irresistibly intertwined in something rare – for a mighty door had opened for us all - for me personally, a door marking my entry to KSA, and a door which the women were marching through. The thousands of young Saudi students and I connected and embraced each other, with me feeling at home and among younger sisters. And we collectively sensed that there was more to come in

Prelude: A Mighty Door Had Opened

time. I respected how fortuitous it was for me to be right there in the middle applying my hand.

In my role I taught, administrated, and consulted on educational and developmental strategies for Saudi women with universities and major Saudi corporations, including Aramco, which was then, the most profitable and powerful corporation, a major sponsor of women's empowerment programs, and the number one employer of Saudi female university graduates. What was expected to be only a standard two-year contract would turn out to be a five-year engagement - much longer than imagined or planned. During that period, I would oversee the education and graduations of many thousands of young Saudi women, including princesses. Those women would go forward, taking on all kinds of professional jobs, becoming business leaders and entrepreneurs in the Kingdom and world - and a host of others going on as empowered artists, wives, and mothers.

The first months and years were rough, to say the least. It was altogether a 2000-piece jigsaw puzzle and roller coaster ride, but things began to fall into place. It got easier as a close Saudi friend would tell me in the coming years. Staying open, engaged, and humble made it worthwhile. There is a definite positive impact on me that endures from living under the abaya. And I can say in earnest that I spent five of the finest years of my life in the Kingdom.

The episodes herewith, are what I witnessed and lived as a professional woman in the Kingdom of Saudi Arabia. This is about the characters and stories of people I knew along the way, and mostly the women, whom I came to love. Venturing into Saudi Arabia to reinvigorate my professional life, for a sense of adventure, and to have a different experience of myself as a woman of color and spiritual being, became more of a homecoming. In the Kingdom I found something that was missing in my life all along and did not know it.

Shemagh – *A headdress traditionally worn by men, fashioned like a scarf.*

Hijab – *A head covering that concealed all of a woman's hair.*

Niqab – *A wrap that concealed a woman's forehead and face except the eyes.*

Za'atar - *Thyme baked into small round pita breads, a Saudi favorite.*

UNDER THE ABAYA

Part One

CULTURE SHOCK, NATURALLY

UNDER THE ABAYA

1
Walking Backwards Without a Plan — And God is Laughing

It was true, what people told me: *"You go there with one mindset and then you adapt."* One had to embrace and acclimate to a drastic change of lifestyle in the Kingdom and above all, to be able to detach, let go and wait. One either adapted or removed themselves from the Kingdom. Those were the terms. I faced that test. The Saudi way of life surely altered my world view. I got on the other side of that challenge and could talk about it five years hence. I could talk about how life in the Kingdom stretched my capacity to detach and let go, and to wait; and how it honed me to face what seemed to be absurd and to laugh at and with it. I found that things did not normally or necessarily go my way, and nowhere near according to my plans; so much so that time-honored 'wisdoms' came to the fore, such as the Serenity Prayer* - *"God grant me the serenity..."* And especially, *"If you want to make God laugh, just tell God your plans."* Saudi taught me the true meaning of those maxims and I would build those understandings into my perspectives and new way of life in KSA. Having a plan was like having a hole in my pocket, and then, unwittingly filling that pocket with coins. Living and working in the Kingdom demanded that people, especially westerners get used to holes in things - holes in arrangements, holes in situations, holes in plans and holes in people. From where we came from, things were not as we knew and as we thought they should be, but turned upside down, literally speaking. And that began to fascinate me. Getting by in the Kingdom was like having to learn as a right-handed person how to use my left hand, and to walk backwards without a plan.

There was solemn wisdom in the country people's often said mantra: *'In sha Allah'*, meaning, it's all in God's hands – which would be uttered in any exchange with anyone, anytime, anyplace, about anything – and always as a parting remark to indicate that that was the one thing a person could be sure of. Funny to me, how it felt more like a verbal reflex than a string of words coming from others. And in time, I would be quick to say *"In sha Allah"* myself in tune with a distant celestial laughter.

When my personal world became enmeshed in Saudi culture - day and night, I observed and experienced how things were seen, done, and understood in ways that were quite 'irregular' to me. I was swept up into the social and cultural decorum and differences and had to structure my thinking and actions around those. That was necessary if I was to truly manage my state of affairs and keep a grip. Of course, I applied my spiritual tools, got my regular sleep and it helped tremendously to get a full body massage every two weeks from Charisma, a gifted Filipino woman. Yet, the impact from the meeting of my western and the Saudi values was intense, and the two blended into 'something' that I took inside me. When I returned to the states after five years, close friends told me that I was a different person. The change in me was more obvious to them than to myself.

There was a wide range of factors that characterized life in the Kingdom above and below the surface – cultural items that I categorized as wondrous, practical, and perplexing. Some were direct, some I learned through inference, and many by trial and error. Most were footnotes and bylaws that demanded my full attention and awareness; in a sense, they were guidelines I had to know and respect and adhere to, and in some cases even more so, as a woman. Some of those above the surface were:

1. Reading and writing was done from **right to left**, as in Hebrew. When juxtaposed to English, the Arabic language looked like a series of lines, scribbles, dots, and waves. But to my eyes, the Arabic written language resembled art. Although English was the second language spoken in the Kingdom, the performance of my responsibilities often required translations which I would easily secure from my students – never an issue and something I enjoyed doing. Yet, I was learning that the Kingdom's rhythms of life were also 'right to left', which could not be readily translated. So, the question for me was: *How does one translate culture?* I could not do that but could only embrace it.

2. **Sunday marked the first day of the work week,** which extended from Sunday through Thursday. That really took some getting used to for me and a lot of ex-pats. In fact, I don't believe that I ever got used to it. My inner clock was rigidly tuned into Friday and Saturday as the weekend. Going to work on Sunday seemed like overtime. Christmas was just another day at the office, as was Thanksgiving, New Year's

Day, the 4th of July, etc. Working on western major holidays seemed surreal. Several Muslim Eids* and holidays were scheduled during the year as official days off, and I was grateful to have them.

3. Observance of the daily prayer times was compulsory for commercial businesses. **Shops and businesses generally shut down at the call of prayer time,** which was five times a day. The exact hour and minutes for prayer were not the same from day to day because it followed the minute by minute changes of the moon cycle. That no doubt treaded into my grocery shopping and errands routines. Checkout stands at the supermarket were literally shut down during prayer – giving people more time to shop or to stand idly around and wait until the checkout cashiers returned from prayer to open the registers and start the lines moving. That was usually 20-25 minutes later - sometimes longer. Shopping after 8:00 pm following the last prayer was too late for me. Initially, I frenetically tried to schedule my shopping runs to avoid being caught up in the prayer rituals, having been delayed at the register one time too many. Sometimes I could get in the store and out in time, and sometimes not, and that was requiring more energy than I wished to expend; it was stressful. I eventually learned to just relax, loosen my schedules, and do what I had to do when I had to do it, and roll with the prayer times when those came and ended. In essence, becoming comfortable with and trusting 'flow' apart from futilely forcing myself into rigid timeframes. I realized that nothing really bad happened and there were no setbacks when I was in that mode.

4. The Saudi tradition that had **women and men co-existing in distinct male and female cultures was all pervasive** in attitudes, behaviors, social mores, and infrastructure. Customary divisions were striking. Sometimes casual separations were made by choice, more often they were built into the culture and required, as public places for men and women were clearly demarcated with separate entrances for men and separate ones for women. Women were sectioned apart from men in workplaces and sometimes in meetings where both sexes were in attendance. Marriage parties were held separately, with one for the bride among women and one for the groom among men. Fathers could not attend their daughters' graduations, nor could mothers

attend those of their sons'. In addition to official customs, there were taboos about genders that influenced separations between men and women in both physical and psychological spheres. I observed the public interface among Saudi men and women to be generally restrained and formal. As a rule, women did not sit next to men, in medical waiting rooms, on the airplane, on buses, and often in the car, unless the man was kin or a husband, otherwise women took the back seat. In many cases women were adamant not to sit next to a man. I observed how women would get up and take a smaller seat or stand rather than sit next to a man she did not know; and how airplane takeoffs were frequently delayed as flight attendants scurried about to switch anxious women whose seats were assigned next to men. One day at the medical clinic while seated in the waiting area for my doctor's appointment, a heavy-set Saudi woman walked in looking for a seat. She was completely covered in black - wearing the black abaya, hijab, niqab, with black gloves and black sunglasses to boot! The only vacant seat was in the middle between a man and me. Instead of taking the available seat, the woman came and stood directly in front of me and motioned that I give her my seat. She did not want to sit next to the man. She was very expressive, motioning me with her hands to move a second time before I could figure out what she wanted and why. I gladly gave her my seat and took the middle one. She thanked me with a frank nod of her head saying, "Shukran." I guessed she assumed that because I was a foreigner that sitting next to a man mattered less to me than it did her. She was right about that. On occasion, a female instructor would hastily seek refuge in my office while men were doing repairs in the passageways; she'd wait behind my closed door until the men were gone. Female security guards, as a rule escorted and oversaw the work of men while they were on the female part of the campus. When I asked women why security escorts were required for men, they said that one reason was due to their belief that the men could not control their impulses and nature and might molest the woman if not with their hands, then certainly with their eyes or their thoughts. At some level, the women felt compromised in those situations where there was proximity to men. On the other end, men avoided touching women who were not their spouse or related to them through blood. That was said to stem in part from their ideas around women's menstrual cycles that rendered them impure. On a few occasions when I extended my hand to a Saudi man, he did not take it. I learned to stop doing that and to extend a smile to a man instead. Those 'gender' customs for women and men tested my idea of myself as a woman. I followed them not because they were right for me, but because not to adhere to them would be wrong.

5. **Censorship was prevalent** both formally and informally. It was ill-advised to say anything defamatory or derogatory about the Kingdom, its leadership and government, neither in speaking or writing. Emails, digital chats, and phone conversations were routinely trolled. It was understood among my academic compatriots to be mindful of what was communicated in digital media and even social forums. Firewalls routinely blocked or scrambled access to outside networks and websites. I religiously used a VPN (Virtual Private Network) to access and stay connected to websites and sources I needed. Publicly, profanity and even mild expletives were shunned and any kind of sensuality; overt displays of affection such as hugging and kissing were censored in television programming and movies. Ironically, the angry emotions, violence and bloodshed characteristic of many western movies were not likewise edited out. With that observation, it seemed to me that the things most censored and problematic in the media were akin to feminine (yin) qualities, whereas those that were akin to masculine (yang) ones were not; and which reflected again, the way that women and men were esteemed in the culture. With me being an outspoken intellectual woman, the censorship became personal, and I was a lot of times walking on eggshells within the Saudi cyberspace maze – it was stifling and at times scary.

6. **Photography in public spaces and publicizing women's images were contrary to social decorum** and was strictly discouraged. It was regarded as rude and an intrusion to take a public picture of someone, a Saudi man or woman that one did not know, and without his or her expressed knowledge and consent. With the modern-day proliferation of smart phones, taking random pictures of people out in the public was a habit in the west, especially among tourists, some saw it as a

right. But not in Saudi, a person could be reapproached and chastised for taking unwarranted photos of Saudi persons. Saudis highly valued and protected their privacy, especially the women who learned early to be modest. Women generally did not want to be photographed, even when they were asked; nor did they want their pictures shared or spread around on social media. Saudi female students explained to me that their fathers expected them to keep their images out of the public eye as much as possible. That was expected even when looking their finest or in their happiest moments, such as graduating. A young lady or woman would stress that a person must refrain from sharing her photo when she made an exception and allowed that person to take it. That happened numerous times with my Saudi students and friends. I have dozens of selfies with students in my phone that no other human eyes have or will ever see. That custom of protecting one's image by extension had a twin sister, which was the invisibility of women in man's wide-open world. Women's images were generally not permitted for public display in advertisements. I noticed on the billboards along the roads and in malls that there were few to no images of women, and if I came across one that was advertising women's garments or products, the faces of the female models were obscured or blurred out. Women were physically everywhere, yet they were not to be seen or to overtly bring attention to themselves – they were to be as invisible as possible. That aspect of the culture further clarified how differently women were regarded and the extent to which those perspectives were preserved. As a woman, I was made conscious of that while out in the open – a thing very new to me.

7. The **verbal trumped the written word** – meaning that except for formal contracts, that which was written in 'black and white' did not carry as much weight as that which was said. What was spoken behind closed doors could handily overrule any written order or agreement. That contrasted with western customs, wherein the written word was binding, no matter what the context. Insofar as the learning process was concerned, with regularity, I had students exclaim to me that what they wrote on paper was not what they meant; and therefore, I should only consider while grading their papers what they were thinking when they wrote it and not what was actually there on the paper.

Students ignored the clearly written instructions on assignments and exams and continually asked me to repeat the instructions. That happened with the students who were fluent in English or not. It dawned on me that it was not that the students were irresponsible or trying to get over on me, but it was really a cultural black hole in most cases. It was something I had to work at - to be patient, and to meet students half-way in those instances where it was warranted. Bottom line, I was exercising a new set of intellectual muscles in order to be an effective educator.

8. One **had to be granted official permission to leave the Kingdom** of Saudi Arabia. That applied especially to contract workers. Visas were not automatically issued. A person wanting to work in or visit the Kingdom was required to undergo the process of being accepted into the country. That usually happened through a sponsor who made a request for a person to enter the country. Saudi Arabia had not been a destination for tourists and historically did not receive many. Most foreigners went there to work and had corporate sponsors. A worker had to have permission to leave as well with an exit visa. One needed to secure a clearance from their sponsors, making sure that they were not leaving behind any debts, unfinished business, or offenses that had not been resolved - otherwise, that they were exiting the Kingdom in good standing. And Saudis were known to have very long memories. Humorously speaking, that requirement kept me on my best behavior! But seriously, I was acutely aware of the moves I made and steps I took – knowing that those could have a long-term effect.

9. In earlier times in the Middle East, Arabs were far more advanced than the West in economics, culture, art, and science. Even some enduring tenets of philosophy and mysticism originated from Arab people such as alchemy. Those strengths remained and were evident in Saudi culture. When it came to architecture, some of Europe's most iconic buildings such as Notre Dame were influenced and copied from early Middle Eastern designs. The **structures and landscapes of cities and towns in KSA were humble and crude by western standards**; that was by design as I learned that the Saudis had a different sense of terrestrial beauty and order. Emphasizing simplicity, mood, and space

to create harmony and balance with the community were values that guided architectural and infrastructural developments. In the city in which I resided, **there was a dearth of sidewalks, and the pathways were not pedestrian friendly.** There were no public bus or rail systems to get around in the city. Automobiles were the essential mode of transportation; and for a woman that was out of reach, unless she had a driver to take her where she wanted to go. So, I walked to places that were nearby, within or a mile or two from my villa. I went walking for recreation or to the market, walking most times on dirt and unpaved roads, or on the narrow curb of the streets alongside passing cars. But I learned that walking around was generally not a common thing to do. When I went walking there were few or no other people on the sidewalks, roads, or curbs that I could see. When I thought about it, who really walked around in that kind of heat. I figured it out that the absence of people out and about reflected the social convention - as the streets, highways and cars were the province of men while women stayed inside and close to home. I continued to periodically walk in the open air while keeping that in mind.

10. Saudi citizens had experienced many years of financial abundance and were big shoppers and consumers, however, theirs was a **throwaway society.** Recycling was not generally practiced. The idea of recycling was not yet on the table. That would be changing given the awareness and consciousness of young adults. Coming from a culture where recycling was the norm, it felt odd, wasteful, and irresponsible for me to toss bottles, cans, and plastics into the trash with everything else. But what could I do?

And below the surface:

11. **Situations were fluid, changeable and flowed, like water.** What was a hard *"NO"* today could be an easy *"YES"* the next day. People reserved the prerogative to change their minds. In most arrangements and discourses, there was the underlying expectation that anything could be negotiated. A person might deny me one day with a series of: *"NO, NO, NO"* and the next day everything would be wide open for discussion and possibilities, with: *"No worries."* And that overnight

shift came without an explanation. So, many times, I took the *"YES"* and ran with it! No questions asked. After unsuccessful wrangling over an issue a learned person who understood that aspect of the culture waited and read the signs to know when to go back and ask or try negotiating again. It was unspoken and understood that exceptions could and might be made for individual cases against an established rule; and which had nothing to do with fairness in a person's mind. That was largely because **ethics and decision-making was based on what was *good or bad* rather than on what was *right or wrong*** – two very different things. It took me a while to figure that out, and to arm myself less with facts, history, and content, and more with process and relationship building, which included letting ambiguity be my friend.

12. **Respect got a lot more done and better** than by being gruff and bossy. Respect and honor were the name of the game in business and professional relationships – even in casual interactions among people. I learned that one had to come with respect first in all interactions with women and men, and never lost sight of that in my verbal and written communications, as well. Disrespecting a person dishonored them. Thus, it was prudent to assume that everyone had a sense of honor they'd want to uphold and protect. In dealing with some caustic and downright evil people in the Kingdom that was hard to accept. Moreover, a good heart and intention were the measure of a person and outweighed how well-educated they might be, or what title they might hold. My manners and social skills had to shine as much and more than my academic degrees and work experience.

13. **Modesty and restraint were woven into the culture.** The modesty rules extended well beyond the required dress codes which forbade tight-fitting clothes for men and women, and which required that women wear the abayas always while in public. Social decency laws were in effect, which outlawed pornographic materials of any kind, and any expressions, written, spoken, or inferred that offended the Kingdom. Homosexuality was a capital crime; it was seen as morally offensive, and punishable by death. Public displays of affection were not common or allowed. I did not see handholding in public between couples. While viewing the 'rare' wedding dance between a bride and

groom, I observed the couple carefully keeping a space between them so that their bodies did not touch as they lightly held one another with their hands at the waist, keeping their movements ever so slight and unexaggerated. Romantic hugging and kissing was done in private, before and after marriage. Couples abided by religious imperatives that prohibited sex and limited physical contact before marriage. That 'encouraged' the couple to focus on developing emotional intimacy before physically becoming man and wife. Restraint and discretion were the informal rules, not only with expressions of love, intimacy, and affection, but to other outward immoderate emotional displays, such as laughter. I would draw surprised, and disapproving looks to me when I belted out one of my hearty laughs - something I was known for and liked to do. I learned to curb my impulses to laugh in public as much as I could. Sometimes that did not work!

14. The norm of modesty extended to an **unspoken rule against being immoral, demeaning or insulting to others.** I never heard a Saudi or Muslim man or woman openly speak harshly about another person. When that individual had been harmed in some way by another, they refrained from saying anything derisive about the perpetrator, even while in our private conversations. I realized how that went beyond restraint and that in their 'mindset' and consciousness, there was just no need to do so. Resorting to say *"In sha'Allah"* was usually their response to a spite or offense, as if as a balm against any 'ill will' they personally might hold. Additionally, it was imprudent to compare a Muslim man or woman and certainly, an Arab person, to animals, i.e., referring to them cows, pigs, horses, etc.; even in jest, it was insulting, defaming, and seriously frowned upon. If a westerner referred to a Saudi using those terms they would have to apologize immediately or pay dearly by being ostracized and avoided. In my first days in the Kingdom a colleague thought that it was important to take me to the side and put that detail among other such footnotes into my ear. I was not in the habit of verbally insulting people, but that precaution helped me to better understand my Saudi friends and students and how best to converse with and support them.

15. **Quantity took priority over quality.** The degree of 'quantity' was emphasized in upper management's assessments of the achievements of my work goals. Progress and success were measured mostly in terms of how much, rather than how well a thing was done, or why. Much of my professional learning and past work experiences were based on achieving quality over quantity. So, going in the opposite direction was a grating diversion for me. However, in a highly unpredictable environment I was finding it an uphill battle to work to achieve 'quality' and easier to reach for an end goal of 'quantity' in my tasks. By default, that unofficial mandate made my work load a lot lighter.

16. **Learning was done in the oral tradition.** Learning by committing information to memory was highly practiced versus critical thinking, reading, and note-taking. Although intrigued, I was finding that tendency of most students to be extremely challenging for me as a professor because it was a cultural dynamic - not due to negligence or malaise. I saw that most students, did not take to the books and instead of writing notes they exhibited an uncanny talent to commit to memory what they were hearing from my lectures or reading from the Power Point presentations. But that was short-lived because the information retained in their heads could not stay there for long, and until it had to be replaced with new information. Therefore, I altered the curricula to include exercises to shore up students' abilities to think critically. I assumed that cultivating the ability to think critically would be augmented by their talent to memorize, thus putting that talent to a higher use; and it worked for most students who were quite adept at critical thinking when presented with the opportunities.

17. The **Saudis had a unique relationship with time.** I observed how Saudis 'danced with time' in some inbred, subconscious, and mystical way. Time was an ally especially for deciding things, wherein the passage of it changed, reshaped, and shifted a situation – yielding more information to the person charged with the decision-making. Also time was deferred to as an 'equalizer' that eased and smoothed out dissensions, conflicts, and misunderstandings where words or gestures alone, could not. To the westerner the Arab says, *"You have the clocks, but we've got the time."* In contrast to westerners, including myself, the

Saudi was not anxious about the ticking of the clock and seemed to ride on an alternate wave of time – at a different momentum. The clock was merely an accessory to time in the Saudi culture. Matters were not as a rule subject to occur within a specific space of time, but in accordance with moods and tendencies, and sometimes even vibrations and the inexorable swings of the pendulum. Situations had their moments. Time was sacred and used to slow things down and allow space. Saudis valued being present in the moment – to get into the essence of an issue or situation - to mine more useful particulars and impressions. There was far less speed, hurry, and rush as in the west. And the culture had its way of making people 'chill' and adhere to its time standards, no matter how much they were programmed and ruled by the clock. That was a major frustration among westerners. It was by being forced into situations where I had to step back and abide by some unfamiliar pace that I began to examine and know more about time and my relationship with it, and consequently, relate to time in a whole new way. I could better appreciate time as a 'helper', by deliberately making room for time – to allow it to weigh in and trusting that I would know when a particular move was necessary. There were fewer regrets and second-guessing, and a deeper meaning when I had to say: *"I'll need to sit with this"* or *"Let me sleep on it."*

18. **Saudis lived at night.** The day began at night for many Saudis. That was the case, especially in the month of Ramadan. During Ramadan the first meal came in the evening after the day of fasting. Throughout the year shopping and activity were bustling into the late evening and wee hours of the morning; dinner at social events usually came after 10 or 11 pm. Soccer practice for schoolboys could begin at around midnight on weekends. Children could be seen and heard playing well after twilight, sometimes before a school day. I enjoyed the sounds of the neighbors' kids outside my villa and got used to hearing them at night. I was early to bed and early to rise and could not hang with that 'night owl' aspect of the culture. I probably missed out on a lot of interesting and fun things which might have made my overall experience in KSA far richer than it was already turning out to be.

19. **Conflict was always happening and easier to step into than to avoid.** The reasons for that I did not know for sure. I supposed that it was an outgrowth of so many people coming together from disparate backgrounds and within a restrictive and ordered society. People were easily frustrated or on edge, and that was ironically juxtaposed with the faithfulness and prayerfulness in the culture. I knew westerners who got so beside themselves and were on the verge of emotional breakdowns, who did not handle the conflicts well that they so easily walked into. I had my share of conflicts. And I observed that Saudis related to conflict differently and feared it less; and it made relations stronger. It seemed that for them, interpersonal conflict was not necessarily catastrophic and relationship-ending.

I witnessed a serious dispute between two Arab men that surely would have ended up with one of them becoming injured or dead if that same conflict occurred in the US. It happened on the road. A car cut in front of the bus that I was on. The driver of that car got upset after the bus driver sped up and drove in front of his car because he was going so slow. Before doing so, the bus driver blew his horn several times to have the slow and erratically moving car get out of the lane, as car drivers were supposed to yield the right of way to buses on the road. But he refused to move. So, when the car driver darted back in front of the bus and continued to block the fast lane by moving deliberately slower, driving like a turtle, things got heated. The car driver then stopped his car, still blocking the bus; he got out of his car, furious, and stormed towards the bus to confront its driver. He was inebriated, out of control, and clearly on the wrong side of the confrontation. In no time, both men were out of their vehicles violently yelling fighting words, flailing their arms about, and pointing at each other with threatening body language. There were no weapons. While there was heavy security in the Kingdom, that was a culture of relatively few firearms in the hands and homes of everyday people. The argument was escalating, until the men were separated by another male passing by, who got out of his car and with effort, physically shoved the two men away from one another. Us on the bus could hear the good Samaritan aggressively counseling the arguing men who reluctantly heeded his words, ceased quarreling, and returned to their vehicles.

The two men let themselves be stilled by the counsel of another which may have surfaced an understanding that they each might have already carried within them – to be selfless in seeking peace with respect. That was what the good Samaritan stressed to them, from Islamic teachings.

Arabic was a language of feeling rather than a language of words, one that I found more emotionally-laced than mental. Perhaps that had something to do with how easily the conflict began and was just as easily quelled and shifted; and which pointed to the Saudis' distinctive capacity to weather conflict. Perhaps there was also some unspoken subtle knowing and acceptance within the culture that conflict served as a necessary release and refresh. My Ph.D. was hard earned and my intellect strong, yet many of my professional and personal relations in the Kingdom and among Saudis pulled me out of my head and into my heart. In that culture I was constantly witnessing situations of how the intellect got us into trouble and how the heart got us out.

20. All of the Saudi people I worked with, taught, and had any association with were Muslim, either Shia or Sunni. That extended to the Indian Pakistani, Egyptian, Sudanese, and other ethnicities in my circle. Most people who were not ex-pats were Muslims – practicing, and mostly devout. Therefore, **Islam was a part of my everyday life and made an impression on me.** My exposure to Islam brought me closer to Arab women and men. Living and working so consummately among Muslims heaped my understanding and appreciation of that faith; and some tenets of Islam rubbed off on me. Experiencing Islam up close and personal taught me more about leading with the heart - allowing the intellect to be guided by the heart in personal and professional matters and being wont to keep things simple. Daily regimens of prayer brought one into an accord where one could rise above the mediocrity and impulses of 'ego' life. I watched the devout cease all activity to rush off to pray; and saw how prayer not religion softened the ego and deepened the spirit, and how my friends and colleagues were applying their faith in their lives. Although I was not Muslim, nor aspiring to Islam, I could not help but be affected by their devotion to their faith, which they brought with them into their relationships with me. Those friendships roused and gave me a lot.

Life was bewildering in the Kingdom. And these and other subtle tenets of the culture had a cumulative effect which impacted me and how I conducted myself. I was a strong professional, but I was one hundred percent of the time made aware that I was a woman in a man's world.

Walking Backwards Away from What We Thought We Knew

Increasingly, western professionals needing job opportunities and relief from their ailing economies were drawn to Saudi Arabia. The Saudi culture, to an extensive degree valued and needed the talent and certain expertise of westerners to move towards modernization. Together and out of mutual need, Saudi and western cultures formed an uneasy, and a far from perfect alliance. Typically, westerners ventured into more exotic and so-called 'developing' lands and expected those cultures, like Saudi Arabia to reflect their lifestyles and keep them comfortable. But, as outsiders came to live and work in the Kingdom of Saudi Arabia, they had to operate in a world that was uniquely different from whence they came and that utterly challenged their views of reality on many levels. Although most westerners tried and made adjustments, the voices of those who did not, could not or would not adjust were loud. If it was not the searing heat, it was certainly the perceived *"bizarre ways"* of the Saudi lifestyle that aroused a chorus of complaints and discontent from many westerners and my fellow compatriots. Westerners harboring attitudes and convictions of their own cultural superiority came with judgment, outright sarcasm and often disrespect for Saudi customs. In the Kingdom, I saw, as my western work comrades snickered at the scratchy broken English spoken by Saudis – who in fact, had to learn English as a second language in order to attend most universities and to work in the majority of companies and fields. I noticed how westerners made fun of and belittled Saudi customs, with one ex-pat professor referring to Arab peoples as *"savages"* in a 'scholarly' presentation.

I reported those remarks to a ranking ex-pat administrator, who took the offense in stride and played it down. I observed how Saudis were aware of those attitudes coming from westerners and therefore, in their own way withheld the vulnerable and real parts of themselves – sharing their deep thoughts and hearts only with those westerners they got to know well and trusted. It was a catch-22 situation; Saudi needed the West and wanted to modernize; and the westerners needed to make a reasonable living, as significant numbers of them could not in their own countries. Both sides had leverage, with westerners applying their talents and expertise, and the Saudis by providing a variety of job opportunities and pockets full of money. But, old, proud, and sovereign, the Kingdom's rules and customs were resolute, unbendable, and not subject to the dictates, whims, or approvals of western peoples. The burden was clearly on westerners like me, to make the greater adjustments in our attitudes and behaviors on how to live in that land – on how to walk backwards without a plan.

To a large extent the Kingdom and corporate sponsors accommodated ex-pats by providing environs and amenities to keep them relatively comfortable. Most professional westerners, including myself, were assigned to live in compounds that were somewhat free from the Kingdom's social restrictions. Those were self-contained and self-governing communities where ex-pats could have some of the comforts and familiarities of home in the west. They could decorate their domiciles to celebrate western holidays such as Christmas, Thanksgiving, even Halloween – with Trick-Or-Treating and all. Women could walk around the compounds in the open air without having to wear the abaya in casual clothes - dresses, tank tops and pants. Some compounds had their own food markets, banks, parks, and medical clinics. Alcohol flowed in some compounds, wherein daring residents had their own stills making and selling wine and a moonshine vodka called 'sid'. Women were even driving cars inside compounds while outside in the public domain it was prohibited. Those activities were kept discreet and strictly contained within the compound. Many ex-pats and some whom I knew well grew so comfortable in their compound lives that they rarely ventured outside socially into the wider Saudi community. They were safe behind the walls of the compounds, protected by the barbed wire and security guards. Within the compound walls, their lives seemed less touched by the upside-down nature of life in the Kingdom. But most still had to face the reality of Saudi life in the office - on their jobs on a day-to-day basis.

Whether living in a compound or not, one would have to get out of their comfort zone of a western mindset to have a real taste and appreciation of Saudi culture. I dove into it and what a ride it was! I walked down the dimly lit and narrow streets at night where few other pedestrians were around, went into the teaming souks, and the night flea markets frequented only by the locals. Most of my friends were Saudi, who were also my closest. I sat at dinner tables with Saudi families in their homes who told me what was on their minds. In one household I was invited into the bedroom of their teenaged daughter and saw her life-sized posters of Johnny Cash and Kanye West which only affirmed what I already knew - that she was a normal teen girl like any other in the world. In a 'behind the scenes' kind of way, I was pursued and charmed by Saudi men - one, a lovelorn official who insisted on hand feeding me dates while proposing that I be a second wife. I attended weddings and Arabic-speaking venues being the only westerner in sight, danced with the women and made the 'nuts and bolts' extra efforts to resource myself within the Saudi subculture. I saw beyond the images of what the world wanted me to see and got a sure taste of Saudi that relatively few others had. Indeed, one could stay safe and tucked inside, or go off-kilter to make being there truly a worthwhile experience. That was a choice every person faced once they set their feet on the ground in KSA. For the most part, the timorous forays of the average westerner into the Kingdom deprived them in more ways than one.

Saudi Arabia evolved from an ancient culture over thousands of years. Surely, a lot that was profound and enduring happened over such an expanse of time. I was beginning to tap into what that was. The culture had evolved in ways that western peoples by and large, may not have acknowledged or understood. There was a mystical undertone that informed everyday life in the Saudi culture, and an amazing subtlety. The country had a soul. Saudi culture was not as sophisticated and cosmopolitan as the cultures of many of the people who transplanted there to live and work. Yet, in the social sphere I observed less haste, less clutter, nor the rancor which often came with so-called culturally developed and civilized nations. By contrast, Saudi was a culture that counseled patience and forbearance, which made room for the shifting of assumptions in the spaces that that engendered; and in those spaces one could take the inward look to access larger parts of themselves, the world, and their connection to it, if they allowed it. How apropos it was symbolically, that in the vacuous desert, free of structures, one could see quite far. And it goes that within that restrictive and isolating landscape of Saudi, there was a lot of room for introspection, self-reflection, and insight; a person could be surprised by what they learned about themselves – for good or for bad. I did.

My main plan that brought me to Saudi Arabia was to earn a living to sustain me while applying my skills and knowledge in the process, and to do that in a two-year period. But in the end, I was groomed by the experience and emerged five years later a modified person. It was a period when I was making constant adjustments to my thinking and behaviors, even my values, spurred by adapting to life in the Kingdom. As I reflected, I thought that sometimes things had to go backwards or sideways in order for people to have the impetus to evolve; or to be jolted to go in a different, albeit a better direction. When a student wrote on her exam: *'I am going to critical my thinks'*, I was at first taken aback by her awkward phrasing. But when I listened into and really 'heard' what she was saying her phrasing made sense, and in a more compelling way than if she were instead to have written: *'I will work on my critical thinking'*. Her way of expressing that seemed to have a meaning that went straight to the point of the matter. Walking backwards became less of a distortion as I delved in further and allowed myself to see and experience more by rewinding and playing things over and over in my mind's eye – which highlighted how there could be many truths around the same issues. I saw how walking backwards without a plan unsettled some and quickened and stretched others – whereby some rose to their own occasions and others let themselves down.

Walking backwards literally strengthened the muscles, improved bodily coordination, and sharpened the senses and mental clarity. In terms of social cultural experiences, it added vivid color and detail to life and gave one the 'esprit de corps' to live in a diverse world, which did the soul a good turn. It was not useful to get too comfortable for too long in one state of mind or way of being. Stagnation set in, which went against the universal course of motion; and becoming content should not prevent one from learning how to learn. The Kingdom had had its way with me, stripping me of preconceived ideas and plans on how I was going to get in, get things done, and get out; and expecting to do so under a preexisting 'persona'. What blew my hair back was realizing that it was fine not to have a plan, that I was still 'OK', which paradoxically brought ease and relief. I put my best foot backwards, reached for the good, kept my expectations low, and would not be too surprised when disappointed. That way I steered clear, lived within myself and with others and peacefully went to sleep at night – still hearing God's laughter, and not minding it at all.

Serenity Prayer – "God grant me the serenity to accept the things I cannot change, courage to change the things I can, and wisdom to know the difference."

Eids – Muslim days of feasting, festivals, and holidays, including Ramadan.

2
The Frustration unto Hell

For several days a female business colleague was fretting, and anguishing to the hilt over an untenable situation involving a male Saudi administrator. No amount of reasoning, placating, or pleading from her as to the obvious right solution would dissuade the administrator. *"That is what happens when you underestimate and go up against the Bedouin mind"* was what another colleague said, chiming in, seeing her angst – and who had been working in the Kingdom a long time. I'd witnessed that kind of 'pulling your hair out' vexation time and time again from ex-pats and even a few Saudis, who seemed to manage it a bit calmer than the ex-pats, however. And many times I had heard people who were veterans and old-hands at working in the Kingdom make that very same comment about the 'Bedouin mind'. The 'Bedouin mind' at work in some situations did not respond well to being questioned, challenged, told what to do or ordered around, even when the position of the other party made perfect sense. That became especially debilitating and maddening when the person on the receiving end had little or no recourse. The plight was their burden to bear. And that was a compelling footnote where business, education, and livelihood were concerned.

Although the nomadic Bedouin lifestyle was a part of Arabia's illustrious past, the modern-day Saudi lifestyle and way of thinking were still influenced by Bedouin traditions – patterned on an age-old design. In Saudi Arabia the nomadic Bedouin comprised most of the population in the early 20th century. Those were the desert dwellers – herders of goats and camels. In the present day they were a small proportion of the country's population, as many had integrated into the urban areas. The 'Bedouin mind' as my colleagues and I understood it was a phenomenon – one that we observed and experienced ourselves, directly from time to time. It was a 'taut' mindset held by some people holding authoritative positions and was evident when they made determinations that significantly impacted others and situations. The Bedouin mind was alive and well in modern Saudi culture; and to many, it was the impetus behind what some westerners experienced as the 'frustration unto hell'

– a phrase that I coined, because that was exactly how it felt when it happened to me. The 'frustration unto hell' was not talked about or made obvious in the public milieu, but it was a very real thing. Whenever he was mystified by how things were decided and happened in the Kingdom, my Pakistani driver Ajmal, summed it up in two words: *"Sah-ooo-dee way!"* And he was matter-of-fact about that.

One realized soon enough that things were not commonly malleable in the Kingdom where decisions were made. In business and organizational governance there were not usually firmly established strategies or formulas to plan and determine outcomes. I found that rules were not clear as I might expect, and those were ever-changing - at times business leaders made things up as they went along. The process of engaging someone in decision-making was more often like fencing, or a game of chance – depending on who was being engaged and sitting behind the big desk. The Bedouin mindset, as I knew it was independent of rules, logic, or reason – even sentiment; and I think it may have even made an art of delay. It was guided by an obscure motivation that was not emotionally, egotistically, or power driven. I found that when the 'Bedouin' had his or her mind set on an idea regarding a person or situation the mind fixated on that idea and would not budge, unless under extreme circumstances that had nothing to do with merit, such as solid justifications or 'points of significance'. It wants what it wants. In a culture where respect was paramount, changing one's mind weakened them and made them appear as not strong or worthy of respect. Bottom line, it was about saving face and/or staying the course.

On a few occasions during my time in the Kingdom, I experienced the 'frustration unto hell'. From that I learned to approach rather delicately, the person in charge whom I saw as holding that mindset and who was making the decisions - to be respectful and having done some prior exploration on how a specific matter was usually handled and decided upon. Because, once an idea, petition, plan, proposal, or cause was presented, the mind that might rule on it was ungoverned. Arab people habitually said: *"In Sha Allah"*, meaning *God willing*, which we were inclined to say in the west. However, the phrase also carried more of an overarching neutralizing quality, I thought. For instance, if I said to another: *"I hope things work out for you with that job"*, the response was *"In Sha Allah"*; if I said: *"It may rain today"*, the response was *"In Sha Allah"*; or if I wished them well by saying: *"Please take care of yourself, I will look forward to seeing you next week"*, their kind comeback was *"In Sha Allah."* When I suggested to a friend that I could help her with a problem she was wrestling with she said, *"In Sha Allah."* And there were many times when I urged students to work harder on their assignments to raise their grades and got the same initial response: *"In Sha Allah miss."* That might explain why many decisions were absent of any discernible rhyme or reason on how conclusions were reached. It was not clear why commitments to plans were soft or why 'dead reckoning' seemed to be applied and trumped over a tried-and-true direction. One surrendered to God when approaching and engaging the 'Bedouin mind'. Because in that mind, things always were as they should be and turned out the way they would. The outcome was beyond the person doing the deciding and holding the reins, and who may have seen their role simply as to 'settle the matter' or to 'take a guess', whether it turned out to be prudent, beneficial or not, because they did not have that kind of power to purposely generate 'a last defining word', or for that matter, useful outcomes.

When it came to business affairs and items that touched upon a person's livelihood the Bedouin mind could really throw that person for a loop. It was like banging one's head against a brick wall. That Bedouin mind at work could be likened to a muscled man who stood stock still while getting repeatedly gut-punched by a feeble lightweight guy. Eventually, when the muscled man had had enough of being punched he would effortlessly lift the little guy with one arm, who by then was worn out, and toss him across the room. For the person going up against the Bedouin mind with all that they had and going nowhere, it could be a 'frustration unto hell'. The more a person prodded, pushed, or fought, the more entrenched the mindset became and the more unlikely an answer or remedy to one's satisfaction would come.

So how did one muster through the 'frustration unto hell'? The 'Bedouin mind' held tight, it remembered, and it might even pay you back. Push back and resistance were not tolerated which could make matters worse. *'Best not to lose yourself and forget who you are'*. The 'Bedouin mind' operated on its own wave of intelligence and had no respect for anyone who lost his or her cool. The unspoken rule was to avoid strongly rebutting or protesting against something that had been decided for or about you, at least initially in the heat of the moment. You go along with it and wait and use time. It was better to acquiesce, humble yourself and retreat to think things through – to avoid wasting efforts trying to devise clever strategic maneuverings, doing mental gymnastics, or looking for some code or written law to produce on your behalf. Eventually, one figured it out and adopted a way to work with the Bedouin mind, not around it. One detached, cultivated patience, resourcefulness. One let go and let time be an ally, and intend to revisit the situation a few days, weeks, or months later when perhaps the rhythms and energies may have shifted; and then try to finagle one's way to a desired change, or reconsideration or adjustment in his or her direction. Maybe then, Mashallah! The Divine would have intervened.

However, there was 'wasta'*, which was the one defense that the Bedouin mind was not immune to and one it could not withstand. Wasta was the power that came from wealth and family and tribal ties that some persons had to wager and even wield. It was potent and changed everything in one sweeping motion. But wasta was leverage that most people did not commonly possess in the Kingdom, and it was totally inaccessible to westerners.

I did not have wasta nor could I get it. Totally out of reach for me. It was a Saudi thing. I was left to fend for myself using my own wiles to win my case when I had a strong medical issue. That was two years into my work assignment in KSA. Up to then as much as possible, I stayed clear from the 'Bedouin mind' in my work affairs. But that time I charged full speed ahead because my health and money were at stake. And in my 'woman's mind' I had nothing to lose. So, I rolled up my sleeves to put up the fight and engaged that 'mind'. I fought the administration that refused to approve a thirty-day doctor's recommended sick leave for me. The leave was a legitimate request to which I was entitled, and it was in total alignment with my contract terms. However, the administration repeatedly and adamantly declined granting the sick leave; no amount of medical documentation or reports from either US or Saudi doctors would satisfy – whether officially stamped or not.

It seemed that the all-male senior leadership simply did not want to grant me the leave because I was a key woman leader - my position was pivotal and my absence would put a strain on the flow of work and on the organization, which was true. But the institution was wealthy and had resources; and the bosses failed to see that my trying to remain on the job in my ailing condition would still be a loss for the organization as well. I was in pain and my body needed rest, medical attention, and rehabilitation. I spent weeks going back and forth with them trying to explain, justify and reason while my health situation was getting worse by the day, and with me still running up against their denial and rejection of my case.

Finally, I took the thirty-day leave anyway without approval and let them 'deal with' my absence; and when I returned healed, I sued. I enlisted the help of savvy Saudi female paralegals who happened to have 'wasta' on their side. The 'mind' backed off. I swiftly won my case and got fully paid for the extended leave retroactively. I did not brag or gloat in my victory but made it a point to show respect and gratitude towards the leadership for 'reaching a desirable solution', and I moved on, resuming my responsibilities. I remained there in that position under contract with no further incident for another three years, and my future requests for leave of any kind were not in the least, questioned or blocked again.

The 'Bedouin mind', hence, the 'frustration unto hell' confounded my notions of what was right, wrong, and reasonable. From that experience I grasped the reality that decisions were often made based on whether the outcome would be good or bad rather than right or wrong; or in other words, judgments were based on whether an act and behavior would have a favorable or unfavorable outcome for the person or business entity doing the deciding. Discernment between 'good or bad' provided more freedom, it was open-ended and allowed room to move around and work with, whereas 'right or wrong' was limiting, finite and linear – too black and white. That was the distinction and the criteria for weighing a dilemma or decision. The institution I worked for decided that granting me the needed extensive sick leave may have been 'good' for me, but it was 'bad' for the institution. And no matter how much I was suffering or tried to defend the need, leadership stuck to that conviction until 'wasta' entered the picture, which would certainly have brought about repercussions that proved to be 'more bad' for the organization's leaders if they did not switch gears.

"In the desert, you do, or you die." My friend who was a cultural expert would say that in jest - but with a hint of seriousness. The desert could be harsh and unyielding. Desert did not fool around. Likewise, the Bedouin mind could be unbending to protect certain interests. It was not evil. It was what it was. In the heart of the Arabian desert, the lone nomadic Bedouin could not wander around aimlessly when searing heat was beating down and when blackest night or a wicked sandstorm were approaching. He knew that things could disappear in the sand when he turned his back. Survival was based on decisiveness. He

had to be quick, focused, and to act instinctively to shield and manage himself, his family, and his animals. His swift choices had to be tight and few to determine a 'good' outcome - minimizing his expenditures of resources and energy. What the nomadic Bedouin decided had to be sure and could not be undone. That was why, 'in the desert, you do, or you die'. And within that context I tried to understand the nature of my confrontation with the Bedouin mind and the 'frustration unto hell'. It was not personal, it hardly ever was, if one were to truly understand that Bedouin mind. Saudi was a culture that decided, but typically did not judge. It was mostly the process rather than the content that ruled one's decisions. And the decisions one made reflected back onto him or her. In some situations, to change one's mind or position was deleterious and placed one in a kind of 'underdog' or loser position with outcomes only they could know. Changing one's mind meant acquiescing to another person's impulses or values, which was not ordinarily the best remedy nor the Bedouin way - an ancient echo forged through eons in the mores and lives of desert men and women. That echo informed those in the present on how to maintain order and stability in the community and society – in the desert. It was to be recognized and respected. The Bedouin knew that the decisions of men were of little consequence in the eyes of Allah. It was not what one did, but how one did it and how one stood standing in the aftermath of what they chose. At the beginning and at the end of the day, the Bedouin knew that all things came full circle to the outcomes that were meant to be. And I could easily see that they could live with that.

Wasta - The power, special privileges, and rights that wealth, social status, position, and tribal ties automatically and unquestionably granted a person – usually a Saudi National.

3
The Bedouin on Friday

Friday was the first day of the weekend in Saudi Arabia; then came Saturday, with a return to work and regular weekday activities on Sunday. I looked forward to Thursdays as my wind down day. Thursday's were like my Friday nights in the states; it was the day reserved for my bi-weekly evening massages or going out to dine. For the average Saudi, Friday was the day to spend with family, inside the home or outside in the public open spaces. Many and major aspects of Saudi life were rooted in nomadic Bedouin traditions – the term 'Bedouin' meaning *desert dweller*. The fiercely independent nomadic Bedouin family was patrilineal. The whole family was involved in making their way of life in the desert which was their home. The Bedouins lived close to the ground and were known for their hospitality and honesty. I saw the modern-day Saudi person, as essentially a Bedouin. Though no longer nomadic, they still placed a high value on family life, togetherness, and allegiances almost to the same extent that they did on religious devotion. On Friday, most businesses except for major food markets were closed until 4:00 pm with many staying closed all day; large food stores that did open were kept to reduced hours. On Friday mornings and into the early afternoon, it was quiet and still outside; there were fewer cars on the roads, no hustle bustle, and very little human presence. It was serene. One could not get gas, go into a bookstore or restaurant, or buy food at many markets. It was the day set aside to honor family throughout the Kingdom. I learned to make sure that I had all I needed for food and supplies by the time Friday came around.

On any given Friday and as weather permitted much of the time – with blue sky and a radiant sun, when I ventured into the open spaces, I would see hundreds of Saudi families sprawled out in the public areas. They were on the grasses, on the dirt grounds, on the promenades and beaches and on the boardwalks for family recreation. It was a sea of families with most of the pedestrian areas taken up. The families came early just after noon and claimed their spots - setting up 'family stations' on whatever slivers of land were free with blankets, rugs, grills, baskets, portable chairs and other odds and ends.

Three or four generations of one family would gather as a unit. Mothers and fathers, sisters, and brothers, and with their children would convene and share the space on the ground with grandparents, and some with their older married children and their spouses as part of the family gathering clan. A familial grouping could be 3 to 10 people or more. There could be a couple with their new baby, or a kinship of a dozen – it was all family. The women were donned in their abayas of mostly black, and by contrast, the men in white thobes or casual clothes. Women were stooping over hot steamy makeshift stoves and grills or laying out the food they prepared at home on blankets and small tables. Fathers were cooking kabobs, spreading that heavenly smoked meat aroma all around. A young man guided his feeble grandfather to wade in the waters at the beach and held on to him as he gently floated about in the shallows; little girls' eyes were peering out from their stark black niqabs – eyes sparkling with curiosity and the sheer joy of being so close with loved ones out in the open, wondering at everything that was going on around them; adolescent girls were whispering among themselves, gigging, and pointing every now and then. Toddlers were running around or chasing balls as babies were having their diapers changed and being soothed. And the low hum of Arabic songs could be heard pouring out from some of the family camps. Before long, it would be time to eat. The family patriarch, the father, would call everyone together and gave a prayer – blessing the food and the family – giving thanks and praise to Allah. After the meal, the family would wile away in their places for the rest of the day until dusk or even later, sitting, playing, snacking, enjoying the scenery and each other.

    It was common for most Saudi families to have a nanny, whom they brought to their Friday family gatherings. As I strolled and observed, I saw the demure Filipino nannies who were firmly attached to their respective 'sponsor' families, focused on helping the mothers and the women arrange and serve the meals, and trying to corral the small children to keep them at bay while playing safely, not too far from their parents. The aromatic smells from the grills and stoves were mouthwatering and made me want to taste the lamb, beef or chicken that was cooking. What's more, I wanted to sit among the families and be a part of what they were doing. It was all so inviting. I could not help but to be pulled in. I must have been a strange sight to the families who regarded me just as much as I regarded them. The scene was new to me as I was new to them. It became a staring fest, but without enmity – just a friendly curiosity from them to me, and me to them. Occasionally, a member of a family would wave me over to join them, and I did – bringing us closer to behold one another and "*Mashallah!!*" My wishes came true! I had a taste of that good smelling food!

I would walk for a long time down the boulevard along the Corniche taking in the view of the families and their nannies. Some were camped right up to the edge of the shoreline; some were nestled in the special booths provided for family gatherings along the beachfront. Some, the latecomers were squatting next to their cars in the sandy parking areas a short distance away from the boulevard, as all of the green and open spaces were gone. The separate family gatherings were in close proximity, often a few feet away from other families – no one seemed to mind, and any open patch of sand or dirt would do. That gay explosion of families would be repeated the following Friday, and the one after that and so on and in the public spaces throughout the Kingdom. As I took in the scene it was easy to see that all of the families there encompassed one big family – that there was a collective 'family mind' prevailing all around. I thought that was a cardinal revelation.

Saudi Arabia was a culture of many tribes. The family was at the center of the tribe and was given number one priority and loyalty. Families tended to be large, irrespective of the size of the household purse, and that family extended beyond immediate blood members to include people who were of the same tribe. A tribe was a grouping of families, which descended from a common ancestor. Tribal associations began with the nomadic Bedouin and went back thousands of years; the tribes could include fifty to hundreds of members. The modern family's tradition of asserting and upholding their tribal identity established their ancient roots in the Arabian Peninsula; as well, affirming one's tribal belonging was an important marker of familial authenticity. The Saudi family name could be different from the tribal name, but the same ancestry was there. The family name was preceded by 'Al' meaning family of or house of, such as Al Dossary, Al Turki, or Al Saud, for which the Kingdom was named. The family name was an important part of one's identity; thus, Arabic women retained their family names when they became married. The Saudis I knew assessed the credibility and trustworthiness of others by their family names, and reputations, more than by their financial status or work positions.

A family's legacy contributed to that of the tribe. As such, a family's virtues of generosity, integrity, honor, and devotion to their faith were more meaningful and carried greater weight than the success of any individual.

Individuation, like the family, was valued in so much as that person kept his and her ties and allegiances to the tribe. Essentially, individuality was tied to the whole family, and by extension, the tribe. For my female students, the concept of perceiving themselves as a self-determined individual was foreign, awkward, even selfish. It was off-putting for them and hard to complete one of my standard individual 'reflection' assignments which required a lot of coaching from me on how to self-reflect and individuate themselves. I wanted them to also value and learn to reflect and get better acquainted with the tenor of their thoughts and emotions – turning inwards for balance and growth. As students did the exercise they reported and journaled how 'knowing' more about themselves enhanced their relationships with 'family'. In assigning them that exercise I learned and appreciated some truths from them on the bliss of the 'family mind' in that it was through family that they were validated and connected to anything else. In that context the Saudi's first responsibility was to family, and secondly to themselves as individuals. That was ingrained early in one's life with family bonds going deep as expressed in an Arab proverb that says: *"My brother and I are against our cousin; my cousin and I are against the stranger."* Overall, the Saudi family unit was expected to be the foremost, central, and stabilizing force in the lives of its members and the tribe. Fridays were the family ritual days to acknowledge and celebrate that.

Any Saudi family may have been as dysfunctional as any in the west; but that was not apparent on the Friday family gatherings. Fridays with family were a duty for the man, who might go out after the family gathering in the day to have fellowship at night with other men. Family problems were kept private and not openly discussed. Family unity mattered over family dissentions - a unity and harmony that was displayed out in the open. What I witnessed on the Bedouin Fridays was the grounding and sovereignty of the Saudi family unit. From that I could better understand and connect with my students and the young women I worked with as well as the many Saudi women and men who became my friends. On occasion on a Friday, I was invited to my Saudi friends' homes to be a part of their family gatherings for dinner. It was there where I gained more insights to 'family' as an inner sanctum of Saudi culture and it gave me lasting guidance throughout my journey into Kingdom life.

4
Hating the Black
- Loving the Black

Each day as I arrived at my university office on the female campus, I was engulfed and immersed in a sea of women - women students, women faculty, women on the phone; and ninety-five percent of the time there were ninety-nine percent women on the bus ride on the way to work and going home. On campus there were women all around and the color black, and no man in sight. Men were not allowed on the female side, unless they were in the 'green zone'* and strictly there to teach. In all other instances, men could not come onto the women's campus unless under the escort of female security. And those security women were severe and no nonsense, themselves cloaked in the black abayas, the black hijabs over their hair, the black niqabs on their faces and wearing black gloves. Their eyes, which were all that could be seen, were intense and focused as they went about the business of escorting the men and tightly seeing to it that the men went directly to their destinations on the female campus to do a specific job and went away without incident. The men might be there to service a copier, turn off the fire alarm, paint, or bring a ladder to replace a light bulb that was too high for the women to reach. And the men knew the rules and were obediently in tow, keeping their eyes diverted away from and off any woman nearby – no eye contact, no sideways glances, no glossing over her body. Their demurring efforts were helped by female students who hastily put back on their abayas or dashed away into ladies' restrooms or classrooms as soon as it was known that men were near and approaching.

The men came first thing in the morning right after I arrived on campus. And no sooner than they could be heard coming, a professor raced into my office to steer clear of the men because her office was too far away for her to get there in time to keep the men from seeing her, and mine was the closest away from the men. She was in sheer panic and did not want to be seen by the men without her abaya on. It was as though she would be caught naked, she said. On a normal day, women faculty and many students relaxed into their routines in casual clothes without wearing their abayas with no men around.

I ordinarily got organized at my desk before plowing into my daily work activities. That was my first task. On any given day I might need to make a trip to the Registrar's office to produce reports or sort out a student issue, which happened to be that particular day. It required me to trek down two flights of stairs and across three building sections, and through long corridors. It was easily a 7–10-minute walk. And along the way I could anticipate stopping and starting as I edged my way through the throng of Saudi female students. It was just about time for the first courses of the morning to begin for the thousands of students who crowded the corridors. I never grew bored of the profusion of female students draped in their black flowing abayas – the 'black' which accentuated their pretty faces, their gorgeous faces - many of them. The tide of black was something to behold during those long walks through the university halls. The energy was high, frenzied and everywhere there was movement with students in black going to classes along with their friends or alone and at all times with cell phones in their hands. Some were taking selfies, some painting their eyes or lips, or one or two stepping right in front of me just to get a good look at me – blocking my path, some racing up beside me to ask something, wanting me to say or do something. There was always something. Students were smiling at me in gladness that I was there among them - an icon, teaching them the ways of the west, a representation of where many of them hoped to go, with education as their relatively new right to exercise. Students were on their knees in supplication anywhere they found a free space, even though it was not an official prayer time. Students, about to take an exam were standing or sitting at study desks along the walls or parked on the floors, anxiously rehearsing memorized answers, rushing through pages of notes.

I saw their handbags: Gucci, Prada, Chanel, Louis Vuitton. I smelled their rich perfumes and ouds. Aside from scholastics, it was a very feminine scene. Numbers of Filipino nannies sat and waited in designated areas ready to take instructions before and during the class sessions from their privileged Saudi female wards; at any time one or several would scramble to attend to them by fetching a cup of coffee for a student who was in a classroom taking her exam or carrying their book bags to the waiting drivers' cars outside. Some students were selling homemade pastries from a small booth stationed near the exit doors. Snack vending machines were sounding off and someone was yelling incoherently in the distance. A lot was going on in those fifteen minutes before the clock would strike 8:00 and students had to be in their seats for the first class of the day to start. I noted how the students did not walk fast, they did not hurry. It was as if that was not how they were supposed to move from one place to another, and as if they had all the time in the world. They sashayed down the halls - their movements, easy, slow, and languid. Most took their time to get where they were going, and they arrived when they arrived; and that was not because it was early in the morning. Lateness to class was an epidemic on the female campus, no matter what time of day; it was a battle that instructors and administrators were losing. I could hear the young ladies talking, speaking Arabic among themselves in the passageways before the start of classes, while in class they had to speak English. That was because the college degree that most of them prized was based on the western model of education. I admired their tenacity to pursue a college degree in a language not their own. I could not do it. And I told them so.

Most female students wore their abayas on the campus, and many did not, except when the men came around. With the men present some had fret and panic on their faces, some had calm and defiance. Some, curious, some amused by it all. When the men finished their work and were no longer in the halls students felt free to toss their abayas aside and expose their shapely bodies in tights, low cleavage tops and dresses. And there were colors. Their clothes were the latest high-end western designs. Their shiny hair bounced about their shoulders and backs as they pranced through the halls. They were breathtaking! Off campus, I'd seen crowds of women do the same instant: 'on with the black, off with the black' changeover in unison at weddings and social events – done the moment a single man entered and exited the room. And I believed that the reasons for the women and the female students were the same, it was important that they present and see themselves at their feminine best, even if no man was able to. As the corridors were thinning it was easier for me to make it to the Registrar's office, that time, eight minutes later and then back to my office. The men were still there, still working with the security women's eyes fastened on them. The halls were now quiet and empty of students. The tide of black ebbed. It would surge again between classes and at the end of the school day with all the pretty girls clad in black filing out of the university doors to meet their waiting male drivers or men of the family who had come to pick them up.

The intensity with which women avoided direct contact with men was one thing, making oneself invisible was an entirely different story. And for me that was an experiment I really got a kick out of and surprised myself with how much I liked it. While traveling in the Middle East I wore the black abaya, hijab, and niqab going to and moving about in the airports, passing through security, boarding, and sitting on the plane for the entire flight. For that singular period of time, I was deliciously invisible. No one asked me to uncover my face, only to produce my Iqama ID; and people, attendants, and officers pretty much left me alone unto myself, as though I was unapproachable. I could see up close and distant, and no one could 'see' me. That was a brand-new thing, and it gave me sensations of delight, mischief, mystery, even boldness and 'faculty' all at once. By not being seen, I was not imposed upon. Because I 'saw' all, I could take in impressions and make inferences about what I was seeing, while no one could comprehend, judge, or evaluate me. I was unknowable.

There was a strange freedom in not being visually controlled or known in a crowd of people out in the public; and how my invisibility was safeguarded by the culture's ethic of modesty and respect for women's privacy, and even the expectation that women should literally go unnoticed. From my intermittent experiments with invisibility I could better fathom the powerful confidence in the gait of those women so completely silhouetted, with their long black abayas dragging over the ground, with matching hijabs, niqabs, black gloves and black sunglasses to top it all off. Surely, a duality was at work there! The 'covering up in the black' custom which was seemingly imposed as a 'repressive' measure, incidentally, protected a woman from certain intrusions. It was a two-sided shield. Something that was limiting was also liberating. Invisibility was not something I could live with on a regular basis, because I abhorred putting the abaya on my body – black or otherwise; it concealed me when I wanted to be seen – most of the time. But, after a taste of it, I'd like to step in and out of invisibility at will and as it suited me – as a strategy and a delightful diversion. Having made myself 'sight unseen' and moved about in the world that way I could understand how women might feel protected under the cloak of 'black' and its sometimes gift of obscurity – and perhaps like me have a hate/love relationship with it.

Green Zone - The only and limited section on the female campus at university where male professors were allowed to enter to teach and without occupying any offices.

5
Crossing that Line – Close Encounter with a Saudi Gent

I am a fervent believer that that which belongs to you to serve your highest good will find you. And so it was, in my encounter with that Saudi Gent.

Because of the way Saudi society was set up to have separate cultures for men and women, most of my interactions and involvements were with women, personally and professionally. I formed friendships with Saudi women and relationships with hundreds of Saudi female students. There was a clear line of demarcation drawn between men and women, especially in the professional world. In that setting, women did not supervise, teach, or lead men; and men were largely the leaders and made policy and decisions for both men and women. Indeed, woman's lifting or offering her voice in man's world was restricted; she had to tread lightly and work harder to make herself understood or to advance a point without threatening the status quo of male power over women. At some meetings that I attended with female colleagues, we were partitioned off to the side of the room away from the men, behind a physical divider where we could not be seen or see the men on the other side, but we could hear them; and in those forums the men's voices were heard and heeded over those of the women. That was the custom and how things were done.

I acclimated and accepted the fact that I must enter only 'Women' or 'Family' sections when banking, dining, or getting take-out food or attending to other everyday affairs. After making the error more than a few times of going into places not designated for women, I learned to look for and heed the signs. The male sections were not marked which were the main entrances, however the areas and entries designated for women were, at a side or back door. For instance, while racing to beat the start of prayer time to get my fried chicken fix, I unknowingly entered the unmarked men's or main entrance of a Popeye's restaurant. Immediately, I was approached by a nervous server who halted me at the door and directed me towards the 'Family Section' entry several yards away around the corner. *Why was that? Why was the women's section marked and the men's section not?* I wondered, and I supposed that it was because the outside world was naturally man's domain in the culture, whereupon men could come and go with ease; all spaces were accessible to them to move around. And men could take that for granted. They could also enter 'Family' sections with their wives and children, whereas women, single or married were strictly relegated to the 'Family' sections. Again, that was the social decorum, which I accepted and adapted to. It was the law of the land.

Men and women had their distinct places, which made it less likely for the seamless everyday mingling of the sexes – something I took for granted coming from the west. Those separations brought women closer, and they bonded with one other and the same was true for men. My Saudi friends and I discussed that a lot; my friends believed that the structural and behavioral splits ingrained since childhood generated psychological schisms that stifled boys' and girls' mutual knowledge, comfortability and connection and strained those interactions in adult life. Lack of familiarity with the opposite sex made it awkward in male/female relationships for young people as they entered courtships – which were often arranged by their mothers and fathers. Men grew up viewing women as remote at best and objects at worst, and women viewing men as shallow and untrustworthy. With such extreme separations, it would seem impossible for me to find myself in close personal company with a Saudi male. But despite the fact that men and women co-existed in different camps, crossing the line betwixt male and female cultures between unrelated people was inevitable and it happened all the time. Likewise, to me, men were similar in the world, and with few distinctions, even when it came to the Saudi male.

A professional colleague asked me to contact his friend who was seeking some advisement with his doctoral program with a western university. The man was a high-ranking executive in a Saudi corporation. He desperately wanted to advance in his company, one of the most powerful organizations in the Kingdom. His need was immediate, and I was advised to call or text him right away. But instead, I told my friend to have the man contact me. I was naturally keeping to my professional ethics, that being, if a person had a need for my services, they should take the initiative to approach me. Also that way they would more likely appreciate the professional relationship and assistance they were seeking to engage. In no time, the gentleman contacted me. Because I could not drive, he agreed to pick me up one evening from my villa and we would go to a public place to discuss his situation. He came dressed in the usual white thobe, red and white checkered shemagh and black oqal* atop – an attire that I found appealing and admired. Up close in an informal setting the male's traditional dress was even more striking and regal. We sat in the hotel lobby area where people were served tea and deserts. He ordered some for us. He was pleasant - tall and with a gentle, nice-looking, bearded face; his body and hand movements were careful, and he spoke softly to me describing his predicament. He was a man in need. Perhaps, in another life, I would have found him to be a potential mate, but not this one. I liked him just the same. Although the meeting that evening was amicable, we did not come to agreeable terms on how to work together. He wanted and probably needed more assistance than I could give and at the time I was preoccupied with other things and was not compelled by his situation. We bid a kind goodbye with wishes for our mutual success. However, I thought about him and our meeting, from time to time.

A few months later he contacted me again, with the same need and questions – he had not progressed much in his doctoral research from where he was when we last met. He was stuck and stressed. We met again in the same hotel lobby. That time, I learned something more about him. His soft-spoken manner made it necessary for me to move closer to him – a tricky thing, as I was fully aware of how we looked – an unlikely pairing on an evening, him Saudi and me a western woman, engrossed in discussion, thumbing through a mass of papers, clearly not married to each other, clearly not romantically involved. Our odd togetherness in the evening lobby drew people's eyes to us. He told me about his mother's terminal illness, how he was taking care of her in his home with his family, and how he wanted to make her proud by becoming a 'Doctor' while she was still alive. He also wanted to become better for his children. For those reasons and to climb further up the corporate ladder, the Ph.D. would be a critical gain for him.

As I listened, I thought about how my reasons for getting my Ph.D. were very different from his, but I totally understood and empathized with his case. For us both, the degree was a matter of qualify of life. And as he spoke I observed the frustration with which he sifted and sorted through the pile of papers he brought, not quite managing his stress. I noted his attempts to express an idea or thought that he could not easily articulate or translate from his Arabic to my English - English being the language for the program he was seeking his doctoral degree and in which the papers were written. I silenced the presumptions in my head that had been fed to me about the aggressive, masochistic, woman-hating attitudes and behaviors of Saudi men and allowed myself to see and read him objectively. I saw that in the absence of ego, there was humility and personal honor. He was respectful of my intelligence and skills, to the point that he was willing to put his trust in me to guide him through his research. Right before me, the so-called 'problem' of the Saudi male dissolved. He was simply a man trying to do something more with his life. More importantly, from what he told me, and the way he engaged and interacted with me, I could assume that he was a man who appreciated women – a wife, a mother, a daughter, women not kin or blood, and by extension, a professional woman like myself. On that basis, I agreed to work with him.

My reasons to work with the gent were also a little selfish. He would pay me for my consulting services; he also said he could build up my connections in the business community in the Kingdom. And I could surely benefit from strengthening my ties in that arena, anytime. That was universally how things got done anyway. Moreover, it seemed that our paths had crossed for other reasons yet to unfold. We were opposites - an independent African American woman and a culturally privileged Saudi man – coming together amidst complex norms and needs in a land where women, generally, on the surface were not supposed to have advantages or positional dominance over men.

In that collaboration there were subtle issues, more or less 'protocols' that were not articulated or thought through, but were nonetheless, operational; pertaining to who was in control, and who managed who – with me as a necessary guest in his country, and with him needing my expertise to finesse a western Ph.D. program for family, esteem, fortune and honor. Within those complexities, there was no road map on how to proceed with our business and academic arrangement. We never got personal, such as talking about the weather and other casual topics; but kept our conversations above board at the professional level, as if there was a threshold that we both knew we should not cross. At the least, we were subtly aware that trying to exercise power and control over the other would be unwise, and that we should rather relate with mutual respect for mutual benefit. We would need to find and ease into a comfortable mode with one another to make our arrangement work.

The Saudi man was in a different category from other men of the world. Yes, there was an assumed privilege, entitlement, and an acute certainty of his formal rights and dominion over women; and there may have been traces of those elements in my interaction with the Saudi gent. There was an exchange during those weeks of working together that he, out of frustration, did an about-face and snapped at me and tried to command me in the research process and on his expectations. His soft charm vanished, and I was to strictly do his bidding. That was when he met Ghetto Girl, my alter ego, who at a moment's notice, appeared on the scene and smacked down any nonsense, attacks, and offensive behaviors that stepped my way. Thereafter, he resumed his usual civil attitude and posture with me. I never forgot that I was the expert, and he was the client. *Was his snapping at me a mental lapse – momentarily letting his frustrations get the best of him? Was he channeling an instinctive resolve about a woman's subordinate place in his world? Was he testing me, or himself?* I didn't know. For, the most part, I saw him humble himself before his need, not before me. I respected that and easily gave him the benefit of the doubt.

It was easy to judge, form assumptions and conclusions about people from a distance or a brief interaction. One had to get up close to appreciate what was really there. The way that the encounter with the Saudi gent played out was an exception to what was typified. And I wished not to and would not entertain negative stereotypes about him. I had seen so much, which put that kind of thinking in check. I had been in the company of Saudi men who openly expounded on the proper roles that men and women should play and who did not understand *"Why women wanted to drive and be independent rather than tend to the home, bear children and service man's physical needs."* I knew that that kind of thinking existed all over the world. In fact, there were western men I knew who were drawn to Saudi Arabia because they saw it as a place where they could freely exercise their own misogynous attitudes towards women. I worked among those kinds of men.

It was not easy to work with the Saudi gent during those few months, which was like walking a tightwire. His impatience with his limited capabilities and me trying to guide him mounted and he began to however tactfully, insinuate that he wanted me to do all the research, organize and write the dissertation for him – for there was just too much going on in his personal and business life and he was struggling with the language. But he still clearly expressed that he needed that Ph.D. Maybe that was his plan all along – to have me do everything, even when I gave him the benefit of the doubt when we first started to meet. It was obvious that his admission was all a point of chagrin for him. Yet, his 'revised' expectations added another dimension to our working engagement. Once that was clear to me, I called it all off. A no brainer. I worked long and hard to obtain my own doctoral credential and was not about to trivialize and cheapen it by just handing an unearned capstone degree over to somebody for money and connections. And that was not the first time I'd been asked to do such a thing – in KSA or elsewhere. After the fact, I confided the incident to Saudi and ex-pat friends who seemed to feel that whatever I decided would have been a toss-up anyway, and between me and my God. We all knew that that kind of academic give-and-take went on all the time and anywhere in the world with nobody really getting hurt by it. My flat 'No' decision was firm, and I walked away from it. He'd find someone else to work with him that way.

Our engagement ran its course, with me taking him as far as I could. It was not about the end result of his getting a Ph.D. – he was surely years away from reaching that goal, but it was about the process of how we were parlaying with one another, which reached its proper conclusion. I did come away with something. Out of all the interactions I'd had with a number of men and women – many of whom were very close, there was gravity to the call to 'assist' that one man. It was not something I wanted to do, but it felt like something I absolutely had to do, regardless of the outcome; and I was not comfortable being caught up in that quandary. Yet, it seemed that there was something about that encounter with him that had my name written all over it, which called me out. It had a certain energy and ring to it – like a benign tug-of-war – of uneasy lessons learned through the execution of a principled act in the continued construction of my life. It felt karmic in that somehow, by engaging him and figuring out our way forward, however messy, seemed right. The encounter went beyond the moment and had a lasting effect. As I reflected, I knew that that was a stage for some fine-tuning and refinements for a reckoning in my soul. I needed to interact with him as much as he needed to do so with me. And I had no doubt that his encounter with a woman like me was a jolt that he would never forget. Some lines needed crossing. People saw us doing that. Perhaps our engaging heralded the softening and closeness of the threshold for continued encounters between disparate men and women, especially the young and for whatever their reasons might be.

Oqal - A black corded ring that held the shemagh (scarf) in place on a man's head.

6
See No Evil, Hear No Evil, Speak No Evil – It's Complicated

Secrecy and protecting one's privacy were a real thing in the Kingdom. That was another layer to the restrictive and 'classified' way the Kingdom had been governed and for which it was known in the wide world. Granted, it was an unspoken code not to discuss religion or politics in the Kingdom, as in other cultures; I cannot recall any discussions I had with a Saudi citizen about the politics of their home country. However, the code of restraint went deeper from my observations and experiences in the grand desert. In my time there, and being a sensing person, I knew that there was far more going on beneath the surface, in the society, within the institution in which I was contracted, and among students, friends and professional colleagues. I learned more about what was going on in Saudi Arabia from sources outside the country rather than from the local broadcasts; but even the news about the Kingdom coming from the outside was most often skewed. It was hard to know the truth of things and get the real scoop. I had to dig, research, and explore to know more about the environment in which I was immersed and learned that truthful knowledge could best emerge from gaining trust and with people opening up to me, which could be a long process. So, save being fully in the 'know', I succumbed under the rule of secrecy and played in the dark for the most part.

News was controlled in the Kingdom as it was in most other countries; control of the media and censorship was intense in the Kingdom – happening to a greater degree. National, regional, and local news stories and information for public consumption were not penetrating and appeared superficial to me; and that trend spilled over into the operations of the institution in which I worked, and even into relationships among people. In the void that 'secrecy' generated and on individual levels, tittle-tattle and hearsay prevailed as people made things up, perhaps out of insecurity, to make life or themselves more interesting, or as just wishful thinking. It was a knotty exercise to discern what was true because rumors filled the vacuum. If there was any truth to be had it would not come forth, all due to the rule of secrecy. Rumors caused trouble and confusion and hurt a person's reputation. There were mistruths spread about me having affairs with colleagues that were utterly false. It was all too easy to be cast as a pariah for the slightest infraction or from a canard that went unchallenged. The intricate workings of 'secrecy' at the individual level in the Kingdom were quite intriguing to me in that a person defaulted into being ultra-discerning - knowing what not to say or do as a way of life and for personal and professional survival. To me, that was not an easy place to be. An expressive, spirited person could have trouble with that. But it was safe to stay between the lines. It was easier to say *"No"* when you meant *"Yes"* and to keep a stiff upper lip, to: *'See no evil, hear no evil, speak no evil'*.

Yet, the Saudis were some of the most gracious and hospitable people I had known throughout my travels in the world and in the US. I sought and enjoyed their company much more than I did with fellow ex-pats. The grace I witnessed and that they extended to me was a ready kindness, respect and welcome that sought nothing in return, and which felt real to me. One could fall out of that grace just as easily when the person extending it was threatened or slighted. I saw how the Saudis avoided and steered clear of people whom they perceived as reckless and behaved in a way that brought negative attention to him or herself. For the Saudi, that behavior could reflect back onto them, jeopardizing the order of their own lives that they were prudent to protect, again by seeing no evil, hearing no evil, and speaking no evil. It made sense.

Saudis were sensitive to how they and the Kingdom were portrayed in the international community. As a traditionally 'closed society' I believed that the negative reporting and images of Saudi Arabia that were rampant in the international community were factors that caused people in the Kingdom to hold things to their chests closely, guarding their secrets and vulnerabilities. Saudis generally refrained from discussing openly what was going on in the Kingdom, especially anything political or pertaining to its leadership. Those were taboo topics, even in my inner circle of friends. People's discretions were also due to the extensive surveillance and trolling of communications such as social media, emails, and telephone conversations, sometimes even snail mail letters and documents, and packages. Within the university, monitoring was common, and we refrained from sharing anything too personal, heavy laden or controversial, unless in person. And that was the same for openly criticizing a person of authority, how a business was run or anything to do with Kingdom governance.

As horrific and internationally scandalous as it was the Jamal Khashoggi murder incident was not openly discussed or mentioned - not even during the heights of the frenzied media attention it garnered throughout the world. Or as my grandmother would say: *"Not a mumbling word"* was said or heard in reference thereof. *Speak no evil.* It was the big elephant in the room that no one dared to acknowledge, certainly not in my zone of students, friends, or business colleagues; and my network was quite wide, having cultivated it over several years. *Hear no evil.* It felt weird. With all that was being daily reported in the headlines around the world, the tragic event, which was also globally held as a conclusive indictment of the Kingdom and its leadership, was hush-hush. As if in a collective silent consensus, the subject was red flagged on conscious and instinctive levels. One kept a straight face about it and simply did not 'go there' keeping whatever thoughts they had about the crime to themselves, even as it was staring us in the face. *See no evil.* One did not know who to trust or who might be listening. One could get reported and there might be repercussions for expressing any opinion, a thought or word in a no-win situation, which at the least could be arousing other people's dismay and distancing, or at worst, losing one's job, being rebuked, targeted, detained, or queried and prosecuted by authorities. There were many easy snares and traps to fall into.

For instance, after the Khashoggi story broke, I received a call from a male professor; he was in a state of panic and having conniptions, lamenting on the aftermath of his engaging a Saudi male student in a 'casual' discussion about the Khashoggi case. In hindsight, the professor regretted making what he thought was an innocent academic inquiry of the student's opinion. Instead, the student flew into an angry rant - expressing his un-wavering support of the Kingdom and the Prince – alluding to a conspiracy headed by the journalist's wife and the Turkish government. Even though the professor had the presence of mind not to express any opinion he might have or to disagree with the student as he ranted, the professor sensed, from the agitation and tone of the student that he was treading on dangerous grounds, nonetheless; and that was not a 'safe' topic for discussion, in any way, shape, or form. My colleague's fear was that he would be *"reported to higher ups"* by the student for simply opening the conversation. He was on pins and needles for several days thereafter until he saw no signs that that would happen. I discussed the Khashoggi story at liberty, but only in closed quarters with a few dear and trusted people.

In matters of 'disclosure' versus 'discretion' the social environment could be more punishing than rewarding, which was also true in the business and professional environments. A somber example was the case of Mr. Vincent. He was a man who greatly influenced me while there and who was at one point highly regarded and central to the institution's governance; he was among the senior officers there, having played a pivotal part in its founding. However, he retired under a cloud. Over the years, he grew discouraged with how things were done at the institution and became vocal about its leadership. Keeping silent was no longer an option for him. Consequently, he was demoted and moved to a smaller office, and ostracized by other leaders who were noticeably absent from his retirement party after his extensive years of service and legacy with the university - as if overnight, he had become 'persona non grata'.

It was complicated. The proverbial maxim to 'see no evil, hear no evil, and speak no evil' was the guiding wisdom – to be of good mind, speech, and action - to play it safe. It was not an impropriety to turn a blind eye. And that 'wisdom' applied to those things that people were not 'OK' with and were problematic. On the other hand, people easily talked about the nice things – as in a *'Don't worry, be happy'* way, that glossed over the slightest contrary notions. I surmised that that in part stemmed from religious values to 'speak only of the good,' which was a universal ideal. In spiritual terms, speaking of the good brought about 'more good'; giving attention to the negative brought more of the same. There was truth in that. Perhaps, in people's minds the adherence to secrecy might in some way discharge that which was not right in one's life or perhaps in the Kingdom. On that note, I was just reasoning from my limited perch, and coming from the US and knowing that no country was without fault.

The fact remained that beneath the whitewash and veneer of secrecy, all was not well in the Kingdom, especially, for women. I continually felt the frustrations around women's issues from the students, colleagues, and personal friends that they would not articulate, minus a few under the breath protests from undaunted students. For the most part women had their personal and collective frustrations as clear points of reference while they secreted their thoughts and would not openly say anything untoward about women's status in the Kingdom. A climate of intolerance for dissenting thoughts and ideas generated reserve and awkwardness among people; it gave freedom to lies, delusions and unwarranted speculations. Truth could be perilous and costly and was best given on a need-to-know basis. Brazing and stretching into the truth became a strategic exercise in bravery that was more easily done when a person clearly knew that she or he had nothing to lose. I saw that kind of courage with Mr. Vincent and in a few other cases.

In another situation, I befriended a really down to earth woman, Layla, who was systemically pushed out of her organization only weeks after she was exalted to a higher position in it. Over time, she confided to me that she was punished because she *"saw too much"* at those executive levels, and that became the death knell for her. She did not do anything wrong, but she was exposed to and witnessed first-hand the corruptions that had been suspected at those levels. She was asked to perform certain tasks that went against her ethics and which she refused to do. I saw her anguish, yet it took a lot for her to confide in me, and even then, she did not provide details of what she saw, naming no names. *Speak no evil.* It was important for her to just move on, which she did, to greater horizons. She put her focus on her next steps, which she revealed to me only after her goals were reached. That surprised me because as 'trusted friends', we regarded one another as sisters. But I eventually got it.

Silence Was Golden

Layla's experience pointed to another aspect of the phenomenon of speaking, seeing, and hearing no evil - silence. Secrecy and silence went hand in hand. Layla's willful silence shielded her from further trouble and harm - she did not 'speak evil' into existence that could be detrimental to her and have ramifications. And speaking out loud of her next steps and goals could push the good away that she desired. Her situation showed how silence was a protection – keeping her safe because she did not give energy to the bad things; and on the flip side, silence energized her aspirations and ambitions as Layla did not diffuse and spill her hopes by 'speaking' them into the air. Thus, silence was golden on both sides of the coin. By not divulging facts to me on the corruptions she witnessed and specifically why she was subsequently fired, nor sharing information on her plans going forward, Layla was heeding a deeply mystical principle. Again, I got that. The mystical undercurrents of Saudi culture were important for me to know, and I was granted a peek at what that meant in the culture – which was cosmic attunement, to put it mildly. I explored further to find that mysticism was consciously held as a factor of life in the Kingdom, although not openly talked about. And now that I knew more about it within Saudi society, I sensed and saw it all around in my interface with students and friends, and even in the public spaces. Some time after Layla's experience, I had an insightful conversation with a student. It seemed that a 'window' had opened, and the student wanted to share some things with me about her culture that I might want to know. She told me that it was Saudi tradition to place certain items or 'charms' in homes to shield its members from the negative energies and thoughts of others who were not family; and that revealing the desires of one's heart was not safe, especially among those not close to you. What I learned from her, Layla and other such 'ways of knowing' enabled me to better understand and appreciate Saudi as a Kingdom of secrets, which brought me closer to my Saudi compatriots.

Whether secrecy was to protect one from reprisals, to preserve faith in the country or to safeguard dreams, desires, and inclinations, what was hardly known to outsiders was the undergirding mysticism in Saudi society, which was a part of that *seeing no evil, hearing no evil, and speaking no evil* convention. That revelation was so cool for me. The power that the subjective life wielded for any person, in any country and for any reason could not be underestimated. There was a profound spiritual meaning to 'see, hear, nor speak evil' that I thought had lessons for us all. I often heard people say: *"Don't speak it or you will bring it into existence."* Yes, there was certainly truth in that.

I witnessed great suffering in the Kingdom, albeit, a collective, silent suffering, among women, because again, it was with women that I spent much of my time. Suffering was woven into a woman's life; and for one to reduce, cope with or overcome suffering, it was prudent not to give it energy by dwelling on it through one's thoughts or words. I saw women rise from hardships and setbacks despite and on account of their sex. Those were women of blithe and indomitable spirit, who spoke little about their troubles as a woman among women. Often, what was not seen, heard, or spoken upfront came through sideways. In their enduring kinship to the mystical, subjective life, and attunement to the rhythms of change and push and pull, Saudis also knew that time intervened in entrenched situations, and new cycles began. Time and change had their own agendas and could care less about the secrets people kept or the truths they looked away from; and in turn, the rubbish got washed away, anyway. With that inevitability in the context of women's lives I could see how the truth did set them free.

7
The Missionary Meets the Muslim – More Questions than Answers

My brother, Robert, an ordained Deacon of a prestigious Baptist church spent extensive time abroad as a missionary since 2008. He traveled into Ecuador and Ghana on regular missions each year to tend to the souls of people living in huts and remote villages. Prior to that, those people had been solely under the pastoral care of village wise men, elders, and chieftains. My brother's wife often traveled with him and played a part in the missionary work. His parish adopted those remote villages and built churches; providing clothing, supplies and books for the children. Christian values were vital and readily received among the people. He and his wife loved their work and helped their parish bring hundreds of people to the Christian faith through teachings of the Bible and worship, with Robert personally baptizing many in the Guinea-Bissau River, off the coast of Ghana. My brother told me of one remarkable incident when his parish elders exorcized what was clear to all present, an evil spirit from one of the village women. I was proud of my brother and his work.

I came to Christianity early in my life being born into a family of Baptists. I recalled as a young girl of about 11 when I sang with my cousins in a children's gospel group. It was really fun. Still, today, I remember the songs we sang. While so young, I took myself to the church on my own because it felt safe and welcoming for a little girl growing up in the crowded, hectic, and low-income southside projects of Chicago. The New Nazareth Baptist was my first church and a sanctuary. It was right downstairs from our thirteenth floor apartment, in view. Church and faith in general were a refuge for a young girl like me. One of my most memorable, touching and life influencing experiences was when a team of white Catholic nuns came regularly into the ghetto during the summer months to gather up and take us little black kids on field trips into the wider metropolitan city. With glad faces and wearing their solemn habits, they loaded as many of us kids that could fit into buses and took us to libraries, parks, to the zoo and museums. That opened my eyes and let me see that there was a big, teaming world outside the ghetto – for me, that I could reach for. From early on, and as I grew, I searched through many religious teachings to have my questions about God and 'life' answered from Pentecostal, Catholic, Buddhist, even Muslim faiths. I evolved my religious understandings and orientation to adopt spirituality in thought and practice.

My brother and sister-in-law, Linda, wanted to visit me in Saudi Arabia. Perhaps, I surmised, it was my brother's way of checking in to see how I was fairing in such a 'strange and obscure' land. I did the lengthy task of securing the permissions and documents through the Saudi authorities for them to enter the Kingdom. Knowing their staunch backgrounds in the Baptist church and as missionaries, I wondered how it was going to turn out with them coming to an exclusive Muslim country. I advised them not to bring their Bible, or at least not a large one, as it might not get through customs, as I was told by my travel advisors when I first came to Saudi Arabia.

They arrived shortly after midnight on the appointed day, and I was there at the airport waiting for them at the gate. Linda was dressed for the occasion with her head covered and wearing loose-fitting clothes. But I chuckled to myself, noting that no matter how loosely she dressed she could not stop those hips. I told her that – we could all use a laugh. They traveled far and for many hours and were arriving in the heat and in the middle of Ramadan.

We planned the next day for shopping after they had some good rest. I put them up in my master bedroom with adjoining bathroom and took the guest room. Ajmal, my driver picked us up, and blocked his entire day to take us shopping and for a little touring to places he thought they might like to see. He was touched that I had family, who would come that distance and to the Kingdom to be with me. It also gave him a new window to know more about me. He had been my driver for four years, up to that time. Ajmal was Pakistani, and a Muslim, through and through. He often arrived to drive me to errands with his newly shaved bald head – an eye-catching contrast to his usual jet-black shiny mass of hair. He'd disappear for days for his regular Hajj and Umrah pilgrimages and when he returned, he was beaming. I saw Ajmal as a sort of 'consigliere', helping me with his insights and wherewithal in the Kingdom; he possessed a fabulously learned and curious mind, something I appreciated about him, next to his good looks.

For twelve years, Ajmal had been a driver in the Kingdom for a mostly female clientele. He spent a month each year with his family in Pakistan, which he supported from his earnings as a driver. He had four children and was putting two through college. I knew that sixty-seven percent of Americans did not know a Muslim personally and I was interested to see how my brother and his wife would get on with Ajmal. After the shopping and touring, Ajmal wanted to linger and hang out with us. That was easy because he had become a close friend and much more than my driver. It felt good to be with people who meant a great deal to me – Ajmal, Robert and Linda. We all found an open time to talk, and the conversation was intriguing. At some points, it took on the feeling of a contest between the two faiths. I observed in the middle as the two sides gingerly approached the other with questions around faith with genuine curiosity; the Muslim and Christians maintained their grounds and did not give an inch in the face of challenges and clear contradictions, even inconsistencies that the dialogue dug up.

There were pointed questions. For instance: *"If Muslim men get the seven virgins after they die, what does the devout Muslim woman receive when she dies?"* and *"Do you Christians set aside a ritual of fasting as we do for Ramadan?" "Do Christians fast at all?" "What is prayer to the Christian?"* and *"What does 'praying' five times a day do for a Muslim's spirit and soul?"* Ultimately, the debate or rather friendly discussion was far more interesting than any answers it might surface – which really did not happen. As it turned out those were unanswerable questions – just meant as a poke from either side to justify or defend where one was coming from. No one was swayed either way, and we were all smiling, just the same. Such was the way of the world. The rift between Christian and Muslim beliefs was legendary, it had been bloody, and was unresolved to that day. The exchange between Robert, Linda and Ajmal was a microcosm of the global impasse around faith. Yet, there remained larger questions, I thought; starting with: *Why was faith, which was an issue so critical to everyone's sense of soul redemption during and at the end of life relegated to such mundane inquiries?*

The Kingdom of Saudi Arabia prided itself as being the custodian of the two holiest sites in Islam, they were Mecca and Medina and declared as such by the Prophet Muhammad. Hundreds of millions of devout Muslims descended upon the two sites throughout each year from all over the world - with more than 2 million coming for their annual Hajj and periodic Umrah pilgrimages. Saudi Arabia was the center of Islam. For that and historical reasons stemming from the Crusades, the Kingdom projected, maintained, and protected an absolute Muslim worship environment. It was one of few nations that did not allow non-Muslim churches on its land. The practice of Christianity among the ex-pat faithful had to be discreet and was done in secret. Bibles and other overt non-Muslim texts were subject to being banned or confiscated at customs. Yet, I found that the protocols on matters of faith were relaxed, but clear on the ground and in a one-on-one parley with a Muslim.

"You stay Christian, and I will stay Muslim." I heard that statement some time ago from a Muslim man and 'would be' convert to Christianity when he felt chided about his faith. His retorted conviction brought the conversion effort to an abrupt end. And that was where the nuanced conversation really began in my villa with Robert, Linda and Ajmal, and for that matter, in the larger faith communities. People of any faith, at the gut level, wanted to know that they were in the right place and doing the right thing; that was my thinking. I believed that my brother and his wife genuinely wanted to know something about the Muslim faith, with no aims to convert. That was not how they operated. For in their understanding, souls had to come freely to the 'faith' once a person had been ministered to and received the 'word'. Conversely, Ajmal's Muslim religion did not proselytize.

A way to validate the virtues of one's beliefs was by holding their faith up against others; and there were a lot of assumptions that went along with that. In the context in which I observed those conversations between the Christian and the Muslim, Islam was a 'pull' and passive religion, in that it did not seek to convert. It did not assert itself to bring non-Muslims into the fold. I had not known of Muslim 'missionaries' going out into the world recruiting *souls*. Additionally, in a Muslim dominated country, I never experienced or observed Muslims as being concerned whether the Christians among them practiced or adhered to the Muslim faith. It was none of their business. I was never asked to attend a prayer service at a mosque but felt welcomed to do so if I chose. Not once, had Ajmal in our years of camaraderie, asked me about my faith. The Muslim did not judge the non-Muslim but turned away from the 'non-believer' – someone who had no faith or religious beliefs. To them, 'faithlessness' was irresponsible and dangerous.

On the other hand, Christianity had historically been an assertive 'push' religion to convert people. Many of the faithful, as with my brother, followed the teachings of the Bible to: *"Go ye therefore, and teach all nations, baptizing them in the name of the Father, and the Son, and the Holy Ghost."* Ex-pats who were my colleagues in the Kingdom made muscular inquiries about my faith and asked me repeatedly to join their secret Christian prayer circles. Their eyes showed confusion and dismay when I declined and indicated that I was not a 'devout' and rather a fringe, spiritual dweller. At an earlier, searching stage in my life, I gave in to that kind of pressure and attended church regularly, until my Pentecostal Baptist minister Reverend Eastman, told me something one Sunday morning after service. He 'saw' and approached me and said: "Sister Taylor, I have been observing you for a while coming here and sitting there in that pew. You are different, and I see you struggling with this. You don't belong here, and you know it. This need not worry you. Your time with this church is done. In the name of the Holy Christ, I am releasing you from this church to go and find the place that you can call your true spiritual home." The Reverend was prophetic and said more to me in that sudden, brief, and private session that I needed to hear.

Eastman's insights and words were staggering but correct and instilled in me a validation that was brand new. From there, with his blessings, I embarked on my avid spiritual journey and never looked back. Along that path, another well-loved Baptist minister, B. T. Anderson, who was also a friend, engaged me in many pointed discussions on religion, faith, and God. We'd go down the proverbial 'rabbit hole' in our long talks, touching upon esoteric, spiritual, and mystical concepts that he did not share in his Sunday sermons in front of his congregation. He gave credit to my pursuit and dive into spirituality. When I asked him why he did not espouse those same concepts in his church, he said: "A minister must meet people where they are." Eastman and Anderson were exceptional men of faith, and so was my brother, and so was Ajmal. That debate between the Missionary and the Muslim in my villa in KSA demonstrated an earnest interest between those two dominant religions of the world. I thought it was a healthy exercise and was glad they did that. All in all, their engagement took me into some deeper thinking on the subject.

Questions that their questions hinted at but were not asked were: *Was Christian belief a more secure pathway to heaven and access to God?* And: *Did either faith make one a better person?* When I looked more closely at each faith and beyond the apparent differences, there were more similarities. Submission to God was at the center of each faith, and that was what the word 'Islam' meant. Muhammad was a messenger, as was Jesus. Recorded history was replete with how the two religions and Judaism had parallel origins and scenarios, of how each grew and evolved with and through the other, and with similar agents of love and themes of an all-inclusive humanity. Muslims had respect for the Bible and were familiar with many of its passages which were referenced in the Qur'an. Islam was said to be a religion of peace, so was Christianity. Those religions were more in concert at their core; it was how they were practiced that varied.

I found Islam to be grounded in cosmic principles. In Islam, the faithful practiced in accordance with the phases of the moon. Ramadan was the annual Muslim purification ritual. It occurred over a thirty-day period in the ninth month of the Muslim year, with the exact time differing by a week or two each year - which was determined by the appearance of the crescent moon. Ramadan was a dedicated time for purging of the spirit through introspection and self-improvement, fasting and intense prayer. During Ramadan, from sunrise to sunset, Muslims were required to abstain from eating food, drinking anything, smoking, chewing gum and sexual activity; they were not even to indulge impure thoughts. Yearly schedules and activities were worked around and secondary to the Ramadan cycle; and to accommodate the month of collective fasting, worship, and spiritual purification. With Ramadan in session or not the daily prayers differed by a few minutes each day – perpetually in sync with the changing phases of the moon.

In Mecca, the faithful pilgrims circled around the Ka'bah in the same counter-clockwise direction as the rotation of the earth. In Islamic teachings, the face of God was 'unknowable' - there were no images of God or holy agents such as Muhammad in the mosques or anyplace else. For the Muslim, 'Divinity' lived in the heart where humanity met the creator. The collection plate was not a tradition in Muslim practices, as mosques were regularly funded by Islamic governments. The temple for prayer could be anyplace, anywhere a person saw appropriate – in the park, in a gangway, a corner or center of a room, or in a designated prayer room at the mall. Any location and spot were sacred where a person could drop to his and her knees in worship of God/Allah. How a person practiced his and her faith was a personal and private matter – left up to the manner with which the individual chose to follow their heart, and to tend to their relationship with God. It was not a public event that was displayed or to be weighed by other people's standards. It was not a group affair.

Where the Christian may have wanted or urged the other to 'be like me', the Muslim had a 'live and let live' posture towards the other. That was what I observed having lived in the Kingdom among Muslims for those many years. I was comfortable, relaxed, and free in a room and in a country full of Muslims.

Yet, I was not one of them, at least, not in faith, but in spirit – as a fellow human being who was moved to live in sync with the cosmic rhythms that undergirds anyone's life.

Faith was good for the soul; and with Christianity as the largest religion in the world, with Islam being the second, both creeds had kept people faithful for centuries, and remained alive and expansive. With that, some apparent questions were: *What gains had Muslim and Christian religions wrought in the world during the centuries other than faith? What victory for humankind? And how much longer would either religion go on massaging that artificial chasm between their beliefs?* I was wondering, *was it possible and time for either religion to convene around a common threat to the mutual perpetuation of their practices?*

Whether it was push or pull, the big question and more was: *Why were there declining numbers of young adults coming into the folds of both religions – Christian and Muslim –* something that was happening all over the world in recent years. The mounting story and around which questions had to be raised was that young adults were not being recruited into the church to the same degree that it was being aged out. Church membership had been steadily declining – yet that was not widely broadcasted on the six o-clock evening news. To a lesser extent than those in the west, young adults in the Kingdom were not breaking down the door to seek salvation or to pursue and grow religious faith through Islam. I wondered who was telling that story. *Where were the young folks gravitating, turning to? Was spirit and soul redemption as much an issue for them as it was for earlier generations? Did the decline have anything to do with stark questions that could not be answered by either religion, however, sincere the intent might be? What consciousness was behind the multitudes of young adults not seeking the church and organized religion? And what kind of world was that consciousness creating?*

Could glimpses of that world be seen from the marches in the streets in the West for economic, political, and racial justice; or in the rise of women in the Kingdom, both spurred in large part by young adult voices – who were becoming the majority population on the planet? Again, I wondered, who would widely disclose some facts on the matter and how should those questions be answered?

My brother and sister-in-law may have come to Saudi Arabia with long-held perceptions on people, culture and faith and may have left with new and revised ones. They may have learned something about the gracious spirit of the

Saudi people, having had direct experiences with some - my friends and regular folks. They did leave knowing that I was safe and not in any kind of danger, neither physically nor spiritually. And I believe that they surely, together with Ajmal acquired a little more confidence in their respective beliefs – an aplomb that was gained, not by winning another soul over to their side, but the resolve that they were 'OK' – that their faith was intact and would not be annihilated when faced with a different point of view. And despite so many unanswered and unanswerable questions, there was certainly a spirit knitted throughout holding the faiths together- speaking to and blessing each one of us.

8
Twice Dry

There were numerous times when I've said and heard others proclaim in earnest: *"I need a drink!"* That included ex-pats, Saudis, Pakistanis, and Indians, men, and women. All realizing with that pronouncement, that it was just an empty promise to themselves – me too. But I knew that the 'dry spell' would come when I made the deal and signed the contract to live and work in the Kingdom. At that time, I felt that I could handle that hurdle. I was accustomed to being able to easily reach for and indulge a casual glass of wine to relax or simply to enjoy the taste of it. I felt that I could manage the absence of such a simple and easy pleasure; but I did not expect that it would be so taxing to go without a glass of 'vino' for months on end. Saudi Arabia was hot, with sparce rainfalls and temperatures averaging well over 100 degrees several months in the year. It was no joke! Having not much to do in the heat fueled a desire for something wet and enlivening. It helped a bit to know that I was not alone - just a little, for the sake of venting to a sympathetic ear.

The Kingdom stretched far and wide over the Arabian desert, including some of the Saharan sands; astonishingly, KSA was ninety-five percent desert. The rainy season was meager, to say the least, with rain falling about a dozen days a year – when I counted. It rained when it got good and ready, sometimes with thunderstorms; and even then, it was not for long. But it was not just the desert that made the Kingdom so 'dry', it was the official absence of alcohol too. Twice dry. Alcohol was illegal and possession and consumption of it was punishable by imprisonment, fines, and in most cases a regimen of lashes with a whip. Exactly when and why alcohol was declared illegal in the Kingdom was unclear. From my inquiries, reports had it that decades ago when alcohol was allowed in the Kingdom, a high-ranking official, while under the influence of drink behaved improperly and over-aggressively with another person, causing harm. Thereafter, the ardent spirits were banned, outright. In that devoutly religious environment, as the center of Islam, imbibing alcohol was seen as *"Satan's handiwork."*

With the absolute ban, it became illegal to buy, sell, import, consume, or produce alcohol – that included drugs and any mind-altering stimulants as well. It was not even prudent to talk about alcohol socially. Not speaking about and avoidance of alcohol was in keeping with the Kingdom's image as a holy nation, as well as its norms of devoutness which it exemplified throughout the world. It was a Muslim country, which adhered to strict interpretations of the Qur'an. It was the home of Mecca and Medina – the two most sacred sites in Islam, to which Muslims trekked from all over the world on their annual and periodic pilgrimages. The Kingdom zealously strived to keep its house clean, and officially, it did. So, those who pined for a drink kept that urge close to the chest and strictly confidential. However, braving the risks of harsh penalties and punishments, those who would drink did find a way.

Non-nationals and Saudis alike drank alcohol both outside and within the Kingdom. Statistics showed that eleven percent of Bedouins consumed alcohol. I'd met and known many who boasted about it. It was not easy for anyone to live with the social restrictions of the Kingdom, especially the ex-pats – with some resorting to reckless drinking which came with a price. One professor frequently entertained men in her villa, drinking at night. Her neighbors noticed, and she was soon after branded as a slut and ostracized. Another woman who drank and smoked hashish with men at the compound pool was swiftly thrown out of the Kingdom. To say that she was 'expelled' would be too mild a term to describe exactly how that happened. Life in the Kingdom could be daunting, and one had to have the diligence and sensibility to get used to it and make it work. Some did, many could not – especially, without a drink. Men and women I knew sought the kind of relief and unwinding that came only from having a drink – privately asking around: *How could they get a taste of vodka?* People fled the Kingdom in droves come Thursday afternoon for the weekend, en route to Bahrain – many, to have a drink, or two, or more.

The causeway from Saudi into Bahrain was typically jammed and it took several hours to get across. Once making it over to Bahrain, people quenched their thirsts for alcohol which was poured freely in the nightclubs and restaurants. They would do the things they could not do in the Kingdom – things that were prohibited in KSA. Not only could they drink to their hearts' delight, but they could go dancing, see movies, and hear live music; and plenty men regularly found refuge in the massage parlors which offered a little something extra, like trouble-free sex with a prostitute. Pork was forbidden in the Kingdom; but in Bahrain, one could buy all the ham, bacon, and sausages they wanted at the Pork Store. It was not mandatory to wear the abaya in Bahrain. Women could and would publicly prance around in regular clothes. How fortunate we were to live so close – only hours away from Bahrain. But the caveat was that one could not bring those same 'letting your hair down' freedoms back into KSA; liquor and pork delicacies had to be consumed outside the Kingdom. All vehicles had to undergo layers of administrative and security checks upon reentering the Kingdom after leaving Bahrain.

During a flight layover in Bahrain, I encountered a Saudi man in the airport lounge. There were plenty of available seats around in the bar area where complimentary wine and spirits were served along with appetizers. But he eyed me and wandered to the area where I was sitting nearby. He had imbibed a little too much and was feeling rather jolly. He, like me, was between flights and on his way back to KSA. He was dressed in the traditional white thobe, checkered scarf and oqal – looking very Saudi. He settled into the chair right next to me. He asked if I was also traveling to Saudi. *"Yes."* Taking my answer as a 'green light', he let loose, his tongue liberated by the high amounts of alcohol he had consumed. He began talking aloud more to himself and into the air than to me - sounding off about the 'extremes' of modern Saudi women: *"Why do they want to drive anyway? These women should be happy to have the man be in control and take care of them. Man protects them and gives them comfortable things. All they need to do is to stay home, cook and keep it clean and spread their legs to appreciate what the man is doing."* He even demonstrated the latter part by widening his legs as he sat. I listened, saying nothing to encourage him. He seemed to be having a good time having his say with no interest or comments coming from me. I was his captive audience in that small airport lounge. I thought it was a useful study. I knew that he knew that he could not drink and act that way once he was back in the Kingdom.

If people could not go to Bahrain to drink, the rare 'spirits' found their way into the hands of those who diligently sought them, and there were many instances of that. I visited ex-pat's and Saudi's homes in the Kingdom where shelves were stocked with bottles of Smirnoff, Jack Daniels, and Johnny Walker – those brands that were easy to obtain on the black market. The hosts took pride in showing off their private stashes. That was also an enticement for some men who wanted to seduce women. I found that out from having to wrestle my way out of an overly amorous Palestinian man's apartment one Saturday afternoon. And there was a secret 'liquor bar' run by an enterprising lady that catered mostly to ex-pats, by personal invitation only. Her speakeasy was a long-standing hideout and hot spot for the ex-pats, until it was shut down because a disgruntled customer snitched on her operation to the authorities.

The Saudi Human Resources Director at one of our partner organizations was relieved from his duties because he came in to work one time too many, stumbling drunk. And the ex-pat 'moonshine circuit' in the less controlled compounds was quite busy producing beer, wine, and vodka/sid. Goodness knows what went into that! They even made a mock Johnny Walker concoction called 'brown'. The homemade whiskey and vodka brews were far cheaper than the real thing, but closer to 'rot gut'. Truth was that: *"Anything a person wanted they could have in the Kingdom"* - said the woman who sequestered a bottle of homemade wine for me, more than once. Yes, I did discreetly partake in the underground availability of spirits, for which I could easily rationalize and did so, guilt free. I had been a good girl for such a long time, helping and doing harm to nobody. And I certainly knew how to hold my liquor!

Lawful drinking was possible under limited and controlled conditions in KSA. That was during the weekly Happy Hours hosted by the US Consulate, which had somewhat of a 'sovereign' status and latitude within the Kingdom. If a person did not own or have access to a car (as women did not) or could not afford the costs to travel to Bahrain, there was the US Consulate where the alcohol flowed for three hours each week from 5:00 -8:00 pm on Thursdays. Not much time in the week for drinking, but it was something. The Consulate was permitted to have its own rules and allowed ex-pats to imbibe within clear-cut parameters – doing its bit to satisfy the cravings of most, and to keep some ex-pats from going stark raving mad from want of a drink. The drinking hours were scheduled in conjunction with the last day of work when people really wanted that drink to unwind. The location was in a designated 'drinking room' on the Embassy grounds, which was chiefly, a highly managed environment reserved for alcohol consumption.

Space was limited in the legal 'drinking room', which could comfortably accommodate 20-30 people at a time. A person had to make a request to attend through a sponsor, or someone who worked at the Consulate a week in advance. Their name was entered on a list, which was only approved after their background was 'system checked'. Upon arrival at the Embassy for the Thursday Happy Hour the person underwent a series of checks. First, their car had to pass through an armed guard security checkpoint. After parking in the designated lot, a passport was required once they approached the Embassy entry gate; their name was verified on the 'list'; handbags were opened and looked through, and body scans were done, then the person was cleared to walk through the gate. All cell phones had to be left behind in the person's car. Cell phones were strictly not allowed in the 'drinking room'. That 'control' was for Consulate security and to offset the chance that drunken selfies would circulate in the community outside the Consulate grounds and offend the religious piety that the Kingdom strived to protect, and indeed out of respect for its laws against drinking. Once clearing the hyper check in protocols, all those arriving were escorted to the 'drinking room' on the expansive Embassy grounds in mini shuttle buses, specifically set aside for that occasion.

The room was nothing fancy, brightly lit, packed and loud with people socializing and enjoying their booze. Plain clothed security people were in the room, mingling among the revelers, closely monitoring everyone's behavior. There was bar food, such as pizza, finger sandwiches, nuts, cookies, and chips. Sometimes there was music piped in; people played cards, and there might be special games and contests to enliven the evening. There was liquor that could be purchased at the bar: Cold beer, wine, well drinks and cocktails – with or without ice, shaken or stirred. People were so happy to be there. I spent numerous Thursdays in that room and with friends. The good times would go on until the lights blinked on and off letting all those present know that the time was nigh to order that last drink for the evening. Alcohol from the bar had to be consumed solely within the confines of that room, which was cleared by 8:00 pm sharp. Many people would not have that kind of alcohol-fueled fun and gaiety again until the following Thursday, and if they cleared the protocols and were allowed to get in the next time - if there was space. No guarantees.

Then there was the black market. With high risk, it procured the regular and premium stuff by name brands - Smirnoff, Jack Daniels, Hennessy, Grey Goose, etc. The black market was primarily run and operated by enterprising Filipino men and women. The first task was to find a person who was willing to procure the alcohol. Black marketeers were sometimes skittish with new customers. A person had to be vetted as trustworthy, discreet, and able to hold their liquor well and not bring negative attention to him or her. The gamble was too high if the procurer was identified and/or caught. The code word used when placing an order for alcohol was 'tea' - *white tea or brown tea* - stipulating either vodka or whiskey, respectively. One never knew who was listening on the phone or scanning text messages in a hyper-surveilled and controlled environment. The cost of vodka, which was usually Smirnoff, came at an exorbitantly high price compared to what one paid in the US or UK or anyplace outside the Kingdom. A pint of vodka that would normally cost about $10 in the US was more than ten times that much, $110, on the black market. Again, one paid for the risk. And delivery could take several weeks. Customers would keep the ill-gotten bottles well hidden in their homes; and would bet their bottom dollar that they would make the contents last as long as possible.

The alcohol was pirated into the Kingdom, smuggled on boats or in the trunks of cars, carefully concealed in secret compartments. Dealing at that level was a sketchy, clandestine business with surprise twists and turns at times. It was criminal activity according to the laws of the land, and it had its shadowy underbelly. While most 'spirits' merchants were 'honest' people trying to make a living like everyone else in the only way they knew how, there were the sometimes, shady characters who did not operate above board or regular. The 'spirits' dealers knew the great risks they took; they were even more aware that their product was in high demand. Some took advantage of the leverage that gave them and the fact that they had people over a barrel. As such, they would do any combination of the following: Jacked up their prices; took their time with delivery; did not deliver exactly what was ordered; or were rude and picked and chose their customers for scant and shifty reasons. A person had to be quite discerning to find an ethical and reliable spirits dealer - a somewhat contradiction of terms. In truth, the risks went both ways. But for many, it was worth having that private bottle at one's disposal in their home when they wanted or needed to reach for it at the end of the day or for whatever.

And Then There Was Shisha!

So, what could people in the Kingdom do when they needed a lift, or a little help to relax and let go of their minds and the affairs of the day; and to do that in a carefree way that was legal and without the stress of black market maneuverings? There was shisha. Shisha smoking involved a water pipe or hookah as westerners called it. It was a luxury that originated in the Middle East as part of its tradition and culture, and a social activity that was becoming popular among young adults in western cultures. Stores that sold shisha proliferated in choice sections of the Saudi coastal city. Shisha was a way of smoking tobacco using an elaborate hose and bottle, with charcoal and ice cold water as a filter system. It came in a variety of flavors, such as apple, lime and mint, strawberry, watermelon and floral. Shisha smoking was pleasurable for me, with 'rose' being my preferred taste. It produced a flavor-filled buzz and was more of a relaxant and mellowing - not mind altering. Shisha smoking in itself was a respite and could be done openly with another person or persons.

People would be people, wherever they were, and would find a way for release and escape, especially when 'the life' was twice dry. Imbibing on the low-down was a part of the life we lived in KSA. Frustrations, loneliness, isolation, nothingness, and a plethora of social restrictions, along with their daily labor and doing without the quality of life they had become accustomed to and left behind in their home countries made alcohol attractive and necessary for many – even the most sagacious of people. It was opportunity and financial necessity that drove foreigners to the Kingdom during that period, with most finding themselves in reduced circumstances, despite the money they made. It was, consequently, a 'dispiritedness' arising from the process of achieving those ends that made a person desire that drink or 'spirits', pun intended. Men and women - westerners and migrants, who were a long time and a long distance from their families were working in that foreign land to send money back home to support their families – much as a mother bird flies off and forages for food to feed her nestlings. Saudis had their own stories to tell, like that inebriated man in the lounge in Bahrain.

The intermittent rainfall on the arid Arabian desert was a real treat when it happened, which put my compadres and me in a 'play-day' and holiday mode, wanting to take a recess and time out to relish the water falling from the sky. So too, was the hard won 'cheerful libation' after a lull, and done in balance, to calm, soothe or granted to oneself as a personal reward. Living a chaste existence, without a drink when a person felt they really could use it, was a tough pill to swallow in the Kingdom for ex-pats, migrants, and Saudis alike. Whatever our circumstances, be they reduced or otherwise, we knew the perils of personally falling short if we were not careful – things could always and easily get worse. It was what us foreigners and the nationals had to reckon with and sort out with our better angels or inner-demons. Some weathered it as best they could, more than others. Shortly before exiting the Kingdom, I heard through the pipeline, perhaps more than once, that in the not-too-distant future some designated liquor bars might be allowed at the Saudi airports and maybe in some hotels. Now that could be a sobering trend. Who knew?

9
An Inch Away from Thirty Lashes

It had been several months since I consumed a glass of wine; and it would be more months until I would travel back home to the states on leave, when and where I could freely savor one. Those musings were prompted when my friend invited me to join her on a weekend jaunt to Bahrain. We would travel there together and return in separate cars because she was going to remain longer for a social event. I'd been to Bahrain several times up to then and knew what it promised; and I enjoyed my friend's company. The decision to go took no thinking about. And now there was a new motivation. Bahrain was a pricey destination and a hub for travelers. It was a lure for Saudis and ex-pats alike, as well as Pakistanis, Indians, and Filipinos, etc. Dubai was a distant alternative. For us living on the Eastern Province of Saudi Arabia, Bahrain was the only game in town that was close where one could venture for 'normalcy' – in other words to 'eat, drink and be merry' and be back home in the same day. The cost for a decent hotel in Bahrain was high, and one needed to rent a car or hire a driver; the lounges and restaurants were also costly; add to that, shopping, and entertainment. A lot of people went there every week. For me, a Friday and Saturday in Bahrain was an occasional delightful sojourn and a rare affordable expense. But when asked, I was more than in the mood to pay for Bahrain's expensive excitement that weekend, and I had no frigging idea just how much that jaunt could cost me in other ways.

Fast forward. "Come out of the car and open your suitcase mam." Said the officer at the Saudi Customs Entry checkpoint - said to me! Looking directly at me! *"What!"* I exclaimed in my mind as panic shot up and through my body – careful at the same time to keep my cool. Obediently, I got out of my driver's SUV, thinking out loud: *"Oh my God!"* I shook, maybe I wobbled around to the back of the vehicle towards the already opened trunk where the customs officer and my driver waited – their eyes pinned on me. My legs were like jelly, my breathing becoming irregular – it seemed to take me forever to get there, fully aware that I was in danger.

An Inch Away from Thirty Lashes

I had given my plan a lot of thought, which was to be put into action once I arrived in Bahrain – to purchase some wine to bring back with me to Saudi. I talked myself into it: *"It's been a while, and you need your wine to help in this life as a single working woman in Saudi Arabia – and with all the sacrifices you are making."* Blah, blah, blah. I convinced myself that it was okay and the right thing for me to do. I was a moderate, casual drinker – a glass of wine or cocktail, now and then. What harm was that? Who was I hurting to imbibe in the privacy and comfort of my villa - a little something to calm my nerves, make me feel warm inside, and fortify me to face the isolation and restrictions – of walking backwards without a plan? *"I deserve this."* I'm still thinking: *"Pouring a glass of wine would be part of an occasional twilight ritual of gratitude - something I could look forward to when I came home from the office and peeled off my clothes and propped up my feet for a respite moment of quiet, relaxation and reflection. It would be offending nobody and enabling me to pick myself up again to 'do' the next day."*

Once I was in Bahrain and commencing to execute the 'vino' plan, those rationalizations accompanied me all the way to the Liquor Outlet, the one place that openly sold alcohol in Bahrain. I knew the risks that the black market smugglers took to provide 'spirits' in the Kingdom, now I was hazarding that risk. By doing so I was sparing myself the high expense of going through the underground dealers and to have the convenience of not waiting the usual 2-3 weeks before they could deliver, if at all. I assured myself that things would turn out fine - I would take care and caution to pack and conceal the wine in my luggage. I was also banking on the positive track record from my past trips in and out of Bahrain. The Liquor Outlet operated during limited hours on a Saturday; people were already lined up waiting outside for the store to open at noon. I waited far away from the crowd and out of the hot sun, entering when the line was gone. I only planned to buy a few bottles of wine, but got inspired, or better yet, greedy, like a kid in a candy store after I saw all that was possible to purchase when I went inside the Liquor Outlet. The impulse kicked in, to meander through and get whatever I wanted.

Alcohol was absolutely forbidden in the Kingdom of Saudi Arabia and had been for many decades. It was reported and I supposed unofficially known, that people who were caught bringing alcohol into the Kingdom were given a punishment of lashes, be they Saudi, ex-pat, man, or woman, young, or old. Thirty lashes from the whip were the average count – that and jail time and a fine. A person could also lose a lot more. Their employer could be notified of their indiscretion, and they would forfeit their job and position, losing all service benefits, and the employer could be automatically absolved of any and all financial obligations to them. The person could be made to leave the Kingdom after serving jail time and taking their allotment of lashes. Alcohol possession and consumption was a serious offense in the land of the two holiest Muslim sites. I knew that.

The fifteen-mile causeway between Bahrain and Saudi was the major and only thoroughfare for personal and commercial traffic, and it had heavy security. But I was not deterred from my plan by that fact. *Why was I so uber-confident to buy the spirits with the intent to bring them back?* I believed that it would be a breeze. I had made numerous previous trips to Bahrain over the causeway - eight to be exact, including the present one; and the vehicles in which I was a passenger were never, never stopped or checked upon reentering the Kingdom. I noted the casual inspections of others and my driver's car from the crew of young energized Saudi customs officers - all male, who would cordially smile and let our car move on ahead, each time; and how a lot more cars were waved through than were being stopped – maybe one out of twenty or more. I saw how when some cars were stopped, the customs officers had the drivers open the trunks, and they gave a quick eye scan inside and OK'd the drivers to pass through the customs station.

I had the impression that the enforcements around contraband were for other people who had been 'profiled' by the authorities or appeared in some way suspicious. Moreover, I was told that the customs authority particularly scrutinized cars carrying several young men. Being a woman, I assumed that the checkpoint authorities would not pry and invade my personal space, as respecting women's privacy was an innate part the culture of modesty. Besides, each time I would wear my abaya when going back into Saudi. With all that, I felt immune to such border searches, which also seemed lax to me. Therefore, equipped with those 'fact checks' and rationalizations, I bought the two bottles of chardonnay and a fifth of vodka. As a sometimes treat I thought I'd sip the vodka mixed with orange juice to make it taste better and last. It was all so easy. I walked from the Liquor Outlet to my hotel carrying the bag of spirits in the warm open air with a spring in my step. But, in the following morning, just before I left the hotel on my way back to the Kingdom, I did a last minute examination of the carefully concealed 'goods' in my suitcase, and there was a pause as I thought, *"Hmmm, maybe I should just leave this all here."*

So, when the crisp, bearded Saudi customs officer ordered me to exit the car and open my suitcase, with my driver standing by, looking hapless, I saw doom. I could run, but where? Turn back the hands of time and do things differently? Not possible! I felt so busted! Fact: I'd been bad and was going to have to pay for it. When caught with alcohol by the Kingdom's authorities, all bets were off; there was no forgiveness, and no exceptions. In my terrorized mind my world and all that I had accomplished in those years in the Kingdom were crashing down in that instant nightmare. And it would bleed into my other life beyond the Kingdom. The future was gone and reduced to what was going to happen next – that was what I was thinking and feeling with every fiber of my being. I finally, arrived at the back of the SUV after what seemed like an eternity, with me seemingly outside my body seeing myself moving in slow motion. I snapped back into it and zoomed in on my suitcase lying in the opened trunk, with a waiting audience. "Please open it, mam." The officer said again. "*So polite, so deadly!*" I shouted in my head. As I unzipped the suitcase, I saw my hands trembling. The customs officer stood close to my left looking 'dead on' at the contents inside that suitcase.

I could see the spot where the alcohol had been placed - in the upper left corner - wrapped in my thick clothing. His hands immediately sprang into the suitcase to probe. "*Is he really gonna do that?!*" I am now screaming in my head. His hands were now digging around in the exact area where the bottles laid snug and sleeping. I stood frozen, but not for long as I saw his hands probing deeper, separating layers of clothing – an inch away from touching the neck of the bottle of vodka. In another 'nanosecond' he would be grabbing the bottle – "*Then what, Elizabeth?! What then!?*" Now howling inside my head. I saw everything hurdling towards the precipice. "*NO!!!*" My 'will', shrieking. At warp speed, I threw my hands into the suitcase on top of the wrapped bottle of vodka and started to lift and move my undergarments around in the area near his searching hands. I did that as though I were trying to help him dig, to show him what was there, to spare him the effort, as it were – redirecting those *evil* hands of his. Me, now speaking. "See, this is my nightgown, and this here is my bra, here are more things." Letting him know that those were my intimate wear – hoping that the Saudi code of modesty would kick in and deter any interest of his to further probe around in a woman's underthings - tempting his hands away from the tips of the vodka and wine bottles which were nestled just beneath the clothes from his fingers and his touch. I did not look at him, but kept my eyes glued on that area of the suitcase, on that spot and his eager hands – willing that something not terribly bad had to happen – not that day! A lifetime slid by and then, Mashallah!

It worked! With that move the officer miraculously, stepped back from the suitcase and away from me saying: "You can go now." Sweeter words had not been spoken to me in a very long time. I think I muttered a *"Shukran"* in his direction with what little breath was left in me but didn't quite remember. What I did remember was that I could not get back to the shelter of that SUV fast enough. But I held steady, after zipping the suitcase closed, I seemingly tip-toed back with the weight of trauma in my bones, but deliberately, with a pace so as not to further incite the officer's attention. I had come within an inch of a punishment of at least thirty lashes, and that was no exaggeration. That much I knew. That epic moment of deliverance when I saw my future receding back from the precipice was a blissful blur. Easing back into the rear seat of the SUV felt safe and warm like a blanket. I escaped danger and peril – had literally dodged a bullet. I heard the car trunk blessedly close. My driver got back into the car and settled into his seat – his movements signaling to only me that all was well, but I was still trying to bring my body back into control. The force of fear and terror was like a heavy metal heaving in spasms inside my chest, such that I could not breathe for a spell. It hurt. It was scary. I pressed my chest to move the energy around and on to the right places. That took several minutes, even after the car started up. That was my body's way of telling me how close I had come to a devastating effect on my life, from which I might not have recovered.

As the driver pulled the car away from the customs check station, I did not recall a time when I felt such sweet relief. Clear turquoise life-giving waters from the bay that sandwiched the causeway on both sides appeared outside the window – claiming my attention. I savored and held that view close to my healing bosom. A refreshing sense of safety set in as I whispered *"Thank you"* again and again, to the Deity in charge, grateful and present in the moment of being so redeemed. I vowed never to do that again, nor take any situation so high-risk for granted. I had a renewed appreciation for the high price I paid for wine and spirits to the black marketeers. Even more, I was regretful and apologized internally for how, in my over-confidence and in being a bit self-centered, I might have compromised my driver, as well. Even though, as a rule, he would not have been implicated in my mischief and would have been sent on his way while I was held back; still, I felt bad about it. A few months later, I learned from a colleague that one of the regular black market dealers who had supplied alcohol to other ex-pats and Saudis was caught, arrested, and assigned a regimen of eighty lashes. While in prison, he was to take ten lashes per week over an eight-week period. After serving his term, he was expelled from the Kingdom.

I could not explain nor fathom why my drivers' cars were not stopped all the other times going back to Saudi from Bahrain but was pulled aside that once when I took the dare, and for what I believed was just cause. Nor why did that come upon me with such focus and vigor on the part of that officious customs inspector. The fact that I came so close to utter calamity and in that same loaded moment was so wondrously delivered from it required some deep reflection. There was a vital message in that episode, most likely, regarding my tenure in the Middle East. It was year five for me in the Kingdom. There had been signs along the way over the past months that my season in the Kingdom had run its course and was coming to a natural close – that it was just about time to return home. I accepted and planned for that. It seemed imprudent to stay longer than I needed. Perhaps, that incident at the customs checkpoint was an affirming omen. When the restrictions in the Kingdom impacted me to the point where I would flirt with such disaster, it surely indicated the dwindling of my capacity to live in such a restrained way.

However, I had become so attached to my experience in the Kingdom and was feeling pangs of sadness knowing that I would soon be leaving. In spite of the social/customary reins on my liberties, I felt a longing for something that I thought was still there in the Kingdom for me, because I had come to feel soulfully connected to it. With that, the tension between the need to go and wanting to stay would just have to sit for a while – left unattended to. The elder women in my family often said to me: *"Be careful not to overstay your welcome with any place, situation or person. Know when it is time to make your exit."* That incident seemed to suggest that staying in the Kingdom past my 'welcome' would not be to my advantage and might cause setbacks in ways unbeknownst to me. If I exited on a high note, in a timely manner, the work I did in the Kingdom would not be for naught.

The multitude of lifestyle restrictions could bring one to a point where she made a choice to act in ways that surprised herself in order to stay tethered to herself. People did things that only they could rationalize and judge, and for which they must forgive themselves. And getting 'busted' and sliding off the rails for an infraction in the Kingdom was an easy likelihood, simply because there was so much that a person could not do, which was forbidden, either officially or as referenced by both clear-cut and nuanced cultural norms.

All of my fine and fashionable clothing hung in my US closets while I donned the drab and dreaded abaya to go outside, anywhere. People looked at me aghast when I laughed out loud in public or averted their eyes if my neckline was a little low. My walking alone in the streets attracted the stares of nine out of ten male drivers passing by – with many insisting to give me a ride because they were certain that I was lost, or as if to just get me - a solitary woman, off the streets. Or maybe they thought I was soliciting. Indeed, keeping myself in check to stay within the lines took a lot of effort, as well as facing the deprivations from the restrictions in the culture. Perhaps 'culture shock' was beginning to wear on me after all. I could only go so long doing without the things that once came so easily. Perhaps, the message and the lesson were about resuming the quality of life I knew which was increasingly required to nourish my life. Knowing when it was time to leave was useful medicine for anyone.

Days later after returning from Bahrain with my contraband or bounty as I preferred to call it, I was in an Uber car going to the mall; the young talkative Saudi driver was broadcasting how he loved going to Bahrain every chance he could to *"Drink some Smirnoff and have fun."* That was all he talked about while seeing me to my destination. He did not know that I had just been there. But I don't think he really noticed or cared if I were listening to him or not.

10
My Beautiful Cage

Shelter was inherently a critical factor in a foreign land, when the things one treasured and took for granted in their homeland loomed large and were missed. I arrived in Saudi Arabia in the wee hours on a sweltering August morning fully drained from almost twenty-five hours of travel – it was still night outside. Once landed, the only thing that I knew for sure would happen was that a driver would meet me at the airport to take me to the place I was to live during my contract period in KSA, and I had no part in making that decision on where that might be. Home had always been a sanctuary for me, where I put much care into creating a sacred place of warmth, comfort, beauty, and peace. How were my new innkeepers to know that? It was part of the chance I was taking to enter something new, knowing and trusting in myself and in the grace of the universe to see to it that things would go well. The ride in the black dark seemed endless, vacuous, yet intriguing – the sweet-looking Pakistani driver, Sheikh, and his buddy with him in the front seats were silent while getting me to my destination. We arrived at the barbed-wire compound where Sheikh presented his Driver's Pass to the armed security guard to go inside. After helping to unload my luggage at my assigned villa, he bid me a welcomed stay in the Kingdom and drove off.

And so it began. Taking deep breaths did not help. My new domicile was nothing charming or awe inspiring. It was basic, quite clean, fully furnished and equipped with the essentials: linens, kitchenware, and cooking staples, coffee and tea, crackers, eggs, milk, etc. An effort had been made to make me a home. That was a start. And I knew and decided that *"I can do this."*

Even though I was told beforehand by people in KSA, it hit me for the first time once there to learn that *other than work, there was just nothing to do.* My villa was the private personal space where I would spend an inordinate amount of my time and life in the Kingdom. Before long, I would retreat there gladly at the end of a day at the office, after dining out, from shopping or just walking back from the compound pool or gym or from taking out the trash. No matter from where or when, retreating inside felt good. The large, thick, wooden door of the villa was becoming an inviting and welcomed site, and when it shut with a solid thud behind me, I was pleased to be on that side of it. And yet, I was no less confined within those walls of the villa. It was not easy to go out and move around – with not much to do, and being out and about felt strange and unnatural, at times unwanted and ill-advised. Reminders were persistent that the best place to be, was inside.

When I went out walking in my residential area during the first months there, I found most often that I was among few persons getting around on my feet – let alone being the only woman moving freely in the open. Men who were the only ones driving cars would pull up to me, perplexed as if something was wrong with that picture. They'd slow their cars and creep alongside me, lean out their windows, and peer at me, wondering what I was doing walking around like that. Although I was fully covered in the required black abaya, that did not stop their stares - their eyes glued, marking my steps on the sandy paths and roads. They'd keep driving close to me even as I stepped faster and tried to ignore them. They were just curious, I thought, and seemed put off by my solitary presence out there, which may have confounded their view and reality.

My walking about alone seemed to be a problem that they had to solve - a situation that needed to be corrected. I was simply out there walking to feel the weather on my body, to go to the store, or to the park where the mothers took their children, where I could swing in the swings if no one was looking or around. Some drivers asked if I needed a ride, or *"Are you looking for someone? Are you lost or trying to find where you are going? Can I take you somewhere?"* Even in Arabic and broken English, their questions and amazement were clear. Eventually, that became too disruptive and made walking alone less enjoyable or necessary for air. I would limit my outside leisurely movements to the confines of the compound or at the least to make my intrepid strolls out in the open on the city streets less regular. The culture was pushing me back inside it seemed, into the cheer and calm that was always there for me. Back inside what had then become my beautiful cage.

My beautiful cage cost me nothing – a perk of my contracted position. The two-story, twenty-five hundred square foot domicile contained most of the accoutrements of a home I could want. The structure and layout were designed in the tradition of the grandeur days of Arabia with new and old furnishings. It had large rooms and a lot of space for one person. It was cool when I wanted it and warm when I needed that. There were generous windows, mirrors and light, an ample staircase, which made me feel like a queen as I ascended and descended it, a laundry room with an all-in-one washer dryer – so clever, a long deep tub for the luxurious baths I often took, with scalding hot water at any time. There was a large self-enclosed kitchen with a pantry; a dining area, two living rooms – one with a wide flat screen TV, an office, guest room, a master bedroom that swallowed the king-sized bed and a lot more furniture, a reading nook, and a patio area for sun and privacy outside. It had four bathrooms. From my window perches I could view a nearby mosque and easily hear the daily prayers it issued. I could see and hear children at play at the adjacent neighbors' villas. Always a welcomed sight and sound. I saw the movements of the people in that horseshoe-shaped up-scale compound and could know what was going on around me outside. From inside I saw the sun and the moon rise and set, and the merry evening lights of buildings and streets off in the distance at dusk. My beautiful cage offered much and never disappointed; there was a diversity of things I could do in there, to see, smell, taste, and savor in there - to touch, to delight, to occupy me. If something needed a repair, a simple call would trigger someone to come fix it. All those amenities with my own decorative touches by and by made it lovely and ultra-livable inside, and just fine with me in a sand-ruled parched place with nothing to do but work and work. My cage was beautiful because I made it so.

I'd think about coming back through those doors of my villa from the moment I left for work in the morning, on the ride to work, at lunch break or in a sharp moment, and certainly on the ride back home. I got strength just knowing that my beautiful cage was there where there was concord for my senses and comfort for my body. And in-home captivity made me resourceful! With a mere handful of western-speaking television channels and firewalls that routinely blocked internet access, I found ways to mine good entertainment from the internet – movies and music, even streamed live sports coming out of the west. I'd kart books there from my US home library after my periodic trips out of the Kingdom. And in the long quiet spaces of time, I discovered the pleasure of throwing myself into 1000–2000-piece jigsaw puzzles - which never failed to produce a desired result. I festooned the walls with elegant scarves and large batik cloths from India and Pakistan to behold, admire, even meditate upon. I scavenged well-kept but discarded pillows and rugs from outside other people's houses, pay to have them scrubbed clean by the local day laborers, and placed them on my floors and sofas. Along with the modern/western style, I opted to have the traditional Arabesque furnishings placed in my villa - a bit gaudy, but I liked it. I appointed an array of Turkish lamps throughout to wake up and highlight the corner tables and credenzas. The fragrant incense of the Middle East and candles burned incessantly in there. The whole interior and mood bore my personality and signature.

I knew that there were countless others feeling the same way as I, benignly semi-quarantined in their homes – with not many nor a variety of places to go. The culture, consequentially, made it habitual and even necessary that people, especially women, become housebound. The interiors of the Saudi homes I visited were typically well-ordered and decorated, often fabulous and dazzling, having every comfort, most even had maids. Home was a destination because there was not much that would get people out of the confines of the home. If one's living quarters were not comfortable or did not satisfy, it could be a real problem. My beautiful cage was a reliable wellspring of contentment, beauty and repose in my life and work in the Kingdom. Unlike the abaya, it fit me. And, whereas my movements were limited to and from work with routine shopping and occasionally dining out, it was where I was most free and myself. I could eat and sleep when I wanted, read, and watch what I wanted, play my music and dance with abandon, entertain guests sometimes – whatever I felt.

In there, I was in control, aloft and immune. No one to take care of in there but me. No questions to answer, or actions to justify, no one peering in. And certainly, there was no BS in there. For some unknown reason all of that seemed more important there in KSA. People and friends who came to visit complimented me on how welcome and homey it felt in there. I liked having people inside my cage with me, and when they left, I could go on happily to bide my time. For the most part, in there I learned how to make peace with isolation. And whenever the lifestyle in the Kingdom or missing home in the US wore me down or when I was just besieged by the vagaries of life, my beautiful cage was a friend. It held me and gave me bear hugs. It grounded and kept me in touch with ME. I knew I could go there and be inside where I could have what I wanted AND needed, leaving that other stuff outside with the hot sand, the inquisitive drivers, and the whining cats. Inside the cage I could choose to turn off the outer noise, not answer the phone calls, and shut down the emails for a required pause, decompression, rest, reflection, and recharging - where I could stay sane and normal – all things so essential in a foreign world of starts and stops.

Things moved at a different pace in the Kingdom. Time was not so much a factor as in other cultures. The Kingdom's pace slowed one down. Time could pass leisurely or fast within those walls one called home. As people kept to their own lives, it made the spaces between human interactions longer. Time, a constant companion, was a teacher, especially when one was alone and socially restricted for hours on end, and the only thing speaking was one's own mind. And that could be tricky. One had choices in that situation. One settled down or busted loose, or one acted out and made a spectacle of herself. There were those foreigners who could not handle the isolation and could not make it. There was too little to do and so much time to do nothing. One worked, shopped, visited with friends, and went back inside. There were business fairs and weddings, which were few and far between and usually attended by others grabbing for recreation. Outside, there were no theatres, shows, concerts, sports events, fairs, dance halls, bars, or clubs; and hardly any socially approved venues where a woman and man could intermingle, and few places where women could be with women or men with men.

When a person ventured out, she and he was most likely to be with and among their same gender of women or men. The culture, grounded in traditions of social modesty and restraint, influenced how men and women interacted with one another, physically and psychologically. It was frowned upon and discouraged for unmarried women to entertain unmarried men in their private residences. There was the curfew that did not allow guests to remain in the compound villas after 11:00 pm, especially of the opposite sex. Overnight visitors, even if they were relatives, were prohibited without prior approvals. Such social restrictions generated a shared experience of isolation and a de facto uptight culture of savoir faire, in which I participated.

With the isolation, the boundaries were many and there would be an unkind reaction to going against the status quo - with barriers around what I could wear, how I could get around, where I could go and what I could say and to whom I could say it. It was easy to make a misstep and be scandalously exposed in a culture so controlled in terms of its customs and social nuances; not being in the 'know' and adhering to those could trip a person up and set them back or make them an outcast - someone to be shunned and avoided. But the culture could also be welcoming and gracious when one met it with respect, humility, prudence, and restraint. If I was not sure of how to approach or handle a situation, I could resolve to put it off for another day. Nothing was so urgent to push me to trifle with my credibility. Time, the eternal ally could be bought, and I could retreat to think things through, saying: *"Tomorrow or the next day, I will know what to do and will respond."* I did a lot of that kind of thinking and consulting with time, made possible by my beautiful cage.

Life for a single woman could be a trial in the Kingdom - much less for men who had wider privileges of social mobility and some relaxed codes of behavior. I often recalled the stoic words of the woman I spoke to before coming: *"Just make sure that your reasons for coming here are strong."* She said that to me twice, to make sure that I heard her. And my reasons for coming were as strong then as they were in moments when I questioned everything – myself and what I was doing, years later. It was for those same reasons that I stayed. The outer environment that restricted and shoved me back inside could not intrude upon the liberty and flight of my spirit in my cage. I was safe and unbridled within those walls. Although, I was not all the time one hundred percent at peace in that resolve, with my moods shifting and becoming sullied and mixed at times. I was human and had episodes of fear and doubt. There were times when my usual and sundry activities would not do to occupy me and fill the slow sticky hours inside, and I'd literally sit and twiddle my thumbs. In those moments my beautiful cage harbored a life on hold. So, I thought.

Yes, at times solitariness seduced me into a state of uncertainty - consumed with thoughts that life was passing me by, feeling limited by environs that stared me down and got me off the streets, behind the high concrete barbed wire walls of the compound and armed security guards, behind the huge solid wood door of my villa. I wanted to be out someplace where things were stirring and moving around. I wanted to be with other people and active outside more often. Sometimes it really, really got to me. I missed my life. Snatches of that life and of the 'me' who should be living it poked through and teased while I was cooped up indoors more than I cared to be. But also, in those anxious moments, I knew instinctively that I was exactly where I was supposed to be at that time and in that place. And that affirmation always won out. Time's passing and diligence would draw me closer to that 'regular' life I knew, and perhaps, as a more evolved person. I understood and accepted that being there was a necessary step, and I could only go forward by having to first dwell within and among those walls. For I had gone to places there in that beautiful cage that I would not have accessed otherwise. I accepted that it was important to be with myself; and I felt blessed that I was one who could appreciate my own company. That appreciation grew as I embraced the epiphany in that luscious spiritual space, that I was moving fast and going far while standing still. One of my most creative achievements during my time in KSA was making a villa my home. And for reasons that I could not fully discern, I knew that when the time came for me to leave that shelter, I would miss it thoroughly. For it was where I got some added seasoning to be the woman I am today.

11
Safe

From the very beginning even before I boarded the plane to Saudi Arabia, people who knew me questioned my safety. Some doubted my sanity and rational mind to go there to work. *"Will you be safe there?"* and when I got there: *"Are you safe?"* Those concerns bounced off me, from then on. Although somewhat awed by the undertaking from the onset, from deep down inside me, I felt no fear about going to the Kingdom, and I did not know why it felt like a most natural thing for me to do. Other than the hassle of traveling long distance in coach, there was no apprehension, no trepidation, no flinching, no alarm, not even a second thought about going to KSA from the start and after the periodic trips home to the US that I would make in the coming years. In fact, I would increasingly feel more like a visitor in the US and out of place than I did in the Kingdom. I trusted my instincts and I trusted in necessity. For me, going to the Kingdom was what had to be done, and it put questions about what it meant to be 'safe' into a whole new light.

There was a reason why barbed wire was strung all around the top of the 10-foot-high concrete wall in the compound where I resided in my villa. Such was the case in other compounds where ex-pats lived in KSA. The idea of housing ex-pats in 'secured' 'compounds' was a protective measure and to provide freedoms that ex-pats could not have in the outer metropolitan spaces. There had been pockets of religious extremists who followed anti-American rhetoric who had attacked areas where ex-pats worked and resided. Those incidents largely occurred in the past years and winded down to be pretty much non-existent as the US/Saudi relationship simmered and improved after 911 and out of economic, political, and militaristic necessity. That was a period when Saudi Arabia relied increasingly on western professionalism and expertise to help boost its economy and modernization agenda. I was there during that window of time where harmony and collaboration reigned and where the Saudi government seemed to bend over backwards to thwart any perceived threats of extremist attacks on westerners. I did not actually 'know' all the details of that while I was there, but nevertheless, it was not top of mind for me, and I felt safe. I wondered what people meant when they asked me *"Are you safe?" Safe from whom and what?* It was not about 911, that much I knew. It was about something else, and I began to realize that it was a distrust of the unknown and an aversion to the dark tunnel, guided by unvetted stories they had been told up to then, much of which was fed by the media.

Once in KSA I found myself safer in ways I had not felt in the states. Surely there were overt hindrances to my liberties in the restrictive culture. I had to conceal my body with the abaya. There were lifestyle things I was accustomed to in the US that were out of reach in the Kingdom and not allowed. I could not enjoy a glass of chardonnay at my leisure. There was no respite or fun to be had by going to a theater, a movie, or to go dancing. Holding hands in public was uncustomary. Life was controlled by a code of modesty and a profusion of norms one just had to 'know'. Social life was limited to shopping, working, occasional visits with friends or dining out. I could not leisurely walk in the open without drawing undo attention to myself, simply because I was a woman walking alone. My communications were surveilled, and so on. But those limitations did not make me feel unsafe. Granted, I knew that culture and society went hand-in-hand; however, it really amounted to the people of the society who made things as they were, and a difference for me.

First, I did not fear for my life or sense of well-being and humanity. I did not fear being robbed or molested or shot. In a densely populated compound, I frequently left my back patio door open; and had been shuttled around regularly by a myriad of male drivers I did not know. With strict, swift and what were viewed as draconian punishments for offenses, the Kingdom had a relatively low crime rate. A contributing factor to the low rate of crime was the earnest and prevailing influence of Islamic values. Fear of offending Allah was as great, if not greater than transgressing against the law, I believed. I found Arab people generally sympathetic, and the Saudis to be a most congenial and forbearing people. I experienced Saudi as a devout country rooted in Islamic traditions that in some subtle way instilled citizens with an elemental elegant courtesy that they readily extended to one another and to foreigners like myself.

Secondly, I became financially safe because the Saudis established me into a sustainable ranking position that complimented my education and abilities during a fallow time where full-time work at my professional level could not easily be obtained in the states.

Thirdly, although by law women were designated as secondary citizens to men, I was safe. I found that what came with the secondary status of being a woman was a 'respect' that most men conferred upon me, and a desire to protect and care for me – however sanctimonious that might be. There was an automatic respect for my privacy, and for the difference I represented as a woman; it was something the men I encountered may have been unable to comprehend or understand, and maybe even were threatened by, but certainly it was a difference they respected - as long as they felt that they could control it! It was complicated. And because I was a bit old fashioned in my views and values, I could deal with that – knowing that women were endowed with qualities that kept them at the level of men.

The thing about 'control over women' in the minds of men only went so far and was just as well an illusion. Nonetheless, that aspect of the Saudi male culture did not cause me grave concern. The 'tactical' repression of women and their rights, from my view, by default nurtured and exalted the feminine. I saw explosions of it all around!

And lastly, the specter of racism was absent in my personal life and work. Any racism that was sensed, observed, or passed me by was imported by some westerners. There was no pervasive counterproductive racial throwback in KSA marking my skin pigment as a blight and a limitation; I was rather, afforded a personal freedom and lightness of being. Despite the constrictions on life, the Saudi air was clean and clear of the toxic psychic racist energies I had long endured in the states. I did not experience assaults or deprivations that were racially motivated. Racial prejudices and assumptions attacked and caused much more harm than being physically assailed, it was a different kind of injury. That stuff did not come at me among people who felt like brothers and sisters. I was grounded, self-assured, and validated as a whole person - not feeling locked into a racial box. I could see more and farther and do more without the intrusions of 'race'. Overall, I was physically and economically safe, and safe as a woman of color and human being, respected, and appreciated for my professional caliber and experience. And that surprised people back home!

Saudi society met and held me well. I likened it to a child wallowing in safety in the care of learned, capable and confident parents. There were aspects that the parents naturally knew from years of trials of what worked and what did not – a matured inbred knowledge of what made sense and what did not, thus engendering and safeguarding a wholesome environment in which young ones could grow and thrive. It was something like that. To put it simply, there was an age-old bearing of safeness in the society and country that I felt intensely.

Feeling so safe, I went below the surface. I engaged the locals, and Saudi families who invited me into their homes – some after just meeting me briefly. They wanted me to sit at their tables and share their stories. I ventured at night onto the dark back alley streets, into the souks, and people's markets, even the ghettos of KSA. I saw into the eyes of the angry man, the defiant student, and of the armed security soldiers and I was safe. I saw and heard the screeching Saudi military jets patrolling overhead, shaking up the sky, watched the news that touted the latest terrorists attacks in the world and in closely neighboring Middle Eastern countries and felt safe. I ate the food, tapped into the country's heart, did my job, made some mistakes, and allowed myself to learn something in the process, and felt safe.

Among other warnings, 'wise ones' told me before I went to KSA that there was absolutely nothing to do there but work, and that reality alone would drive me mad or out. Ironically, with the turmoil in the world and with me apparently at the epicenter of the everlasting conflict in the Middle East, living within the Kingdom and under its mantle of devoutness gave me a break and kept me feeling safe and sheltered for a long while. The natural grounding of the ancient Middle East connected with me entirely - making me feel as though I had come home. I had ample space and time to stretch out and be myself in Saudi society, and in some odd way, life felt less precarious and complicated and more predictable in that vacuum of seeming nothingness which I could also equate with a quality of safeness. Surely, the society had its Mr. Hyde. There were regularly scheduled public executions, Sunni and Shia conflictual fallout reverberated around the Kingdom, deadly skirmishes were happening in border towns and over in Bahrain, and there was even youth gang activity in the Kingdom. Still, it was different in a country that I could see and feel had a noble old soul. Its staunch 'ways of knowing' and 'being' presented me with few distractions, no diversions and minimal social demands on my energy and resources – with less to try to figure out and press myself into. And, as a *'Big Girl'*, there was little likelihood of my getting in harm's way unless I made the concerted effort to do so. Ha!

Part Two

IN THE LIVES OF WOMEN AND MEN

UNDER THE ABAYA

12
Womb Room

Beautiful Noura texted me on a Wednesday inviting me to an evening gathering at her home the coming Friday. It was a regular affair held periodically – every couple of months or so, and one that I looked forward to. The ding of her texted invites pleased me and brightened the moment. Having been there before, I knew what to expect – always a good memory. Getting invites in Saudi was typically from women to women to come together for dinner and visiting. Being welcomed into a Saudi family's home was something I did not take for granted; I knew many ex-pat colleagues who had been in the Kingdom much longer than I and were yet to receive those personal invitations. I was a newcomer to the close-knit group of women who had been faithfully meeting that way for many years.

    My driver got me there in a round-a-bout way at around 8:00 pm, taking longer than it should. But one learned patience in the Kingdom. When the evening ended Noura would surely have her driver take me home as a courtesy. Noura, physically stunning and voluptuous in her pastel flowing attire, greeted me and other arriving women with many kisses on the cheek, and led us into a sitting room where the family received their guests. Once inside, off went the abayas to hang in the closet during our time indoors, and we'd settle in to enjoy an evening of talking, laughing, eating, music, and sometimes dancing in a resplendent Arabesque setting. It was like entering a sacred inner-sanctum, into the bowels of their comfortably stylish home – a warm and enveloping space. The room was aflush with the sumptuous glows of assorted ornate lamps, stationed in their corners. Walls bedecked with tiles framed the room in a kaleidoscope of colors. Perched against the walls were intimate sofas of gentle earth browns. Cozy and pillowed. Facing the sofas were small accent tables topped with dellas* of coffee; there was Turkish tea and delights, nut plates, cookies, pastries, chocolates, and tiny balls of coconut 'somethings'. A smoky old incense fragrance hugged the air and mingled with the woody floral scents of the ouds softly emitting from the women's bodies. The room spoke to my senses as I sipped the hot caramel-colored Arabic coffee that was poured and served to me the moment I settled into my seat.

I could not help but to look up to take in the comely carved painted ceiling which told the story of a happy garden of day green leaves and vivid fuchsia blossoms. Very well done. The room was a consummate welcoming heaven that I wanted to hold and press into me. Women, young, elder, mothers and daughters continued to arrive and were welcomed in an exchange of 'kisses' as they entered the room in soft voices. They greeted in the traditional Saudi way of caressing at the shoulders with their hands and tapping a cheek to the other one's several times in succession, making low kissing sounds – at times two, four or five. I counted eight 'tap-kisses' between women who had known each other a long time. There would be nine of us in attendance that evening with the calm and sweet company of the hosts' cat and three dogs. What would take place was culled from an ancient ritual of dialogue where tribal members sat around in a loose circle and followed whatever thoughts, words or impressions that came up. The conversation flowed from one topic to another about anything that crossed our minds, having no specific agenda. It could be about the madness in global politics, the trials and the joys of plastic surgery - already done or contemplated, jazz, education for our children, the good-looking and single men we knew, California and food – personal stories.

Food silently appeared on the long table in the adjoining dining room as we were talking and visiting. The dinner was mostly prepared by the Filipino house helpers. Samia, the host of the evening, Noura's mother and a beauty herself, would then summon us all to come and sit. Samia insisted that I, their newest guest, take the chair at the head of the table. Spread along the table were plenty dishes: hummus, dolmas, spaghetti casserole, lamb kabobs, rice with lentils, chicken schwarma, eggplant moussaka, tabouli salad, pita bread and sweet drinks. More than enough. Samia would direct the Filipino house servant to put food on a plate for me – something of everything. All I could do was receive and smile. We ate and enjoyed the food, as Samia who prepared some of it, beamed over the scene. We finished eating the meal close to 10:00 pm and were just getting started. The food feast was its own celebration to precede what was still ahead for us that evening.

Us women rejoined in the sitting area to visit some more with coffee, tea, and desserts. That time, we moved closer to each other from our places on the sofas, to better hear and understand what was being said and to know what lived in another's heart. *"These are my sisters"*, came to my thoughts both as a realization and a resolve. The alchemy of the women coming together with 'intention' begat a female energy cocoon that was alive, creative, intelligent, and strong - like a womb. And I would from that moment on know it as the *'Womb Room'*, for it was there that the inspiration for me to write this book was birthed.

As the men's and the women's cultures in the Kingdom co-existed side by side, seldom, did those cultures coalesce except within the close bonds of family, and even then, they remained distinct. No one would or could clearly explain to me why men and women had separate cultures. It was just something that was and had been an adopted way of life for a long time. That drew women closer to women and men closer to men. It was true that men and women universally saw the world differently and played their unique roles in it – which went to another level in Saudi culture. Men historically had dominion over women's lives under the *male guardianship** system, and within that landscape, women tended to need one another more. Consequentially, the male/female cultures and the limitations set upon women generated mature and forceful alliances among women - something that men could hardly penetrate, know, or understand.

Women gathered incessantly in the Kingdom and Middle East as they had done for hundreds of years, at weddings, parties and engagements, fundraisers, for zaghrouta* singing, or just privately in their homes. They did that in the same manner as western and eastern men in their private clubs and majlises, albeit with some refinements. There were no cigars, cognac, or mock beers; no strategizing on how to rule in the world or pats on the back on how well that was being done. Yes, women were ambitious and competed, everywhere and all the time – publicly and in the exclusive domains of their minds; yet in that 'womb room' women's communion superseded any need for that. With the stage being set for the unrestricted mixing of women they concentrated among themselves; and that intensive female cauldron evoked a quality of the feminine that was 'divine' - a quality that women reflected and delivered in their everyday experiences and that was apparent to me in the 'womb room'. In the gathering of women, there was no bitching or bemoaning the travails of womanhood, there was no complaining about our lives or of the singular oppression we experienced compared to other women of the world, nor aims or talk on trying to be like men; there were no victims in the 'womb room'. It was not said but agreed, to open a space where we were safe and wanted and respected - telling and holding our stories – of speaking, hearing, and witnessing, and the subtle recognition of the sacred energy and haven fashioned and shared when we were being fully honest with ourselves and one another. We sat in 'the' circle of utter support, with the absence of pettiness or low-level attitudes. Authenticity was the unspoken rule: *'If it is not true and if you don't mean it, don't say it'*. *'Speak of what is good and useful'* - to keep the energy pure, raised and at a high pitch in the company of one another as if for our emotional, spiritual, and feminine survival! Nourishment at all costs – in the way that an embryo needs it while inside the mother's belly.

Because Noura and the women had dinner gatherings on a regular basis, I could tell how essential those get-togethers were to their welfare, and for me to be invited into the circle was really something special. Once having entered the circle it was clear that their invite was also to reach out and enable me to feel comfortable and welcome in their country, and so that I could get to know and to see who they were as women. Yet, I was not so naïve as to assume that the women were not naturally reading me to know the kind of woman I was and my interests and motivations. Saudi women did that quite well – one of their tools to intelligently navigate their way in society. As a matter of fact, I was expecting and hoping they were assessing me, knowing that they would be just fine with what they saw. As such, having lived my entire life in the US I had not felt closer to women as I did in that room. Even though I had an affinity for things Arabic, that connection with the women went beyond that. I was not just joined with the women as a group, but also more connected to certain aspects of myself. In that embracing, intimate circle I was opened and fed. My disclosures and unfolding were met with kindness, empathy and useful nonjudgmental input that warranted my consideration. I experienced an instinctive rush of the joy, if not the majesty, of being female. And they let me in on their open secret that women operate with the 'knowing' that they possess unassailable qualities and 'advantage' over the men who appeared to run their lives, and that the women were a real force in the land.

The evening turned very late before we knew it. And having bathed in one another's light and energy we fell into a satisfied mode of departure. We put back on our abayas, hugged and went our separate ways. Once more, lifted from the experience I was grateful for that and for the certainly that I would go there again.

Male Guardianship – A system in Saudi Arabia that by law, designated men to make key decisions and determinations in women's lives, i.e. traveling, working, getting an education, etc.

Zaghrouta - A form of high-pitched trilling vocalizing women made. The sounds generally represented trills of joy and jubilation – performed by individuals or in groups.

Dellas - Stylish pitchers used specifically to serve Arabic coffee.

13
Abiding the Abaya

The way that women appeared and presented themselves in public was of utter importance in the Middle East. The abaya was the traditional garment for women in Saudi Arabia and in most Middle Eastern Muslim countries including Egypt, Iran, Oman, Jordan, Syria, Lebanon, Afghanistan, Iraq, and Yemen. Within those cultures, women, whether they were Muslim or not were expected to be modestly dressed when outside. Covering one's head and body was a choice that women made in some Muslim countries, and although full body covering was not required in some countries, women were discouraged from showing their bare arms or legs above the knees and wearing revealing and suggestive clothing. The dress code was more strict and enforced in Saudi Arabia; wearing the abaya in public was mandatory for women. Women's bodies had to be fully covered while it was optional to cover one's hair with a hijab and to cover the face with a niqab, leaving the eyes exposed.

The official requirement of the abaya for women was central to Saudi Arabia, largely because the country prided itself as being the center of Islamic faith in the world and was committed to upholding long held traditions of modesty and religious mindfulness. Up to recent years, the religious police known as the Mutaween enforced modesty codes by stopping and arresting people for dressing offenses; they also directed people to go to 'prayer' when the call came. The Mutaween were a part of the Committee for the Promotion of Virtue and the Prevention of Vice, and also the preservers of Wahhabism, which was the literal and strict interpretation of the Qur'an. They were the austere branch of Islam (Sunni) which eschewed modernization, polytheistic worship and even mysticism, whereas Shia was more spiritual. The Mutaween were everywhere and monitored and aggressively enforced the social rules for anyone in that vein. My dear and rather idiocentric male ex-pat colleague was arrested by the Mutaween for wearing flaming red pants in a shopping mall and not going to prayer, although he was not a Muslim. The influences of the religious police and clerics were waning due to the Crown Prince's emergent policies of modernization in KSA towards a more open society. However, the abaya remained a staple of Saudi society. Women's abaya stores lined the streets and proliferated in the malls with racks upon racks of hundreds of abayas filling up the store and on display in windows. Abayas could be tailored to fit within fifteen minutes to an hour, while a woman shopped for more abayas. Abayas were the foremost, singular garments that any woman had to own, which dominated her closets, and she could not have enough or too many of them.

The abaya was basically a full-length robe-like dress; it was by design very loose-fitting and pretty much 'hung' on a woman without clinging to her body. Westerners called it a 'burka', a crude name that was foreign and generally not used by Middle Easterners who used the term 'abaya' and which I thought was more suitable; the word had a fluidity and elegance to it that befit what the garment represented and how a woman donned it on her body. The abaya covered the woman, draping from her shoulders to her feet. It had to be worn in such a way that the woman's flesh and natural shape and curves were hidden and not discernable, with her arms and legs concealed, even her ankles and wrists. Hair, especially when it was long and flowing about the head and shoulders highlighted a woman's attractiveness. Thus, hair should be covered with the hijab. The niqab face covering rendered the woman nearly invisible and unrecognizable, except by those who knew her well enough. And that was the effect that the customary attire for women was meant to achieve.

Black was the traditional and predominant color for the abaya until that began to change, particularly among younger Saudi women and in recent years. Not only was the standard black shade problematic, but the requirement of women to cover themselves in public was increasingly becoming an unspoken point of contention in the Kingdom, again, especially among the younger women. And they would use whatever leeway they could to get around those requirements. I witnessed the gradually changing abaya culture as women began sporting abayas in grey, blue, white, even polka dot, and striped and floral. Still women wore mostly the 'black' which came in a variety of designs - with sparkles and spangles, with beads, and lace, in soft black, and in blackest black, and with elaborate embroideries. There were black abayas in light just-so sheer fabrics for hot weather, and heavy for the cold.

I owned several abayas, hijabs and niqabs. For me, wearing the abaya was a major hurdle in the Kingdom regardless of its changing colors and styles. It really was, with me being a woman whose identity was reflected in what I wore as with any modern woman. I must admit that I did not like wearing the abaya;

I had a peculiar relationship with it. The abayas misshaped me, no matter how much I had them tailored, they hung on me like a burlap sack, looking all frumpy. Maybe it was the broad shoulders I inherited from my grandmother that made them hang that way. The requirement for it did shorten and simplify getting dressed in the morning by boiling down my choices to which 'black' abaya I was going to wear. But even still, there was some reticence, and muss and fuss involved in that irksome exercise each day of picking one from my collection of abayas and putting it on. And as I often let my angst run away with me, I felt awkward, unattractive, and not myself with it on. But I wore it just the same. As time passed I slowly adjusted my attitude about the abaya and found it intriguing to cover my body, hair, and face on occasions when I wanted to try something different and travel incognito. I was in full gear with black abaya, niqab and hijab in my excursions to Qatar or Egypt or Dubai and found being 'invisible' in public strangely invigorating, especially on those flights with ninety-seven percent men and all that testosterone.

The abaya symbolized women's role and status in society in relationship to men, who by contrast, uniformly wore the white thobes. The Islamic reasoning behind that was that women represented the moon (mother) and wore black; whereas men represented the sun (father) and wore white. That corresponded to Daoist theology where the 'feminine' (yin) was represented by the color black and the 'masculine' (yang) by the color white. The Islamic tradition espoused that a woman's role was to be keeper of home and hearth, which was her domain. Like the moon, women represented the interior life, birth, receptivity, and passivity. Men, like the sun, represented benevolent authority, moral strength, and command. Man's role was to navigate the world outside the home - that of commerce, business, and activity. In Saudi Arabian traditional thought when a woman ventured out into the public spaces she was in 'man's' domain and she must, by wearing the abaya, make herself appear as indistinct as possible - or invisible, as a show of non-intrusiveness and respect in man's world. The thobe as the traditional attire for men was a long white loose-fitting shirt; it was accompanied by a shemagh or scarf which was draped over the man's head and crowned with an oqal. The oqal also had a symbolic meaning, which was: To be knowledgeable and helpful towards others. The traditional attire for men was not required to be worn, as men also dressed any way they wanted in public – casually, in jeans, shirts, or suits and ties.

Abiding the Abaya

The mandate for women to wear the abaya was firmly in place, however. I was sent back home to put on an abaya when I was arriving to attend an event that was formerly a US sponsored abaya-free affair that I had attended a few times before. But not anymore and I didn't know that. *"This is not accepted."* That was what the security officer told me, insisting that I leave and return wearing an abaya. So, I called my driver to come pick me up and take me to my villa, wait outside while I put on the abaya and take me back to the event. It was an abrupt inconvenience, but I did not waste my time getting too upset about it. It was what it was, and must be accepted, was my resolve. I wore the abaya diligently in public except for times when I went directly from car door to house door to visit a friend in her home. On one occasion, to my surprise, I felt naked and vulnerable without the black sack on me while waiting at the door for my friend to let me in, for fear that I would be caught right there and chastised or reined in for not wearing it in the open spaces, even for a few short minutes outside a domicile.

It was not easy navigating the world as a woman, on several levels. And in some odd way I saw how the abaya was an instrument that aided women in that regard. Any woman by consequence, established a relationship with her abaya. It became a part of her persona, whether she wanted that or not. The abaya was her passkey to go 'to and fro' without causing concern, raising an eyebrow from others, or triggering disapproval, let alone being reapproached by security people or a person of authority. The abaya normalized the woman while she was in public. A woman could wear anything underneath the abaya – pants, casual clothes, underwear, or nothing at all, as long as she had it on when she ventured out, and in many common cases, when men who were not family were present in her own home.

There were mysteries surrounding the abaya custom. The origins of the abaya 'rule' were generally not clear and answers did not come easily. However, some did, and they were mixed. In earlier Arabian tribal life, the abaya was required for women and girls to protect them from being carried off by rival tribes. The black color was used because it was readily available; black was the most durable shade and material at the time, and it made the women and girls indistinct from one another – as a protective concealment measure.

The abaya was not originally intended to have religious and faith-based connotations in the tribal nomadic lifestyle, it later took those on. The Qur'an stated, *"Tell your wives and daughters, and the believing women to cover themselves with a loose garment...to be recognised and no harm will come to them."* According to ancient Islamic texts, the custom of women covering themselves was inspired by Mary, the Christian mother of Jesus. Her convention of concealing her head and body was seen as a reverence for God, and such demonstrations of 'piety and purity', were proper and necessary for women of faith. Islam respected and adopted that thread by requiring Arabic women to emulate holiness, piety, and modesty as did Mary. Henceforth, for women, the abaya became a habit – like a nun's habit, to use a pun. The hijab was worn by a woman to identify herself as a 'Muslim woman'; and she expected to be treated as such by doing so. The more devout and fastidious women put on dark sunglasses and black gloves, and no parts nor an inch of their skin was exposed. Combined with the black abaya, hijab, and niqab, that look literally turned them into black silhouettes; and as one man put it at the sight of one of those completely 'blacked out' women: *"When she puts on those glasses and gloves, forget about it. She is finished!"*

Modesty and virtue were essential to keep religion and faith at the center of everyday life in the Kingdom. Islam taught that constant prayer purified the soul and kept one close to God, Allah. Prayer was a central in the culture where distractions to keeping one's faith were minimized through social rules and edicts. A woman uncovered was an interference for men and women, which took their minds away from Allah. The abaya kept women from inadvertently disrupting faithfulness. It shielded their bodies and *'adornment'* from the eyes and the advances of men, whose nature was regarded as aggressive, lustful, and had to be tempered. Overtly dressing for sexual attraction in the public sphere was not allowed in Islamic cultures because it also stigmatized women and jeopardized male/female relationships. Saudi men I met prided themselves in keeping their wives covered so as not to invite the attention of other men - to keep the peace and to protect their *"crystal"* as one Uber driver professed to me. Privacy was also a right for women. My female students often told me that wearing the abaya protected them from being evaluated by others. They said that when a woman's body was accentuated by the way she dressed, it invited people in general, including other women to evaluate and judge them. They said that people were always being evaluated and judged in public - which was true when I thought about it; but it was an unwelcome intrusion into their privacy, and it was an offense in Islam. My most physically attractive students expressed that they *"did not like being assessed that way in public"* - not by men or women. For them, the abaya was a necessary and trusted shield against that.

Nonetheless, Saudi women had differing views of the necessity of wearing the abaya to cover themselves. A dominant minority of Saudis were 'hard-core traditionalists' Wahhabis (forty percent from the last 2008-2009 count). And where the abaya was a nuisance and imposition to some women, others found solace in it and wore the abaya with a vengeance. In fact, covering their heads and hair was relaxing for many women, while some would like to break free from the abaya and all manners of concealing their womanly virtues. Abayas were not required within the residential compounds or at weddings and public events where only women attended. Even still, at those affairs, the abayas were tucked away into nifty little sachet bags that any woman would carry in her purse, ready to be put on before men entered the room or when she left the event. There was increasing talk that the rules on wearing the abaya might become more relaxed, as part of the Kingdom's move towards modernization. And there was growing evidence of that. Yet, given the culture of the Kingdom and the deep-seated traditions people held onto, it was likely that a majority of Saudi women would be faithful and astute to abide the abaya. The modern day Saudi woman's embrace and acceptance of the abaya began at an early age. I'd see small girls alongside their mothers wearing miniature black abayas and hijabs with their pretty faces beaming against the coarse black fabric. They were cute little copies of their mothers. And with that, I understood the power of the abaya and how my own relationship with it might have been different had I been weaned on it in the same way.

I observed that the custom of concealment with the abaya and hijab often had the opposite effect for which it was intended. A woman's hijab naturally became loose from talking and moving her head about during the day. That required frequent adjustments to keep the long scarf tight around her head – it became an incessant preening ritual, performed dozens of times a day. I often observed my Saudi friends making the adjustments several times during a conversation or meal. The way that the hijab was fitted around the head did not stay for a long time not even when pinned down; to keep her hair concealed the woman had to unwrap and rewrap the hijab around her head and tuck it back into place or secure it with hair pins. As they were speaking and gesturing, I watched in fascination as women and my friends loosened the scarves around their heads to tighten and tuck them neatly back into place and do it again a short time later. Their hijab adjustments involved several directed and careful movements of the hands so as not to reveal a single strand of hair in the process

– taking a few minutes each time to do that, and while still talking. It was a reluctant tease about the head, trying to control hair that was so painstakingly pushed underneath the hijab, which to me the women performed as an art. It pulled me in. I saw the persistent hijab readjustment rituals as being done out of necessity and in some cases by design. The preening naturally drew attention to women's faces, which were often, carefully made up - with emphasis on the eyes – lined and mascara rich and framed by precisely sculpted eyebrows. With the Saudi/Arabic women, it was all about the eyes. Beautification and cosmetics were, after all, a multi-billion-dollar industry in Saudi Arabia.

Being attractive would always be a value and priority for Saudi women, which the abaya and hijab surreptitiously seemed to aid. The abaya culture went beyond the physical garment. The more ardent wearers of the abaya did so with a distinctive flair and elan as displayed in their poise and carriage such that as they walked by, I would stop and stare after them in wonderment and admiration on how the abaya accentuated their femininity. I'm thinking: *"She knows how to walk so that the hem, which brushes the ground, does not trip her feet whether she is wearing heels, pumps, flats, or sneakers."* I noted how her fluid stride down the path called attention to her as the abaya mildly folded around her shape, allowing hints of what was moving around underneath. The woman walked, not so fast, which was part of the appeal. Of course, I learned that while wearing the black abaya in the Saudi heat, one had to at best walk slowly. But there was deliberateness in her walk - a saunter, a lilt and ballet to her steps. Still, I'm thinking, as I watch, *"These women do have a way of 'working that abaya'. Like a dance, they have turned the abaya into an arresting event!"* With the abaya the Saudi woman was more captivating than if she were traipsing down the street with nothing on at all. *"How do they do that?"* Still wondering. And then again, there were the eyes. With her body, hair and face completely concealed, the eyes stood out, not merely because the Saudi woman really knew how to 'do' her eyes, but because of what was behind them, and her way of communicating lots of things through them. The 'eyes' conspired with the abaya, hijab and niqab and made me want to look at her more and see that which was not hidden but coming through loud and clear. The eyes were alive, they spoke - took me in and showed me a whole new thing about beauty; for theirs was such that could not be halted by yards upon yards of black cloth. The abaya with all its trappings raised an ultra-feminine essence to the surface and rendered the Saudi woman as a mystery far more alluring than ever - staring me in the face. *"Now, isn't that something!"* I thought.

14
Beneath the Sparkling Chandeliers

Socializing was deep-seated in the culture of Saudi women, and I would even venture to say that they got together more than the men. Compared to other cultures, women were most often with women and men with men. And with the women, being close with one another on a regular basis in various settings was somewhat of a lifeline.

Since arriving in the Kingdom, and into my first year there, I had been looking forward to attending an event put on by Saudi women. Invites to women's events were not easy to come by for a western woman. That was not because they were not welcome, but because many western women did not orient or position themselves to receive invitations and such offers. By and large, western women tended to congregate among themselves and stayed within their comfort zones in places, situations, and associations with other westerners. I chose to step away from that pattern, from curiosity and out of necessity, and by doing so I got the invites. At those social affairs attended by hundreds of Saudi women I was practically the only western woman there or one of two at best. In those settings surrounded by closely knit Saudi mothers and daughters, friends, and relatives a western woman could easily feel left out. Those were primarily Arabic-speaking venues, both on the written invitations and spoken there. Naturally, the Saudi women attending knew one another and they were cliquish, making me feel even more like an outsider – which I was – but to an extreme. However, for me, in those inner circles I was to learn more about and engage the culture of Saudi women, and perhaps to become a part of it – which, eventually, I did.

Saudi women were very organized and active, and they tended to their social milieus with diligent care. Not just anyone outside their social circles got invited. My most memorable one came when least expected and from an unlikely person. A student gingerly approached me one day at the end of the class I taught and asked me if I would like to buy a ticket to attend a fundraiser that her mother was hosting to combat Alzheimer's disease. Her mother was

UNDER THE ABAYA

part of a society of women who regularly organized events for charities. My immediate answer was yes. The ticket cost 500 riyals, which was the equivalent of $125 US dollars. That ticket would take me into a highly impressionable event - from the many that I attended in a room one hundred percent filled with Saudi women, where men could not come. And no matter what the official occasion or event headliner was, there was always a lot more going on in those great rooms of Arabic women and beneath the sparkling chandeliers.

It was a warm spring evening. I arrived at around 7:00 pm along with other women. We were dropped off by our drivers at the Sheraton Hotel near the downtown area. We all came covered in our abayas – some wearing hijabs and niqabs. I was in my splashy abaya – the one with rhinestone trimmings that I naively wore on the first day of my job appointment in Saudi. That time I wore it with smug assurance that it fit the right occasion! I presented my invitation card to a man in the foyer who directed me towards the curtained entrance to the fundraising ballroom. The thick curtains shielded the women attendees from the views of men ambling about in the hotel lobby. Passing through the curtains I entered an uncommon scene – a room of Saudi women uncovered, en masse, without the abayas over their bodies nor the hijabs or niqabs - all dressed to the nines there in that room at that moment in time. I shuffled myself with the arriving crowd of women into the decorative grand ballroom, none of whom I knew. But they noticed and smiled at me, and I smiled back – glad to be there with them.

We moved into the room to find our seats. The room was massive, it was the grand ballroom after all – crowned with an array of crystalline chandeliers overhead. From the front stage there was a runway extending to the center of the room separating both sides of the room – forming a 'T' with the stage, and which suggested that there would be a modeling showcase that evening as part of the fundraiser. Since I went there on the invite of my student, to my delight she arranged a VIP seat for me in the second row away from the runway not far from the stage. It was an exclusive area where I was seated near some obviously prominent and affluent women in the community. My, did they look and smell good! The grand ballroom was nothing less than opulent. Dozens of tables covered with eggshell-tinted tablecloths were neatly arranged on both sides of the runway topped with shy miniature lamps and fresh floral art - fancier ones were in the VIP section. Bite-sized, delectable desserts, a variety of chocolates with Arabic coffee, Turkish tea, and tropical juice drinks were offered by a never-ending parade of female Filipino servers to those seated in the first few VIP rows of tables. The husky lilt of Arabic chatter from the excited and energized crowd of women cheered the room. Throughout the ballroom women were seated with family, other women, or friends. Most were in perpetual motion roaming around from table to table, laughing pleasurably while conversing in their random visits with one another. Although I was attending alone, I felt connected and a part of it all. I made eye contact with women across the room and at nearby tables, who acknowledged me in welcome, and I was just fine.

While seated I observed the women, young and mature, embracing one another as they came into the room. They performed their customary way of greeting by gently clutching one another at the shoulders and 'kiss-tapping' their cheeks together several times in succession – two times, three times, four – sometimes eight and nine kisses; the stronger and longer their relationship was, the more kisses they exchanged. I shared that kissing custom many times with my friends and liked the way it made me feel - a sublime expression of affection, sisterhood, welcome, and even love.

Glamour and sensory delights reigned supreme in the room beneath the sparkling chandeliers. It was such a contrast to the drab and sandy outdoors from whence I just came. The elegant décor spared no expense. The air was an intoxicating blend of the finest earthy fragrances of ouds that the women were wearing. The explosion of female charm and fashion artistry in that room was irresistibly felt. I took it all in as it took my breath away. The ladies wore high-end, one of a kind, evening gowns that I easily assumed were tailored or mostly bought during their trips to European hot spots such as Paris and Milan - gowns that rode perfectly on their sleek, to rotund body types; they wore exclusive designer shoes and the jewelry to match; their faces were professionally made up; their finger and toenails freshly groomed; and their hair precisely coiffed and lucent; the eyes were dark and bewitching; and to top it all they exuded a grace and decorum that bespoke their evolved femininity. It was a feast for the senses for those who could appreciate it. While outside the world commanded them to cover up, in that room the women were proud and defiant in the display of their God-given gifts. And they even took it up a notch!

What I witnessed was the Saudi women's rare collective expression of beauty - uncontested when combined with fashion and style. They afforded themselves the best in attire, shoes, ouds and perfumes, and jewelry whether they were wealthy or not. In a subliminal way, together they seemed to make the statement that: *'We own this – all that you see. This is us!'* As a lover of beauty and a believer in the power of the feminine, I was benefiting and fed from the scene set before me which was part of the pleasure of being there and for venturing out into Saudi women's society. To me the Saudis were uniquely a physically attractive people - both the women and the men. I realized that 'fact' early on, after I arrived in the Kingdom. Nine out of ten of my students were beyond pretty, and I had seen Saudi men who were so beauteous that it damn near brought me to tears. As I sat and took in the festival of the feminine, I could not help but wonder if the men really knew what they were missing. But of course they did, how could they not!

Money, knowledge, and beauty were regarded as the three most powerful things to possess in the known physical world. Surely, health, relationships and spirituality were important too. But money, knowledge, and beauty held sway in hard reality over attack, evil or want. It was obvious that there were a lot of women of means in that ballroom, who were part of the female populace who possessed much of the Kingdom's wealth. Money gravitated to the Saudi woman. Built into the social code was that a woman be provided for. If she had no husband or father, the government gave her a stipend. And it was well understood that: *'Man's money was his and the woman's, while woman's money was solely her own'* – an idea put to action that helped to generate hidden and obvious wealth for women – with most of the savings in banks being owned by women. Regarding beauty, I had long observed and been fascinated with Saudi women's allure which when accentuated by their brand of haute couture could outdo any Paris runway. From my view, it was not the clothes, the shoes, nor the makeup that characterized their appeal – Saudi women just knew how to do 'feminine'. And with women acquiring university degrees like never before at that time, there was no doubt that all the power that could be had was in that room, and the women were free to indulge it, particularly, beneath the sparkling chandeliers. In that setting I knew that I was witnessing a private, alive, and remarkable sub-culture of women in the Kingdom – brought to bear, above and beyond the abaya. And I had a ringside seat!

Women's social events were serious affairs; they were the headquarters for social gaming. Marriage was a key goal for most Saudi women, and a priority for mothers more than fathers. At those happenings, be they fundraisers, family celebrations or wedding parties, there were always the mothers strategically seeking wives for their sons. It was an arena where young ladies had to look their regal best; and in that ballroom, they did! Making no pretense, mothers were eyeing the younger women, each weighing the ladies with their unique criteria of who was worthy of her son and would be a good daughter-in-law. The young ladies, in turn were expecting, even hoping that they were being watched, assessed, and scrutinized by the aged and wise eyes of mothers, which in that venue was utterly appropriate. All dressed up, they were busy gliding about and flitting from table to table, acutely aware that they were a part of the 'show' and getting a 'going over'; and likewise, they projected and postured themselves in the most favorable way. Every word, gesture, and step mattered. I could see that they knew that that night was a marker for their future lives.

Speaking of marriage and weddings, on a previous occasion I went to a wedding party of one of my students, with hundreds of women in attendance. It was called a 'wedding party' because the couple had already been married in a private ceremony, maybe days or weeks prior. The party was a formality to allow the bride and groom in separate venues to commemorate their union among family and friends of women and men, respectively. The wedding party experience was similar to the fundraising event of Saudi women, however, something rather phenomenal happened. The evening began at about 7:00 pm and guests were served hors d'oeuvres up to the time when it was announced that the bride and groom were about to enter the room. It was close to 9:00 pm. It was not typical that the bride and groom appeared together. That was left up to the discretion of the host family. However, at that wedding party the bride and groom were going to enter the room together and momentarily. The announcement gave the audience of one hundred percent women the time to reach into their sachet bags which they carried in their purses, and to remove and put on their abayas which had been waiting silently in abeyance to be donned at the presence of a man. Incidentally, sachet bags were handed out to women before they entered the wedding party room in anticipation that their abayas would be needed during the course of the evening. Hence, the chamber that was moments earlier a free-ranging, eye-popping display of female gaiety, panache and flair instantly turned into a solemn sea of black as all of the women uniformly and hastily covered themselves and only minutes before the groom entered with his bride - altogether, having a Venus fly trap effect.

It was a dramatic transformation of the room, made to accommodate the entry of a man into a space filled with women, even though he was to be there ever so briefly to escort his bride to oversee the festivities. At that wedding, the groom would sit beside his bride at the front stage for a short period and leave – and then, off went the abayas! In any event that a man would enter a room of Saudi women for any reason, the women would instantly put on the abayas, hijabs and niqabs that were reliably nearby. In most cases at those events, there would be a forewarning that a man was about to enter the room. And once the man exited, the extravaganza of beauty, style, and color reappeared, with the abayas, hijabs and niqabs taken off and stored away just as quickly as they were put on - like a light switching off and back on. There was nothing like it. It was fascinating to watch and to partake in that custom, regardless of how contrary it was to me as a western woman. Covering in the presence of men was required on the authority of the Qur'an, and for me among the women, it was also a measure of respect. The women's synchronized removal of the abayas was symbolically akin to the lifting of the societal veil if only for an interval to reveal the vast treasures behind it. At yet another wedding party that I attended with a colleague, the young bride made a moving appearance, entering the ballroom all by herself, dreamily strolling down the center aisle towards the front stage clutching her bridal bouquet. Two little girls held up the long trail of her white petticoated tulle wedding gown as she walked. She sat upon the stage alone throughout to preside over the celebration of her marriage brought to her by her female family and friends. Us in attendance were informed that the bridegroom was close by in another location and was remotely watching by video as his bride made her entrance and sat upon the stage. And yes, us women had the option to cover ourselves. As in the wedding parties, at the fundraiser, the abayas were not far away, but tucked into little sachet bags to be put on at a moment's notice when a man was coming, which in that case did not happen.

    The first few hours at the fundraiser were spent with the ritzy women socializing and partaking in the hors d' oeuvres and beverages. There were soft Arabic instrumentals playing in the background from the saz, the oud, the doumbek and tabor drum. The Filipino servers diligently kept filling our ornate mirra* cups with Arabic coffee and producing trays of tasty nibbles. They wore ruffled white blouses and dainty hats – showing pride in their duties on their faces, with ladylike bows and lasting smiles. They would make their rounds again and again until it was time for the banquet meal, which would be served between midnight and 1:00 am. I fought hard to resist the tempting finger food and cautioned myself to hold my appetite until then.

The venue took its own time, nothing was rushed, for time was not an issue that evening. Things would commence not by the clock but when the ballroom was filled with enough attendees and upon the arrival of certain women dignitaries. At some point after a few hours an announcement was made, of which I did not understand a word. I could not speak Arabic which was spoken entirely there. I asked a woman at a neighboring table who told me that the modeling show was about to begin. The chattering visiting women returned to their seats as the modeling was to be preceded by the Saudi national anthem. We all stood to listen and sing. Following the showcase, which was a preview of evening fashions, not abayas, the runway was cleared for the women to dance. They leisurely left their tables and stepped on to the runway which had become their dancing platform. And they began - the younger with the older women danced with one another, as a unit. In tune with pulsating Arabic music, mothers, daughters, friends, and relatives danced across the platform in a loose line, one behind the other in their rich gowns and finery. They stepped smoothly about in understated movements – with a gentle waving of their hands in the air and a slight twitch and swivel of the hips. In rhythmic unison their feet seemed to skim over the floor - like the prancing of flamingos across a soft shallow pond. Pleasure was on their faces as the women were enthralled in their dancing and subtle communion with one another. It was hypnotic, lovely, and easy to watch.

After the dancing we were told that the banquet was ready in an adjacent room. It was just after midnight. I was not hungry from all the tidbits I'd eaten, but I could not resist digging into the self-serve buffet. There was no mincing on the feast which featured: various mutton and beef dishes, baked fish, fried chicken, baked chicken, savory basmati rice dishes, macaroni and cheese, traditional dishes and casseroles, spaghetti, humus, breads, cheeses, non-pork cold-cuts, figs and melons, desserts of all kinds, salads and greens, soft drinks. The banquet tables were stationed on both sides of the room and were filling fast with hungry women coming in from the ballroom. The energy that started off the evening began to ebb with the approaching early morning hours. The mothers were talking to other mothers and to the young women in low tones, and young women were talking among themselves – perhaps comparing notes – all were eating and winding down. And shortly thereafter we all began departing after calling for our drivers who were steadily arriving. Us women removed our abayas from the sachets and put them on, with some donning the hijabs, and niqabs - covering before leaving the hotel, going home in the night.

The festivities were over, and I had made a few new acquaintances. My eyes, ears, nose, and taste buds had feasted well with great satisfaction. I went away knowing that unleashing and honoring themselves under the sparkling chandeliers was important to the Saudi women and it was important for those who witnessed it. It was important for me. And I had another takeaway to remember. Whether it was a lone woman walking along the sunlit Corniche promenade, a solemn sea of black abaya clad women, or women gadding about in posh evening gowns, the Saudi woman was consummately feminine, and in a class all unto herself. En masse, they honed a beauty that could not and would not rest upon attire or adornments alone. They were unapologetic, happy, and even reveling in the privilege of being female. Their incessant socializing and gathering afforded them the occasions to collectively retreat into the power of being a woman in the face of oppression - making the most and the best of female qualities in a way that rendered them irresistible and compelling. From what I was fortunate and allowed to see, theirs was a womanhood culled from a concoction of fragrance, make-up, gait, mannerisms, voice, and a cast of the eyes - all blending with female instinct, love and devotion, a fierce sisterhood, and a design to be the heart in man.

* *Mirra* – *A tiny, usually ornate cup expressly used for drinking Arabic coffee or teas.*

15
Reem – She Who Would Run with Wolves

Noted author, Clarissa Pinkola Estes (Women Who Run with the Wolves), wrote: *'Within every woman there is a wild and natural creature, a powerful force, filled with good instincts, passionate creativity, and ageless knowing. Her name is Wild Woman, but she is an endangered species. Though the gifts of wildish nature come to us at birth, society's attempt to civilize us into rigid roles has plundered this treasure and muffled the deep life-giving messages of our own souls. Without, Wild Woman, we become over-domesticated, fearful, uncreative, trapped'.*

I knew such a woman, who nursed and gave reign to her wildish nature during my time in Saudi Arabia. She was my good friend, Reem. When most women would go along to be safe, she said 'NO' and braced for the suffering she knew would surely come with that.

The few times that I saw Reem joyful and at ease was when her children were near. Otherwise, she carried the weighty countenance of a woman trying to hold it together – to maintain a standard and live on her own terms in difficult circumstances. She was not afraid to talk about anything that was on her mind, and what she had to say was interesting. Reem was not a pretty, but a smooth-complexioned, charming woman in her 40s. She wore her abayas and hijabs in the shades of gray, powdered blue or taupe, and even before diverging from the 'black' was becoming common in the Kingdom. She was full-figured, warm-hearted and a foodie, like me. We often dined together in traditional Middle Eastern restaurants; we'd sit on cushions planted on the floor and eat the savory food with our fingers. It tasted better that way for me. "Order more, anything you want and something to take home for tomorrow. The owner is a friend of my family, it's OK," she would say to me and indulge, I did.

Women's development and uplift initiatives and movements were on the rise in Saudi, gaining strength since 2015. I became involved in one of those forums whose mission was to support women's entrepreneurial development and business independence. Bringing more women into the workplace and supporting them as business leaders would boost the economy at a time when it was needed due to decisive shifts in the oil markets, the war in Yemen, and the overall move towards modernization in fulfillment of the Crown Prince's, Vision 2030*. Many of those organizations for women were in partnerships with or sponsored by universities and large Saudi and US corporations, such as Aramco, Baker-Hughes, Schlumberger, Saudia Airlines, and major Saudi banks. In tandem with sponsors, the women's groups regularly hosted conferences, elaborate luncheons, workshops, and training in rooms packed with women and men. It was in that setting that I met Reem. I found her to be personable and present, fierce, and harboring some inner ache. She came across as a woman whose past and even her present life was riddled with trials and sacrifices, and with hard lessons learned. Her stories touched me. I grew to love her, and we started to say that to one another as friends. And we meant it.

Although the climate for women's advancement was improving in the Kingdom, there were still barriers and just so much that could be done. Despite the strides women were making in the business world, their lives remained subject to male authority. The male guardianship system remained firmly in place, which imposed limits on women's liberties; men determined the degree to which women could get educated, get a job, get married, and travel, etc. Women's upward mobility had to occur within the parameters of 'male guardianship and permissions' – in terms of what men decided was right and appropriate for them, and from which, as many saw it, women needed to be emancipated. I saw how women's groups and organizations had to tread lightly and not advocate too strongly for anything that would upset the balance of power and control between male and female cultures. For instance, I initiated a film project that would feature and profile successful Saudi women across the board – as artists and professionals. I organized a group of Saudi women and a Saudi male filmmaker around the concept.

The idea felt so right to us all and we were excited about the project; it even gained traction with a local media network that would air the finished project. And money to produce the film was not a problem. However, as we began our planning process, we were soon informed that the Saudi Ministry of Communications required us to have permission to hold planning meetings for our media project as a standard rule. That apparently was a footnote we overlooked. At the mention that 'permission' was required and because our project had attracted the eye of the Ministry, most of the key women players involved in the project got cold feet and backed away from it. The project fell apart. My sense was that the women did not want to be on any radar as advocates for women's development. That made sense at the time, and I could not or did not judge them for that. But I was dismayed at the degree to which women chose to stay safe and careful and were pressured and conditioned to do so.

Reem was married to a member of one of Saudi Arabia's prestigious and influential tribal families. With that background and asset to her advantage, Reem chose to get out of the house and be a part of what was changing in the Kingdom, placing herself on the front line of women's causes. Apart from many other women I knew in the movement, Reem was led by her heart and not the need for position or recognition. She avoided the limelight and did not seek to bring attention to her work. She was a silent and humble agent for the women's cause, making significant moves behind the scenes to help women get educated, get good jobs that led to advancement, and help them to own businesses, essentially, to lead empowered, self-determined lives. Reem knew and understood that while the male guardianship laws were in place that there were limits to what could be done – that her work with women's groups could only go so far, and that there were slim margins in which progress could be made. Although she did not need to, Reem made it clear to me that she worked because she wanted to do something for women's lives. But it was the plague in her personal life that would increasingly demand her attention and for which her work with women was grooming her to address.

Reem's husband was strikingly attractive, about her same age; he had a 'wandering eye' which was fed by his drinking problem. It was pulling him away from the home and causing persistent marital tensions. During one of our dinners together, Reem shared with me how she and her husband had known each other since their youth – professing to me in earnest that she knew she loved him the moment they met that long ago. And she still did. Married many years now, they had four children. But now, growing apart from him as a marriage partner wracked her soul. Reem was not under the illusion that she was unaffected by the setbacks of the women she put herself out to help; and she lamented on how she could not travel with her children for shopping or recreation outside the Kingdom to nearby Bahrain without her estranged husband's approval in the social data and monitoring systems. He would need to register his approval, directly and timely. Getting his permission was too often a humiliating ordeal for her because of his changing moods and it was not easy to pin him down when he was away from home. On a most recent request to travel with the children he reluctantly granted her permission to leave the country for a two-hour trip to Bahrain to see a movie with the children, and she practically begged him to allow that. Reem was developing health problems from the stress of his alcoholism, infidelity, and recalcitrance.

It stood that alcohol, and its consumption was illegal in the Kingdom and punishable by imprisonment and physical lashings. So, to satisfy his growing drinking addiction, her pretty husband was spending longer periods away from home, weeks at a time, in neighboring countries such as the UAE (Dubai) or Bahrain drinking and in the company of women who also liked to drink - leaving Reem to tend to all matters concerning their children. She complained that the drinking changed him and that he was becoming increasingly mean-spirited in his stupors, and during a more recent drinking weekend away from home he entirely refused to grant her permission to travel with the children.

Reem ordered the husband out of the house at one point and took him back in when he pleaded to rejoin his family, but he would not commit to stop the drinking. She allowed him back in the home but would not share the same bedroom with her husband until she was sure that things were going to be right with him. That did not happen. All while Reem was sharing that with me over dinner, she was emotional and fraught with anxiety, and was unwrapping and rewrapping her hijab as it kept coming loose as she spoke. The constant hijab adjustments seemed to be part of telling the story of her world that was falling apart amidst her efforts of trying to hold it together. As her husband's drinking binges continued, Reem as a last resort, asked him to take her with him so that he could consume his liquor in her company instead of with other women. His answer was an outright *"No."* He did not want her with him in his frequent drinking outings; he saw her place as being in the home with their children. In his reasoning there were certain kinds of women he wanted to drink with - party women, or *"bitches"* as Reem called them.

In the culture, women suffered quietly and submitted to the whims and dictates of husbands who had more leeway in the society, and they put up with it. Reem told me how she was dying inside with the knowing that her husband would not stop the drinking and that he preferred the company of *those women*. But she was getting really clear that it was not within her to be a part of her husband's continued *"alcoholism and whoring"* lifestyle and the drama and angst it generated for herself and the children any longer. Yet, in that clarity it was still a struggle for her to decide what to do as a Muslim wife, and mother. Reem was a devout woman and tenderly watched over her children who showed her much love when they were around her - with the youngest one habitually clinging to and whispering softly into her mother's ear and with Reem soothingly whispering back. I saw.

In the Kingdom, family should be given priority over personal desires, and Reem felt that she owed it to her children to keep their father close to them. I asked her, "Would you drink to satisfy him?" "No," was her ready answer, emphasizing: "That is a line I will not cross" and, "Whatever I do about this, it is going to hurt, because I know that after him there will never be another man for me or in my life to bring around my children." She added, that closing men out of her life would be her choice. Upon yet another drinking weekend to Bahrain, and with his rejecting her request to go with him, Reem made the decision that she was going to divorce her husband. It was not typical for a woman to initiate divorce in that or most circumstances, especially from a husband born into wealth and prestige and with her having four children to care for. Divorce placed more of a stigma on the woman than the man. People would assume that it was something she did wrong that resulted in the divorce - that it was all 'her' fault. Reem also knew that she could fall from favor with the tribal family she married into. Yet, she did not fear any of that. In her choices, Reem knew that she was pressing up against the heavy weight of a culture where women abided and self-sacrificed to stay safe, and were expected to. She knew that, for her soul's sake she was going to push into a hard future that she was ready to face alone.

Months later, after returning to KSA from my annual vacation, I learned that Reem had divorced her husband. And I was made aware that as a divorced woman her freedom to make important decisions to govern her life were now her own, according to the law; however, not regarding the children, whereas those decisions had to involve the father. I met with her several times, making a visit to her home one evening for tea and desserts and to have henna painted on our hands and arms. Reem called in her henna artist friend to do that especially for us. It was a gay evening, and a happy time with my friend. Reem was still warm and full, with that quiet ferocity; there were lesser traces of that old inner ache. She looked 'different' - self-possessed and in charge of her life - seeing a lot of good days ahead. Months ago, I was concerned and even afraid for her because of her unrelenting spirit and the strong choices she was making

– going her own way against what was expected of her and considered 'safe'. I admit that I was surprised that she really did divorce her husband – the love of her life and moved on. Really, I did not have any sense of how she would come out on the other side; because I had little witnessed, both in the Kingdom and in the states, a woman, who so lovingly let go of what she had and knew, who did not tarry to 'walk her talk' and run with wolves. That raised my esteem for Reem, and I loved her even more.

Women not made docile from oppression, grew fierce. It may not have been overt, but it was there. Innumerable women bore stories like Reem in the Kingdom who made the rough choices that they knew would leave their arms and their beds empty. With *wild woman,* 'seeing' was knowing and doing - there was something pure in that. In the coming times when I would be with Reem, without a doubt she was making fresh and atypical choices, willfully creating a life in tune with her nature.

*Vision 2030 - A comprehensive blueprint for transformative economic and social reforms throughout Saudi Arabia. It was launched in 2016.

16
Dying To Be With One Another

It was not apparent to me that Luluh was in love until she burst into my office one day with an 'emergency', asking me for a *"hard favor."* Her 'love' was a secret that she kept away from relatives and friends, including me. For her, it was a high-risk secret. I did not know that she had a boyfriend until then - four long years into my relationship with Luluh as student and teacher, which was surprising, because we had grown to be so close.

Luluh and Omar developed a liking for one another many years ago when she was 16 and he, 17. When Luluh's father learned about their budding relationship he put a quick stop to it; not that Luluh was too young, but because the father kept a tight guard and clamps on Luluh's world. That was what she told me, and what I witnessed personally. It was an aspect of her young life that she woefully accepted, her father's authority was iron law. Luluh and Omar kept their enduring attachment to each other from afar under wraps for as long as they could, even though their feelings were intensifying as they grew older. In Saudi Arabian culture, relations among friends and family could be extremely tight knit. The society of family and friends, even neighbors was often a small world where people know a lot about each other; and odds were good that *'there was someone who knew someone who knew something about you'*. Having her father and other family members know about her feelings and contact with Omar was the last thing Luluh wanted. So, she and he distanced themselves from one another and communicated essentially via discreet texts and phone calls over a period of months and years – with rarely any physical contact. Over time, what started out and seemed to be a teen fancy evolved into a friendship, and a remote courtship with ever-growing affection and love that could make them husband and wife one day.

Before Luluh revealed to me her secret love that day, she'd come to my office when she wanted any kind of support: To rest from her studies, to tell a story or to entice me into doing silly things such as magic hand bumps, making dance videos, and taking wacky selfies. There'd be balloons coming through the door with her and cakes, she'd bring me Arabic coffee and dates, leaving the ornate dellas behind for me to keep. I made room to visit with her whenever she wanted. Luluh was considered a 'dark' Saudi in the culture – with light amber hued skin. She was self-conscious about that and that she was not alabaster complexioned as other young women. However, she was exquisitely lovely just the same. As I watched her blossom into a woman, I also saw her cry and anguish over the repeated spites from her father and other male family members who seemed to be a unified front against anything that was her heart's desire. To hear her tell it, they thought that her spirit was too strong and her personality too feisty and willful – seeing those not as attributes but as a curse upon her. They believed that those traits would cause her to be reckless and make regrettable mistakes; and they had to protect Luluh from herself. Luluh stood out from other Saudi students, with a different mind. She had a quick grasp of things spiritual, and she could easily let her views explore and roam outside the boundaries of Islam, of which she was a 'devout'. All the same, she was eagerly open to ideas from other perspectives. Luluh came to me the week of her 23rd birthday, her face bearing the strained weight of urgency and sadness, so heavy that she practically vomited out the words: "Doctor, I have a hard favor to ask you. Me and Omar are dying to be with one another. It has been so long." That would be the first time I heard Omar's name, Luluh's boyfriend, in hiding.

Courting a boyfriend or girlfriend out in the open was something young adults took for granted in most other countries. In the Kingdom, togetherness did not come easily with the distinct cultures of men and women that were deeply woven into society, along with the norms of modesty, religiosity, and few venues where a 'boy' and a 'girl' could enjoy carefree mixing; marriage was the bedrock in the culture over independence and being 'single'; but couples, married or not, could not be 'forward' to express their affections in public. The disassociation of the sexes in childhood and adolescence was also a factor; all of which made relationships challenging. That was why young adults opted to marry early or otherwise became resourceful in finding ways to be together.

Luluh and Omar had been attending the same university but on separate male and female campuses. That added to their being apart not only in time, but in place. She told me that she wanted to see him, which would be the third time in years and after a long lull in their relationship due to her father's insistence that she not entertain any interest in young men. Like a modern-day Romeo and Juliet, they were in confusion and self-reproach for having feelings for each other because of the pressures against them and having no support that might validate that what they felt was right. That was also a reason why she waited years before confiding to me that she had a private romance. I supposed I had gained her trust by then as someone outside her family, or she was simply growing into her own self as a woman. The favor she asked for was to allow her and Omar to visit with each other at my villa for a few hours; and to keep that strictly to myself and only between us. My answer was a no-brainer. "Just tell me when you want to do this, dear."

Luluh dinged me on What's App the very next day to set the time when she and Omar would arrive at my villa on the coming Friday. She said that it was OK if I had to leave and do something, which I took as a strong hint that they wanted to be alone. Again, a no-brainer, and something I wanted for them. The thought of opening my living space to a young couple was soothing to me, and I sincerely believed that it would do just as much for me as it would for them, and in ways I could not spell out.

The morning of the day when they were to arrive I dusted, cleaned, and prepared the villa for them. I made plans to do several hours of shopping and some sightseeing with a friend. Later in the afternoon at around 4:00 they arrived, one after the other, in separate vehicles. Luluh came first with her driver. I watched her petite form hop out of the driver's car and approach my villa door, dressed in a romantic pastel colored abaya with matching hijab. She was nervous, and I smiled easily to help her relax. Omar arrived five minutes later after Luluh's driver had taken off. I suspected that he was stalling, waiting, and watching nearby to see that she was there and to make sure that her driver was gone. You see, drivers often made it their business to know as much as possible what was going on with their clients, and especially the comings and goings of young Saudi women – some were even paid more money to do that for parents or guardians. The drivers 'watch and tell'. The coast being clear, Omar pulled his car into view and parked farther down the street. After exiting his SUV, Omar, as an extra precaution, walked around to the back door of my villa to make his entrance instead of through the front door. He was dressed in regular street clothes, no thobe. My spirits were high in the presence of the two lovers who once near one another hardly knew I was there. I was clear with no doubt that having them be together in my place was the sure thing to do. I am still blushing in the telling of this today.

Omar was taller than I expected, masculine and quite cute with jet black hair, mustache, and a closely-cropped beard. He had a friendly open face. A big guy, who I thought could have easily scooped Luluh up with just one arm. I could see how Luluh's headstrong and lively temperament intrigued him and brought out his patience and protective urges, and how he made her feel safe and adored. Together they were an appealing couple. I fussed around a bit putting on music and incense, but that was not important to them. I stored the lemon cake away that they brought me as a gift, knowing that it was my favorite and left, going on my way, wearing the widest smile on my face I had in a long time. When I returned hours later there were telltale signs that the enamored couple made the most of their few hours together, alone.

In the culture, matters were ordered and had their proper places in the lives of women and men. It was a way of life where marriages were customarily arranged by mothers and fathers. It went without saying that Sunni and Shia mixing was irregular. And the public display of mutual attractions between persons was outside the norm. Men were on automatic to avert their eyes away from an oncoming woman; women were partitioned off from men at formal meetings; and of course, a woman was covered to stave off the unwanted stares, advances, and admiration of men. I respected and did not criticize that way of life in the Kingdom, which had its pros and its cons; not ideal - it was just different. As the social gender rift would leave people 'connection-starved', it had its virtues and redeeming qualities. In fact, I found that the culture's interrelation mores had a way of retaining some degree of innocence in how women and men related. There was a pearl there. From my view, those mores made it less likely that relationships or intimate encounters would be taken for granted, whereby separations, however forced or artificial they might be, allowed space and room for relationships to breathe. In my thinking it was possible to see too much of a person. Human beings needed space whether most people realized, understood, or accepted that or not. Longing nurtured love. From a distance one could see more and the other better and appreciate what they had. With longing there was time to reflect and to contemplate. Love and affection could percolate and form in the spaces between embraces. There was time to get to know oneself and one's real needs and become better able to be whole with another.

With distance and separations lovers could think about the relationship more and were better able to cultivate and bring their best selves to their intermittent amorous encounters to make the most of that time together. I thought. I experienced a taste of that in the relationship I was having in the Kingdom which remains vibrant and pleasing in my reminiscences to the day. I savored the times I could spend with my male companion in the Kingdom, whereas before in the US I treated those times as a given. In KSA our occasions together had to be finessed by navigating between work schedules and cultural restraints. I looked forward to the weekend dates we could reserve, knowing that that time was borrowed, limited, measured and fleeting, as it was with Luluh and Omar. When we had to part until the next rendezvous I'd go back to the moments we lived – stretching and playing them over again. Memories held fast, and what we mindfully created in snatches of time was not quickly washed away by distance and social walls; and that made our 'next' times more alive and precious.

Young love abounded, and hormones raged an environment of walls and restrictions; and there was a prevailing sense that the mixing of young men and women could lead to evil outcomes. What could those evil things be, and which could not be stopped: Licentious sex, an unwanted pregnancy, a marriage to someone the family did not approve of? I saw how those things happened. Pregnant and troubled young women came to me for support and counsel. Married female students showed up with mysterious bruises or were pressured by family to suddenly drop their studies for messy reasons. Drivers complained about the prostitutes who insisted on smoking and soliciting in their cars. It was well known that young Saudi men, in groups of approximately ten to fifteen, would combine their money to lease a large room or apartment. None of them lived there but kept the space to freely enjoy the fraternity of other men in a private setting. They shared the space in their spare and off time where, among other things they watched TV, smoked shisha, or played a card game called baloot; and on occasion, if not often, a guy would claim the apartment for a day or evening to entertain a young lady. I asked Omar if he was involved in any of the male group rentals, to which he flat out said that he would not remotely consider inviting Luluh to be with him in such a setting. They would wait for a better time and a better place.

That evening, Luluh and Omar amply thanked me for allowing them to have those few hours together and departed with the same tip-toed caution as they arrived. Luluh was due back at her home an hour earlier; it was 8:30 pm but she was too dreamy to worry about the consequences of her being late getting home. She had already prepared her story for where she was – *"shopping and visiting with friends."* She called for her driver who soon arrived and was waiting outside. She put back on her abaya and head covering, hugged me, and stepped with very light feet, as if floating, out the back door with Omar following closely behind. A few minutes went by before one of them appeared from the narrow gangway between villas where they could not be seen. Luluh came first to the villa front with Omar hanging behind unseen to give her time to get into her driver's car and depart. Omar then came out in the open and to the front of the villa after Luluh's car had gone. He walked down the street to his SUV, got in and drove off. Before emerging from the gangway I was sure that the two held back and stole a private parting moment – a lingering goodbye, until when?

There was much to be said and to know about the longing that came with having a distant lover for any culture. Perhaps in the Kingdom, it paused one to take the relationship less for granted; crafting a way to be together through the obstacles of time, distance and cultural norms made 'togetherness' sweeter. Marriages and relationships in the Kingdom tended to have a longer life span than in western cultures. That was even true of arranged marriages. Love in those marriages was not instant, but it could grow over time. I'd seen that happen. Love could then be keener, more tender, and more abiding. I thought. But that was changing in the Kingdom with the trend among the younger adults towards demanding gratification in the here and now that was served up by modernization and the integration of western values. Opening the door for love and togetherness and the destined couple did my heart a lot of good – to see Luluh so radiant and nourished from being with Omar that day and knowing that it would have a lasting effect. I wanted that she would come to me when she needed to be with him again, alone. And she did.

It was a complete love story - maybe and likely because the 'longing' helped to make it so. Luluh and Omar had their engagement ceremony two years later and were wed a few months afterwards. I saw. She was a ravishing bride! Luluh had grown stronger in the ensuing years since those few days at my villa, and the force of her desires and right to be in love in the open air could no longer be denied by anyone, nor the truth that she and Omar were soul mates and meant to be with one another. They found their way. And a year after they wed there was a baby on board!

17
Tryst

Cars, vans and other forms of personal vehicles were the primary means for people to get around within the dense metropolitan areas in the Kingdom, as public transportation was limited or nonexistent within most cities. To get about the town or to go anywhere, women depended on the men in their circles to drive them – their husbands, fathers, brothers, sons, or hired drivers which could also include taxis, Uber or Careem*. All roads were the province of men. That was interesting, because women were the key persons in the household who needed to move about in public spaces more often than the men to shop, run errands or tend to personal matters such as going to the doctor or getting their hair and nails done, or to take the children places. 'She' had to get out in the open to go here and there to sustain and keep home life and herself aright, which was frequently - just about every day.

So, when the men in their circle of life were not available to drive them, which was often the case, women handily had their personal drivers. And they commonly had two or more regular drivers, with one as the main wheelman. That was to ensure that the women were mobile as they needed to be and in a timely manner. The plus side was that having a personal driver at one's beck and call was somewhat of a luxury – no hassles with pumping gas or car repairs and affording the woman the experience of being serviced like the wealthy class. To be able to say: *I'll have my driver take me here and there* or: *I'll have my driver pick you up and bring you to my house* had a certain ring of privilege and elevation to it. That was a two-edged sword however, for where having a personal chauffer or driver may have been a luxury for the wealthy, it was still a sharp reminder of 'any' woman's second-class status, and that she was not free to come and go as she pleased under her own auspices. Nonetheless, for every woman, driving was an elusive freedom, and a liberty that only men of any status could partake. Drivers became the one requisite constant in a woman's life, and she could realistically see and spend more time with her driver than her husband. Some women complained that they felt at the mercy of male drivers, who could sometimes be aggressive and threatening to them. But that likelihood could go in either direction.

I had my personal drivers, and one specifically who was my 'go-to' guy whom I could count on much of the time. He was Ajmal. Ajmal was a Pakistani man and devilishly attractive to my eyes. He had thick coal-black hair set perfectly against his smooth bronze skin. He'd seasonally shave to sport a bald head for Hajj or Umrah. Even then, he was nice to look at. He had a sexy compact body, nice hands, and an easy non-assuming manner. He spoke perfect English, the common language among all nationalities in the Kingdom, he spoke Arabic also. Ajmal had a keen mind which he liked to exercise by sharing his thoughts and insights and to indulge in questions while driving me to and fro. He could find anyplace I wanted to go and would offer to wait for me as I tended to my errands and then take me back home. I referred to him as my 'consigliere' as he was helpful at giving me advice and wisdom on the ways and mores of life in the Kingdom. Ajmal was a humble Muslim man dutifully attentive to the rites of Islam – even keeping special time on his watch that marked the daily changing times for prayer – to the minute. After being my driver for nearly two years, Ajmal asked me to marry him so that he could take on a lucrative job in the US. I entertained that idea for a while but eventually, told him it would be a bad move for us both. The relationship between the US and Pakistan was on the rocks at that time, and Pakistanis' visas were not getting approved as much as other nationalities; and such a marriage would be put under the microscope in the US. I felt sad about that whole situation, but it did not affect our driver/client friendship.

One morning while taking me to the mall to shop Ajmal was noticeably restless, and said he immediately had to tell me about something that happened to him the day before. It must have been intense because he was so agitated leading up to the telling of his story, repeating that he really had to tell me right then and hoped it was okay. Ajmal had seen a lot in his twelve years in the Kingdom, even a public execution which he declared he'd never want to see again. And the recent thing a day ago still had that grown man oddly unsettled. He told me that he had taken one of his other regular female clients to run some errands and, again, *"Something happened!"* She was a middle-aged Saudi woman – "a nice-looking, nice lady" he began to tell. Here is how it went.

It was nearing noon. Ajmal noticed that his long-term regular client had been unusually quiet on the ride back to her house after grocery shopping –

the car trunk filled with bags. Sitting on the back seat of Ajmal's car the fully black abaya, hijab and niqab clad woman's mind was moving fast. She was thinking hard on something, for a while, at least she was after the trip with him to the mall for groceries. In hindsight in how Ajmal read her from the rearview mirror, her eyes and posture told that she had made up her mind on something. What that was he had no idea. In the woman's mind: *Now was the right time and she was going to do it. She could and would no longer hold off. Her husband was away on an overnight business trip to Riyadh. With her next shopping and errands with Ajmal being next week it would have to be today.*

Upon arriving at her home, the woman paid Ajmal before exiting the car, and thus removing the awkwardness of payment coming up later, considering what she had in mind. Ajmal as he typically did after taking women shopping carried the grocery bags into the house, placing them on the kitchen floor and counters. The woman watched him steadily from behind, saying nothing then proceeded to shut the front door. As Ajmal was about to leave she moved quickly and blocked him as he approached the door – spreading her arms across the width of the door with her back against it – facing Ajmal, sternly. *"You cannot go out now."* She said in Arabic. Then in her confidence and in his words, "She moved into me" – speaking only with her eyes. Ajmal, as if in a dream state was stunned and off-guard and frozen where he stood - letting her *"Take control of the dream."* She pulled away her black abaya from her body and the hijab and niqab from her hair and face, letting those fall to the floor. No words, just motion. Ajmal yielded to her lead. "And she was forceful!"

Now Ajmal was relaxing into his regurgitation of the afternoon dalliance - describing it to me with glee, grinning even more in the telling, saying that "It was all new" to him, that something like that had never happened to him.

"That Saudi woman stopped me at the door after dropping her off from shopping, she refused to let me leave and then, she, she 'raped' me. She raped me for six hours! Her husband was not there. And that woman was not normal – she did things – she took me over!"

"How could she have done that for six hours Ajmal?" I asked.

"I don't know, I just know that six hours passed. And it was time for me to leave!"

"Will you see her again Ajmal?" I asked.

"No, I scared! I would only see her if she was any woman other than Saudi, I would like to do that again. She made me new."

"Why won't you be with her that way again?" I asked.

"With Saudi woman, it's too dangerous. But otherwise, I could use a woman like that every day!"

And he was correct in that assertion because the Sharia law permitted husbands to exact punishments with impunity on their unfaithful wives and their lovers. I asked, "So how are you 'new' now my dear friend?"

To that question, he expressed how he needed a woman - that the event "Put that to a reality" for him.

Ajmal had his family living in Pakistan while he worked to earn a living for them in Saudi Arabia for eleven months out of the year. He sent almost all of his pay to his family while he lived a thread-bare lifestyle in the Kingdom. And he worked hard, I could attest to that. Ajmal had been a long-time driver for a faithful clientele of Saudi and ex-pat women in the Kingdom, and it seemed from his telling it that the encounter with the woman, refreshed and gave him a new lease on life.

Lastly, I said to him, "I am not surprised that that happened to and with you Ajmal, you have the kind of charm that would drive any woman crazy over you." He liked hearing that and produced an easy knowing smirk. Ajmal was a close, trusted, and precious friend to me. Yet, afterwards, I could not wait to get back inside behind my villa door and have a good loud laugh! And I really did not think he would mind, and probably found himself laughing about it too once he settled his nerves.

It took that hot Saudi woman to remind Ajmal that he was an attractive and desirable man. And in the act of seducing him, she may have also been affirming her own independence and sexuality. The woman may not have desired her husband or maybe there was something going on between them that led her to the sexual intrigue with Ajmal. We will never know, and that was between the husband and wife. The Saudi woman and the Pakistani driver were nonetheless caught up in a culture of heightened modesty and limits, and where terrible repercussions could happen when sexual and marital protocols were broken. It was taking a huge gamble for a married Saudi woman to be romantically or sexual involved with a Pakistani man. Ajmal knew that and told me that: "Pakistani man was the worst person to get involved with Saudi woman" – adding that his life was "put to the edge with her." The woman fully knew that she was going against the rules and placing Ajmal and herself in peril in her moment of 'need'. But *'catch me if you can'* was sometimes a safe bet in such capers.

Sex happened in the Kingdom; it happened a lot and between those one would least suspect and with unlikely partners; it happened between women, and it happened between men. As in any place on earth the allure and appeal around sexuality were at the core of who men and women were in their lives, every day. Like magnets, sensual attractions were indelible and could not be duly regulated or stopped, and despite the precariousness of it all, would find ways to be eased – on the desert sands, in the back seat of a car, in a private room in the office building, or in someone's borrowed apartment. *"That Saudi woman"* took control and directed her passion, like a missile if only for that afternoon rush that we know. Whether it was a right or a wrong thing or even good or bad, she must have felt so much better for it, and it certainly lifted the spirits and opened new vistas for the beguiled Ajmal.

*Careem - A popular Saudi Arabian version of the Uber taxi system.

18
A Little Flirtation on the Way to Oud

A one inch bottle of oud was gifted to me as a 'welcome' from a work colleague, Dr. Bonita, in my early days in the Kingdom. She may not have realized it when she gave it to me, but she was doing me a sho' nuff good turn. Once I smelled and put the oud on my body, I was hooked. Although the amount of amber liquid in the vial could last for months, it was not enough. Thus, I began my quest for more of the uniquely Arabic fragrance which was like nothing I'd ever worn on my neck and wrists and behind my ears. And I was not the only one so instantly captivated by the power of oud. During my periodic trips back to the states, the musky scent of oud on me would draw the interests of other western women, who would gladly pay me big money with no questions asked to bring some back for them the next time I was home.

Oud was principally and plentifully found in the Middle East – used by women and men. It could be expensive depending on the derivatives of the scent and how it was blended with other natural elements. I was not fazed by that fact, which did not stop my pursuit of oud. Unlike perfume, oud was one hundred percent alcohol free and made from dark resins derived from an assortment of tree woods. Some of those trees were quite old such as the agarwood. Oud was called 'liquid gold' because of the finer qualities of its aroma. The fragrance was a pungent blend of old wood and essences of flowers and other perfume ingredients; it was rendered as an oil that came in small amounts - in one ounce, half ounce, or quarter once bottles. The aromatic amber, golden, or dark musk colored oil was drawn from the bottle with an inserted slender rod and gingerly applied to the skin. The Prophet Muhammad, held the tradition of rendering the 'heavenly' resin, referring to the agarwood as a *"Distinct thing to be found in Paradise."* And Louis XIV, lauded for his extravagances was known to have his clothes washed in oud, and even bathed in it. Oud had rich notes and was long-lasting - colluding with the body's natural oil and forming a bouquet that was distinct to the wearer. The arcane scents released with oud on the skin influenced the mood and behavior of a person and enticed and attracted others. It was an entirely intoxicating aroma that no French perfume could match. Some in Saudi society said that certain oud concoctions played a key role in the making of babies. No doubt. For me oud was more than a fragrance, it was a lure, as I was to learn on my way to acquire more of it.

On an easygoing Saturday morning after being dropped off at the souk by my driver, Ajmal I walked into a small perfume shop that specialized in oud. Going inside the shop felt super nice, and not because I was coming in from the heat outside. Cheerful little bottles of oud decorated the shelves behind the counter and throughout the shop like Christmas ornaments. The solitary purveyor was a man of about 45. He was attractive as I had found many Saudi men and women to be. He had flawless creamy skin and bore a dark shiny beard and mustache; intense eyebrows framed his deep piercing eyes. He wore a suit and tie, not the traditional dress for Saudi men. I was his only customer, and we had the store all to ourselves to indulge my slow and diligent pondering over the many wondrous scents in the shop.

As I perused over the bottles on display - touching this and handling that, I could feel his eyes on me. And not wasting any time he invited me over to the counter for him to present some samples of oud. There was a pensiveness in his look as he watched me while moving his hands to select a fragrance for me to sample from the many bottles in the glass counter cabinet between us. He presented me with several types of aromas, with each aroma lovelier than the one before. He knew his product, which was also an opening for him to explore and come close to women – an observation that was not my imagination. When I chose a fragrance that I liked and was about to test it on myself, he dismissed my hand, coaxing the bottle from me. He explained that there were certain areas of the body where the oud should be applied, that I should know. A tender demand in his eyes sought my approval which was at once wordlessly granted. And he proceeded to demonstrate. Drawing the oud liquid from the sample bottle with the slender rod, he applied amounts to one side of my neck, then the other, searching my eyes for my reaction to the aroma. It was a fabulous moody musk with mature rose accents. When he saw that I liked the scent, he nodded and delicately brushed open the top of my abaya ever so slightly to expose my collar bone where he applied more of the oud. He took my hands, turning them over and rubbed the oud onto my inner wrists, and then opening my abaya a bit wider to free up more of my skin, applied some at the top of my breast line and ending with a dab at the tip of my exposed cleavage.

There were no words, and a lot going on. I was amazed at his assumption that it was okay for him to take such liberties and amazed at myself for so easily allowing it. It did not feel bold or indelicate – but more of an entreaty. *Was it a spell cast by the oud that made him and me so free to carry on that way?* I did not know, but it felt like the most natural thing to do and the appropriate way to try and experience the precious aromas of oud. The Saudi oud merchant did not ask, nor was it necessary for him to ask to apply the oil on my skin, although we both knew subjectively that it was not the usual thing a merchant would or should do. But also, at a subtle level he and I knew that he would not do anything I would not allow. And I sensed that he wanted nothing more than for me to relish the scent of his product - enhanced by him, not me, applying it directly onto my skin, which I did. It was an innocent, playful, spicy moment that we gifted to one another – one of those sensual adult interplays that slipped under the radar – it was sacred and private with motives that may not have even be known to us, but it felt easy and affirmed who we were as a man and woman in our self-made hinterland.

There was no panic or reject reaction from me as he uncapped another bottle and held it close to my nose to take in the aroma before repeating the ritual of his applying the oud onto me. I nodded a yes and he wiped the prior oud off me, unclipped the rod from the bottle and lapped the next liquid sample onto new areas of the sides and front of my neck, and the other places as he did before. Words would have been an intrusion. My pleasure was his pleasure, and his, mine - of the delight and the flirtatiousness of his actions and my ultra-feminine allowing - of his giving and sampling my female space. Yes, we were caught up in the spell of oud and thoroughly enjoying ourselves. And the point of sale would go no further than that. I bought a good-sized bottle of the best one of the oud fragrances. Happily, paid a lot for it and left the shop pleased. I knew that he too, was pleased behind me at the counter. That secreted lush persuasion would color the way I would know and wear the oud from then on.

A desire that was repressed would find a way to be expressed – even with more fight. What we denied ourselves would knock and eat away at us until it was heard and appeased. The behavior of the oud merchant was forward, even defiant in the Saudi culture of modesty and discretion between the sexes. And yet, there was something redeeming about how the curbing of the sensual and the separation of men and women could unfurl such intensely erotic and subtle occasions that a man and woman might be more determined to share. On that supple morning in the souk perfume shop I rallied such an occasion. That flirtation on the way to oud put a spring in my step and woke up my day. My femininity was tapped and enjoyed. And that charmed me - something I had been missing from having so little social contact with men in the land. The oud merchant sipped me softly as if to sniff a flower or to take in a sunset, and I allowed myself to be appreciated as such. It was grace.

 I revisited that dallying brush in reminiscence of how fine it was to be so sampled – and against the odds. I didn't believe that the natural urges of man to connect with woman and woman to man, or persons to persons always had to lead to sex. Even better, we came away sated from having given ourselves over to an instinctive encounter that was destined to happen. And perfectly so, between consenting adults in a sweet room alone, appreciating that something so intimate would go well and just so far - like the lingering smear of oud from tiny bottles onto skin to be savored by the wearer and those who came near.

19
Planet of the Women
– To Know Their Voices

The parallel existence of women's and man's worlds in Saudi Arabia was a carry-over from Arabia's ancient Islamic heritage going back thousands of years and from its Bedouin traditions, and perhaps dating as far back to the time of the Ottomans. In that context it was inferred that the separations originated from the *"Extreme concern to protect female purity and family honor."* It was a complex history. In my time in the Kingdom, the cultural separation of the sexes was apparent and pervasive in work environments and in public places including banks, hospitals, restaurants, and other commercial business establishments, with most having designated entrances for women marked on the outside of the buildings apart and away from the general entrance for men. Universities had separate fully operational campuses for young women and men, each mirroring the other with respective administrative bodies - one for men and one for women. In hospital and clinic waiting rooms there were assigned areas for women to sit away from men; and in some supermarkets there were separate checkout stations for women. Those demarcations also pervaded social life such as in parties and gatherings. There were times when I could go through my entire day, from working to running errands without interacting at all with a man, except for the intermittent drivers.

To be thrust into a world of women was something like being on another planet where the ones surrounding me and with whom I was engaged much of the time, day and night, were of one gender. There was a sameness to it – a sameness that at times was stifling for me. The women had to deal with one another from day to day with some input from men but without men's physical presence. The women could be catty, irritating, gossipy, and generated a lot of drama among themselves. For me, they could be a lot of times boring. Yet, there was also a familiarity and the shared experience of being somewhat exiled from the world community which brought a comfort and safety, a bonding, and the peculiar freedom to let our hair down and just be women! After the initial culture shock of being in a world of women I acquiesced; I settled in and stepped more into it and began to see and listen into it; there I found a vitality and a durable energy beneath the surface of the planet of the women.

I came and lived and worked in the Kingdom during the time when women were on the rise – or at least, incipient campaigning and support for women's upward mobility was afoot. Still, as the parallel cultures of women to men was the prevailing law of the land I associated and worked exclusively with and around women within that timeframe of epic change. Men were primarily the leaders and administrators, and that too, was slowly changing. The surge of activities around women could not be labeled as 'women's rights' or called a women's movement, nor compared to any in other cultures. It was quiet, moderate, and not aggressive. The campaign to support and lift women did not toot its horn or seek to draw attention to it, nor did it have a name or unifying message around which women could organize. It was not in the news, there was no legislation for it, nor was there marching in the streets. It was sponsored by a resolve in the minds of some, if not many, both women and men to generate openings and pathways for women to participate to a greater degree in the Kingdom's economy, i.e., in the workplace, and as business leaders and owners. They saw the need for it and the promise behind it.

It was said that *'a man who cannot change his mind would never change anything'*. But even change did not rely upon the whims of men. Besides, the ordinary affairs of peoples was like a pendulum - when circumstances reached an extreme in one direction the 'pendulum' unerringly swung the other way; it could swing from the 'ideal' to 'chaos' and go back and forth – which was all about growth and evolution. That was universal law. When that occurred, the only clear options were to resist change and subsequently self-destruct or go in the opposite direction. That principle applied to nations and kingdoms as well. In a world with few and lessening oversight on how a country was governed, to revise a national mindset came as a voluntary act, which could call up a deep and courageous vision. That was what I saw first-hand as what was happening in the Kingdom, and I thought that the mounting pressures against women's repression was giving that proverbial pendulum a big and decisive shove from left to right. In the eyes of the world and from the internal rumblings among the citizenry, the Kingdom had reached a low point with regard to freedoms and rights for women; and gradually, the tide of the old ways was ebbing.

It was a rare and remarkable thing when a great country changed its mind. It was humbling to witness and to stand in the vortex of such an event. Few times in the history of peoples had that occurred – most notably with the Russian glasnost and the tearing down of the Berlin wall. The Kingdom of Saudi Arabia had gone through internal upheavals before with Saudi society historically remaining closed about its traditions and customs. However, *this time* it was a momentous transforming event and with implications for the world. The Saudi Vision 2030 was generating a marked shift in communities and among individuals. The precise objectives decreed within the Vision 2030 generated a stir that would impact the Kingdom's status and its role in global relationships, societies, and governments alike. The world was watching.

Living and working in the Kingdom during its dawning days of modern transformation was a wonder and a privilege. I thought that being there during that time and doing what I was doing contributed however minutely, to the shift. Where women were specifically concerned, the changes were varied, seemingly relevant only to women but the changes were unilaterally updating everyday life in the Kingdom; several objectives espoused in the vision opened socio/economic doors for women such as increased job opportunities and levels of responsibility for armies of women and appointing women into Ministry positions. Concurrent with the vision, some notable 'coming' changes were: Putting women behind the wheel of a car and a soft promise that the abaya and hijab would no longer be mandated. The changes were making room for a young woman to know that it was 'okay' to reflect and look deeply within to better 'know' herself, and to put her voice into the world; or for young Saudi men to openly take a stand for a woman's right to decide for herself on all matters vital to her quality of life – staring down the emblematic and long-standing 'male guardianship' rule.

Their voices were coming forth, more easily - the thousands of young women who were graduating from university and becoming a strong part of the emerging Saudi society. For years they had been tuned in with their fingers on the pulse of what was going on. And now they had a lot to say to those who would listen. What they voiced was important for me to hear, and I kept a record of their thoughts verbatim from the papers they wrote and from what they said to me, which told the story of refresh and a welcomed era through their eyes. In their words they said:

Farah: "The country is taking a step forward and losing its rigidity."

Mariam: "Regardless of how careless I was, I have grown up before it's too late."

Sukinah: "People (women) are increasing their awareness to working and self-reliance rather than sitting in their homes and living the life of the past generations."

Fatimah: "I think the community will start thinking differently and more openly, especially in the women's cases. I don't have to worry about my career."

Benazir: "I have the responsibility to work hard and support this vision for our country."

Bedoor: "I learned from this vision that it is never too late to change, and change does not happen in one day."

Hussah: "I see our country in a flourish period. Nowadays, as a Saudi woman, it is impacted on me personally because now we are more involved in the community and being treated equally as men. Some of the new vision is reflecting my passion. For example, allowing the woman to drive and punish anyone that tries to stop women from driving."

Noor: "I've changed a lot to a hopeful personality."

Zaineb: "Saudi vision means to me as a citizen of Saudi Arabia life, a better future and better country. The vision is unlocking the talent, potential and dedication of the young men and women."

Falak: "I realized on me."

Hadeel: "The technological and environmental changes will attract people from all around the world to come and see the new edition of Saudi Arabia. As a Saudi citizen words cannot describe how proud I am of this vision and the fact that the land of the two holy mosques will develop and improve in every aspect like technology, health, entertainment, productions, economy, education, politics, and many more to mention and be stronger and independent now. No country can improve with not the improvement of its people. As a future, I should never lose hope of my country because Saudi Arabia is building its new history."

Ayat: "The vision makes me aware about my thoughts and the disposal of my weaknesses. Before the vision, I wasn't known. I can do everything with only myself. I can spread my leadership now. I am able to reach my goals with no hesitations or judgments."

Munirah: "The vision freed up the wrong thinking of women's work. Most of my female family members and friends are working now and the negative thinking of a woman's work has been freed. As Prince Mohammed bin Salman said, 'The sky is the limit, and we are aiming to elevate the standards of living and quality which will allow people of Saudi Arabia to make a positive impact on the entire world."

Nouf: "I am so proud that most of the society are aware and awake. Getting ready for the future that is what Saudis are doing."

Khadijah: "These days I can start my own business without needing a man or a husband to work beside me. I can depend on myself greatly. This vision makes many of my friends dream after they can only depend on others for their living. Women are free now and can share in the progress of their society."

Those women and legions more were the harbingers of the country's transformations. I could not have known the power of the shifts taking place in Saudi society had I not witnessed and heard it from my station up close and personal in the planet of the women. Those were virgin words in the Kingdom coming from young Saudi women as if from out of an abyss. And so much more was said. There was a time when words like those would have been jeopardous and were restrained and kept hidden, like women's bodies under the abaya. Upon hearing those words then and there out loud I knew that it was a seminal moment in time when the women could speak openly, unbridled and to someone like me. To know their voices was to know their hearts and intent, which gave a preview on where their country was headed. When a country educated and freed its women, it educated and freed itself - an act that raised the energy in the land and prompted things to grow. Women's plans were measured in centuries, it seemed. And slouching towards a probable future, the Kingdom was rethinking and rearranging itself and its possibilities - coming to terms with the new reality that nothing would come true without the women.

20
Graduation Night

The female students were crowding into and jamming the campus corridors, with hundreds of the seniors energetically chatting about their graduations set for that night. They were sharing their winning grades with each other in amazement and release now that they had passed their courses. Many of them exceeded the usual 12-15 semester course credits by taking on a load of 21 credits to finish off their college education in record time – and with high marks*. An A+ was the only option for the high achievers who wanted that 4.00 GPA which would secure them good jobs and praises from family, and even money from proud mothers and fathers – 1000 – 2000 riyals for each A they received. Against university policy, they graffitied the campus walls with murals to tell their stories, with poems and drawings of their 'sheros' and of themselves wearing caps and gowns and wide triumphant smiles. As I walked through the halls, I watched them and took it all in myself, smiling with and for them – pleased with my work which played a part in generating that scene.

With regularity during the last days of the semester, students would bum rush me in the corridors or mobs crammed into my office eager to know about their final grades. *"Did I pass, miss?"* All echoing one another. It was not advisable to give students that information before final grades were officially recorded with the Registrar to minimize the spiral of bargaining, pleading, anger and protests that occurred among dissatisfied students and parents, sometimes husbands. But I did so anyway. It was usually the low achieving students who raced in to know how they did, high performing students knew they did well, they just wanted to affirm whether they got the A+ or not. Two students, Rawah and Fanan, who were best friends throughout the semester and took my course together came to see me, anxious about their grades. And they should have been because they barely passed with D+s. They were such beauties whose friendship seemed to come before anything else, even their studies. When I told them their grades, they leapt into hugs with one another; they thanked me profusely and went screaming down the hall with glee, holding hands as they ran. I would remember and chuckle on that sight of them for a long time. The two came back a few days later to present me with a gift box full of vanity 'lady' things: nail polish, a mini nail polish dryer, a fan, lipstick, false eyelashes, etc. Theirs was a typical response to receiving a passing grade, which meant that they could and would walk across the stage come graduation night, and that was a big deal.

I was not an easy professor. I was known as Doctor Rigor, and that fit. It was critical that the female graduates were well learned and prepared to meet the work world, and had staying power, be it as an employee, a business leader, or entrepreneur. The gap between students' capacities and what organizations were demanding was huge and was confirmed in the conferences and meetings I attended in the business community and women's 'upward mobility' forums. I knew that the graduates could not assume that they could waltz into a good job just because they were pretty or wealthy or even had 'wasta'.

Fluctuations in the economy and deep-seated changes that were afoot in the Kingdom made businesses more competitive and serious about who they hired, and I wove that understanding into how and what I taught. High grades were to be earned not doled out as many professors were seduced to do by their students. Needless to say, there was a lot of bribery going on to get passing grades. Of course, the female students were reaching from a great disadvantage of not having had the same extensive opportunities to attend college as males had long been privileged to enjoy. It was only in recent years that large numbers of Saudi females were able to attend universities and have access to the same learning curriculums as males. The fact remained that 'earned' good grades and achievement would help female students in the long run and stay with them; and I wanted them to graduate with pride - that they did their very best and on their own. Many and most of them did just that, like Sarah. She was a former student who told me that during a job interview it was pointed out that her GPA was low. She then said to the interviewer: *"My GPA may not be as high as I would like, but I earned it all by myself."* Needless to say, Sarah got the job.

On the few days leading up to the long awaited graduation night, I could look out of my office window at any given hour and see clusters of female students gathered in the courtyard below. They were trying on their gowns and caps, posing, and taking pictures, chasing, and grabbing at each other, playfully swinging one another around, and laughing - their dark lustrous hair dancing about their heads and shoulders. I viewed them as long as they were out there fooling around, because their frolicking celebrations were confirmation of what professors and students had achieved together.

Graduation day was notoriously lengthy, with the regular 8:00 to 4:00 office hours plus the ceremony all through the evening hours. The female administrators and professors were picked up from their compounds by university buses and taxis and shuttled to the auditorium which was located on the male campus; it was vacated by the male faculty and students for the night to allow the women's graduation festivities. I had attended several graduations there and was used to the process and prepared myself for a long evening. We were to arrive at about 6:00 pm with the ceremony beginning at 8:00 pm.

In the spacious lobby adjacent to the auditorium there were tables and tables stocked with cakes, chocolates, and finger sandwiches; there were faculty, administrators, female students in their regalia, mothers, and women relatives milling about. Along the walls were several portraits of the all-male university founders and leaders. Pictured were the Rector with male dignitaries who seemed to be overseeing and approving the women-only event – all looking stern and regal in their thobes and checkered shemaghs and oqals. Dozens of Filipino staff women in crisp white blouses and long black skirts stood by at the food tables to assist the crowd in filling their small plates or walked around with an assortment of edibles, pouring Arabic coffee and tea into tiny mirra cups. Most of the female students were oblivious to the food fare and were instead caught up in the moment and the frenzy – gathering with friends, giggling, hugging, posing with each other for selfies. The room was electric.

After a period of greeting students and their families in the lobby, fellow professors and I retired to an upstairs lounge area where we would wait, rest, relax and visit among ourselves until the ceremony began, which would officially be when the Princess arrived. She would officiate the graduation as she had done in previous years. The Princess was the wife of the university's founder. At the announcement that the ceremony was about to begin, we entered the auditorium and took our seats. Mothers and other female family members were seated in designated rows behind faculty and administrators who were occupying the first several rows from the stage. Hundreds of students were seated in rows at the very back and according to their specific Colleges of learning. Men were not allowed, that included fathers, brothers, and husbands.

Once the Princess arrived and took her seat at the stage, the ceremony began. She was seated in the plush VIP section at the foot of the stage, along with the graduation coordinators. Standing as ushers and 'eyes' along the walls, I spotted some staff women I worked closely with, but now found them unrecognizable – their persons had been transformed by make-up and fancy clothes and shoes, and for the first time, I saw their hair! Everyone stood for the Saudi national anthem, which was followed by an Arabic hymn sung ever so angelically by a student. The Honor's student and keynote commencement speaker was one of my graduating seniors, whom I recommended for that role. She was the brightest learner in my 'capstone' course – Hala. It felt good to see her up there. She directed her speech to the student audience, giving them praise on their accomplishments and words of hope for the world they were about to enter. That was followed by an inspirational speech in Arabic by another student, as most of the graduation program was in Arabic. There was no translation; that was the Saudi students' celebratory venue; although some ex-pat faculty members furiously complained about the lack of spoken English at the graduations and refused to attend them for that reason. But, in my mind, if one could get into the spirit of it, there was really no need to know exactly what was being said. The joy pouring off the students and their mothers more than adequately articulated the whole story for me and others.

As the students' specific Colleges of learning were called, they lined up accordingly and began to approach the stage. Some still giddy, some suddenly pensive, all in their navy-blue caps and gowns bearing the insignia of the degree program from which they were graduating. The College of Business where I was the leader and professor had the most graduates. Each graduate ascended and walked across the stage when her name was called simultaneously with the blown-up photo of her appearing on the projector screen above. The Princess now standing on the stage shook the hand and smiled her blessing at each one. She stood taller than those around her looking like a towering benevolent fairy in her silken layered abaya of yellow, peach and cream with golden highlights streaming through from the top to the hem – her hair shining, auburn, and full, flowed around her shoulders and down her back. She was impressive. Next to the Princess, a staff woman handed the graduates their degree portfolios. The actual degree would be placed inside days later once the graduates were fully cleared by the Registrar – a typical protocol for most graduations. As the graduates exited the stage they jubilantly released, as if in those few seconds they had finally crossed a coveted threshold and they need not worry again, because their education could never be taken away from them.

I watched with satisfaction and pride as those students I knew, taught and was close to, descended from the stage to pass by my seat going towards the atrium at the rear of the auditorium. I had strategically chosen to sit in the last seat in the row and along the aisle the graduates would walk down and where I could see them up close at their very best, with their faces all made up, their hair styled and their shoes. Oh! How they really made a 'statement' with their expensive designer shoes! Most of all I wanted to be with them to share their triumph in that fleeting moment. In my excitement, I left my seat and made haste to the atrium to congratulate them. There were hugs and tap-kisses on the cheeks, appreciations and 'thank yous' – and selfies, of course were taken on the condition that the pictures would not be shared with anyone - archiving that snapshot in time as a personal and private one among women.

Graduation night was over for that year. It was now close to 10:00 pm and I was looking forward to returning to my villa to fall into bed. The graduates were off and running, they were done. Some were lingering, now with a higher-pitched chatter than it was earlier that day, and the majority were exiting the auditorium with friends and family going off to feast and party into the night. I would not see most of them again. Some would return to my office weeks or months later to announce the new job they got, or to tell me about their wedding plans, or how they were helping their fathers with their businesses. Some would come by to report how they were applying the things they learned in their new positions or seeking graduate degrees at universities in the Kingdom or abroad – asking me for letters of recommendation. I would even run into some of them around and about the city in various places. An untested army of women had been groomed and set loose into the world - women who were now better able to benefit from the positive shifts in the Kingdom. My wish was that there'd be a welcoming grace for them in the dynamically changing fabric of Saudi society – one that needed and respected their input, productivity, and leadership more than ever. In time I would receive good reports back from the employers who hired and worked with many of them and from the people who crossed their paths.

*Mark - *The term used in the Saudi educational system referring to points towards a final grade; 66 out of 100 marks were required to pass a course. Accumulated high marks over a semester increased a student's GPA.*

21
In the Men's Gathering Place – The Majlis

I am thrilled to report on my strays as a happy interloper into gatherings commonly and exclusively held for men. I kind of stumbled into those sanctums where women infrequently visited. It happened one time in the Kingdom and again in Qatar, where I by happenstance, came to be in closed settings as the lone woman among dozens of Arab and Saudi men. As most of my interactions in the Kingdom were among women, the deviations into 'man's domain' were awkward yet refreshing intrigues for me. After being surrounded by women most of the time, I found that I was relieved when in the sheer company of men. Those experiences were meaningful to me. Perhaps I needed them, for they provided an added dimension, as it were, which mitigated how life in the Kingdom was affecting me.

The weekend could not come fast enough with me so much looking forward to being with Ronald, my ex-pat male companion. We were going on a short road trip into the desert to visit the camel farms, about seventy-five miles away. Sharing close company with a man was like cool air in the heat, and on that day, I would get a healthy dose of that. He'd rent a car and call me to say that he was on his way, he'd pull up to my villa, and with me ready with my abaya on, off we'd go leaving the city behind. On the road we knew when we were rural and near the camels because of the smell, not a bad smell, but a strong pungent animal odor – from a lot of camels. We were in an area where there were many farms where camels were bred and sold. At one farm we got out of the car and went up close to the camels, they were fenced in, but we could reach out our hands to them. The camels came close to look at us too and let us feel them. I thought that they were such sweet and intelligent beings, even unreal and otherworldly.

As the heat started to get to us, we looked for a place to go inside for relief. We spotted a small one-story modest building nearby and went there because it looked accessible although the surrounding area was deserted. The door opened into a spacious sparsely furnished room where ten Arab male camel herders were sitting, barefooted - lounging about on the floor, having tea and all dressed in the traditional thobes with the red and white checkered shemaghs draped over their heads. The men looked as astonished as we did. Ronald and I had unknowingly entered a prayer and social room for men, which was called a majlis*. "I should leave," was my first impulse. But as soon as I said that one of the men got up from the floor and approached us. He was one of the Saudi owners of the camels. He knew that we were hot and thirsty and insisted that we come in, remove our shoes, and have a seat on the floor and refreshments with them. I asked if it was okay for me, a woman to come inside. "No worries, come, come inside with us," he said. Inside the large room were dozens of pillows and seat cushions situated against the wall. No chairs, no tables – but a lavish Arabesque rug spread across the entire length of the room. The men cleared a space around us to sit, giving me a wide berth because I was a woman.

A young boy of about 11-years old, upon being told to bring us drinks seemed to pop out of nowhere and promptly began to serve us while cheerfully proclaiming that his name was Fez. Fez was proud and happy in what he was doing in his boy-sized thobe and turban – preparing and serving the beverages to the men and now their sudden guests. He was talented in the way he poured the tea into the small clear glasses from a high arch. Fez stayed nearby and on watch, waiting for the next time he could pour for us. Ronald launched into a conversation with the man sitting beside him – they were speaking alternately in English and Arabic. I sat quietly taking in the room, accepting my place in the whole scene, and letting Fez continue to pour me tea. Soon, the muezzin* was calling for prayer – a call that was heard everywhere. The men and Fez solemnly clustered in the center of the room, forming three rows. They asked that Ronald and I be silent as they prayed. For the next fifteen minutes they went through the prayer rituals making salutations of devotion with bowing and kneeling and rising again and raising and lowering their cupped hands – murmuring silently to themselves. There was no Imam present, but the men knew what to do. After prayer, the men invited Ronald to take a picture with them as a keepsake of our visit. It was a 'man' picture. As a woman, the men could not be near me, and my image was not allowed in the photo with them.

An hour had passed, and it was time to leave and to get something to eat. I asked Ronald what he was talking about with the man sitting next to him. He told me that the man was asking questions about the kind of work we did and how did we like the Kingdom. He wanted to know if I was Ronald's wife and if either of us had children. The man spoke about his wife and family and how he had become a camel herder like his father, whose father was also a camel herder. Some of the men in the room were his brothers. He told Ronald that the camels came from Qatar, and the men took care of them until they were sold for traveling, carrying goods through the desert, or for meat. Ronald said that the man was curious about the ways of the West and asked what we thought about Donald Trump. The cordial camel herder was also taking the opportunity to practice his English on Ronald, and vice versa with Ronald practicing his Arabic – a fair exchange. Before departing back into the heat, I shook Fez's hand and thanked him for his service. When I extended my hand to one of the men he flinched and pulled away, telling me with his eyes that it was not allowed. That was how I learned that men were not to touch a woman who was not of their blood – not unless she was a wife, mother, sister, child, or cousin, etc. Being in the room with the men as a woman was an exception for them that they welcomed, and even then, protocols had to be followed.

My second 'fluke' appearance in the man's gathering place was in Qatar; that time I was the solitary woman among fifteen men in a private social room. It was at the end of a day of touring Qatar with my friend Dr. Khalid and we were about to settle into the soft spring evening – visiting more with each other. There was a group of men, some of his close friends who regularly shared an evening meal in their majlis. They, like him were mostly businessmen and owners. Dr. Khalid wanted me to meet them and drove us there. The Qatari men's gathering place or majlis was a simple ordinary apartment inside a two-story building just off the street. The physicality of the majlis had nothing to do with its name; it was termed the majlis in the spirit of being a designated space where men could gather and have fellowship on a regular basis, like the Saudi camel herders inside the one-story structure.

Four men sat with Dr. Khalid and me on the steps outside the majlis – we were waiting for the rain to fall, and for the dinner to arrive. If anyone was uncomfortable with my presence there, they would not say anything, but just abide by some unspoken code that it was okay for that time; either that, or they would not dare to go up against Dr. Khalid who brought me there as his guest. Obviously to me, he was the alpha male in the group – a status attained no doubt, by his refined looks and bearing, his wealth, influence, and ties with the greater community, as well as the strong friendships he had cultivated among the men over many years. The respect among the men was plain to see. And if

Dr. Khalid said it was 'OK' for me to be there among them, it was 'OK'. I was not a distraction or amusement for the men, who left me to myself, no one said much directly to me other than casual greetings and asking how I was enjoying Qatar. There was an occasional smile or nod, and I could tell that the men were appreciative of my company and of my physical appearance.

In Qatar the abaya was not mandated for women to wear. And I took full advantage of that freedom by dressing fashionably yet in appropriate loose clothing. The bright colors of my sweater stood out against the all-white thobes and scarves the men wore. And as I was self-conscious of keeping my sweater buttoned all the way up and kept pulling at it to stay closed a button popped off landing somewhere on the ground nearby. It was a tiny white button. Noticing that, three of Dr. Khalid's friends jumped into action. They were immediately scrounging around over the concrete pavement searching for the tiny button. That unlikely sight of the men so regally dressed in their thobes and headdresses, relentlessly peeking, poking, bending, and stooping to find the button made me more self-conscious. I asked them several times not to bother, that it was nothing. But they ignored those words and kept looking. Round and round they searched, over here, over there, behind and under this and that, seeming to be making a contest of who could find the little button for the little lady. That went on for several minutes until one of them found it – snatching it up from the ground and showing it off for all to see in victory. Wow! I was not quite prepared for all the attention brought upon me by the men during the hunt and retrieval of that button. Such chivalry!! I was humbled, although the frenzy was amusing and priceless. I put the button in my purse and no longer cared whether my sweater left a little bit more of my flesh exposed. Some threshold had already been crossed with the button search episode. No worries. It was time to eat, as the dinner had arrived.

We were called to enter the majlis for the meal, which had been prepared and sent over by one of the men's wives. Inside, I was escorted to a seat away from the men towards the edge of the room, with most of the men making a deliberate attempt not to notice me. There were men already inside watching a soccer game on a small television and speaking silently among themselves, occasionally rooting, and cheering the Qatari team on. More men filed into the room – young, and middle-aged pot-bellied men; most of them had beards and wore the thobes with shemaghs and oqals about their heads. Some of the elder men were feeble and hunched over – entering the room slowly alongside men who were hefty and lean. I could easily surmise that having the elders in the room was, nonetheless, essential and grounding in the gathering.

The food was served by the male Filipino servants on hand who brought it from the kitchen and laid the platters of baked chicken, rice, pasta, and bread on the table in the sitting area. A man motioned me to remain seated as more than one of the Qatari men served me – one prepared my plate and gave it to me as another handed me a can of soda. Not speaking anything to me and making sure that I had everything I needed, they left me alone. In the men's gathering place I was in a bubble. My presence could not, would not and did not intrude upon the men's business – their bond and solidarity. It was understood that I was to eat and enjoy my food having nothing to say or do with any of the men, including my friend Dr. Khalid who was steadily talking and visiting among his comrades. With all the male talking and clamor going on around me I could not understand a single word that was being said, even though English was a commonly spoken language in the Middle East and most likely among the men in the room. I noticed that before, outside the majlis on the steps the men interacted with me a little – asking me a few light questions, whereas inside the majlis I was completely isolated and on my own.

I often wondered what Arab men did among themselves in arranged private settings, and whether my presence among them may have inhibited what they would normally do. But that probability was not the case. In Saudi and Qatar I was *in* the room of men, not *with* them; I was experiencing three levels of separation in the majlises: Male culture, male privacy, and Arabic. That was not at issue. Words made up twenty percent of the communications between people, whereas volumes of information was transmitted through attitudes, body language and tone all the time. There was a lot of information for me in those majlises in Qatar and Saudi. Ultimately, I was getting so much from listening, sensing, and observing – being there *with* the men in their sacred space.

Male gathering was a regular ritual in Middle Eastern cultures, just as men came together in 'men only' private clubs in the west. It was a universal thing and a rational aspect of any society. A distinction I noted was that the Arabic men in the majlises in the Kingdom and in Qatar tended to converse and interact closely as an entity as if there was one deliberate collective 'male' mind at work, whereas in western private clubs the men tended to be present as individuals - pairing off with another, or in smaller groups, or some sitting alone enjoying their singular company, as if on their own private island.

Given the male/female separations in the Kingdom and from some prior incidents, I did have reservations about entering 'men only' spaces with the expectation that the men would be hostile and make me leave. There were times when I accidently entered a place occupied by men and was quickly however, 'gently' ordered out. In those instances I had not noticed nor was I aware of the Women's Entrance that was marked around the corner or several doors down. However, in the majlises, although I was secluded in their space and was not there to participate in any manner, rarely had I experienced a welcome and safety among such cohesive groups of men. I might say that I even had a feeling of importance in some benign way.

Being in the majlises brought me closer to the Arab male where I gained a better glimpse and a useful understanding of 'him'. With the little that they could or allowed themselves to express and gesture to me – the camel herders and the Qatari men, they did so with an eloquence, a kindness and a reverence that piqued my femininity. I came away enlivened from that dense male energy and appreciated how good it felt to be in the company of men, realizing how much I was missing that in my daily affairs in the Kingdom. I gladly thanked my good friend, Dr. Khalid for hosting my visit in Qatar that afternoon and evening, without touching him of course.

Majlis – 'Sitting room', a term that described a special gathering place, usually among Arabic men with common interests.

Muezzin – Or mu'azzin, was the person who called for the prayers five times a day from the mosque which could be heard throughout the outer spaces. The person leading the prayer for the gathering faithful was the Imam.

22
Men Die Alone

During the time I lived and worked in the Kingdom I knew of the deaths of five men within my circle of business colleagues. Each man was a western citizen, middle-aged - averaging 55 years-old; they were Caucasian and African American. Their deaths occurred on separate days over a period of five years. Concern was raised when the men did not show up to their offices or to teach their classes – and after several days had passed; it was then that their apartment doors were forcibly opened, and they were found dead inside. That came as a shock to those who knew the men well and those who did not. Death in the ordered life in the Kingdom was making its presence known. And those 'passings' seemed to follow a disquieting pattern.

Police arrived to take any evidence of what might have happened and recorded the deaths, and the bodies were removed as the people living nearby in the gated residential compound stood by looking with sad eyes, wondering about it all. Some of them probably thinking, that that could have been them, and maybe it might be in a coming time, but all of them no doubt, feeling helpless that there was nothing they could have done for the men.

The men died mostly of heart disease, with one falling into a diabetic coma. They died in their sleep or had a medical emergency that they had to deal with alone. Some had been lying on the floor after life had left their bodies for days. Their names were Keith, Emet, Jon, Anthony, and Simon. All were single, unmarried men working to make a living in KSA, far away from their native countries of the UK and US. It was how a lot of men and women 'made do' to have a life and to support the welfare of their loved ones back home.

I met Keith a few months before he transitioned from life. We attended the same faculty forums regularly, whereupon he approached me wanting to exchange phone numbers and get to know me better - hinting at a date. He was African-American, tall, with a nice handsome face, and I noted that his body did not look fit or healthy. I liked Keith's demeanor and wanted to be his friend - choosing not to entertain his interest in me personally, because I avoided dating men within my work organization. I was also preoccupied with my position and its extended responsibilities, which at the time was consuming. So, I pushed his interest to 'engage' me off to be considered at a later time, perhaps, once I got settled into and in control of my leadership post and office affairs. I really meant to do that and kept his phone number close at hand and assumed that there was all the time in the world to get in touch with him. I was taken aback when I learned that he was found lifeless in his apartment a few months later. I kept his number and the text he sent to me in my phone. Not sure why. *Was Keith's reaching out to me a call for something that might have helped and kept him alive?* Another one of the men was a withdrawn, sullen guy, who was known to be exceptional with numbers and accounting. The few interactions I had with him left a sour taste in my mouth, so I avoided him, thankful that the duties of my office did not involve him in any way. That was not worth thinking about when I learned of his unforeseen death alone in his apartment, lying on the floor at the side of his bed.

Other than Keith, I did not know or had any casual associations with the other men, only a remote working relationship with them. And their stories carried the same weight of a loss all too soon. A man departed life without immediate notice; it happened again, and again, and again, and again. That had a somber effect on me. Men died alone in the Kingdom – at least they did in my sphere of professionals, contractors, and educators. Not just I, but we as a community noticed that it was the 'men' who were dying that way. What made those deaths so poignant was that they occurred within one organization with five deaths in the same number of years, with the men, all living alone and around the same age, and all within the same residential compound. Even the police who were repeatedly called to the scenes observed that it was unusual, and that it was the men who had been dying – not the women.

Some time following the last death I overheard a conversation among a group of colleagues with one person saying that it was *"the loneliness."* And that *"Men were not good at handling the isolation and aloneness"* - a stark factor inherent in the lives of ex-pats. While some people were predisposed to be loners, some were alone against their will and were more vulnerable to emotional and physical withering in an isolating environment. Women and men were sequestered unto their work with little room or an outlet for a social life. Unlike women, it was granted that single men did not have the 'coping' skills or the networks that kept them engaged and kept them going. My male ex-pat companion mentioned to me how our relationship *"really helped"* him get through those few years in KSA and was a *"lifeline"* to him. He expressed that to me more than once and I do believe, in earnest. Perhaps there was some biological/psychological difference between women and men - some quality that women could draw upon to cope. I didn't know. But it pointed to a larger issue that impacted both men and women: *That no one can do this life alone.*

Human beings were meant to be with other humans. Newborn babies weakened and died or did not grow normally if they were not touched and had human contact on a regular basis. Human warmth, intimacy and relationships filled the heart and kept it activated. It was well documented that people died of broken hearts; science had proven that acute emotional stress can shock and paralyze the left ventricle causing a heart attack. I had an uncle who was in his prime and whose heart failed and stopped shortly after the woman who was the love of his life left him. In a relatively short period of time, I witnessed his decline from being happy and healthy in love to despondent, decrepit, and sick of life. Human contact and closeness were not something to be taken for granted in the Kingdom for men or women. Yet, for the most part, it was improbable to engage with the opposite sex in the Kingdom. I knew men and women who struggled daily with the ordeal of loneliness or being alone too much – two very different things. Saudis generally mixed, dated and married within their own ethnicity. And if the average Saudi met the opposite sex through their parents, one could imagine how less easy it was for a foreigner to meet another of the opposite sex. Although there was a greater ratio of men to women in the Kingdom, it did not make much difference in terms of the opportunities in which available men could connect with available women.

The divisions between the sexes as it was imbedded into the social fabric applied to all men and women in the Kingdom – it was inferred and structural through informal social mores, codes, and even taboos. That was stifling and it reduced the occasions for opposite sexes to easily meet. In Saudi culture, men were not supposed to look at women directly; they would avert their eyes away from a woman if she was, for example, walking facing in their direction in passing. That happened to me all the time, from Saudi, and particularly, from Pakistani, Bangladeshi, and Indian men. The 'averted eye' syndrome caught on among many ex-pats too. Among strangers, direct eye contact from man to woman was not encouraged and viewed as a sign of disrespect and an intrusion. Conversely, from a woman to a man, eye contact was seen as a 'come on' or an invitation, which may not have been the woman's intent. Casual, male/female social 'dis-interactions' were all so confusing, neurotic, and fragile. People just avoided acknowledging or approaching each other as strangers in public spaces altogether – even me much of the time. And the more formalized male/female contact and communications were complicated, i.e. in business settings, etc. All of the above were exacerbated as there were few to no public venues set up for men and women to freely interact that might facilitate familiarity and comfort between the sexes.

There were no bars, clubs, regular concerts, dance halls, etc. Restaurants were set up to accommodate either men in separate areas or families in another – not boy and girl together. Unmarried men and women were discouraged from visiting one another's private residence or spending too much time within a domicile alone. Overnight stays between unmarried men and women were prohibited as a long-standing rule in most residential compounds. And when that rule was broken there were usually dozens of busy eyes in the community ready to fabricate gossip about the forbidden visits and spread it around – reporting the goings on behind closed doors between consenting adults. Intermingling, let alone, dating, therefore, became an action one needed to finesse. One worked during the week and what they had left was the weekend, Friday, and Saturday for themselves – and for many, most of that time was spent alone. Some men who had a car drove to Bahrain for the weekend where there was openness, where they had easier access to women, which by and large was with prostitutes – it was their choice. They eventually had to return to their villas and apartments to be alone again.

But wait! There were ways of getting around the aloneness. Driving to Bahrain for a weekend fling was not the only way men made off from the isolation in the Kingdom. A colleague of mine, who was deeply affected by the deaths of those men, confided in me his intensifying need for companionship, a desire that was beginning to preempt his professional goals. Those deaths made it *"absolutely clear"* to him how alone he was and how threatening that void was becoming to his well-being and quality of life. He was reconsidering his priorities and planning to relocate to another region, maybe the UAE, where he could enjoy a change of scenery and more freedoms. He wanted to date and be out in the open with a woman – to walk down the street holding hands, to have her over at his place for dinner – without all of the hindrances, secrecy, and shaming. Those kinds of freedoms were starting to mean more to him than the security of continuing in his present high-level position. Another colleague took control of his loneliness. The specter of his approaching the age of 60 as a career man, and alone had no appeal whatsoever, and it was scary. He went online and spent weeks and months scouring the profiles of women in the world until he found the woman he soon married.

Moreover, after years of sending money back to their home countries in the west, many professional men who came to the Kingdom to earn a living for their families eventually transported their families to live with them in the Kingdom – a decision that helped them find a way to make life work for them all. And of course, there was the savvy Filipino 'Madam' being all too aware of the plight of the single ex-pat male in the Kingdom, she specialized in matching young Filipino women as wives for older single western men. Such pairings were magical. Undoubtedly, she had a successful practice, for I had seen how some of those men became quite content from her services.

At some point after the fifth death, a circle of professionals including me agreed to establish a personal directory of our contact information; and to regularly check in on those who had health issues and especially to do so on the same day if they did not come in for work without giving notice. *Overseeing and being our 'brother's keeper' could save a life*, we thought.

In the few years since I left the Kingdom my friends there told me that two men at the university died suddenly of health issues. I worked closely and well with one of them - Allan, a conscientious man and a rare professional, barely forty, who was supporting his wife and three children in the Philippines.

A pertinent fact remained, that we could not do this life alone. With that in mind I rhetorically asked speaking aloft: *"Isn't that what the love songs have been saying to us all along? And was that increasingly the case as the world got crazier, less safe and life was not fulfilling for more men and more women?"* I wondered if endearing words, close relationships, compassion, or a constant warm and human touch might have prolonged the lives of some of the five men, now seven. I was thinking: '*We are all beings composed of energy which we rely upon in various forms for succor, especially in trying times. Food, rest, and validation are some forms of energy that sustains a human life – validation for who we are and what we do. We need the energy of love, affection, and intimacy – things we can only beget from one another; we can go only so far without that or some form of nourishing human contact*'. If those truths were more top of mind during my first encounters with Keith when he reached out to me, I would have responded much differently – if even to decide in that moment to be present with him as a close and caring friend.

UNDER THE ABAYA

Part Three

INTRIGUES OF THE ADVENTURE

UNDER THE ABAYA

23
Such Devotion

A whisper of song cradled me as I was stirred from a deep dream at daybreak, just past 5 am. More song sauntered in, to my hearing and sensing, entering as a soft hello like the pastels of the dawn. It was the first chant, the singular call of the muezzin, a muscular baritone cry that reached for higher crescendos, as it was echoed by the sonorous choruses of other muezzins pouring out from the distant towers of fellow mosques. Those sounds were amplified through loudspeakers perched atop the many Muslim temples that served the populace of the coastal Arabian city and were what awakened and greeted me from slumber each day.

The 'a cappella' of the faithful was irresistible as they conspired in the praying in of a brand new day and could be heard everywhere by anyone and everyone. I lie there and listened, taking it all in. Not wanting to lose a second of those lovely Arabic hymns by getting out of bed too soon. I leaned into them, as they brought pleasurable feelings to me. Those morning devotions never failed to lift my sleepy mind and body into the day.

The prayer call from the nearest mosque seeped in through the windows – registering its presence as though it were the breeze that was moving the fluttering curtains, lightly spraying into the room. It moaned and shimmered and rose to a wail that was glorious, then settled back down to a hushed rejoice. I did not understand the words, but they comforted me because I allowed them. The solemn alpha male voice held the center of song with other devout brothers' voices streaming in and folding around it, holding it steady in an authority that beckoned, but did not demand as they lovingly adored their God. The morning devotions from the mosques within hearing went on for long minutes, culminating at a lofty pitch and then trailing off in a distant accord of gentler accents of adoration – rescinding back into the silence of dawn. I wanted to follow - and missed them when they were no longer there.

The calls to prayer would be repeated intermittently four more times during the day, but not with the same rapture and 'effect' as the calls riding on the newborn sunrise. At that time a person was roused and fresh, between dozing and waking in a netherworld where one was more susceptible to the seductive sounds of prayer which seemed to issue from an ancient portal. Morning, with the Fajr prayer, was the time when such fierce devotion could be heard. Whenever I heard and listened to it, I knew that I was in a place like no other.

In the Kingdom, prayer was central, and it governed the rhythms of everyday life. Wherever one might be, the prayers were there. And whether one was faithful or not, the prayers would affect whatever they were doing. The prayer times did not exactly align with the clock but were set in time in accordance with the movements of the moon, which was different by a few minutes each day. Many devout Muslims had a special calendar app on their cell phones to tell them the exact timing of the prayers.

The daily summons to prayer were called adhan. The adhan calls to prayer came again at around noon for Dhuhr; then in mid-afternoon as Asr; at sunset as Maghrib. The last and evening prayer came as Isha'a, which was the longest and most beautiful - a completion that celebrated how the faithful had made it through another twenty-four hours on earth. In all of the prayers of the day, including Isha'a, the clerics' recitations of sacred texts from the Qur'an were melodiously rendered - as chants in resplendent prayerful intonations; no words were read verbatim.

The sounds of Isha'a were a beauteous ache – a plea, an oath, a hope, and a promise all expressed as one vow. The night prayer was especially enchanting. It could be a lone tenor's tender recital - a perfect devotional to Allah, or it could be a baritone's haunting howl – when combined they were an anthem that just set itself down into one's soul. Nothing else in all I experienced and knew could rival such sounds. When I heard the prayers during the day, I would stop what I was doing to go to the window or better still, outside to listen all the way and through to the unearthly harmonies of the all-male ensemble of voices. So compelling were the songs of prayer, not only to the Muslim soul, but to the Christians and peoples of other faiths. The melodic prayers would enthrall anyone who would stop, listen, and allow themselves to be moved and touched by them. How a country's culture that so notably sanctioned restraint could produce such loose richness, release, and depth in daily rituals of worship and adulation was extraordinary to me!

The calls for prayer came while I was spending an afternoon with a male friend in Qatar. We had been enjoying walking and talking for hours, stopping now and then for a beverage or coffee and sweets. Upon the muezzins' calls for the afternoon prayers of Dhuhr and Asr my friend politely and immediately suspended our visit - excusing himself to vanish into a nearby mosque to pray. All I could do was find a place to sit and wait the twenty minutes to half hour for him to return. And when he did, prayer was not discussed. We simply carried on with what we had been doing prior. His departures and absences to pray were seamlessly woven into his daily activities and there was usually a mosque close by where he knew he could go. Such was the devotion.

The call to prayer took over and shifted people into a different mode. Shops closed and bared their doors. Customers were gingerly ushered outside to wait until prayer time ended. Business transactions ceased. Patients were told to wait as their doctors went off to pray. Restaurants turned away incoming diners; the shades were lowered over windows and the entry doors locked. Those customers already inside and seated were told that the waiter would stop taking orders, and they would be served after prayer time. Sometimes dining customers were forewarned just before prayer time was announced to put their food orders in before the kitchen shut down for a while.

Food markets closed the check-out registers, leaving in place long lines of shoppers ready to pay for their groceries; they had to then wait in the stopped lines or just use the extra time to shop some more. Deli staff ceased slicing and serving from behind the counters. The shoppers stood and watched as cashiers and food servers abandoned their posts and slowly walked away towards the back of the store where there was most likely a prayer room, or to the mosques elsewhere in the mall or neighborhood. I must admit to my own frustration and folly when once a cashier, smiling with apologies closed the register just as I was next to check out. I only had a few items and asked him to quickly ring them up. He shook his head, smiling and apologizing all the same, and walked off. I left the store in a huff, leaving my groceries in the cart where I had stood. I guess I had been standing there in line too long to take that. It wasn't as if I had another thing I had to rush off to, prayer time was happening everywhere. I was just perturbed about having my time and rhythms usurped that way in that moment. But I was the one who lost that round – going home without items I needed. I would have to make a second trip back to the store which would cost more time and money to pay the driver. Ha Ha! Now I was laughing at myself! In time, I learned to plan my shopping better to avoid the prayer times as best I could, which more often was not easily possible because the times were always changing. So, patience!

When the calls to prayer came, men and boys entered the nearby mosques in droves, removing their shoes before going inside to kneel shoulder to shoulder with other men and boys. The mosques were primarily where the men went to pray, and they were plentiful. There were 'ladies' prayer rooms nearby or inside the women's restrooms; and when there was none close by women found other places, which was any area. Shrouded in the traditional black, women dropped down on their knees wherever they might be and where it was reasonable. Every place and any place became sacred ground when 'she' designated it as a place to pray. Although prayer affected everyone's routine and activities, non-Muslims, like me were not required to conform or participate in the rites. But I watched and waited, just the same.

As prayer time ended, activity resumed. Shops sprang open. Medical appointments resumed. Cashiers reappeared and returned to their stations, jumpstarting the registers. The lines moved. Shoppers could get cheese and cold cuts sliced or have some marinated olives or salads portioned into plastic containers by pleasant and prayer-refreshed deli staff. One could get that fabulous chicken tikka dish from the ever busy and crowded hot food counter to take home for supper. In the restaurants, the waiters returned and might even bring the already seated diners a treat in appreciation for their 'wait'. The women were up and moving around again. I could complete my errands and call my driver to come pick me up to take me home. I was grateful to have my time and freedom of movements bestowed back to me in that interval before the next call for prayer.

Those who openly objected to the calls to prayer, especially the morning prayer, were usually ex-pats; but to whom, and to what effect? I wondered and could not fathom why they were so disturbed by something so lovely and blessed. But no time was wasted on trying to figure that out. Even though many tended to cast a cynical glare and thought at that tradition, or declaring the culture as crude, backwards or even evil, in terms of religious beliefs, the typical Arab person in Saudi Arabia was noble, and the nation - extremely devout.

The average Muslim spent a significant amount of time in prayer, which was five times a day and seven days a week; that amounted to thirty-five rituals of prayer a week – with each prayer lasting from 15 to 20 minutes. Chiefly, prayer constituted 9 to 12 hours of every week for the Muslim, all year long.

Prayer shaped and informed their day – every day. In truth and in wisdom, such devotion was a story to be known and contemplated. Could that intensive regimen of prayer have something to do with the rare graciousness of the people I met and knew? Or how did that relate to what was considered 'developing' or 'civilized' where nations and cultures were concerned? The daily diet of prayer quickened and refreshed the spirit, infused a 'quality' in the soul, and it tempered the ego like no other faith I had known.

The always soothing chants of the muezzins were a diurnal reminder and surrounding comfort of humanity in awe of the Divine – a solemnity that had been going on for nearly fourteen hundred years. Though I was not Muslim, that mattered to me. And I would anticipate the prayers each night when lying down in bed – to come upon me at dawn, like a lullaby for a reverie.

24
The Surprising Things I Learned in the Grand Mosque

The Kingdom of Saudi Arabia was the center of Islam, it was where Islam's history began and the home of the two holy cities of Mecca and Medina. The Kingdom was the heartland of Islamic devotion and practice. There were approximately 94,000 mosques in Saudi Arabia in my time there.

Mosques proliferated in the Kingdom, all of which were flanked by one or two towering minarets to mark their location and fidelity. The minarets were easily seen from far distances. Some were ornate, some, humble and plain. From within the mosques, the adhan, or calls to prayer were voiced by the muezzin; the cleric leading the prayer for the gathering faithful was the Imam.

Mosques were the designated holy places for men to go and pray. Often, I had in fascination observed the men immediately cease their activities at the call of the muezzin for adhan and collectively, as though under a shared spell, proceed to a nearby mosque for prayer. Before entering the mosque, they removed their shoes, leaving them outside in stacked shoe-sized wooden compartments just outside the entrance. The doors were kept open at some mosques and I could see inside the sea of white thobes the men wore as they uniformly bowed and kneeled at the prayer ritual promptings from the Imam at the forefront of the temple. Some were boys with their fathers, uncles, or brothers. Outside the mosque and in outlying areas, women in black, who could not enter many of the mosques, would also faithfully attend to the call. With no Imam present, the women and girls fell into prayer wherever they happened to be in that moment – performing their own prayers from what was instilled in them and that they always knew. They would pray on the steps outside the mosque, in a passageway along the street, in an alcove in the mall, or in a special prayer room within the women's restrooms. Anyplace was a sacred spot for prayer – they made it so with their intentions, and the prayer rugs they handily carried with them. Before and/or after prayer, the women, wherever it was convenient, would wash their hands and feet – some prayer rooms and women's restrooms had special basins for the washing of feet – as it was the same for men, with basins outside some mosques.

Some mosques had a separate entrance for women where they could go inside and pray - partitioned away from the men, in an adjoining room, or in the balcony or mezzanine. The assignment of women and men to different areas in the mosque during prayer was meant to eliminate distractions and keep everyone's mind, especially the men's minds on prayer and to maintain a countenance of devoutness. Being restricted from entering most mosques first as a woman, and second as a non-Muslim in Saudi made me want to go inside one even more. I went to the Grand Mosque in Bahrain, which had the same designs and interior appointments as the large mosques in the Kingdom. The Grand Mosque Al Fateh in Bahrain had a special appeal for me. It was one of the world's most splendid and imposing mosques, and one that hosted tourists from around the world. I felt that I could learn some important things – things that would expand my perspectives on aspects of Islam. It was close enough, just a day's trip across the causeway from Saudi Arabia to Bahrain, and there were plenty of other activities for me to do while there.

In the reception room at the Al Fateh Mosque I removed my shoes and was given a black abaya and hijab. Wearing the abaya in Bahrain was not mandated – an abaya and a head covering were however, required inside the Grand Mosque. That was my first time at a mosque of its size and grandeur. Much love, care and intelligence went into the making of that stunning, all-white piece of architecture.

The 'English Speaking' tour was led by a young Arab man who was thorough and proud of all that he was sharing with our mixed group of men and women; he took his time making sure that all of our questions were answered, even inviting a nearby Muslim cleric in the mosque to add to what he was explaining to us. He told us while pointing out the relevant areas and artifacts that:

It was important that the supplicant came to prayer with a pure intention and was cleansed in their heart – free of anger, or bad thoughts and with an attitude of surrender to receive. Washing the hands and feet were symbolic of that cleansing, which was called 'wudu'. The 'salah' were the motions that the supplicant performed in the prayer ritual, which was a sequence of hand movements, and bending, kneeling, and prostrating while reciting the holy words. That was done in supplication and to embody the prayer so that it would be sensate and have 'effect' on the worshiper's overall being – mental, spiritual, and physical. The person must be fully present with the salah, which was not to be hurried.

The erudite young man explained that: Anyone could be an Imam – even a child. The sole requirement to be an Imam was to be able to recite from memory a portion of the Qur'an. The concept upheld that no one person was better qualified than another to shepherd souls to pray before Allah. However, the calling of the adhan was assigned to men to do and was not permissible for women. It was also reiterated at the grand mosque that men and women prayed in separate areas within the mosque to maintain religious piety.

Within any mosque during prayer, the Imam and devout followers faced in the direction of the Ka'bah in distant Mecca, which was the most sacred site in Islam. The Ka'bah was the black monolithic cubical structure situated at the center of Islam's most important mosque: Masjid al-Haram also called the Great Mosque. It was draped with an ornate thick brocade cloth (kiswa) that was changed every year in the ninth month. Within the Ka'bah was wide open space containing very little; three pillars inside held up the Ka'bah. Embedded outside at the eastern corner of the Ka'bah was the encased black stone known as the Hajr e Aswad which was *'the most venerated stone on the face of the earth'*. Stories of the origins of the stone and how it came to be there were mixed. It was said to have been a meteorite or a stone from heaven given to Abraham and Ishmael as a symbol of God's covenant with the Muslim community; and there was some connection of the stone to Adam and Eve. During prayer the Imam's back was towards those who prayed. And as the Imams led the prayers from the thousands of mosques throughout the Kingdom, they were doing so mindfully and in solidarity with the devout pilgrims who had journeyed to Mecca on their pilgrimages and were simultaneously in that moment on the ground in Mecca circling around the Ka'bah.

A strong thing I learned was about the ritual of the Hajj and Umrah pilgrimages – the 'Tawaf'. The pilgrims circled the Ka'bah intentionally in sync with the counterclockwise rotation of the earth! That was a deeply mystical aspect of Islam for me to note. The pilgrims circled seven times while reciting supplications to Allah - seven also being a significant and sacred number in Christianity, meaning fullness and completeness. As the mass of pilgrims circled, each one would try to kiss or touch the sacred stone, or at least to point in its direction. The entire rite was to bring the pilgrim closer to God – with the Hajj being a once in a lifetime requirement. Going further, the tour guide explained that the moon and its phases represented *'God's guidance through life's path'* – it was a symbol, by which one tuned in. Moon impacted the pace of life and shaped Arab people's relationship with time. As the moon's movements were different by the minute each day, so too were the daily prayer times, accordingly. The daily prayer time fluctuations were also in keeping with the notion that time was perpetually changing and never the same. With that, the Arab's relationship with time was loose and casual – very different from the west. They were not tied to or hooked into rigid rudimentary timeframes but were closer to cosmic/sacred time rather than linear. I saw the Arab moving slower and in flow with changing time and they were not in a race to keep up with or to beat the clock. They did not seem to fret about time, as their lives were more ordered and measured in rhythms. Those were surprising facts and revelations to me - that the deep practices of Islam were in alignment with cosmic forces and universal laws! I began to see the ancient religion afresh, which also illuminated to me how I was experiencing Arabic people and their culture in Saudi Arabia, many of whom were close friends.

The guide explained: Within the mosque there were no images of God (Allah). That was because to the Muslim, the face of God was not known or knowable. For the same reasons, there were no images of holy deities or humans in Muslim mosques. The parallels and intersections among Islamic, Christian, and Jewish faiths were strong, wherein stories from their histories were intertwined as with the black stone, also in the lives of Abraham and Mary. Ishmael who was born to Abraham by Hagar became the progenitor of the Arab peoples – the Ishmaelites. As a part of Hajj and Umrah, pilgrims were to run seven times between the two nearby hills of Hagar (Safa and Marwa) in honor of Hagar's commitment to her son, Ishmael. And the Qur'an depicted Mary, giving her recognition and adoration as the iconic representation of the holy feminine. According to the Qur'an, it was from Mary that the covering of women in Islam was inspired and referenced. Those and other parallels between the faiths were such that my Muslim friends said that *"A person had to be a Christian first before becoming a Muslim"* - at least in spirit.

What struck me as also intriguing in the tour was learning that the recital of the Qur'an was not done as in the rote reading of words from a page in a book, but the words were sang as a song. In essence, one sang the Qur'an! That confirmed what I had personally observed while touring a museum with a male friend in Qatar as we happened upon an aged Qur'an that was splayed open on display behind a glass case. From some inner prompting my friend began singing the words from the book. It was spellbinding, not only the sound of his euphonious crooning, but to realize that he in all seriousness, was actually reading in song, which was how the Qur'an was read, and it could and should not be comprehended or communicated in any other way - my friend said to me. The guide explained that the Qur'an could only be recited as a song, which became personalized when its rendition was colored by the differing voices of those who sang it, be it in the mosque during prayer, or in the leisurely reading in one's private room. For Muslims, singing the Qur'an was their way of beautifying the holy words, and elevating the energies and vibrations within and around - singing in one's fullest heart. I then understood why I had never heard the Qur'an mechanically 'read' word-by-word by any Arab person. Hence, when ending the tour our inspired guide launched into a delivery of a verse from the Qur'an with his own voice in song.

At the conclusion of the tour it was not said but inferred that Islam respected the faithful and fellow-believer of other religions, yet, had no care for those who did not possess a belief in a higher Deity. There was a natural bias in Islam that: *There is a God.*

So why were there no Christian churches in the Kingdom up to that time? For I had been repeatedly invited to secret Christian prayer circles in the Kingdom. Among Muslims, Islam was regarded as the purest and official form of religion, with the Qur'an and Sunnah (the tradition or 'way of life' of Muhammad) to be the country's constitution. It was not illegal or forbidden to be a Christian or Jew in the Kingdom, but it was prohibited to espouse and spread those religions. That was possibly changing with 'agreements' recently made between KSA and the Vatican that might or would allow some Christian churches to be built in the Kingdom. At least, that was what I was hearing.

I came away more surprised than amazed from my time in the Grand Mosque al Fateh. Learning more about the undergirding mystical nature of the Muslim culture was an eye-opener and registered with parts of me that were inclined in that direction. I came away informed and enlightened on the commonalities among the religions of the world and encouraged to know how faith in any form was rooted in primal and universal wisdoms, above and beyond all the words.

25
Touching a Prince

I'm going to say right off the bat that I was never one to be enthralled with so-called 'royalty' - of queens and kings, princes and princesses, dukes and duchesses, and earls and such. To me, they were people just like anybody else, who happened to be dealt a different set of cards in terms of wealth, privilege, and social status. I did not concern myself with what they thought, said or did, nor with who was married to whom, or what they named their children. It was simply not my cup of tea. Pun intended. I did not judge those who found the aristocracy of any nation state interesting and who marveled at their lives; I recognized how they might get a lot of joy from that. No doubt there may be many good and fine people among 'royals', but that was where my look in that direction ended. Like everyone else, they had to meet the call of soul evolution in the here and now. Wise men, women and prophets throughout the ages had expounded that what set one person apart from another in terms of quality and merit was the evolutionary trajectory of their soul. In that sense, yes, there were superior and inferior peoples. That being said, it came as a huge surprise when I had an experience with a Saudi prince that made a lasting impression on me.

Royals abounded in Saudi Arabia, with a King and a host of princes and princesses. On recent count, the family of the House of Saud had approximately 15,000 members, 2000 of which carried the lion's share of the family's wealth, and the majority of the power in the Kingdom. From the very beginning my professional colleagues and I were informally advised to be prudent with anyone bearing the name of 'Al Saud' among the students and young people we worked with; for they were related to the royal family and for which the Kingdom was named. There were Al Saud Princesses in some of my classes. They were studious and well earned their high grades from me. In fact, their comportment as young ladies was as regular as any other student - not pulling attention to themselves or expecting special treatments. Other than their name, I would never have surmised that they were Princesses, ergo, the culture of modesty in the Kingdom. Their low-key haute couture attire and accessories gave them away; but for that matter, most of the Saudi ladies were from wealth and showed it in the way they dressed, in the expensive handbags they carried, the shoes they wore, the chichi pets they showed off, and from their ever-present personal nannies nearby and ready to do what the ladies could not or did not wish to do. There was however, one occasion when I had already set the semester schedule of classes, when senior management abruptly instructed me, in no uncertain terms, to change the schedule to arrange a particular class date/time according to what was convenient for one Princess. I had no choice in the matter; I understood how power worked. She turned out to be an excellent student who was also a pleasant and appealing person.

On the day, which I expected to be hectic, it was fifteen minutes before the first of two back-to-back classes I was to teach for sixty female students. That would be followed by a department meeting where I was to lead the agenda, and review and send out the notes afterwards. There were dozens of emails to plow through with several of them red-flagged as High Priority; and students were incessantly rapping at my office door - drop-ins, who constantly ignored my protocol to make an appointment to see me. They were twisting at the doorknob trying to come in – which was kept locked so that I could focus. I also had to review and put the final touches to a rigorous report that was due by 4:00 pm. All in all, a full lineup for the day with no intrigues or drama – yet. Then my secretary Jane, forcefully banged on my door telling me that she had an urgent message to give. I let her in. From her lips, it turned out that selected members of the female leadership were summoned to appear immediately on the male campus. We were to be a part of the welcoming party for the Saudi Prince, who was the main benefactor of our university. He would be arriving within the hour and our appearance there was mandatory. Thus, my classes and meeting were cancelled. Us women leaders put on our abayas, some with their hijabs and niqabs, and we hastily loaded ourselves into a few cars provided to shuttle us over to the male complex. Once there, we were sequestered in the foyer off the main entrance, away from the lobby, which was filling with men – some wearing suits, and many in the traditional Saudi male attire. The women were then escorted to a seating area and instructed to remain there where we were also served Arabic coffee and water.

We did not talk much in that environment - on the men's turf. But on the ride over to the men's complex, the more outspoken of us women could not stop grumbling and complaining - in vivid color, about the disruption to our day and how rudely we were treated. We did not care if the male car drivers were listening and might even inform on us; we had a stinging right to feel inconvenienced. Now, on the male side we were quiet and still, waiting for what was next. We watched as the men gathered jovially and talked together in the lobby, each of us women weighing our own thoughts and impressions. Outside the glass doors of the foyer and entrance, men were dutifully waiting for the arrival of the Prince's entourage. A nervous, middle-aged man clad in a perfectly white starched thobe and trimmings came to our area to give us instructions on the proper way to greet the Prince; another person had given the men the same prep talk:. *"Wait your turn as the Prince makes his greeting to everyone; extend your hand to his only if he extends his hand to you; look him in the eye, but do not initiate any conversation other than to say your name and title."*

    The Prince's motorcade was said to be minutes away. The same man who gave us the greeting protocols led us women to the center of the capacious lobby to form a large semi-circle adjoining the men at the entrance of the building. The men were lined up first and then the women. There were about sixty of us; we were arranged according to height, with the shortest coming before the tallest of the men and women, respectfully. The semi-circle naturally had the men on one side facing the women on the other. We stood there in formality for about twenty minutes - the waiting was the only thing heard. My legs were growing tired. One woman asked for a chair as her back was starting to hurt. The time came. We could see the motorcade of several long black shiny SUV Suburbans as it slowly crept up to the curb outside. Out of the hush came the bustle and commotion of activity of security men and senior university officials who seemed to appear out of nowhere – dotting the 'I's' and crossing the 'T's', as it were, to make sure that things were perfectly in place and ready to receive the Prince. The Prince's own security detail was there, seeing him out of his vehicle and walking him towards the building. They stood aside to survey all as a few of the university's security and senior leadership took over and began to escort him through the procession around the semi-circle, starting at the male end. The Prince was going to approach and greet every single person.

    The Prince moved into the horseshoe-shaped alignment of men and women with ease, it seemed. He was an imposing figure in flowing layered robes of black, white, and gold, with a tasteful matching headdress. He was lofty in his height and dwarfed those surrounding and walking him through his greetings. He was now making his way towards the section of women. I was no longer annoyed but became fascinated by the spectacle in which I was an involuntary participant, assuming that it was all rather perfunctory and an exaggerated self-serving show of power. I thought I knew where it was going from the way we were ordered on a moment's notice, to stop what we were doing, no matter what, to get there and cue up for some dignitary's impromptu appearance. I assumed that it was another demonstration of how 'power' would and could impose upon me and my fellow colleagues standing there – to feed on our energy of compliance and subordination as lesser persons and 'subjects'.

All were silent, with the only sounds uttered and heard being the one-by-one saying of a person's name and title and the Prince's heavy low voice, who would nod now and then. The university president walked close to the Prince, keenly eyeing each person the Prince greeted as if to ward off any untoward gesture or comment from anyone; and as he studied us, I studied the Prince. He was getting close, and it was my turn. He stopped, standing square before me, looked into my eyes and extended his hand, inviting me with his eyes to say something to him. *"I am Dr. Elizabeth Taylor; I lead the women's Business degree program."* He looked around fifty, not only tall and august, but OMG, was he good-looking, wearing, so well, that textured Arabic masculinity. But that was not the catch. I was smarter than that. His hand was large and warm – it wrapped around mine. He articulated something along with a nod that I could not comprehend then and there because I was reading him in another way. Whatever he said got communicated to me at an elemental level. He was 'present' with a quality and pitch of energy that registered in me - which was more spirit than mental or physical. There was a depth and something old in his face, suggesting a benign cosmic link between us. He 'saw' me. With his eyes and his grip, he extended to me a vitality that did not take anything away from me but left me with a feeling of uplift – of validation and connection.

I cannot say if he was a good, bad or a kind person. There was no ego or intent, but a grace and a resounding sense of who he was, which enlivened most of us in that semi-circle. He was not bigger than life but was big in life. That was the impression he left as he moved on from me to greet the next person and the next. Without the title of Prince, his immense wealth and power, and the regalia, I think he still could have pulled that off. Rarely had I met a person with such a large and magnanimous energy. I had not experienced that kind of personal impact with colleagues I had known for months and years, regardless of their station in life. I realized that that might have been what the Prince came there to do, to give us a real piece of him, and to 'see' us, beyond the pomp and circumstance. In the eternity of that moment, I was not touching a Prince, but in his magnificence, I was communing with a *conscious* human being.

At the conclusion of his greetings, the Prince was ushered into the great hall where congratulatory speeches would be made and most likely a feast would be had among the men. Us women were cordially escorted back to our waiting cars with the same drivers who would now return us to our offices to resume our work. The entire affair took about three hours from the time we were pulled away. I surprisingly felt more energized and pumped to finish what remained on my desk for the day; and to muse about what just happened on the men's side of the block.

In my musings: People needed to be comfortable with themselves; being validated helped that, which was the best thing that one person could do for another. That simple gesture intrinsically fed and nurtured any and everyone. At the core of much of the suffering in the world there were everyday people who did not have their worth and legitimacy witnessed and appreciated by another, especially in the context of a relationship or some human engagement. Each person's responsibility to validate another was something that indigenous peoples and ancient cultures deeply understood. That harkened to a tribe in South Africa, in the northern Natal region, which had the spirit of 'validation' built into its daily greetings. When they said to one another: "*Sawa bona*" as a *Hello*, what they were actually saying was *'I see you'*. The other member of the tribe replied by saying "*Sikhona*", which meant, *'I am here.'* The logic was, by 'seeing' the other person *'you bring them into existence'*. Also, native peoples of Africa in the sub-Saharan desert practice the awareness that *'a person is only a person because of other people'*. I discussed those traditions in my graduate courses on diversity, inclusiveness, and behavioral science, and such. It was a profound and telling custom. It seemed prudent to seek to validate another wherever possible, regardless of one's station in life. It came back around. With Saudi Arabia being a tribal desert country having old Arabic roots, and close to Africa, I wondered if the Prince's personal and validating way of greeting us that day was informed by those customs.

My world said hello to that of the Prince's. Not just a link, but perhaps, there was a cosmic 'wink' exchanged between us two. The experience left a positive, memorable impression, enough to tell about; and which had me wondering: *What really made a Prince? Did he become that way from the title, or did he bring credibility to that title by virtue of his personhood?*

26
Magda's Meals

When I arrived home to my compound villa at the end of the workday, I already had in mind what I would have for dinner. Most people do. But for me that was the one act of efficiency and control that gave my days some semblance of predictability. I was highly conscientious of that. Meal planning was different for me in the Kingdom – what with having to be precise when shopping for all that was needed for meals for several days out - a week to ten days or longer. That was because going to the store for anything was not merely a hop, a skip, and a jump. It was time consuming. A trip to the market and back required scheduling and waiting for personal drivers or Uber/Careem and planning around prayer times. Going to the store was a big expenditure of time which I could not afford during the workweek, and grocery delivery was not an option. By the time I got home after work there were about four hours for me to settle in, prepare dinner, eat, and enjoy what remained of the evening until I would go to bed at about 9:30 pm. I would rise at around 5 am to get ready for the 7:15 am transport bus which would take me to the office with the day's assignment or classes starting at 8:00 am – my workday ended at 4:00 pm. All of that, including the trip there and back took close to twelve hours of my daily waking time.

One evening, just as I was about to take the first bite of dinner, my cell phone rang. The number was not recognizable. *"Hello."* It was Magda, my next-door neighbor calling to say that she had prepared some food for me. That was the first time I heard her voice or even knew she existed. And I did not know how she got my number – did not want to ask. I had lived in that villa #94 for several months and never met Magda. I knew her family, who were Egyptian – but somehow, she was not in that picture because she stayed indoors most of the time – and in the kitchen. Her brother, Mohammad was an administrator at the university and knew me. I was to learn that Magda was in her late sixties or early seventies; she was a retired engineer who played a strong hand in the construction of several prestigious buildings in Cairo – of which she was quite proud. She was now living with her sister, her brother and his wife and their son, next door to me. Somehow, Magda had been keenly aware of who I was as she was quite particular about her neighbors and made it a point to know who was living next door – so close.

Our villas shared a partition wall in the back area where I could easily see into Magda's family's patio. But still, I never saw her before. She said on the phone, speaking very little English, "Come to the back wall, I have food for you." From her tone, it sounded as though I needed to go right away. "Food is warm for you." She confirmed that. So, I put my dinner aside and went out the back door to meet her at our villas' shared wall. Magda was a mid-sized woman about five inches shorter than me, her round face held an infectious dancing smile; her eyes beamed from behind her black rimmed eyeglasses. She greeted me handing over the wall a tray with several small plates of Egyptian savories and a little carton of juice. "Tomorrow I will have more food for you", she said as I received the tray from her, and thanked her, with curiosity on my face. Back inside my villa I compared what she cooked with what I had already prepared for myself - it was a no brainer. I ate her food. She called later to see how I liked the food. Kudos, delicious, and all of that I said; but more humbled that she thought to share what she cooked with me – even following up on that. She told me again that she would have a meal for me the next evening and she would call to let me know when it was time to meet at the back wall. She did just that and promised to do so every night. Magda's handing over and my receiving the nightly dinner trays would go on from that time forward every day of the weeks to come; what I did not eat that same night, I would store or freeze for another day. I always had food! And if I were going out for the evening, I'd call Magda to tell her, please not to bother. But she still insisted to have food waiting for me when I got back!

Magda knew her way around the kitchen. And not only were her meals so tantalizing and far superior to anything I could have prepared for myself, but I was immeasurably overcome by her gestures of goodwill and generosity. And at times I did not know what to do with that feeling. *"How could I expect someone to feed me every day like that? Did it pose a burden on her and what could I and should I do in return? What was it that moved Magda to do that, day after day, and with such delight?"* I checked myself to see if my questions had anything to do with an underdeveloped ability to 'receive' and came up with an empty answer. Because I knew how to do that; I taught that kind of stuff, after all.

Magda's giving for me to receive, just was. Yet, I could not help but to be a stern believer in reciprocity in relationships.

I went over, knocked on her door and asked Magda to please tell me what she liked because I wanted to give her something in return. I had begun to look forward to her fabulous meals at the end of the day! They were also handy and relieved me of cooking most evenings. At my question, Magda threw up her hands in effusive rejection of the idea that I give her anything, stating: "Wallah! I am so proud of everything you are saying. Alhamdulillah! All I want for you is to give love and to love everyone, and for your smile. I am so happy for your smile. You encourage me to love life. Really, you are my daughter from the first time I saw you, and because of this world, I want you to be happy and to love everybody." What was central to all that Magda was saying to me was *'love'*. It was as simple as that. Even though she refused to receive anything from me, on one occasion I took it upon myself to take a large platter of fruits and sweets to Magda's family. Mohammad called me soon after to tell me that I did not have to do that, saying that I was the one who needed to be taken care of, not them. He said that the family's wish was only that I be happy to accept what they had to offer. And Mohammad said more along those lines to make his point clear.

Life in the Kingdom as a single woman could be excruciatingly solitary. And for another person to have me in her heart and mind so steadfast and sure, made a difference in my days and my nights. In her way, Magda touched and blessed vulnerable parts of me. Magda's meals were a gift and a testament of love. Through them, she was telling and affirming that love was ever present, and it did not go where it was not needed, nor asked for anything in return – that life was 'wonder-filled', and that the force of love within her *had* to give.

The nightly meals consisted of several small plates and bowls – sometimes two or three at a time and with something to drink – sometimes a dessert plate. They were complete and filling. She prepared fish, lamb, and chicken in various ways with indescribable exotic Egyptian sauces. She had a way with spices that gave a lift to any meat and vegetable – especially with the eggplant. Each dish came with plenty of basmati rice - buttered, infused with saffron or mixed with pistachios and raisins. Magda called me between 6 and 7 pm just before she did her evening prayers to say: "I am waiting for you at the back Ms. Elizabeth." I would immediately go to meet her at the wall where she eagerly presented me with my meal for the night. She'd be fully covered from head to feet with her black hijab wrapped tightly around her face and abaya hugging her mature shape. Each time, her eyes came bright with the joy of sharing something that she made with someone whom she knew would appreciate it – elevating her body on her toes to stretch her arms above and over the patio wall to extend the food to me with both her hands. Magda was giving with all that she had. And I surrendered to that, as Magda's meals were a motherly nudge and an enticement for me to remember and embrace my Arabic soul.

Weeks passed with no meals coming from Magda. Her nightly calls abruptly stopped. I did not want to intrude upon the family, but I was getting worried, and it was not about missing the meals. When I went next door to check in, I was told that she had a serious illness several weeks back. It was difficult for her to move around, and she was spending less time in the kitchen. A male Filipino was hired to be Magda's hands to do the cooking for the family. Magda told me that the hired cook was not really all that good, not adequate, and hard to instruct in the kitchen, and she was making the best of it. Sitting with Magda in her living room, having tea, she told me that she would not want me to have the food he cooked – that she did not want to give me anything that did not come directly from her. Surely, the meals prepared by the family's new chef did not have her special touches or the love she put into cooking. Thereafter, I continued to visit Magda with tea and conversation, as we had grown close over the many months and were easily so happy to see each other. And every time, she would have me leave with some cakes or biscuits. Her eyes still lit and intelligent, Magda would continue to say to me: "You know that I am your mother." She would lean in closer to say the words again, making sure that I heard and understood.

27
His Robust Attention

The Muslim male in Saudi, whether single or married, was not entitled to assume that he could overtly approach a woman to express any interest. Here, states the Qur'an, *"Tell the believing men to lower their gaze and be modest. That is purer for them."* And so it was, that within the social sphere of the Kingdom, women's bodily curves and their lovely faces were not to be ogled at, peeked at, or even causally looked at. In men's eyes, the woman was to be invisible and asexual, and they were to maintain physical and emotional distance from women who were not of kin in public; and beyond that, public displays of attraction from persons to other persons went against the custom of modesty and discretion. With all of that, plus the fact that I was not a Muslim woman, made the attraction more dicey when it came to 'him'.

I reluctantly lived within the rule not to invite and to avoid the attentions of men, which was in part influenced by the belief that man's sexual nature was most often troublesome and could not be trusted. My friends and students explained to me that it was an intrusion to have their physical selves assessed, evaluated, or desired by men in the open. Those were their words: 'assessed' and 'evaluated'. And still, from my disposition I had no problem having my physical attributes patently appreciated, by the men. I was not a rebel, nor a loose woman. I just could not get my head around that idea of shunning male attention and did not quite know what to do about it. More than that, I simply had to confess, I was glad to be a girl, and savored the occasions that affirmed my femininity – whether in the Kingdom or anyplace I happened to be in all of creation. It was my right.

The men in the Kingdom adhered to that rule, as I'd seen. They averted their eyes, kept a social distance, and behaved cordially with women who they were not in any kind of a relationship with. It must have been hard for them, I thought, because the Saudi women were so fetching, hands down! In my opinion, collectively they ranked among the most beautiful women in the world. So, in truth, some men were looking when they knew they were not supposed to look; and in my case, it was with my most effusive silent consent.

His Robust Attention

The 'ardent male' subject was a Saudi bus driver who shuttled mostly us women who were ex-pat professors, and ranking administrators, along with staff personnel from the residential compound to the female campus at university. The shuttles operated Sunday through Thursday between the hours of 6:00 am to 9:00 am for the morning shifts going to work and between 2:00 pm to 4:00-4:15 pm in the afternoons, taking women home after work. That male driver's days were not regular; he was periodically transferred to a different route elsewhere for weeks at a time. On those days when he was driving our route, he made several back-and-forth rounds during those hours. I was most times on his 8:00 am and last 4:00 pm rounds. Us women agreed that he was the best driver. We trusted that he would get us to our destinations safely and in reasonable time, through smog, drenching rain and heavy traffic.

The university transport bus drivers operated in a tiered system; the very best drivers were allowed to transport the women, and who were usually Saudi and Pakistani. Morning and afternoon buses were normally filled with women and few men because the men could drive, and the men had their own buses leaving the university campus going home. That minimized having men and women sitting next to one another on the buses, as the women did not want to sit next to a man in the bus enclosure if they could help it. Already generally annoyed by their low status, the women were not that easy to please and tended to be skittish and complained about drivers being reckless behind the wheel, going too fast, or when they just did not like the way the driver looked or acted – which was sometimes behaving too familiar with the ladies. Drivers had been swiftly fired because of those complaints. And although he was a 'trusted favorite' among the women, that singular bus driver was doing what the 'bus women' accused men of – publicly laying his eyes on a woman - me. He, in his way, treaded close and closer to me - straddling that line to let me know that I had his attention; and it was robust! Well, he certainly had mine.

I could not help but notice him in the first year of my job assignment at the university. He had 'presence', dressed in his white thobe, and the checkered red and white shemagh crowned with the black oqal. He was about 45 to 50 years of age, a few inches over six feet, bearded, with a prominent nose and chin, and dark eyes. He seemed arcane - a pensive man with some unnamed urges coursing through him. He spoke very little, in Arabic, to some of the women who knew him by name, and even then, it was just as a greeting. But most times he said nothing, as he stood stoic outside the bus while the women piled in, standing respectfully away, with his arms folded high and tight across his barrel chest, staring away into the distance. He'd automatically turn from whatever was occupying his gaze to acknowledge me with a glance and a nod when I came on board. I preferred the bucket seat at the very front of the bus, next to the driver's seat. There, I took in the panoramic view of the road ahead on our rides to the office and back home to the compound, not to mention the sights of life whizzing by with the sand hued buildings and local people doing their day; an occasional herd of camels could be seen trotting on the dirt paths off to the side of the road. So much 'eye candy' for me. I never tired of looking out of the front and side windows, which was worth the awkward effort it took for me to get into that 'cockpit' seat at the very front of the bus. Maneuvering my body within a tight space, I had to step up onto a small platform - almost touching my head to the bus ceiling, balance myself, then bend over and carefully step down to the right and plop into the bucket seat. Once seated, it felt perfect to be there. A lot was going on while in that seat near my venturous bus driver who was ever aware and attentive to my presence.

As I and the other women passengers got settled into our seats and it was time to go, he climbed on board and took to the controls of the bus. He would turn to me with an acknowledgement that he saw me – that he was now there next to and with me. And 'here we'd go'. He spoke no English and I spoke no Arabic – worlds apart in status and culture. But we were in a communication beyond words. I did not mind what he might be thinking or imagining with me sitting next to him or what my yielding proximity inspired in him. He let me know in subtle ways that he expected and wanted me there seated up front, beside him. I could pretend that we were going on a trip together – the other passengers were invisible - not there – just us two. Perhaps, he also pretended. He would motion for me to fasten my seatbelt. Sometimes I would just wait for him to remind me of that – a thread, a verbal tendril. As the bus moved and at stop intervals, I felt him looking at me in a way he ought not – scanning the lines from my face to my hair to my neckline and hands and fingers – nails polished, often just for him. I reveled and relaxed into the feel of him taking me in - my essence. I sank into his off-put gaze, just so - as not to let him know that I knew he was looking. But he did know.

I riveted my eyes, not my head to see him gripping the wheel and working the clutch to move the bus. His caramel hands were long and slender. I watched when the bus was stopped or idling how he carefully adjusted the scarf and oqal around his head with those hands. I saw his things: The Saudi national flag with the emblem of the white palm and crossed swords against a green background, prominently displayed in the front window; his big Samsung phone on the console, the scattered husks from the sunflower seeds on the floor that he snacked on; the tiny round Exotica can in the dashboard, containing some secret – it was all the time there in that same place. Sometimes I dabbed a touch of my most fragrant oud onto my wrists for him. I saw how he noticed that. I could not do much else, wearing the abaya, which by its design was meant to keep women from being alluring. Still, I gave him something to notice – dressing in gay colors. He noticed my hat one day and pointed to it nodding to let me know that he saw and liked it.

    I would see him with the other men drivers standing outside their buses as the women were boarding at the end of the workday. He stood out among them, as if he belonged someplace else. He listened more than he talked, but when he did, he shared in a male playfulness and liveliness with his comrades like men on a sports team. I watched as he and the male drivers removed their shoes and sandals to walk barefoot on the grass – that would help them sleep well at night. At times, he'd take a string of prayer beads from his thobe pocket and roll them over and through his hands and fingers. I liked what I saw about him; it was good for my eyes. And I also liked that he took the dare to see me.

    He looked and waited for me to exit the building at the end of the day and motioned me over to his bus. One time when I boarded another bus by mistake, he caught that and pointed to his bus and 'my' bucket seat as if to assert: *'Why are you not here? That is your seat, next to me'*. I did not do that on purpose but was just a bit distracted and rushed that day. I made sure to locate and get on his bus from then on.

    I wanted to at least know his name, as we had become so familiar in the subtle – with our dance of the senses – our little waltz. He knew my name because it was sometimes mentioned and called out from other people on the bus who knew and spoke to me. And as the fates would have it, one morning, I overhead my name mentioned in an exchange he was having with a woman passenger. "What did he say?" I asked her as he was watching. "Abdullah says you are a nice lady." Now I knew his name. I smiled at what she told me and in his direction. Between us we knew that that was as much as he could say to or about me - sideways, at best. He made the comment to the woman when I was close by - him expecting, maybe knowing that I would hear and ask about it. So there it was, another thread. Even if he did speak English and I spoke Arabic, words between us would be reckless, and against the social decorum for men and women. But, later that day he was deliberate, adroit, and zoomed in as he gently brought the bus to a crawl to stop and release me right at my front door. It was almost 5:00 pm at the end of the 40-minute ride home. I was his last passenger. Stepping off the bus and turning to him, I said "Shukran"; looking directly at me his eyes spoke loudly. Abdullah steadied the bus there at my door until I let myself inside my villa, taking my time.

Aside from the speechless interludes with 'him', I had my own life, and I was certain, so did he. The bus ride home at the end of days with the caresses of Abdullah's attentions gave me a reprieve from the planet of the women. It felt nice to have a man's eyes on me – and for his view to linger there awhile. I don't think I could have enjoyed being looked at that way as much as I did from him in the Kingdom. *Was it because it was forbidden?* No. *Because it was out of context and not common or proper?* Again, no. Yes, because I missed it and wanted it. *Did he have a wife and children – more than one wife?* Not knowing those things, I could only surmise. Whatever the case might be, it did not concern me. What I had and which was enough was that I was his treat for a little while on a given day that he made room for, in his way, that felt so pure!

In my musings I supposed that in another time and setting we might have dated. And I also knew that our measured attraction need not go any further than the 'here and now'. Nothing actual or actionable was meant to happen between us. Somehow, we knew that. It was just a 'something' - something that needed to be lived - something he had to do, despite himself, maybe to pet and soothe nagging urges inside - something I had to allow with my fullest acquiescence - something that gave a glimmer to humdrum days – something that affirmed the unavoidable attraction between two people of quite different worlds – something that bespoke the wordless language that men and women would always understand.

I knew the difference when a man's eyes were assaulting and undressing me and when, with his eyes he was appreciating and enjoying what he saw. The latter made me into a flower. Whether the day at the office was easy or tough, Abdullah's robust attention had me walking through my villa door at day's end wearing mellow gratification on my face, so much so that I could testify to any and all that: *"I am a woman, and a rose ain't got nothing on me."*

28
Next Oasis

The desert was not a giving place, what with the barren landscapes sparsely littered with spiny cacti and fauna that would prick you at the slightest touch. That was their way of protecting the precious water inside for them to live where water was generally not around. But deserts could by chance bear delights in the middle of an expanse of nothing. In a desert within a desert where the lives people led were bereft on top of the heat and sand, there could also be found a life-giving oasis. That oasis was not a set place or space, but an occasion – an event. In that desert within a desert, I came upon such an oasis - one that I could plan for and anticipate with the specific passage of time – a 'next oasis'.

Meaningful companionship could be like the scarce spiny cacti in the vast Arabian desert – especially for a single western woman. In the Kingdom, the absence of venues for social intercourse no doubt, made it hard for people to meet and establish relationships, which were more often, hit and miss. As well, the restrictions and taboos that warned unmarried couples from spending time together behind closed doors were all so prickly. Couples most often had to find inventive ways to pair up in private and be ultra-discreet about it.

The good news for me was that the ratio of men to women was high – with more men to go around in KSA, either Saudi nationals or men from other countries and nationalities. But even so, it was still a question of quality. There were a lot of men, but not necessarily ones for a right match. Before I met him – the guy, I had been proposed to several times and dated just as many men. In the first years in Saudi, work was all I did and could look forward to. That changed as the solitude mounted and wasting my time on empty dates was no longer acceptable.

On one of those evenings when I simply had to get out of my villa, I went to a social event hosted by InterNations – an international meet-up forum for ex-pats. It provided periodic venues for dinner and outdoor activities where people could socialize with others like themselves, and who had the same experiences of living and working in Saudi Arabia. InterNations was the only venue of its kind in KSA that I knew about. There were many people in the room milling around, and the food was good. I mingled and ate, and just before leaving, I saw him come to my table. After he sat, he was soon engaged in conversation by others at the table. He was about 6 feet tall, he had a slim well-conditioned body frame, nice eyes, and an easy air about him. I watched, noticing mostly his graceful and beautiful hands, and how he spoke with them. I liked his face, and not hearing all that he was saying to the others, I could still tell that he had a sophisticated intelligence that also appealed to me. I had to leave, but not before going over to him and handing him my business card – interrupting the conversation he was having. "Call me." was all I said and left the room.

And he, Ronald, called the next day.

We began to date, and fell into each other so easily, starting off with a day trip to the ancient sand caves of Al Hofuf - a popular destination about one hundred miles away. It was Friday, a day of long exploratory driving through the desert, and dining at a homespun Arabic family food restaurant just off the route. That was the beginning of our two and a half years together. A window of time and space seemed to open for us and bless our togetherness. We found private beaches where we lazed all day, guzzling refreshing non-alcoholic beer. We toured historical sites, did weekend getaways to Bahrain – ending most days smoking shisha, ordering food in, or taking our own sweet time cooking the evening meal. We'd cozy up with a bowl of goodies and a late-night movie and then, lovemaking and sound sleep. Fine and mellow were the intervals when he would get suddenly quiet, regard me intently, and slowly lift those beautiful hands to remove his spectacles on his way to kissing me. I liked knowing that it was coming.

Weekends were our time, feeling like forever, until those precious two days ended with the dawn of the workday Sunday morning. Work dominated our days and weeks, yet most times we had the weekends, Friday, and Saturday, to look forward to – our 'next oasis'. He'd have some light adventure planned – however basic it was, did not matter. We had our off-beat favorite place to dine, and our routine stroll through the nighttime flea markets – the only westerners around. We'd wander through the emptying ink-black night of unlit Saudi streets – me in my abayas, he in his jeans and fitted shirts. His shoulders erect as he led me on – sometimes holding my hand when no one was looking. We'd walk for long spells, ambling through the malls and alleyways, peering into shops, going in to handle objects that caught our eyes, tasting, testing, and fraternizing with Turkish and Pakistani store merchants, some who gave us tea and sweets. With no particular place to go, we were secure in knowing that we had each other in the night ahead. He would park the car far away from my villa so as not to bring attention to the fact that I had an overnight visitor, and he would leave just before the folks in the compound began to stir into the weekday morning.

The outside chance of our meeting as we did was not a given. We were from very different worlds yet found solace in one another – he, Dutch, and me, African American; me, the mystic, and he, an engineer; left brain, right brain – brought together by desert magic. Beneath it all, we knew that we were 'easing' one another through a strenuous period of time in the Kingdom. In the desert within the desert, we pushed past the surface trappings that made us so different to embrace the subtle and more profound things that connected us. We made our coupling work. The physical and intellectual attraction was certainly there. In our relationship, he was a rare man and I, a good woman who consciously embraced an understanding that kept things simple and interesting. In our implicit consent we were creating an exclusive sacred space, bringing our best selves to each other because our 'stroke of luck' was not to be played around with nor taken for granted. To share in a relational joy and spree was what we both wanted. We knew that it was within us to do, and what we had to do in the desert.

In the 'oasis', we exhaled, languished, and indulged – caught in the grasp of an easy romance. Trusting that there was room, and we would be soft and safe to stretch our moments. There was laughter, and colors for two. I showed him my music and danced for him. He gave me his desire to know more. We had sun, cool waters, and our secluded beach where we'd idle into twilight and 'til the red, yellow, and blue lanterns dotting the shoreline flickered on and glowed – inviting us to stay a little longer. Grapes – hands down! Play. Amusing one another with our stories and quirks. We were happy with the time we had for those things. Touching. Seeing. Things he said, what he heard from me. Grown-ups blushing. Saying nothing. Gazing as the moon eclipsed the sun. Two days . . . with our delights so real, like being inside a love song, in a pairing synced to the zest and sway of a bossa nova. I stepped back from the dream now and then to see that it was really happening. Yes, it was. No mirage. Hours . . . seconds . . . and it ended as surely as the water found in the desert would, after a spell sink into the sand. For just as we were high in our adult frolic and felicity, time moved us along. The workweek approached with each tick of the clock, ending us, and we'd say our goodbyes, nourished from what was and in anticipation of our 'next oasis'.

As the weekend came to an end, we'd gear up and put on our game faces to trudge through the next five days. Our 'next oasis' re-fueled, replenished and from it we were made ready. For us two, that could be counted on. The dry expansive desert demanded that we be alert; for in the desert: *You do, or you die.* The desert did not care. It allowed little room for dawdling, missteps, error, or the lack of discernment. The wrong word or gesture, an unwarranted frown or a failed attempt had consequences that were hard to 'walk back'. One needed to have their act together to make it and to last. Getting through the coming five days was an 'intensive', but it would clearly end as the 'next oasis' loomed closer ahead – when our mornings, afternoons and nights were finer – where love bloomed over time. Even so, we knew that all we really had was the present, in the Saudi desert and at some future point we would necessarily go our separate ways for good. We were ultimately wound in a tenuous web that would not hold us together for long, and when that inevitability arrived, we would deal with it.

And we did. Our halcyon days in those 'next oases' in the desert within the Saudi desert stayed alive in our memories, reminding, and lauding what two people can do. An appetizer for the love of a lifetime. We met one another well and made an art of intimacy that kept on giving. That keeps on giving.

29
The Watch

The 30ish year-old bronze-skinned Egyptian strode out of the warm bay spread before me. As I lazed there, my eyes were drawn to how his muscles throbbed and glistened with soft water that trickled down his body - all like some torrid scene from a Hollywood movie. He was looking at and coming directly to me – and gripping something that he plucked from the water that sparkled in his hand. *"Oh boy"*, I thought, *"This is gonna be good."*

Earlier, the young Egyptian spotted my male companion, Ronald, and me as we entered the private beach; making no pretense, he studied us intensely as we sought and picked a perfectly secluded spot to park ourselves for our long easy day at the beach. We were in Jubail, Saudi Arabia, it was an early Friday afternoon. It was the end of summer and those were the best days for the beach - not too hot, not too cool. That was one of few private commercial beaches we found and where I could wear a swimsuit. The beach front was opened on weekends only and space was limited, but that was not really a problem as the beach was not well-publicized or known. Discretion was still advised for women to cover when going to the restroom or food bar. I noted that still the one or two Saudi women on the beach remained fully covered, wading in the water wearing the black abayas and hijabs and I was the only woman sporting a swimsuit. I looked forward to those beach days – they were simple, serene, and restful and well-worth the fee we paid to get in.

Shortly after we unpacked our goods and set up our lounge chairs on the sand near the shore, we saw the Egyptian sauntering our way. He'd come to introduce himself and to *"make friends"*, he said, all the while with his eyes shamelessly on me. By then in my life in the Middle East, I had become quite familiar with the charm and uncanny aggressiveness of the Egyptian male. His name was Amon. Ronald and I allowed ourselves to entertain Amon's unsolicited 'friendly' company. No worries. He was an interesting character with stories to tell, and we liked meeting people. Ronald was an avid swimmer, and it was getting warmer, so he let himself be lured into the water by the Egyptian for what Amon called some *"nice swimming and diving off the banks."*

That was fifteen minutes ago. Now Amon was standing over me, stock still, dripping wet, and self-assured as I basked in my chair. And Ronald was nowhere in sight. Amon did not ask but smoothly ordered me to open my hand in which he placed a woman's sterling silver watch. "This is for you" he said. I was right, said my mind: *"Yeah, this is really good!"* "Where is Ronald?" I asked. "Oh, he is still in the water, decided to swim far out there." He said, as if to assure me that that was part of his design. "You sure you want to give this to me?" My eyes steady on him more so than the watch and I dared to ask why he wanted me to have the watch. "Yes, I am, it belongs to you." He spoke. "Thank you, Amon." And I'm still trying to fathom what was going on, with Amon, with Ronald, and how to react entirely. "Let's go find Ronald", I said starkly in the awkward pregnant minutes with him idling there looking so composed and expecting us to make something more of his gift to me – within that little space of time. But that was not to be. Again, I said:. "Yes, let's go find him." I was not about to 'go there' with Amon, but to take his gift as a 'random kindness'. I had no idea of exactly how Amon expected things to play out, for I was a one-man woman.

With my insistence we walked the rim around the shore and spotted Ronald pulling himself out of the waters from a rocky embankment. He enjoyed his swim. He sensed from the moment that Amon invited him into the water that he was up to something but did not worry about it. He needed to swim, and he knew what he and I had established together - he knew who I was. I showed Ronald the watch and told how it came to be in my hands. We'd soon send Amon on his way with smiles and appreciations for our time with him. I thought that the three of us knew it was all a joust on the part of Amon, a ploy - testing his nerves, playing a game to see if he could win, and not being attached to even that outcome. He'd be just fine.

When I had a moment to myself and after Amon was gone, and Ronald back in the water, I turned the lady's silver timepiece over in my hands taking a closer look. I saw that it was not only diamond encrusted, but a Versace. I thought that Amon was so caught up in his haughty pursuit that he did not realize what a 'jewel' he held in his hand. Yet, I revised that thought to resolve that had he known, he still would have bestowed it upon me in the same knightly fashion – which was a part of his act. I smiled, eased back into the lounge chair, and allowed the shade to shield me from the burning sun, and for a feeling of well-being to envelop me as I sank into a reverie. I saw the whole picture. I saw how on a hot sunny day a young well-heeled Saudi woman kept cool as she swam about vigorously in those same shallow waters wearing the diamond encrusted designer watch with its loose clasp, and how it slipped off her dainty wrist without her knowing. I saw how afterwards she and her brothers or father, or husband may have trolled the waters in vain to find it, and eventually, how she would handily, without a second thought go on to buy a new comparable one. I could see how weeks, months or maybe years later the strapping Egyptian attracted by its shine dived low and scooped up the watch as he made his way out of the water - his eyes fixed on a woman he thought he could bait and possess as he placed it into her hands. And he was grandiose, presumptuous, and well scripted in saying: *"This belongs to you."* Amon was right. Yes, in my hands, in my 'keep' now, it did belong to me. A ritualized drama was played out in his offering at the beach that day, which brought the storyline of the lost watch to completion. It was a thing rehearsed in another realm - that was meant to happen, and with the same cast of three. Again. *"Yes. I shall treasure and protect your gift to me Amon and remember you."*

30
Yankee Doodle Dandy and Me

If you ever have the incomparable opportunity to ride a camel, please do it. I had long desired to ride a camel before going to Saudi Arabia, and even more while I was there and certainly to do it before leaving the Kingdom. Once on the land, time and busyness got the best of me and the occasion to ride a camel came late in my fifth and last year there before returning to the states. But I got it done. And I did not fully come to grips with my obsession to ride a camel in the Saudi desert until I did. I was positive that I had already ridden a camel, but that was many, many years ago when I was much younger, and it was too far back to have any meaning in the present day.

Camels were herbivores and lived on dried hay and water; they were built for the desert with wide hooves that kept them from sinking in the sand and it took a long time for them to dehydrate. Camels never ventured far from watering holes – knowing instinctively where those could be found. Camels were abundant in Saudi, especially at farms located way out in the desert. One knew that they were near the farms from the overbearing sharp and stinging smell. Large numbers of camels could be found at farms in Al Qassim and Al Hofuf. Herds could range from a dozen to more than a thousand camels, that included adult camels and calves – all in a sea of tan and brown. At that time many of the camels were sheltered in Saudi Arabia, transported from Bahrain and Qatar as part of a commercial trade agreement. Camel farmers housed and traded them for specific purposes. They were bred to carry goods long distances through the desert; people rode them for recreation; and camels were sold for meat and milk in markets, which were staple foods in family homes.

The camels were typically managed and conducted by a herder or a guide. He might be the owner of the camel or hired to train and tend to the animal. He used a small whip to steer the camel and to do his bidding – rapping it lightly on its fanny, speaking softly – as if cooing, directing the animal on when to go, where to go, and to stop. The guide worked with the animal with care and respect and would not and did not want the camel to be abused.

I made it my mission one day to go out far to find a camel to ride. The very moment I beheld those marvelous animals, I could not wait to get up on top of one. When I approached the camel and it walked up to me, I was greeted by and in the presence of a most splendid being. "His name is Yankee Doodle Dandy" said Barak, his guide – gripping the camel's reins. "And for a donation of whatever you want to give, you can ride him." Interesting how a camel's eyes spoke, and it was not the double rows of long eyelashes that made their eyes and faces so sweet. The upward curve of the camels' mouths made it appear as though they were smiling. *"Well, that was because they really were!"* I thought. Smiling about what? I had no idea. And they had an enviable way of seeming generally unperturbed. They groaned now and then, but not as a complaint. Stepping closer to touch him, Yankee Doodle Dandy had an aura. What's more, Yankee seemed old and to know a lot - most likely plenty more than me. Perhaps from some memory encoded in his DNA he'd know some things about the nature of man, or about certain events that happened long before the sands filled the desert. Maybe even, Yankee knew when the rains would come again.

Barak had Yankee bedecked in an array of multicolored beaded necklaces around his neck, and with small garish sandbags slung over his back with long tassels that dangled below his belly; it was all topped off with over-sized day-glow green sunglasses on his ever-smiling face for attitude. Yankee did not need those trimmings for me to appreciate his majesty – outlandish, but majestic all the same. At least the brightness of it all deflected flies - part of what him being a walking circus was intended to do. The tassels swayed with his languid gait - showing off his swagger as he approached me closer. He was a riding and show camel. And he had a mind of his own.

Yankee Doodle Dandy looked me directly in the eyes as he stood and towered over my head – I'm thinking, *"He is possibly discerning if I was a good person or not and worthy to ride him."* But whatever was true about me, the camel would let me ride him anyway – Barak would see to that. It just seemed that Yankee needed to do his own assessment of me before I could get on his back. I thought that Yankee might even speak to me! And the way he eyed me showed that he did not and could not fear me. The camel seemed to know what I was thinking and what I wanted, and he was going to help me do that. Yankee read me right. My state of mind in that moment was like that of an excited little girl ready to have an experience of a lifetime, something she really wanted – to ride the camel. And that little girl was about to have some fun!

With Yankee's 'OK', I felt welcomed and keen to ride him on the sandy earth. Of course, he was too lofty to hop on top, and I was not sure how to situate my body with the hump. Barak cheered me on telling me that I was to "*Sit right on top of the hump of the dromedary camel – the one with just one hump!*"

At Barak's egging, Yankee Doodle Dandy shuffled his huge bulk and eased himself down to my level, settling upon his front knees first, then his hind knees so that I could straddle his hump. Having the massive camel lower himself to accommodate me that way felt strangely honoring. As instructed by Barak, I grabbed hold of the front and high end of the saddle and hoisted my leg up and over the camel's hump – I was on. Although Barak was right nearby, Yankee and I did not need his help on what to do next after that. I felt as though Yankee Doodle Dandy allowed me a minute or two once seated to get my confidence and bearings before he nonchalantly rose from the ground and began his slow, deliberate, lolling motions forward. I felt a whoosh and a tingling in my head as he lifted his body from the ground, rising and hitting the air. I was like a rocket that shot straight to the top of the sky! I shrieked and laughed as the thrill of it rushed all the way through me. "Wheee!" And smiling Yankee took his time.

There was no hurry. I knew his every long lazy stride, all I had to do was hold on, perched atop his great padded hump; where we were going, we would get there - my body rocking from side to side, like a baby in a cradle. Yankee Doodle Dandy and I were in pure sync - with Barak speaking low to him, holding the reins, walking close at hand. From that high place, I could see all around. I saw the exquisite sights of the desert, and sand, and sand, and sand; there was a hamlet in the distance with specks of people looking like insects, and much more that could be seen but not heard. My whole body and my senses were happy with the gentle, rhythmic march of Yankee Doodle Dandy inside that landscape. It was serene up there. I wanted to stay on and go on and on and on. But too soon, and much too soon, the ride came to its end and the camel lowered himself for me to dismount in the same measured way he did at the start. I touched Yankee's kind face and was sad that I had to walk away.

Now stoked and really hooked, I would ride camels several more times before leaving the country to return home. Those rides would be similar, but not like it was with Yankee. With him, it was singular, like a first love.

31
Bacon, Lettuce and Tomato Sandwiches

It was a foregone conclusion and open secret that there was a lot of sex going on in the Kingdom – among the married and unmarried, crossing interracial and cultural lines, between men and women and the same genders. But I thought that more than sex, food was the buzz in Saudi Arabia. What with certain social curbs on the senses in the Kingdom, people indulged ferociously in rituals of eating – something they could freely do two to three times a day, even more. Food was on the menu and on the minds of the average man and woman from the time they woke up in the morning 'til night – thinking about what they were going to prepare or eat for lunch or cook for dinner - becoming mildly preoccupied with which restaurant to dine at or what they needed to get from the store to cook, regardless of the interceptions of prayer times.

Food was everywhere, all the time. I could find all kinds of fare in the Kingdom: Chinese, Thai, Vietnamese, Italian, French, Spanish, Greek, Sushi, Creole, Vegetarian, Vegan, Soul Food, etc. It was all there, along with American restaurants, even fast-food chains such as McDonalds, Burger King, Chili's, and Five Guys. I was pleasantly surprised to find so many Popeye's fried chicken outlets there. Glad to see 'em. One time when I had a hankering for some pizza, I arrived at the Domino's franchise and had to wait the twenty minutes for prayer time to end before it would open and let me in. I had arrived just as the doors were closing for prayer. But it was well worth the wait. I was a hardcore foodie. And I had plenty of company in that regard in the Kingdom – ex-pats, Arabs, Filipinos, Pakistani - even those who were not foodies before, turned that way as a release and as a source of pleasure when pleasures were few.

It was said in Saudi that *"When we share the meal it means we will never betray one another."* Most of my memorable moments involved food, such as dining in my friend Wafa's family's French and Jordanian restaurants – just she and I with an army of waiters fussing over us, and how she never failed to prevail upon me to order food to take home in her warm-hearted way. Wafa and I just liked to eat and talk, in that order - together; it was like that. Food accentuated my many times with Haifa - sitting on the floor in private rooms in traditional Middle Eastern restaurants, indulging humus, rice, kabobs, and mocktails. One evening at dinner she symbolically removed the timepiece from her wrist and insisted that I have it when I complimented her on it – placing the watch into my hand with a smile like no other from a friend. Indeed, food was the thing, it was the glue to affirm and consolidate relations – to mark the beginnings, endings, and the heights of things. Food was plentiful and we could have all that we wanted, except for pork, which in the Muslim tradition, was forbidden and not sold anywhere in the Kingdom.

The date with Charles was notable in my Saudi escapades. He called me 'Sugar'. And I liked that, which was a food thing too. Food was at the center of our short dating spell. We met at a professional business dinner and decided that it would be nice to try to get to know each other. Interesting guy, yet I saw that we were much too different from the start. Like oil and water. He was a staunch conservative cowboy businessman – ceaselessly on the phone and hot on the trail of the next big deal and more money; and me - a liberal, modestly salaried professor with a bent for things spiritual and mystical. But the physical attraction was surely there. We'd take it as far as it needed to go, I knew.

Charles called me up for a Thursday night date at the start of the weekend. Said he had something very special planned for his 'Sugar'. The evening began with him arriving early before 7:00 pm, fetching me from my villa; me gladly greeting him at the door wearing my abaya, and high heels that he urged me to wear whenever we planned a date. He'd look me up and down and give his unspoken approval and proceed to escort me by my arm, the short distance to his black SUV – being such a gentleman by opening the passenger door, and gingerly helping me into the seat. I liked that too. We'd had several dinner dates, but that night we would dine in his apartment. I had reservations about that. We had just met a month prior, and I was not quite ready to be physically intimate with him – not sure whether that would happen either. But I wanted a 'surprise' and went with the flow, trusting that I could handle things. He lived on the top floor in a luxury executive high-rise apartment in the business district. It had separate living quarters within for the maid – whom he made sure was gone for the night. "*Wow*" says me quietly to myself at the size and elegance of his place. And the moment I saw the large Bible on his coffee table in the living room, I assumed that I could relax and feel at ease about being there. Off went the abaya to reveal bare shoulders and the full view of halter top and leggings with the heels – making me more comfortable and adding something more than 'bacon' to play with his senses, perhaps in return for my 'surprise'. Us women did tend to think that way!

Not wasting a minute, he led me into the spacious kitchen, equipped with all the modern high-tech accoutrements any professional's kitchen would have. Playing at being clandestine, and cloak-and-dagger he teasingly beckoned me to come closer, flicking his index finger. He opened the refrigerator and as a magician would pull a rabbit out of a hat, he produced two packages of bacon. "Tah dah!" Says he. "Wow!" Says I, that time out loud. Now that *was* a surprise, a big one! "You rock dude! How did you do that Charles!?" Says I. And he said, "I brought these back from Bahrain concealed in a secret compartment in my briefcase. You can take one home with you. With the other, we are having bacon, lettuce and tomato sandwiches for dinner." Charles then brought out a bottle of red wine from the cabinet. *"What a resourceful man."* I thought and said to him: "Now you are being twice as naughty!!"

We hurried down to the market on the ground level of the apartment building where we purchased tomatoes, lettuce, mayonnaise, and bread; came back to the apartment kitchen where we immediately launched into preparing the meal. Charles was pan-frying the bacon, while I cut up the lettuce, sliced the tomatoes and toasted the bread with my taste buds watering at that all too familiar smell of bacon, which also seemed out of place. He burned incense to disguise the unmistakable scent of bacon being cooked, which was filling the air inside. It could not get done fast enough; and when it was, we as a tight team slapped all of the ingredients between the toasted bread– the mayo, tomatoes, lettuce, and the star of the show: BACON. With the sandwiches made, we went into the dining room and sat at the table to view the metropolis lights of our small coastal city from high above. He said a Christian blessing, poured the wine, and we ate slowly and in silence, as if in a trance agreement, to mark the moment, to savor our bites – making the secretly sequestered meal last. We had two sandwiches each. For me it was like having bacon, lettuce, and tomato sandwiches for the very first time, and it ranked among the most delicious meals I had in the Kingdom. And truth be told, that 'rush' was the highlight of our evening together!

I had bacon, lettuce, and tomato sandwiches for the next two days at home in my villa, from the package Charles gifted me, and cooked the last slices to eat with eggs over easy on a leisurely weekend morning. It would be quite a while before I would enjoy that again.

I grew up eating pork – everything from sausages, ham and bacon to neck bones, chitterlings and pig feet and tails; and I found that suddenly going without that taste was 'not right' and an annoying deficit in my life in the Kingdom. Thus, when I periodically went home to the US on holiday I would tear into BBQ, pork chops, sausages, and ham – all things in moderation, of course. My family was amused by my pork starvation and enabled me every chance they got by taking me to places where pork was king.

Who were we harming by granting ourselves that little treat? A gambit which most likely would not be repeated, because it was not easy. I'd visited the homes of fine upstanding Saudi families where wine was on the table, and where liquor was tucked away in the cupboards. And I never forgot what a purveyor in the black market told me: *"You can get and have anything you want in the Kingdom"*, which was true, and still that actuality was not a walk in the park. It seemed that the things we put in an extra effort to acquire made them more special, worthwhile, and stimulating once those things were in hand. For Charles and me, stepping outside of the rules was not fun or enjoyable, only having something that we had been missing. My monkish life in the Kingdom raised my appreciation for the simple things that I too often took for granted. In that land of contrasts and schisms, the things that were most familiar to me were what helped to keep me grounded, focused and more capable to produce, however basic they were.

I made a choice to be in the Kingdom, to harvest a new experience for myself and to bring value where there was growth and need. In doing so I, nonetheless, sacrificed having access to some pleasures that had been staples in my life. I'd done more good than any harm that I could imagine, working with and for the people of Saudi Arabia – the women. Still, although no one was looking, I could not help but to be conscientious of the fact that I ingested more than a morsel of meat that was contrary to the food consumption laws of the land. I thought about those things. No guilt, no worries. In the final analysis, and how I saw it, putting a little pork in my belly was a fair trade off. For I had come to understand and respect - which was also a footnote taken directly from the Saudi culture, that *'all was forgiven when one did off things in good heart'*. Knowing that, it was okay and warranted; and I could self-attest that *"I can have my bacon and eat it too!"*

32
Why Stay? Because IT DOES Get Better

Before I decided to pack my bags and venture into Saudi Arabia, I was sure to conduct the necessary due diligence – homework, investigation and research into the land that was calling to me. I was going there for sustainable work that was scarce for academic professionals in the US in the aftermath of the economic downturn, and where recovery throughout the nation was slow in the following years. The market for educators was saturated and fiercely competitive, leaving people like me, female, African American and middle-aged on the sidelines. Thriving in the profession in which I was educated, trained, and established was my right. And I was not about to wear myself out as an adjunct professor teaching at several universities per semester in order to live well – which was becoming a fast trend for many seasoned academics. And, truly, it was time for me to take a break from the US and have a change of scenery for a while. For those reasons and with my natural sense of adventure, Saudi Arabia was an intriguing destination.

Well ahead of my departure I talked to people who were in Saudi via Skype – to know what was going on there beyond what was being reported in the national and international media. I searched behind the headlines and images that were brandished about that would have me believe that Saudi was a haunted, backwards, oppressive, and evil place – and that I would not be safe there. The Kingdom needed and welcomed educators, professors, and teachers, and preferably those with a western orientation. And the Saudis paid well. The most reliable and influencing information about the Kingdom came from Dr. Bonita, another American woman who was already working there. Through the fuzzy Skype transmission coming out of Saudi Arabia, she looked me unwaveringly in the eyes and calmly said: "You must make sure that your reasons for coming to Saudi Arabia are strong." Her countenance on the Skype screen was cryptic which I was to later realize was because of the routine monitoring of communications in KSA. She said that was the only advice she could give me. That advice was medicine which told me all I needed to know, because *"Of course"*, my reasons were quite strong. But no amount of cogent research and investigation would prepare me for what lie ahead in KSA.

On the plane I sat next to a demure Sudanese woman, also on her way to Saudi Arabia. She had a sweet face that was sad. The lovely Arabesque pastels she wore that covered her head and body were pleasant. We did not speak but exchanged glances. Yes, she was sad. I remembered her, not sure why – *was that telling me something?* Arriving in the Kingdom in the deep part of night was a first learning adventure. There were long lines at the entry check-in stations: A line for new arrivals – first timers; a line for migrants and/or short stay laborers who were mostly Pakistani, Indian, and Bangladeshi; a line for Saudi residents; and one for returning non-citizens – ex-pats. On future trips back into the Kingdom from short stints at home in the US, I learned to walk swiftly, even race after deboarding the plane to get ahead of the crowd and to avoid standing caught at the tail end of the line for retuning non-citizens, which was invariably the longest, slowest line. When I got there the intake at that line was extremely tedious and tortuous, processing hundreds of weary people arriving in the wee hours. The brief check-in interviews were performed entirely by sharp, young Saudi men working their apt hands and fingers at handling passports and visas, taking pictures, and rapidly clicking away at computer terminals. They were looking very uniform in their traditional male garb of immaculate white thobes and checkered red and white scarves - an arresting sight that held my attention, for I was beat from twenty-five hours of traveling and flying economy class! But, after all of that I now had boots on the ground!

The 'IT' that got and made things better was the 'mindset' I had to adopt to afford a lease on a reasonably comfortable life in the Kingdom, which enabled me to fulfill the objectives that brought me there; and not becoming prematurely discouraged by the trials I met nor defeated by my presumptions, inhibitions, and fears. Long sentence. That was a big 'IT'. But IT did get better, aided by time and stable friends. One needed friends in that environment, which were easier to make than to keep. If one had a friendship that withstood the test of time, they were blessed. What I found phenomenal was how life on the ground could bring out the best and the worst in people – how kernels of tendencies within people got magnified. Many foreigners were hard put. There were those who had not cultivated the wherewithal to cope and instead, preyed upon others to stay steady and resourced. They fed upon other people for their energies, money, expertise, support, contacts, and favors that were not returned

– siphoning off vital things that others needed for themselves. They came my way. The weak preying on the capable happened everywhere in life, for sure, but it seemed more pronounced in the microcosm of the Kingdom. One had to be discerning. And that discernment had to be done with an inward glance as well as outward.

The culture in KSA did not bend, adjust, or change to accommodate anyone; nor did the slow process of adapting to it. Fine tuning my 'frame of mind' was the best option – relaxing my ego and trusting my decision to come to KSA. It was not a conscious act, done in the light of awareness, it was just something that I morphed into by letting the Middle East's enigmatic charm work on me as running water made smooth a jagged stone. And while it was happening, I did not resist or fight it. I knew that I was affected in some subtle way and went along with it, as it did not hurt, and it was not killing me. Most of the people I knew were like me - finding their way around in neutral mode. But many were not in the middle and were instead, on edge.

One of the major assumptions that many outsiders brought with them into KSA was that they were being imposed upon. They came convinced that there was an active force working against them - that they were constantly under siege. They'd see themselves as square pegs resisting being fitted into round holes and compromised. The 'phantoms' they created in their minds drove them to set themselves up with self-fabricated obstacles. When in fact, their 'assumptions' were the edges that may have needed rounding out. There was nothing innately evil or malicious in the culture; it was just of an abruptly different design. By coming with a defensive mindset, even though coming there may have been out of necessity, many foreigners all too often found themselves waking up in a war zone. If the angst was not a result of being held hostage by one's own false assumptions, then it was the extreme discomfort, physically, socially, and psychologically, that became a 'thing', and got to the most resilient of people, even me. It was hard. I had crying spells. I did not feel that I was at war, but I began my trek into most days with the heebie-jeebies, just the same. However, that angst subsided as I got busy.

The first year was hellish. That was what I felt overwhelmingly, in my mind and spirit, which was a long story. In part it was the stark, non-negotiable adjustment I had to make in Saudi; I 'parachuted' in – into a mire and got a huge dose of culture shock. Being bound to the wearing of the abaya when in public was daunting for me. In my vanity, at home, I spoiled myself with loads of high fashion and designer attire, and in fact, was a recovering shopaholic. The abaya mandate would certainly expedite a cure for that, I thought. It was especially difficult to adjust to the assorted restrictions on liberties that I took for granted in the US. It seemed that a gigantic 'NO' was everywhere, i.e. limited mobility and not permitted to drive a car; alcohol was illegal; pork was forbidden; there were no live theatres, nightclubs, concerts or music halls, no symphonies, or places to dance, watch a movie, see an opera; there were no festivals or sports events, etc. Technological glitches happened with regularity, and the slightest thing could trigger total shutdowns in a digital landscape that was highly controlled and monitored. TV entertainment was mainly Middle Eastern programming with a handful of western channels such as CNN and movie stations – which were heavily edited – no strong language or sensual scenes – not even kissing. There were scarcely any venues for women and men to mingle, and certain places I could enter, and certain areas I could not. It was uncustomary for me to walk all by myself in the public thoroughfare which predictably invited undue attention and scrutiny. There were lots of below the surface social 'dos' and 'don'ts', and 'should nots' that no one coached me on - that I had to learn by trial and error. However, I kept remembering the words of Dr. Bonita, who was now my friend, that my reasons had to be strong.

Hardly a day went by without me lamenting to those close to me on how I desperately needed to cancel the two-year contract I signed onto and leave. Some of those same people just up and left - giving no notice – 'contract be dammed!' I counted time on my calendar - checking off the days left until I could take my leave and go home for several weeks. Escaping back to the lifestyle I knew was a long, tired dream. I was, however, enjoying my work in the Kingdom. I felt privileged to work with and among the thousands of female Saudi students, women administrators, and my faculty. It was fresh to me, and I felt as though I was making a tangible difference in so many lives. It tapped my spirit. But it was not the work that drove me to tears, it was the flip side of my professional activities - the isolation, the dearth of activity, the restrictions, of doing without – of the tricky parts of having to learn how to play in the dark.

The second year was uneasy and took effort. That was my 'grin and bear it' year - toughing it through. Now I was systemically marking off the days remaining until the two-year contract ended, not just the days until vacation. There were consequences for breaching a contract, such as losing the 'End of Service' bonus and vacation pay, which could be substantial; and getting expelled from the Kingdom in bad standing and not allowed to return for several years. And I did not like burning bridges if it were avoidable, no matter how rickety they were. There could be other surprise punitive measures. Negotiating out of contract could ease some of the consequences, but not entirely; plus, it was hard to do. And it could still leave a mark on me. More would be lost than I could and was gaining. There was unfinished business back home in the US; I had to pay my bills and needed to get a leg up on finances. As long as I was and felt stagnated, I was miserable. So, I just dug in. Although I was healthy and made sure to stay on top of that, the stress was still in my body. I started to get bi-weekly full body massages to ease the anxiety and to help me stay the course. I began putting more energy into establishing inroads into the culture - getting out there - navigating the business landscape and social environment; I made it a priority to master the essential technologies to keep things running smoothly; not to mention regularly checking myself with that 'inward glance' about my attitude – and to avoid feeling sorry for myself. Those efforts started to pay off.

My two-year contract was finally completed. The date I had long awaited and pined for had arrived. I had the option to renew for another two years and with a knee-jerk response in a hot minute, I declined. I was already out of the gate and charting the life I would resume back home in the US: Getting back to my soft bed, reading my books; going to the places I would drive to in my car; sitting at the piano bar, sipping wine; wearing my regular clothes; walking outside with the sun on my bare shoulders, and so on. Upon receiving my 'Decline to Renew' letter senior leadership immediately scheduled a meeting with me and asked: "What can we do to continue to have you here?" By then I had given leaving versus staying more thought – weighing the pros and cons. I was seeing encouraging evidence from my efforts to adapt; that evidence and management's obvious sincerity and need for me shifted my thinking. But I was clear: "Give me a lot more money and a larger villa." Done. In hindsight I wondered to myself, *"Why did I so easily decide to stay, given all of my mental and emotional wrangling over the past two years – the counting of the days and all that?"* I could not answer my question just yet. But it surely felt swell to be needed.

Before that meeting with senior management and signing on for another two years as my second year was ending, I sought the advice from a Saudi friend, Amal. I asked her: "Why should I stay?" She told me: "In the third year, it does get better." There were some blanks to her other statements that weren't quite filled in. But it was largely those words, spoken so caringly, reassuringly, and with certainty while looking me straight in the eyes that also influenced my decision to stay. I believed her and she was right.

Shifts happened. The third year found me having good friends in the Saudi community – both men and women, being invited to weddings and into their homes for meals and gatherings. And there was something new - I was content and a 'native' in Saudi society – with Saudi folk - enlivened with their company more than with many of my ex-pat comrades. I found to no surprise that Saudis had real issues too, like divorce, losing a job, abusive bosses and being lovelorn. While making friends, I was stretching into the business community and had a constant male companion. I had turned a corner and started to settle in. Staying with the momentum, I dove deeper into the Saudi communal scene, putting my driver, Ajmal to work and venturing out of the compound more to go toe-to-toe with the culture. I went places where no one spoke English; trekked into the market areas tucked away and off the beaten roads where only the locals congregated; I got involved with women's uplift activities, working on special projects, knocking on doors, so to speak; and I went anywhere my students invited me.

Saudi did not get better, I did. And what helped that? Several factors. Time, of course. Time took care of problems where words or maneuverings fell short. Time moved matters along and brought insights, relief, and useful things my way. With me, it began to sink in that I was fulfilling my goal to help make a difference in KSA, and that was doing me a heap of personal good. It was working with so many radiant, young, up and coming Saudi ladies that charged me and gave my work meaning; it was being truly needed. By recognizing and aligning with a deeper purpose, it all made sense. Spiritually, I was appreciating the wisdom and perfection of the universe that assured me that I was in the right place at the right time – assured that I was meeting the moment well, and darned sure that I was not missing my 'calling' nor was life passing me by. I no longer marked time or kept the countdown calendar and put that aside. And in a more temporal sense, despite the restrictions, I realized how connected I was to the land and how I was falling in love with the Middle East – falling in love with its beauty, with its heart, with its oldness, with its grace. And in some obscure way while in that part of the world, I felt in the thick of life.

Into the fourth year, things clicked. Whereas in those initial years it felt as though I was losing my grip, it became clear that I found my home in the

Middle East. It seemed to be the place where I belonged. That new 'mindset' I was cooking was the 'me' awakening to that reality. I realized that the company leaders who recruited me to Saudi Arabia to live and work did not promise me a rose garden, and they were, after all, keeping their end of the bargain. I had my health, I was meeting my objectives, contributing something of value and moving forward. Acclimating to Saudi and waiting on time was not so bad and kind of a relief, and I could not put a price on that.

At the end of the second two-year contract, I was torn. I could see that the threshold was approaching for me to formally exit the Kingdom, but I felt undone. I noticed that I was starting to like the way I felt there - the way it made me feel. Maybe that feeling was always there, but I failed to sense it through all of the noise. I wanted to explore that feeling and stay a little longer, so I struck a balance and negotiated for one additional year, which would be number five. That fifth year was so easy, in fact, it was glorious. Five years for me in the Kingdom of Saudi Arabia, who would have thought!!!

Time helped to temper my frame of mind, hence my perspectives, and to the point where cultural restraints became secondary; the anguish receded, isolation turned into something else, and truth spoke through the tears. The sobering question that stayed in the back of my mind and that kept me in check was: *"When I leave Saudi what am I really going back to in the US?"* I really could not say, but it was not about what I thought I missed.

The Saudi desert mojo had taken a hold of me, and its alchemy made me into someone else - more myself. I looked 'through a glass darkly' and viewed what worked, and that which did not. I hadn't forgotten the struggle, it never left, but I became more relaxed with it. I got to know how to get things done – how and when to run errands; where to find things, better at navigating the human and technological terrains. I was mastering money, food, and energy management; knowing when to take a good rest, and when to do a thing so elemental as to seal the windows and stuff a towel at the base of the doors well ahead of the coming sandstorm. I was learning how life tasted when I took it in bite-sized pieces with no need to gulp. The finer moments lasted longer; and I felt sure more often, as I marveled at how things fell into their right places when left alone. *Life was good!* Saudi and the Middle East resonated with my soul, and I resolved to remain tethered to that 'destination' whatever my next steps might be. The strong reasons that took me there were replaced by stronger ones to linger and to make my way back in a future time.

UNDER THE ABAYA

Part Four

JUST BELOW THE SURFACE

UNDER THE ABAYA

33
Dark Truths – Fear of Women

Ajmal, my astute Pakistani driver of several years solemnly told me of an incident in which a Saudi 'girl' approached him in the parking lot of a food market one night. "She was not looking for a ride", he said. The girl, a teenager came up to him as he was getting into his car and asked if he had a room. Because Ajmal spoke Arabic well there was no mistaking what he heard her say. I said to him in jest: "She came to you because you are so good looking, the ladies like you."

"No!" he chirped back, saying that it was something else. In that culture it was rare and extremely unadvised for a young Saudi woman to cross the line to approach a man she did not know for anything. He did not know what to say nor how to respond to such an invitation coming out of nowhere, in the dark, and one that had an element of illegal danger to it. Despite his many years of driving women in the Kingdom, Ajmal did not know how to deal with the situation and did not understand why she chose him with such a request. I knew that the honesty and integrity that lived within Ajmal was obvious to anyone. Even she, with her adolescent eyes could probably discern it through whatever distress she was experiencing. Saudis can be very perceptive people.

"I am not a prostitute!" The girl quickly exclaimed. "I just need a room. Can I stay with you in your room?" "No, I don't have a room." He told her. "Then can you help me get a room? Can you rent a room for me? And I need some money." Ajmal gave her twenty riyals - the equivalent of about $5 US dollars, which could go far in the Kingdom - telling her that he could not rent a room for her. He said that to her while keenly looking her over for some sign that would tell him more about her and where she was 'coming from' beyond what she was telling him. Her words were just spilling out all over the place, he said, and it was not the full story. She showed him a man's Rolex watch. Ajmal took a close look at it and saw that it was real and expensive. "This is real isn't it?" He said. "Yes, and so it this." She said, showing him a handful of fine jewelry. Again, she said, pleading, "I am not a prostitute, I just have some issues."

As much as he was an honorable man, Ajmal was a cautious man, and especially when it came to encounters with Saudi women. He kept a respectful distance and did not tread against cultural norms where Pakistani men and Saudi women were concerned, except for one occurrence he shared with me, that he *"could not help"* – and involving two consenting adults. The situation now facing him was quite different.

Handing her back the watch he decided not to go any further with the encounter. He said to me that he felt sad for her but could do no more than to give her the riyals and leave her where she stood. He knew that to try to do more would certainly put him in a jeopardous position. The Saudi laws and norms governing male and female interactions were precise and strict, and it would be foolish to try to go up against them, for whatever reasons. With him, especially being a Pakistani driver, involving himself to help her would cost him dearly if it were found out. However, the incident made a strong enough impression on Ajmal that it was the first thing he mentioned to me when he picked me up for my errands. He retold it so vividly that in my mind's eye I could clearly see that young lady standing, left in the dark empty parking lot as he drove away. I felt something for her too and sent her a prayer.

"I think she ran away from her home." Ajmal said, still processing, and concluding his thoughts on what happened that night. He was probably right. "You've been here awhile Ajmal and dealt with a lot of women. Do you have any idea what she was running away from?" I asked him. "It could be anything, but I am sure she was running away from home. These women are just plain prisoners in this country and even in their own homes. There are just some dark truths here" he responded. From what I learned and knew about the underside of the culture, that young lady most probably ran away from a husband or family, and having no claim to money of her own, she secretly snatched the watch and jewelry to get by. *Like anyplace else in the world, Saudi had its dark truths*, I affirmed in my thoughts. And the tragedy of that desperate vulnerable adolescent girl in the night pointed to a much larger story.

The oppression of women was long-standing and inbred in the culture, stemming from an ancient script informed by the mood of men. It was a code that ranked women as second-class citizens – as having no rights equal to men, and who were like property, possessions, or objects to be controlled, dominated and lead by men – outside and within the home. Like that unnamed teenage girl who found herself in a no-win situation, a woman who had had 'enough' might have little other recourse than to run to strangers for help. *Why couldn't that girl seek out a friend, a sister, a mother?* More than likely, her girlfriends and the women in her family circle were caught up in similar circumstances. Moreover, the women and friends may have long acquiesced to the 'code' and were compliant and at worst, complicit. They may not have had the will or the resources to help those who decided to resist and/or flee. They might have even tried to appeal to the young woman to find a way to stay. I'd seen that scenario played out again and again, among my students and some friends.

The formalized repression of women in KSA gave rise to abuses that further impeded women's upward mobility and potential to create and learn and grow well. A woman was supposed to be and make herself 'invisible' in every possible way from covering herself with the abaya, not walking alone on most streets, to being on the fringes of the business thoroughfare, or absent from it altogether. Women's low status was not a popular subject; but it was apparent in most aspects of society and was something that the young female university students were increasingly speaking up about. It was common knowledge that young women and girls were often required to assist their mothers and families by doing the cooking, cleaning, shopping, and caring for their younger siblings. That was their role in the family when education, career opportunities and mobility were not generally available to them. And as opportunities began to rise for women, some abuses persisted. Also, their lives remained stunted and controlled, largely by fathers, husbands, even brothers.

The woman-child who approached Ajmal may not have been a typical spoiled run-away teen who was mad because she could not have 'her way' but was most likely escaping an impossible situation where she had no one to turn to – only an outsider. Obviously, her troubles was so unbearable that it did not matter who real help came from, and she made a run for it with purloined items to barter her way to a different, perhaps a healthier environment. A grown man's watch and a grown woman's jewelry were not freely given to her but were valuables she confiscated to finance her next steps. The bonds in the Saudi family ran deep, and I knew that it would take a lot to impel a young woman to run away as she did. It was a disquieting thing in my mind when I tried to imagine what became of her. Whatever her reasons for running away may have been, her plight got me to thinking hard on the 'issue' that I was also frequently dealing with in one way or another with my students.

Unfortunately, as in every place in the world, young women and girls were physically abused and preyed upon sexually by the men in their families. I recalled a private and sensitive talk I had with a student, Munirah, about twenty years old, a sultry beauty and budding artist. She told me that she was having recurring bad dreams, which were actually *"true 'rememberings"* of how her father repeatedly sexually abused her *"for a lot of years."* As she got older, the reality of what happened was becoming more lucid, strong, and troubling - creeping into her dreams and causing her to lose sleep and being chronically late for her first morning class.

I too, was affected and an indirect target of the corruptions that may have generated the circumstances of that distressed teenager and my students. As I witnessed women's oppression I experienced it myself as a professional woman – covertly and overtly. It was in the very air I breathed. And believe me when I say that it was no fun. I consciously chose not to be shamed, diminished, or compromised by that, but made alive with awareness of how critical the matter was to us all.

Fear was at the root of most oppressive acts by a person or group in the drive to dominate, control and even harm those they did not understand. Hatred entered that dynamic as well, which was a close cousin of fear. I could say that by coming to Saudi Arabia I had entered the lion's den where the 'fear of women' was given full vent and perpetuated, and the Saudi brand of female oppression was stark and *'in your face'*, so to speak. But globally, the 'fear of women' was the big elephant in the room. I witnessed and experienced female oppression in the Kingdom, but also in western countries. I saw that the fear and 'dis-ease' were not different in the West, just more covert.

Ironically, that girl ran away from the 'danger' in the sanctity of her home among family but saw no threat in asking a stranger for help in a dark vacant parking lot – an older foreign man. The crime rate against women in Saudi Arabia was comparatively lower than it was in the west, with the headlines in the US regularly reporting on the heartbreaking stories of women being kidnapped, molested, raped, missing, enslaved, and murdered. Women in western cultures were by and large the most victims of crime and violence that was usually perpetrated by men. Young women also ran away from their homes in the West and for the same reasons; and women still struggled for economic and social justice all over the world. Although the global spotlight was fixed on the oppression of women in Saudi Arabia, fear and even 'hatred' of women was universal - an errant drive in most cultures and nation states. The Kingdom, of course, officially made its case about the second-class status of women through laws and codes designed to control and restrain women. In truth, the Kingdom was a vivid depiction of how that was played out in other forms on the world stage. There was a thin line between suppressing to control women, as in Saudi and sidelining them, as in the West – both were destructive. I saw that Saudi Arabia had become a scapegoat for the world's collective fear of womankind, and that the finger pointing was likened to the *'pot calling the kettle black'*.

A dark truth was not only about the hidden 'abuse' that woman-child may have been escaping, nor about what western women confronted daily in the streets, in the workplace, or in their homes, it was about the age old pernicious 'fear of women' which had many faces around the world. Humankind had made strident advances in space technologies, communications, robotics, miracle cures, test-tube babies, and controlling the temperatures on the planet, yet humankind had not confronted its own collective shadow about the fear and oppression of the feminine. There still seemed to be 'a ways to go' before the 'fear of women' was universally acknowledged and righteously addressed.

Having spent precious extensive time in the Kingdom and seeing and experiencing so much, I could speak and wax philosophical about women and men and fear, and from the benefit of having lived both in the East and West. And even though both women and men participated in the universal 'fear of the feminine', the fact remained, that men in suits still ran the world. The math on the subject was simple: When men dominantly ruled, there was imbalance.

Qualities such as wisdom, compassion, laughter, nourishment, creativity, diversity, collaboration, acceptance and so on, were feminine - soft things that kept social morality, business acumen, economics, logic, and the body politic in check. On a micro scale, embracing the feminine could make relationships, families, home life, and marriages happier - better. On a macro scale embracing the feminine could bring vibrancy and progressiveness to any nation. It looked as though the leadership in the Kingdom was beginning to move in that direction. The churning social climate that was 'tapping into women' in Saudi Arabia could symbolically be seen as the genesis of what was needed in the world - a lot more. The unleashing of women's power and potential would, I believed, save the Kingdom. Something that was pent up for so long would eventually explode gloriously all over the place. Maybe the world would still be watching.

That teenager's story stirred my compassion and moved me to better understand and work stronger with the women in Saudi – in the classrooms and with women's progressive movements - helping them to not fear each other and themselves. I wondered about that woman-child roaming the streets, alone with despair in the night, reaching for anyone who could save her. I thought that from her actions with Ajmal, perhaps the 'danger' might be less in her own land as she searched out there to find her way; and that she would have an advantage over others like her who flee in the night in other lands. I had the big hope that she kept on going and did not turn to look nor go back.

34
"Miss, I Am Broken."

Ramadan was several days away. Saudis were planning for their month-long fasting and introspection. It was late spring, and the semester was ending with the university corridors becoming emptier and quieter as students were finishing with their final exams. Ex-pats were preparing to travel back to their home countries for extended breaks – so was I. The usual everyday activities in the Kingdom would lessen to some extent during the period of Ramadan. Business hours would change to reflect the 'fasting' schedule, and Muslims would begin to live by night, when their daily fasting rituals ended at sundown and would come again at sunup. Non-Muslims would nonetheless, be caught up in the Ramadan time changes and rhythms.

At the office, the day started off rather serenely. There was no teaming agenda on my desk, but I trained myself to be poised for the unexpected – between the calm and the drama. There was never a dull day in my position and always something to fill my time – organizing, planning, teaching, trouble-shooting – wearing a lot of hats. Some of those hats were being the counselor, sage, confidante, and mentor – all rolled into one to students, faculty, and fellow administrators, and being an adopted 'mother' to one exceptional young Saudi woman. I welcomed those roles which were more rewarding to me than being a central leader and authority figure. The pace of that day reminded me about my love/hate relationship with the clock. Some days it ticked too fast, steeling time that I needed. Other days it ticked too slowly, making room for something unexpected to barge in off the cuff that had to be dealt with before I wanted to go home – causing delays. The slow clock ticking and the mounting stillness in the air for Ramadan widened the space more so, for 'stuff' to waltz in, and a lot of it was time eating trivia and trifling schemes, sometimes it was not – it was a draw. Today was one of those vapid mornings where I woke up longing for the moment when I would walk back through the huge wooden door returning to the embrace of my villa. The clock was not my friend that day. It was taking too long for the afternoon hours to pass, with no classes to teach, no meetings and most of my faculty gone. It was getting close to the hour to take the early transport bus home as I had planned and was starting to wrap things up. Then came a barely audible tapping at my office door.

"This is not McDonald's." I announced – more like yelled at the repeated rapping - a phrase I borrowed from an esteemed colleague. I often said that smiling wryly to students who insisted on ignoring my office hours and not making an appointment. They popped by, burst open my door, and haughtily strode in with their mouths already moving - griping about their self-made mishaps, and needs and what they wanted or hoped I would do for them – all that before I could settle into my seat at the start of the day. It was annoying and disrespectful, and after all, it went against the professionalism ethics I tried to instill in my darling female students of Arabic heritage. The little princesses incessantly expected me to stop what I was doing to serve them on the spot at their whims – like McDonald's. I worked at McDonald's in my early teens, I should know. And it was around semester's end that pesky problems liked to walk through my door. Not in the mood for that, I was tempted to get up and command whoever was there to go away. The door was not locked, and the wee self-effacing young lady stepped in. "Give me a minute. You can wait outside." I said to her, clearly annoyed. I took my time hoping that she'd get tired of waiting outside and leave. Indeed, I was becoming jaded by all of the false emergencies and entitlement driven ploys that kept coming through my office door – draining my time and energy. Case in point, a few days earlier I had to forcefully order a student out who stomped into my office, belligerent in her demand that I bend the rules and make my faculty member increase her grade. I even had to call for security.

With the door slightly ajar I could see the meek young lady still waiting outside and being patient. *"I was probably a bit gruff with her"*, I thought. But she remained there, determined to see me. I'm thinking while clearing time-sensitive emails, that there must be a real issue that brought her to me and made her stay, despite my sharp manner. Maybe she was not just another person bringing me the blues on the kinds of implausible issues that could not wait, imploring me to 'please do something about something'. I went to open the door wider to let her in. She was seated in a lotus position on the floor now, adjacent to my office, wearing a black shawl and abaya, staring into her lap where her small hands lay, cupped. I asked her to come in.

She entered on tiny, timid steps and stood still, casting her eyes down – saying nothing. "What is it my dear?" She looked up at me. Her face was burdened with a sadness much too old for her – a heaviness and depletion. It did not take long to know that she wanted something important from me - my time, my energy – some favor I could grant from my position. I fished around for the right tone and words to pull some reasons out of her, to help her speak and say what was troubling her – to open up. She had to know that she was safe to talk to me now; though it seemed that just getting to my office to see me was half the battle for her. With effort she said: "There is something not happy with me Doctor. I need to talk to you, and I was told by someone something good about you. That is why I came to you. Please, I am sorry. Please, I need to talk." She had my full attention. There was a critical matter happening – caught between her woes and a need. "Close the door and sit down dear."

Her name was Yara – a young Saudi woman of twenty-one years old – not one of my students, but one I may have walked past without noticing in the corridors. There were so many in the crowded university passageways in the fullness of the semester. She said again as if it were painstakingly rehearsed: "I need to talk to someone, and somebody told me something good about you. So that is why I came to talk to you." She seemed overwhelmed and had difficulty with the English words to express herself. "What is making you so unhappy dear?"

Young Saudi women were not typically forthcoming about their personal lives. They were rather secretive with their thoughts and feelings. They held back and held in, until a real trust was established. Fighting through the English, Yara was working her way through that reserve because she had reached a point where she had no choice. A lot was coming through her eyes and demeanor - reaching across the wide chasm from her culture to my understanding.

As if surrendering to her own words, Yara uttered: "Miss, I am broken."

"You are so young to be so sad." I said to her - moved with how direct she was with those words.

"I am not too young and not too old to have problems miss. My mother is sick. She is big and getting bigger. This is because of the medicine they are giving her. My husband left me. I do not know why. I was married for only a year. My problems are so too big."

I urged her to say more with gentle questions. Yara continued. "My husband, he is blocking me on the Absher* so I cannot do anything or go anywhere. The life is too much for me. I am depressing with life."

Unloading the words and the emotions with them tired her. She stopped talking, now looking directly at me expectantly, as if she wanted me to say or give her something – to extend a lifeline. A silence clothed the air. She may not have really known what or if she wanted something from me – perhaps just having someone else hold the weight of her young, troubled life with her may have been enough. She did not ask me for anything but there was surely a gap that needed to be filled. Yara's face was plain and her complexion smooth like a small child's. That with her short petite physical frame and shy manner made her seem so fragile. But she was not helpless, and I was not going to allow her to leave my office feeling that way. I saw how she could feel that she was breaking under the heaviness of those problems. Whatever I said to her would be to empower Yara to hold on to herself. My words would have to be direct and simple enough for her to hear and understand. And there was just a fleeting moment to try to make a difference in how she was feeling. Given her being Muslim, I was not sure how that would come across as I could only speak from my spiritual values in the context of her personal crisis.

"My dear, when life gets too much, you have to focus on what you can control." She was quiet, listening and perking her face to acknowledge what I was saying. "I am sorry to know that your mother is so ill and hope that she will be better. That is in God's hands, In sha Allah. And now you cannot control what is happening with your mother. You can only pray for her. Do you understand?" She nodded.

"You cannot control what your husband is doing and why he left you. Right?" She was not sure of that, and not quite ready to say anything.

I continued: "When life gets too much for me, and the picture is too big for me, I take a small piece to work with. I take what I can handle. So, you must do this. Take a small piece of the life. And only focus on what you can handle. You can only focus on what you can control. And that should be something that is the most important thing for you right now. What is that thing Yara?"

"I am going to take the final exams next week miss; this is a problem with me."

"So what is it that you can do right now to feel better? What is the most important thing now?" Yara could not get clear to find the answer but agreed when I suggested that it was that she passed the exams and her courses.

"I am so sorry to be bothering you, miss."

"No dear, talking with you now is the most important thing I can do today." And I meant that. I knew that there was a university counselor that I could have sent her to see, but chose not, because I knew that the matter at hand was for me.

I continued by saying: "When God closes one door" . . . and Yara finished the sentence, saying: "Another door opens." That was the nexus in our talk and where I hoped Yara's catharsis might begin. From there I knew that Yara and I were now speaking a universal spiritual language, despite her limited English and my teensy-weensy Arabic. I let some space enter before asking her: "Can you close that door on your husband Yara, and not be afraid?" She nodded her head, as she wiped away the tear that was rolling down her cheek.

The spirituality and mysticism that existed beneath the surface of the religious culture among Saudi people was not easily accessed by foreigners. I learned that broaching the subject was a door that a Saudi person did not readily open. I had to open it first. In the spiritual intelligence we raised, by me opening that door, and Yara by stepping through it, we put together a plan on how she should and could approach her professors about her final exams; pray for her ailing mother; and let go of her husband and anything that he was doing to try to hurt her. I advised her to be careful of what she focused on and where she put her energy, which she now needed for her goal to graduate. Yara appreciated and accepted my every word and I believed that she needed to hear what she already knew. Beyond her sadness she was radiant with an inner quality of light and depth that I had witnessed up close in a few other young ladies. Still, she warily accepted a hug from me before leaving my office.

Having missed the early transport bus, due to my session with Yara I stayed around to get more things done and thought that I just might call a driver to take me home. Walking through the sparsely populated corridors a few hours later I spotted Yara. She approached me beaming, with excitement in her body and footsteps. She was eager to tell me her news and progress. In the emptiness and quietude of the female campus she wasted no time putting the plan into action that we discussed. She told me that after she left my office she contacted her professors about her final exams, and that they would work with her on how to study and pass the tests coming up next week. She added that she felt lucky that she could reach them in those last days. Yara was lighter, she was smiling. I could tell that despite her outward gloom earlier that afternoon that what we talked about really sank in with her and she got what she needed to act on. I told Yara to come see me anytime she wanted. Final exams were huge stumbling blocks for a significant amount of students; passing and succeeding over that hurdle meant that they could get on with their lives. I knew that would give Yara the boost to manage and put her life in order. Her report to me showed that she was well on her way.

Sometimes the words of guidance and counsel I gave to students and other professionals was wasted on those who were just sucking up my energy; the energy in the form of my time and supportive counsel was not applied by them to lift or improve their lot, but instead went in one ear and out the other. Their beseeching me for help was just to satisfy the moment – to get a short-term fix, with that person wanting to come back for more. Yara was not that way. She was earnest. She inspired me. That 'broken' young woman had the courage to take care of herself by seeking me out in the trust that she would be safe and receive the help she needed; and she had the gumption to almost immediately do a lot with the advice that she was given. Her actions took her closer to overcoming a key obstacle she was facing. That wee shy woman was sturdy enough to do all that.

Working with Yara affirmed the universal truths and languages that linked us all in our journeys through life, no matter what paths we took. As for Yara, certainly, when the student was ready, the teacher would appear. I felt privileged to have had the encounter with a no longer 'broken' woman, who was a marker for the resilience and progressive-mindedness of the young Saudi women who surrounded me. And I continued to guard my doors to know who was knocking – the physical ones and those of psyche. There was always wisdom in that.

Absher - An electronic system in KSA that was a recording and tracking service for the economic activities of all citizens and foreigners. It was also through that system that approvals and clearances were made for people to purchase goods and receive payments of any kind and to travel.

35
Dowa's Tears

When Dowa launched into her tears, I did not know whether to laugh, to hug her or to run her out of my office. It was such a con and such an irresistible con. She knew that I knew exactly what she was doing, and I knew that she knew that I knew. Crazy stuff. But most times we both played along with it anyway. So, in that sense, it was not manipulative, but rather like a parlor game – the afterthought of it would serve as my amusement for the rest of the day! Seems that the crying tactic was all that Dowa had to work with, for she was not the brightest student trying to reach that spring semester finish line to pass her courses and graduate. And Dowa was not a beauty like the other ninety-five percent of her fellow students. But she was endowed with a sprightly energy that grabbed onto me, and which I knew came from a genuine and uncorrupt place. She did not use her tears glibly, but only when she thought that she had no other option. At times, I let the tears move me on purpose, to grant her the satisfaction of knowing that she did try to get what she wanted and needed, even if it had to be with tears. Her signature burst of tears was not rehearsed – in no way practiced, Dowa just knew how to cry.

I did not make exceptions for Dowa, not in the least bit. A lot of crying went on in my office with a considerable number of female students. Dowa made token efforts to earn the favors she wanted, and she did not ask for much nor expected me to move mountains for her; she wanted things such as a late pass to other classes, extra time to complete a paper well past the deadline, to switch to work with a project team with more smart and capable students after all teams had been established, or extended time to get a doctor's note to save her from being docked for absences – things I could easily do, but not without her showing an appropriate amount of contrition and self-reproach. Every inch forward mattered to Dowa, and she would eagerly take it; and she did have the courtesy to make an appointment to see me, to cry. Sometimes she would arrive with a gang of friends for support, but those friends had to wait outside with the door closed, as witnesses or audiences were not allowed when I met with individual students, even Dowa.

One day Dowa came to ask me to change the grades on an exam in which she scored poorly. She barely passed with a low grade of D+. On that day, she was in for a surprise. Whereas she prompted my hand before, that time she was overreaching. If I changed a grade for her, I would also have to do so for other students, and that would compromise my learning standards. Students did talk and shared among themselves about the accommodations professors made to help them get by, and which would bring more students with the same requests pounding on my door. Dowa was going to try to convince me that what she wrote on the exam was not really what she meant to say and that her grade should have been much higher – more like a C. And I'd heard that one before. Dowa had to learn to try harder with her studies and learning discipline. When I told her that and said *"No"*, she brought on the tears.

Dowa's tears were an avalanche, with the force to impact things. When all else failed, she instantaneously started fretting, weeping, and bawling which could be heard through the door and way down the hall – putting on her show. Her tears were a loud, hungry, incorrigible accusation and pleading all at once determined to wash away the NO; and those tears would vanish just as abruptly as they started when and if she got her way. There was no controlling or containing her reflexes to feign injury when she was denied. Only the result that she wanted would stop Dowa from crying.

Dowa's tears were an introduction for me into some truths of the culture of women in the Kingdom. Exceptions were the rule in Dowa's mind and the same with many young Saudi students and women like her. For them it was always a buyer's market, particularly in the field of education; and 'choice goods' could always be had with a little finessing such as: A higher mark on an assignment, a free passing grade - an unearned reward. Bartering was respected and expected, and if the tears did not work, 'wasta' certainly would. I saw how the 'tears' were an in-bred part of the student culture, which to some degree extended into the larger social dynamic of women. Tears were the handy and reliable 'go to' tactic to make things right; and made it so that any and everything was negotiable. One applied the resources they had at their disposal; and the tears were ready tools used by many to engineer a life.

With doors opening wider for Saudi women to obtain a college education young women clamored for at least a bachelor's degree, as their young lives increasingly hinged on that, as it might and did for other women in the world. However, with young Saudi women, it was for more acute reasons. Up to 1956,

Saudi women were not allowed to be formally educated. The education that was available to them, was somewhat remedial – to prepare them to be good wives according to Sharia Law* and the Qur'an. Over the ensuing decades things began to gradually open for women to receive a formal college education, which in its initial stages was not equal to or on par with that of men. King Abdullah, also known as Ibn Saud, was called the 'reformist'; under his reign up until his death in 2015 he opened more doors and equal pathways for women's college education, most substantially with the establishment of scholarships. That opened the floodgates and masses of young Saudi women were flocking to universities that would accept and provide them with a curriculum the same as men. At my university the female enrollment doubled and at times, tripled that of males; courses for females had to be extended to add several sections to accommodate the fast multiplying numbers of female students; and hiring professors in order to meet the demand was an ongoing top priority. I directly knew that the reasons and motivations to get an education and a degree were a matter of national and personal pride for many female students. Students realized that their country was changing, and they eagerly wanted to acquire the knowledges and skills to contribute to the Kingdom's developing progressive agenda.

On an individual note, at university, I observed that there was a race and competition for a college education among young Saudi women, particularly, to graduate with a 4.00 grade point average (GPA) or as close to it as possible. Additionally, employers were preferring to hire those with high GPAs. For the Saudi women and their families, a university degree raised their social status. Young Saudi women and their families were increasingly appreciating the fact that having a college education was crucial to their success in life – not only for employment and work, but having a degree made them more appealing as marriage partners and enhanced their prospects of being wedded to 'select' men. The college degree was becoming a key part of a Saudi lady's dowry. Marriages were conditioned around the university degree and GPA a woman acquired – the high GPA and college degree raised the value of the dowry. Together, those constituted free passage and access to a higher quality of life – a 'good' husband and job, social mobility, etc. The females' families often made a precondition on the marriage contract that the young woman *"Be allowed to continue her education and to get a job after marriage."* The husband 'to be' must agree to those terms. Perceiving that so much was at stake, the female students would bitch, goad, scratch, and claw to an nth degree over half a mark (.50) to increase their grades. That could spell the difference between barely passing to failing or going from a B+ to an A, with the A+ as the most coveted final grade. Mothers and fathers, but more mothers than fathers awarded their daughters with 1000 – 2000 riyals for every A or A+ they received.

So, let me talk about the mothers and the fathers. Mothers worked overtime in the background on anything having to do with their daughters' educations. The fathers were visibly active on the front lines, using their positions and influence or just plain male authority to have their daughters' educations vouchsafed at the highest marks possible; they dealt directly with the university top leadership anytime they had a concern or sought considerations for their daughters. It was not a matter of whether the daughter was a good or worthy student, or even making the effort to excel, just as long as she got through and passed the courses and semester. Husbands would call me on their student wives' behalf to defend the wives' positions or to push for grading exemptions. There were never-ending gifts; and one was obliged to accept a gift that was offered in the culture, even when it did not suit one's taste. Refusing a gift was an affront, which made things tricky. And despite the lovely faces, the ornate dellas of luscious Arabic coffee and dates, the ouds, the chocolates, the cakes, the selfies that students liked to take with their professors, the jewelry, the endearing kisses on the cheek from hopeful mothers, and of course, the tears, the professors were simply a means to an end. Reaching the top of that ladder was the 'end all'. Bottom line, *"Please give my daughter a pass!"* And sometimes things got ugly.

There was a scary spectacle in which an irate mother accosted, berated, and *cursed* a faculty member for ruining her daughter's life by failing her. The mother came to the campus, found, and confronted the professor, and shouted for all to hear that she *hoped* the female professor would never find a husband, among other things. And that was not an isolated incident. As such, come grading time and semester's end, faculty did not answer their phones, they kept their office doors closed and locked – not letting anyone inside at all, and otherwise, made their presence on campus scarce to avoid the onslaught of unhappy students, their parents, and spouses.

The high premium placed on education drove students to flagrant and widespread cheating and deceptions. There were 'anti-math' campaigns and an epidemic of students contracting out their major course assignments for non-university professionals to do. A growing shadow industry of 'consultants' who would do mock research, editing, paraphrasing, and any kind of doctoring of assignments for students for a modest fee was a hex for educators. And the use of those services was not limited to female students. By comparison, male students were not as studious and 'smart' as the females – maybe they were, but the females were famous for applying themselves and going the extra mile to obtain college degrees than the males because education meant so much more to them and benefited them at that epic time in the Kingdom. Along with a passion to learn, many females still used whatever means necessary to get that degree. And as in anyplace else in the world, there were plenty of men and women taking on and holding plum jobs and positions with degrees that were not earned but bought or bargained for.

Such furtive activity went on in the states also; I have stories to tell from my extensive tenure as a professor and Chair in US universities. There was no difference in how things were done and how grades and degrees were obtained between East and West. In KSA the bartering and gaming was no less similar to the father who pulled strings to get his son accepted into an ivy-league university in the US; or the ingenue who slept with her professor to pass the course, or the instructor who altered grades for students who did him or her favors, also at US colleges. To me, it seemed more colorful and frenzied in the Kingdom, not different. But it certainly wore us down – the endless charades of students who were hell-bent on moving my hand from right to left, as with the culture. Culture aside, in their cases regarding grades and passing, it was more burlesque than legitimate.

It was such that I had to challenge the students by asking them that in their reverent Muslim culture, "Wasn't it 'haram'* to manipulate situations to get something that was not earned?" Their reply was: "Yes miss, but then we pray to Allah and ask for forgiveness and we are forgiven." With that, I tossed up my hands, resigning to the idea that: *Most anything could be justified with a tweak and adjustment of perspective.* With the exception of hard crime, the students were most likely correct in implying that if the 'intention' was not corrupt, the action, however grievous, was rendered innocent and forgivable; and that God, the Divine weighed the intention over the deed. I would ponder that 'logic' for a while. I had to say that despite their theatrics and shenanigans over grading and passing courses, the students by and large, were respectful and revered their teachers, and far more than I experienced from all of my years teaching in US universities. Saudi students and their parents knew that their teachers played a mighty and pivotal role in their futures.

The crux of the matter was that the Kingdom was expanding its need of educated people for its rapidly changing and developing economy. Businesses had to recruit great numbers of qualified people for new and existing jobs as a lot of people were retiring from the workplace and reductions in financial benefits were systematically moving ex-pats out of their jobs. As a result, 800,000 ex-pats left the Kingdom in 2017 and double that number in 2018, and that decline was continuing. The pace of exits was unexpected and had a great impact on the Kingdom. As well, the Kingdom needed entrepreneurs to help ignite its new Vision 2030. Those factors were beginning to point to the population of seventy percent younger adults under 35 years of age who would fill the increasingly available jobs and take on the emerging roles as business leaders and entrepreneurs – shoring up the labor force. That would be aided by the Kingdom-wide campaign of Saudization* in a major way.

With Saudization, more and more jobs were opening for Saudi citizens, which was a good thing and in alignment with the Kingdom's new vision. But the vacated and available jobs far outnumbered the pool of 'qualified' people with college degrees to fill them. The job market in the Kingdom was literally playing catch up. In my eyes, that was part of what spurred the 'rush' and 'angst' to secure a degreed education, and especially for the army of young women for whom working professionally was a relatively new 'privilege' in recent years. Hence, Dowa's tears may have been a portend to the economic calamity that her country was facing if the gap between need and qualified Saudi employees, entrepreneurs and business leaders could not be filled in reasonable time.

And there was a conundrum overriding the entire situation: Saudi Arabia favored and wanted to integrate the 'western' way of business and education. It identified with 'westernization' as the model to grow and develop as a country in the world. Yet, at the same time, the Kingdom sought to retain its strict adherence to Muslim values and its way of life. Some cultural aspects and ways of being that were indelible and built into Muslim life were irreconcilable and prone to render the 'western way' as anathema. I saw. Understandable. I observed firsthand that it wasn't that Saudi did not want to but could not, and perhaps would not entirely integrate the western education model with how people 'learn' and 'know' in that culture. For instance: Speaking English was required for business effectiveness and upward mobility; so were western business-mindedness, protocols, professional decorum, and standards. Yet, those brushed up against and clashed with the Saudi mindset and business mentality which was rooted in nomadic values and traditions. In academia students did not easily adhere to reading books and note taking but applied an uncanny skill at memorizing in their learning processes. Learning was and would fundamentally be based on an 'oral tradition'. It was the Saudi culture that won out, for the time being. Which took me back to the tears.

I saw the Saudi Vision 2030 as being driven by the need for economic growth and diversification away from the sole dependence on oil rather than as the 'will' to liberate women; women did gain new opportunities from the Vision, and they were still crying. Women would continue to resort to manipulations to get buy in a culture that systematically suppressed them, institutionally, socially, economically, and religiously; again, that came from my perspectives based on observations and experiences. And even with the changes and openings in the Kingdom, the long-standing guardianship rule was in force, which had men, by law, making key decisions over women's lives. That cultural root, along with prevailing traditions and mindsets would forestall the Kingdom from actually becoming westernized.

Later in my years in the Kingdom and having broader experiences under my belt, I became more than immune to the tears, I became entirely vexed by them. Here's this. Rihana came to me to appeal that I change her grade from failing to passing. That outcome was no contest. Rihana clearly earned the failing grade, based on her lack of commitment to learning and performance. But she came in to plea-bargain just the same, and I listened, noticing her drastically altered appearance. She did not have the shine that she had while classes were in session during the semester. There was no luster in her hair, no sparkle in her eyes like before. Her lips were ruddy and there was no blush in her cheeks. She looked haggard in her black abaya - hunched over like an old woman waiting – pacing outside my office – seeming depressed and as though she had gone to hell and back. She did not bother to call or email prior to set up an appointment but traveled almost ninety miles from her home in a distant town, Al Qassim, to see me. That was her second time making the long trip and she caught me by 'dumb luck' in my office on the last day of the semester. It seemed pertinent and strategic that she made her appeal to me in person and impromptu. So, I gave her my 'audience', knowing also, how hard it was, but unavoidable, for me to fail her. Passing a semester required at least 66 out of

100 marks, and Rihana was 2.5 marks shy of that. Up to that point in the semester, Rihana had been trying to do things to win my good graces, as if she knew that she was going to fail and hoping that her gestures to me would 'break her fall' – things such as offering to host me in her home and a tour of sights in her town – even sending a driver to pick me up from so far away. I declined, or rather postponed accepting her offers until after the semester. Standing before me now, the evidence of her fall was clear.

Rihana was set to get married in the coming summer and because she failed my course it dropped her GPA substantially, and everything changed. She said that she could not get married now, and a *"bunch of other things"* could not happen and were falling apart because she did not pass that critical course. She was desperate and imploring me to change my mind, to grant her the 2.5 marks, and allow her to pass the course so that she could get her life back on track. And before I could say anything, the tears began to well up. At which point I raised my hand and commanded, "Khallas! Stop it right there! When you start to cry, I dig in and become your worst enemy. I am not inclined to hear you – because then, you are being manipulative. So tell your story straight and speak from truth and what is real, not with tears. Be strong in this. I cannot hear you through those tears. And tears will only make me make up my mind against you." And just as quickly as they began to form, the tears retreated behind her eyes. Crying was too easy. I made Rihana do the hard thing, which was to speak the raw, gospel of her plight on her own, using her words. She strained to do that, it took a few minutes, but she did; that was the price, and maybe that lesson would stick with her.

I thought about the fairness of it all, and how much did a life really weigh when it came down to marks and degrees and such. I saw a person before me, pleading for a 'rescue' – a reprieve. Rihana's was a story about a life - made evident without the tears. Seeing that, I knew that I could keep my integrity and sense of fairness close, and in the same spirit, I could also let go. That was grace - a sometimes thing. I did not want to be that person to offset the rhythm of her nascent journey in life, with a future that was not yet written; and it was a thin line to cross to give it a jumpstart. I granted her appeal, which was what I was wanting to do all along, even before she came to see me, as I knew she should and would. With that pardon, Rihana, now a bit composed, swooned back into the sunny, pretty girl I knew; and hugs and kisses and selfies ensued. I was human after all.

It was a dilemma. There was no right or wrong to it. Only, what felt good to do versus what would have been the bad thing. I guessed, I was starting to become 'Saudi' in my own ways and logic after all, by following that code which was: Deciding based on what was good or bad rather than right or wrong. Dowa's tears told lies; they were a demand for something that was not earned. But then those tears also spelled the truth of woman's pain and gave a shaky voice to that which could best speak through tears. Even though those two students, Dowa and Rihana came armed with their arsenal of tears, there was a genuine need and a pull. I wondered if being on the threshold of tears for so many women for so long was also an effect of abiding behind the veil; and that in some elemental way, it deeply mattered for one person to help and lift another, one-by-one and so on.

I will always hold dear the unforgettable sight of the dozens, if not scores of young Saudi ladies clustered and waiting for me outside my office as I arrived to work on many days. They were in their black abayas sitting on the floor, standing against the wall, or in thick groupings right at the door - each with some request of me that would give them an edge or a step forward in their education and careers. The lives of women were held in the balance and woven into the molding fabric of legacy repression. That was happening even with the Kingdom in the deepest throes of change, and which continued to generate situations like Dowa's, Rihana's and those anxious students outside my office. I began to see that the day was nigh when women would not have to cry that much anymore, for they would have fashioned more formidable tools to work with. From the openings being made for them, I could see that they were beginning to do that.

As it turned out, despite upping her efforts, Dowa was on her way to failing my class, as were many others, and they would have to repeat it come next semester. Students and colleagues did not peg me as Dr. Rigor for nothing. So, I gave the entire class the option to do a bonus assignment, which was an opportunity to earn extra marks and raise their grades a notch. The assignment was to perform volunteer work and report to me on what they did and to give me official verifying documents. That would also support the Saudi Vision 2030, wherein increasing volunteerism in the Kingdom was a key objective. Dowa completed the assignment; she passed the course, and without shedding a tear.

*Haram - That which strictly went against Islam and offended Allah.

*Saudization - A system of laws enacted in the Kingdom to generate and provide increased job opportunities to Saudi citizens, the equivalent of Equal Opportunity Laws in the US.

*Sharia Laws - Laws derived from the religious precepts of Islam and part of the Islamic traditions.

36
Wegdan

She routinely arrived several minutes before the start of class and preferred to sit in the first row taking the seat closest to the professor's desk, my desk. With her large book satchel on the floor at her side and computer splayed open on the desk, and greeting me with intelligent eyes, she was ready to go. She was about 5 ft 2 inches and draped in black/black. Her abaya and hijab left just enough area to show off her round, alabaster, pixie cute face; curious, keen, and smart, all in one. That was Wegdan.

To me her name sounded like something out of rap culture. I don't know why, but it did. While recording the class attendance I often teased her about her 'rap' sounding name by mimicking the iconic hip-hop moves – head cocked, crouching body leaned to the side with arms crisscrossed with the two-fingers sticking up, etc. Looking right at her I called out: "Wegdan!" Then I did the moves and she'd answer all too loudly: "I'm here!" She would snicker, and the others laughed too. The students told me that I was *"hyper"* which was their cultural word for 'animated' and 'entertaining'. Well, throughout my career I held teaching as 'edutainment'. Having students with names like 'Wegdan' just gave me license to respectfully amuse them and myself while providing necessary instruction. My lessons had Wegdan's rapt and fullest attention unlike some other students who could not help busying themselves on their phones. When caught, and they usually were, they were docked a full mark off their final course grade for disobeying class Rule Number 1 – absolutely NO Texting!

Although I could be comic at the front of the class, I held them to a high standard. I did not play around with that, neither did Wegdan. Wegdan was a stellar student – a superior learner; and she was a good study for me, as I grew from teaching and guiding her. She was an agile scholar who soaked up what she was learning like a sponge. She had ideas and brought those to share to see what I thought. She enhanced my delight and joy of teaching. "Tell me about your name", I asked her on a day. "It seems unusual compared to the other names Arabic parents give their daughters." She told me that it meant "The love and conscience of God." That fit, I thought, also thinking to myself that if I had to choose a favorite Arabic female name, it would certainly be Wegdan, and the next favorite would be Sukinah. I liked the sound of Wegdan's name and saying it also; it conjured up *'ballsy girl'* imagery for me, which incidentally, matched her. There was a spunk and activity and motion to her name and about her as if it were proclaiming: *'Watch me do this. I'm ready to go. I've got power and I'm not standing still!'*

The majority of Saudi students' educations were financed by generous government scholarships, which at one time proliferated and were easily granted to anyone who wanted to attend university. And although such scholarships became causalities of the changing economy from cutbacks to the educational fund that did not stem the tide of young men and women pursing college degrees. Most university undergraduate courses were in English. Therefore, before entering college the majority, if not all of the Saudi female and male students had to first learn English - to proficiently read, write and comprehend in a language that was not native to them in order to proceed with their education. Intermediary ESL and math courses were provided for students to take for two years before entering university at the freshman level. The Arabic language was a long way from English, and I applauded students on their tenacity to obtain a college degree in a foreign language, which I thought was a laudable accomplishment given how disparate Arabic was to English in speaking, comprehension, writing and flow – from right to left! And again, to orient themselves to English and demonstrate that in a four-year college degree program?! Come on now! I told students how difficult and amazing that would be for anyone to do, even said that to Wegdan, which she took in stride.

By the time they reached the senior level, some students still did not have a grasp on English and had concealed that deficit quite well to get that far. They did so with the help of 'sisterly' friends who were more proficient and did assignments for them, or by getting easy passes from some soft and willing instructors. But the business world was mandating that English be learned at the university before graduating. Wegdan mastered the English language. Her reflection, critical thinking, and writing skills were superior to what the average Saudi student could do, and evidently, well above some of the master's students I taught in the US. She pursued her education with zeal and willpower. She wanted it all and could do it all. And yes, she would eventually get the A+ from my class, and in all of her other classes. Sharp as a tack.

Walking through the campus corridors I would notice the groupings of students during the lunch and breaks between classes. There were the 'pretty girls' – primping, giggling and taking selfies; there were the 'girls of wealth' sashaying about in high fashion abayas, sipping fancy coffee drinks, with their Filipino nannies in tow; there were the 'goof offs' yelling and talking loudly – sprawled out in the café areas, clowning around, and not a book in sight; and there were the studious ones, huddled together off in a secluded spot thumbing through their books and notes, talking quietly. It was in the latter group that I would see Wegdan. She kept with the brainy and focused ladies. They were in another zone altogether. *Someday they are going to run things.* I would ruminate to myself, smiling as I passed them by. They saw me too. One time, Wegdan pointed at me, whispering something to her smart girl group. But I was not concerned with what she might be saying. I saw no ill intent in Wegdan. She would volunteer to tell me days later that she was telling her friends to take my course in the next semester; by that time she would have graduated and with flying colors, I knew for sure. But all was not rosy in Wegdan's world. All was not as it appeared. She was Shia in a sea of Sunnis.

Sunni and Shia were the two denominations of Islam. The difference between them was their interpretations of Islamic laws and words – most chiefly, on who should be the successor of the prophet Muhammed. For the Sunni it should be Abu Bakr and after his death, Umar; for the Shia, it should be Ali. Shia also had their separate religious days, for which the Shia students discretely asked me to grant them excuses from class. They would wait for class to end before asking so as not to have questions raised from the Sunni students about their special requests, which I easily approved. Active isolated skirmishes between Sunnis and Shias were happening in neighboring towns like Al Qassim. Ex-pats were strongly advised by the US Consulate to steer clear of that town for that reason. Major riots and conflicts across the causeway in Bahrain were drawing international media attention. People were dying, being arrested, and imprisoned as Shia rebels were demanding fair trials and the release of political prisoners. Bahrain was seventy-five percent Shia and ruled by the Sunni royal family, Al Khalifa.

There was a distinct quiet tension between the Shia and Sunni students attending the same university, who had the same professors and sat next to one another in their classes. Yet there were never any open hostilities or conflicts between the two religious sects on the female campus. Shia students, who were the minority in the student population, hung together. Sunni and Shia students distanced themselves from each other with the respectful acceptance that they ideologically occupied separate sides of the same fence. They easily kept things civil, peaceful and in their places. Despite the standoff I believed that the Sunni and Shia students did not really dislike each other; they were preoccupied with their classes, learning agendas and goals and separate friendships.

I developed the ability to distinguish the Shia from Sunni students. That was important for me to know as a professor and academic leader. No one could or would tell me how to do that, but I could instruct and manage the student populace better when I could discern their differences, ergo being more sensitive and aware of their needs, learning styles and habits. I could tell if students were Shia by their behavioral patterns and physical appearances. Shias tended to cloister unto themselves; they were plain clothed and faced, and unadorned, with no frills or makeup. They were typically shrouded in the 'black' from head to feet, whereas the Sunni young women were all over the place. They took the freedoms to dress in regular casual clothes while on the female campus and they must have spent small fortunes on their hair, eyes, and makeup. The Shia students expressed themselves in a low-key and guarded manner, often self-effacing. Being hundreds among thousands of Sunni students, they sought not to bring attention to themselves. Where Shia students were concerned, it was obvious to me that the dichotomy of having schisms while daily rubbing elbows with Sunni students in an enclosed university environment was a strain, especially with them being a minority. Given the restraints that that situation likely imposed on their behaviors and fullest self-expressions, I knew that there was a lot more to Wegdan; and the parts of herself that she did not make known were a cause for wonderment.

I regularly set aside time in my schedule to meet with the graduating female seniors in my office, and only when they were willing to have counsel with me. "What are your plans after graduation Wegdan?" I asked her. "I am going to do something to help my country." She would proudly say without hesitation. Clear as a bell. That was the sentiment of most of the graduating young Saudi women, Sunni, and Shia, which was not just about loyalty but a deep understanding, resonance, love, and faith in their country. The Kingdom was their mother and their father. I gleaned from my conversations with them that they felt halted and inconvenienced by the laws that stifled women's liberties; they were upset with it all, but they were not resigned to suffering. And then I knew that they knew that the future was in their hands.

A few months after she walked across the graduation stage, Wegdan came to my office to present me with a fancy abaya that she had tailor-made for me and totally without my knowledge. She also gave me an invitation to her upcoming July wedding. She reported that she was recently hired into a Human Resources job with a major bank. So much good news! But I was not surprised. In the spring of the following year she came to see me again, now a married woman to show me a picture of her new baby girl. It was clear to me that the *"great news"* of her childbirth was equally as important as her announcement in the same sentence that she was about to return to her job. She set few and specific goals for herself in her senior year and reached them all within that year! Earning her college degree with the high GPA was a factor in her overall achievements; marriage and motherhood were important and in keeping with family tradition; and sustaining a good job was Wegdan's emergent right as a woman. Now that she was out of academia, and beyond university walls, Wegdan was giving me a fuller view of herself. Yes, she was a 'doer' and as her name professed in my mind, she wanted it all and was doing it all; and the pride and rare determination on her face told that Wegdan was far from done. Now, armed to the teeth!

Wegdan was not the exception, there were so many others, and all too, with such winsome names. I could not count them all; there was Alkwother, Zara, Sukinah, Asma, Maryam, Farah, Nouf, Aisha, Alaa . . . the list went on. And whether they were Sunni or Shia, I continued to affirm with conviction that those women were bound to be noteworthy in whatever they were driven to do in the world.

37
Sultan

The university's residential compound kept on hand a team of laborers. They were mostly Pakistani and Indian men who migrated to the Kingdom leaving dirt-poor villages in their home countries. They came to KSA to obtain the only source of income they could to support their families back home. And the paltry remittances they received in the Kingdom was much more than they would have earned in Pakistan or India. They earned an average of 900 SAR (riyals) a month, with the Indian man who supervised them earning about 1100 SAR. One US dollar was the equivalent of 3.75 Saudi riyals. So, those men made about $240 with the supervisor earning about $293 dollars each month. The men were on call eight hours during the day and performed general duties such as mowing the lawns, repairs, plumbing, and systems maintenance and upkeep. Their duties were to keep life in the compound of ninety-six upscale villas comfortable for residents like myself. For the residences the men did everything such as fixing the TV cable, AC systems and door jams, repairing and replacing appliances, decorating, painting, hanging curtains, moving furniture and any related job in between. With just a call to the supervisor making a request, a resident would have one or two workers assigned to the villa to perform a service or solve a problem – if they could. Compound residents were advised not to pay the men anything, but tips were welcomed and readily accepted. The men were not generally on time or neat, but eventually, they came and made the best of the situation – as they were not actually skilled laborers. They were rather, the most available and more destitute laborers that the institution would employ on the cheap. They were the exploited underclass. One of the 'off-putting' practices of the Kingdom - a practice not unique to Saudi Arabia.

Within that scenario, I noticed Sultan, he stood out. I first met and spoke with Sultan when I moved into my villa. He hardly spoke English but made every effort to understand and be understood. His job was to do the garbage detail for all ninety-six villas in the compound. Trash had to be collected daily from receptacles outside each villa and discarded in the large refuse dumpster at the secured and guarded entrance of the compound. His job was to also keep the streets clear of any debris such as empty bottles, the mess left by children at play, scraps of paper, dead leaves, and anything else. Sultan did odd jobs such as washing residents' cars, and other clean-up work for needed money when he could fit those chores into his regular trash detail, and only once the streets were clean.

I would often look out my living room or upper bedroom windows and see Sultan at work on the road at neighboring villas. He wore the traditional dhoti tunic - and loose pants of the Indian and Pakistani men, but unlike the other male laborers, he was wearing a turban around his head that seemed to accentuate his personal dignity. Like his name, he had the air of a Sultan, which he might have been in some past life – perhaps incarnated now in this existence to balance the scales. I could see him fitting in a bygone era, holding court in some far-off citadel, being honored, revered, and obeyed, receiving kisses on his hand - beloved by his consort, flanked by dutiful viziers. He'd be riding high upon a mighty horse, crowned with a bejeweled turban, in command - issuing vaulted strategies around countries, conquests and men. Sultan pushed a little yellow refuse cart around the compound streets collecting the trash in a slow deliberate style. Sultan did not hurry, but he was not lazy. Working in the heat, he found his own pace that would keep him going from morning to night. Whenever Sultan saw me as I was carrying a trash bag from my villa towards the large dumpster, he would dart my way to relieve me of the bag no matter how far away from me he was at the time. Begging the trash bag from my hand, I understood when he said: "This is for me to do."

Standing 6'1" in a scrawny physique, looking about 40-45 years old, Sultan still exuded a 'quality', like that of an Islamic nobleman. No mustache or beard on his face, which bore rough-hewn facial features so scarred by want and toil that it was not easy to discern if his age was set by his years or the hard life he endured. I thought he might be much younger than he looked. What could have been a ruggedly handsome face was beset by endless hefty labor and perhaps the disrespect and abuse that came with it. He must have routinely worked twelve-hour days. I suspected that because I could observe him at work when I left my villa at the start of my day in the morning and when I returned home in the late afternoon, and with him sometimes still toiling into the twilight hours. Perhaps he was told to work longer, perhaps he wanted to, perhaps that was all he had to do. I did not know.

The Pakistanis and Indians were ranked at the bottom of the social scale in the Kingdom. They were relegated to perform the most menial tasks, with the lowest pay and to live in sub-standard housing conditions – assigned in large groups to tight living quarters – sleeping on very small beds. Sultan shared a room on the compound with six of his countrymen next to a makeshift temple where they went several times daily to pray. He would tell me at some point that he made 800 riyals a month, 500 of which he sent to Pakistan for his wife and children, whom he was happy and allowed to visit for one month out of the year – a trip home that was subsidized by the university.

Among all the laborers I saw and from those who came to my villa to service something, Sultan was a singular man. There was something about the way he went about his work that warranted attention – my attention. He seemed proud to work strong and thorough and performed his tasks with all that he had. The compound streets were just about squeaky clean on his patrol, with nothing tossed, no litter, not even a candy wrapper. If someone dropped something on the ground with him around, he was right behind to arrest and deposit the item into the yellow cart that was always at his side. He left no trash waiting in the containers outside each villa to be carried off. There was elegance in the way he guarded the compound streets against wayward trash, as if it were personally offensive to him to see anything other than spotless streets. And that he did when no one was even looking – or it seemed. I watched often when he was out there tending to the streets, turning his low-skilled job into art.

Because Sultan was working his garbage detail or washing a car outside whenever I left my villa early in the morning I often wondered if he did that on purpose because he had by then become familiar with my schedule. I could not help but to walk past him on my way out the door. When I would leave going to work he was there, nearby. As if he were waiting, Sultan stopped what he was doing and stood up straight from stooping over, with his shoulders folded back to present a pierced smile and greeting of, "Assalamualaikum mam", to which I would say, "Alaikum Salam." He did his morning greeting as if it were the most important thing he could do in that moment, looking at me head on, not averting or casting his eyes away as the others of his class of laborers trained themselves to do. And I regarded him back, speaking into his eyes, 'seeing' him. That might have been a meaningful instance in Sultan's day to have his humanity affirmed by someone else. After our greetings, I sensed him contemplating me as I continued my way down the road.

I engaged Sultan to clean two large rugs and observed from my window as he laid the heavily soiled rugs on the ground and got down on his hands and knees to scrub them with soapy water from a bucket. I had found the rugs in a compound dumpster, which were in fairly good shape but needed a good washing and I wanted them to cover the cool tiled floors inside. Whoever previously owned the Persian rugs must not have known that Sultan was around to transform them back to nearly new. The spendthrift residents of the compound threw away a lot of things that still had good use in them.

"Whatever amount you want to pay miss" was what he said when it came time to pay him for cleaning the rugs. When I paid him well and gave a tip, he accepted it straight on, with a: "Shukran mam", being fully present with the receiving. He was too proud to squabble over money. But he did knock on my door one evening to show me a hospital bill that he could not afford to pay – hoping to collect a donation. That was the one time I saw Sultan afraid, and I knew that coming to me that way was not easy for him to do. The money that Sultan needed to survive came in small doses and what he made for his hard work was never enough. I could see that Sultan suffered; and he knew that I knew that he was a man doing what he had to do. I felt that he wanted me to know and appreciate that about him and to 'see' him. Sultan's nobility showed through the haunted and tattered look of him. He became an exemplar for me of character and grace under fire.

The long Saudi summer had gone by, and I returned to the Kingdom after spending several weeks at home for a break in the US. Things changed in the summer – people and pieces of life shifted around and were not the same come fall. The days bore a different cast, especially the mornings. That time, I heard that Sultan had left the Kingdom when I asked about him. No one knew for sure where he had gone or wanted to say. Maybe he went back to Pakistan to be with his family or found better paying work elsewhere in the Kingdom. I hoped so. With him gone there was no one to share a genuine greeting in the morning, or to gently relieve me of the tiny burden of carrying a bag of trash. It was not about the trash – but a blessing from one human to another. Sultan brought something to my days that I missed. Now there was one less sincere smile and human spark, one less male voice, one less friendly rescue for my sometimes 'damsel in distress' feminine self by male strength and wherewithal for the simple repairs and odd jobs; there was one less reminder of the divinity a person could radiate despite the anguish and exertions in life. Sultan was abruptly, and too soon, gone away; and so were his countrymen who worked and were a part of that compound life who followed his exit soon after – Wassim, Hamza, Renji, Abu, Shaikh. They were all gone now, leaving some who stayed behind to wonder why.

38
The Filipinos

In the Kingdom, I observed that class distinguished peoples in the social strata, more than race; that was so, even though Saudi Arabia was a melting pot for the races of the world. Saudi was clearly an Arab country; however, Arabs were more identified as an ethnicity and culture, united by a common history. It was a well-known fact and unmistakably obvious that a class system was in place in KSA. At the top of the social scale were the Saudi nationals and western ex-pats - those people who possessed the coveted blue passports from the US or the burgundy ones from the UK and other parts of Europe; ex-pats from other Middle Eastern countries were in the mix as well; all came for lucrative work in KSA. Ex-pats like me, were paid modest to high professional salaries and given generous benefit packages. As a perk, we were provided with fully furnished and in many cases luxury apartments and villas, complete with flat-screen televisions, kitchenware, and linens. The Kingdom, as a so-called 'developing' country had become reliant on foreign workers from the top of the social scale to the lower ones.

Slavery was abolished in the Kingdom in 1962 by the decree of King Faisal. Forty years hence, a permanent underclass consisting predominantly of migrant workers evolved and would be indispensable to the economy in the Kingdom for years to come. The migrants were largely from Africa, Asia, and Middle Eastern and poor countries. The unemployed, underemployed, and impoverished peoples streamed into the Kingdom from humble housing, mud-brick shacks, and hovels in dense communities in their home countries where finding work was difficult, if not impossible. Those peoples performed a variety of menial blue-collar jobs, often working long hours at the lowest wages. They were single or married men and women with families and children to support, taking the only opportunities they saw available to them to earn a living.

The foundation had been laid for the modern-day Kingdom, by which professional, migrant, and blue-collar worker positions and statuses were clearly demarcated. Saudis and ex-pats held the white-collar jobs, such as company executives, business leaders and managers, educators, engineers, bankers, etc. Ex-pats made up the bulk of the professional positions, especially, in the field of education, making up approximately ninety-five percent of teachers at the college level. By contrast, the permanent underclass that came to be in 1962 remained in place doing non-professional work. Migrants held jobs that greased and kept the wheels turning in most business organizations and establishments, and in Saudi homes. Those were the jobs that Saudis did not want and that ex-pats were not meant to perform nor came to Saudi Arabia to do – a similar scenario to what had been happening in the US with Mexican laborers. Most of the migrants in KSA were Pakistanis, Sudanese, Indians, Bangladeshi, and Filipinos and composed approximately forty percent of the overall labor force in Saudi. They were cleaners, maintenance and repair staff, delivery workers and drivers, garbage collectors, bakers, construction workers, day laborers, housekeepers, chefs, etc. Filipino women held most of the jobs as nurses and as domestic servants within the Saudi household. Filipino men and women almost exclusively made up the office support apparatuses – the grey area between white and blue-collar jobs - in clerical, administrative assistant, and secretarial jobs, and as junior functionaries in Human Resources and IT. Their salaries were approximately $1/20^{th}$ of the average salary paid to ex-pats and Saudis holding professional jobs, and they were not awarded the same standard of health insurance as others – which was third-rate with minimal sick day allowances. They held down the offices; however, they hardly ever rose higher from those positions, which they kept for many, many years. Although they were socially classed at the lower rung of the scale, I came to realize what a powerful force and group of people the Filipinos were; and how they were so underestimated.

Crossing the social status line was 'taboo', and one did not know just how much against the grain it was until they crossed that line. The Filipinos knew that – most people knew that. People generally stayed in their places. Saudi or western men who did marry Filipino women were shunned and looked down upon by their colleagues. I took great interest in the Filipino culture. They made an impression on me, and I learned a lot from them. In fact, the Filipinos were some of my favorite people in the Kingdom and a central part of my life. A Filipino woman was the first person to greet and give me the 'tour' on the day I began my work assignment in KSA, and she was to be my assistant. That was Jane, whom I thought was about thirty, but later learned that she was much older - in solid physical shape. Our professional relationship was easy with a lot of casual highlights. On many days, we tickled each other into such laughter that we could be heard through the walls and all the way down the hall. She'd request that I bring her souvenir key chains from my travels which she said gave her a taste of the world. Jane was a cheerful spark of life and considerable help to me, and I was her muse.

The Filipino men did not as a rule work as drivers for Saudi and ex-pat women; that was done mostly by the Pakistani and Indian men. Driving was one of few non-professional jobs that the Filipinos did not dominate. While Filipino men held the office and administrative positions the Filipino woman who was a domestic servant often functioned as a nanny, cook and maid. She was usually in her thirties, forties, or fifties and sometimes older, whose job was to provide multifaceted services in almost every aspect of life for families, which were typically Saudi. In every Saudi home I visited, there was a domestic servant, and even with the families I saw in public, shopping, or riding in cars. They traveled and went places with families - tagging along behind or in close proximity. I believed that the 'all-around', 'ever-present' domestic servant possibly played the most crucial role in Saudi society – facilitating family life, so to speak – the heartbeat of any nation.

The domestic servant attended to the major daily household chores, and additionally, some accompanied young Saudi female students to universities and tended to their needs. At university, there was a special section reserved in the corridors for the domestics in their roles as 'nannies' to stand by and wait for their wards to finish their classes and see them home. One of my faculty members reported to me that during an exam, a female student requested to text and ask her 'nanny' who was waiting in the halls, to bring her a cup of coffee to the classroom. That frivolous request was denied outright. The point was that there was no limit to what the domestic servant could be expected to do. What could be a luxury in western cultures was a 'given' in Saudi family life. Domestic servants came cheap and were an affordable 'necessity' for the average Saudi household with children, who were their 'sponsors'. Some domestic servants lived in separate quarters within the sponsor's home. She was expected to be nimble, handy, and available on-demand.

The female Filipino domestic was an appendage to the mother – serving as a spare set of arms and hands – preparing meals, setting the table, cleaning, being nursemaid to the sick, and tending to small children with the mother often nearby, watching and supervising. They were more or less, a fixture in the lives of the women of the household - the unerringly dedicated caretakers emulating 'mother love' on behalf of too busy, overwhelmed, or privileged parents. From my windows I could glimpse a domestic in the early mornings taking young children off to school or packing them onto the school bus, and then seeing the children back home later in the day, when she would certainly then prepare the evening meal for the family and may play with the children. She answered the door, she did repairs around the house and troubleshooting, and was the 'aunt' - at times providing an ear to listen. The domestic might have her own family but spent most of her time looking after the Saudi family who utterly depended on her. Some domestics were proud to say that they had been working for, or better still, *"taking care of"* their family sponsors for decades. I'd met several. On the dark side, it was well known that the domestic would discreetly service the sexual appetites of males in the household – usually not her choice. A few years back, a Filipino maid was executed for killing her Saudi male sponsor for *"Gross abuse and rape."* She was decapitated with the long sword in the public square in Riyadh on a bright January morning.

Just as family and tribal loyalties were a priority for Saudis, the Filipinos were bound to their own families; it was the primary reason that many of them came to the Kingdom to work, and which kept them there - to earn money to support children and families in the Philippines. Some had relatives in the Kingdom, and most did not. My secretary Jane was sending money to her kin in the Philippines. Central to their values was 'sacrifice'. Back home in the Philippines among their families and countrymen, the men and women who traveled abroad to work were called 'heroes' because they were not only supporting their families, but also their country's economy through their selflessness; keeping their families afloat, consequentially kept villages and communities thriving, hence, the entire country.

In their lives within the Kingdom, the Filipinos' sense of community was powerful and enabled them to withstand and make the most of their crowded, sub-standard living conditions. Most were housed in small domiciles or units called 'clinics' – five to ten at a time and slept on beds not much larger than cots. The women's units were on the university compounds amid apartments and villas occupied by the teachers, professors, and administrators, while Filipino men were mostly housed in low-income districts, with some in Saudi ghettos. In the women's units there was a common kitchen, bathroom and living area; having no TV the women streamed movies, music, and a variety of entertainment on their laptops. My secretary, Jane shared a small bedroom with two to three other women. Other housing accommodations were 'fair to middling' and all housing for the Filipinos was never permanent. Jane often told me how they disliked being moved around whenever the university institution needed added space. *"I feel like a nomad"*, Jane would lament; but she and the women became accustomed to that reality. I often wondered if they looked forward to going home to rest and relax as I did at the end of the workday. The office spaces they occupied during work hours were far roomier and more private than the living units they went to after working. And to my question, I found that they did look forward to going 'home' – for there, they had each other. I saw them in the mornings on the transport bus with their damp freshly washed hair and sleek bodies dressed in shiny black abayas. Their phones were constant companions, stuck to their hands it seemed, with them clicking pictures of themselves and each other, talking, and endlessly texting, and once in a while singing into their phones – sending a song for someone back home. If they were not chatting or working their phones, some were catching a little more sleep on the bus ride before the start of work; and then, after work at the end of the bus ride home they'd pile out of the transport bus retreating as a 'group entity' into their small living spaces.

With the money remaining in their purses after sending half or more of their monthly earnings to their families or kin they lived frugally on carefully managed budgets. The women pooled their money for food shopping and cooked and ate in a communal setting. In summer months I often observed them gathered and eating together outside their domiciles, as it was cramped and hot inside with no air conditioning. The Filipinos were cliquish; some of that was by virtue of their low status and cultural bonds. However, it was also their Christian beliefs in a Muslim country that by happenstance, pushed them together and made them a cohesive group. But that did not keep them from assembling by the hundreds to pray for the Kingdom at times. Unlike other migrants, Filipinos were largely Roman Catholic, and low-key about it. They created their own cultural world within a world, with festivities, fashion shows, cookouts, and matchmaking, etc. When squabbles and conflicts arose, there was usually a person within the close-knit group to step forward to help fix things and keep the peace. Holding together and maintaining a unified front in the midst of their hardships and low status was carefully guarded. The stories of self-sacrifice they shared and that I witnessed punched into my heart.

The resourcefulness of the Filipino community of men and women was no joke. For many office workers, they tactfully went about their regular contracted work, and on off-hours pursued other avenues to supplement their meager wages. Doing 'moonlight' work to boost their incomes was not permitted for the Filipinos - so they asked those clients on the receiving end of their extracurricular services to, *"Kindly keep this on the quiet."* Of course, that was the easiest thing that clients such as I could do to support them - we even referred customers to them. They trusted us with that. It was our secret pact; and as far as I knew with all of the things they were doing under the table, none of the women ever got caught. That was the case as it was a foregone conclusion that the university's 'no permission' policy that forbade Filipinos from having 'side hustles' was no more than a 'pretend policy'. Everybody and their mama knew that despite the gratuitous housing, that the low wages they took for the essential work they did made it damned near impossible to sustain a living as an individual, let alone a family, and especially with a majority sending most of their earnings to folks back home – whatever the case might be.

The black market was predominantly run by Filipinos who could get goods that were not found or allowed in the Kingdom, and a lot more. The more intrepid black marketeers procured and sold alcohol to a ready clientele of ex-pats and Saudis who could and would pay the high cost for the risk to smuggle the 'goods' into the Kingdom – more than ten times the normal US price for a bottle of vodka or whiskey. My secretary, Jane baked on the side and prepared Filipino dishes for people who had the taste for it. She made the yummiest, moist, and tart lemon cakes, at my request, many times. The Filipino woman who relaxed my body with weekly massages came to me in the early evening following her full-time day of work. Other women regularly cleaned the apartments and villas of ex-pats and cooked for bachelors who could not. Some provided technical services - helping with computers, software, and mobile phones for pennies on the dollar. Filipino men hired out their services to conduct mock research, do homework and ghost-writing assignments for university students.

Once every year each Filipino man and woman took a month-long paid vacation to go home to their families. The Filipinos' passports were generally retained by the university institution and given to them when it was time for them to take their leaves going home. The institution would collect and retain their passports when they returned. That practice was not done for ex-pats who kept possession of their passports. When things went wrong or mistakes were made, the finger was more often than not, pointed at the Filipino; they were easy targets for blame by those who lorded over them. They were vulnerable in untenable circumstances, but discreet about how they were treated, and dared to complain or speak up for fear of making their situations worse or losing their jobs. I asked my masseuse what she thought about the people who routinely scapegoated and mistreated her countrymen and women, to which she said, smiling thinly: "They have small minds, Doctor."

The Filipinos lived and worked with the full knowledge of their low status in the Kingdom. They knew that they were an economic convenience, but expendable, even though their functions were essential and fixed within the Saudi lifestyle, both in the workplace and in the home. What struck me most about the Filipinos was the resilience, resourcefulness, indomitable spirit of community, and selflessness that they displayed given their financial privations and third-class treatment, such that I had rarely witnessed among any culture of people. The Filipinos' advantage and part of their strength was that they possessed a shrewd knowledge and understanding of how the system worked, and they knew how to work it, i.e. the university and Saudi. They knew the causes and the effects – the pitfalls, the gaps, and apertures, and how to navigate those. They knew how to recognize, even anticipate, and avert traps and to scout out openings. They were the real survivors, with many having outlasted most of the ex-pats that came and went; and barring Kingdom regulatory changes, they would be there longer still. What was not known was that the Filipinos knew a lot more than people thought they knew. They were the information keepers and had the 'poker face' down pat, even added a smile and a wink to it. They'd been through a lot which constantly reminded them of their lesser status. On the surface they may seem to have become null and went along; but they never accepted that, and revealed nothing of what they really felt, at least not to those not of their race and class. A wise and good rule of thumb was that you *"Do not fuck with the Filipinos"*, for they had a certain collective passive aggressive indignation that could bring your house down.

Thursday was the start of the weekend, and it was also a special time for the Filipino women - it was shopping night! It was the one time when the women gussied themselves up and took to the night air. In early evening the younger women and the older ones emerged from their domiciles wearing lipstick, blush, and eye shadow. It was a stark contrast to their unadorned work faces of earlier in the day. Some to me, were hardly recognizable. All dolled up, they piled onto the transport buses that made evening shopping runs to the major malls, or they slid into drivers' cars and went off into the 'nighttime' to popular Filipino markets and hang-out areas. And they hardly ever faulted on returning home within the curfew set for them around 10:00 pm. Where they went at nightfall on the 'shopping' furloughs was a mystery to me, and even those close to me would not tell a word; they would just give a vague smile as if to say: *'That is not for you to know'*. Maybe, it was to rendezvous with secret boyfriends for there were plenty available men around. I found the Filipino women's Thursday evening escapades intriguing and was pleased that they had that outlet for fun and pleasure and left the women to their business.

Mothering was a natural part of the Filipino women's community, which was extended to outsiders when they felt like it. They'd experienced and seen it all and little surprised them. I observed that from being more exposed to and able to know the women. Feeding and seeing other people eat their food may have been one of their favorite pastimes. Whenever I walked near their periodic cookouts on the compound, they would predictably invite me over; if I politely declined, they'd strongly insist that I come sit and eat with them. With my belly satisfied, they'd ask if there was any special Filipino dish that they could make for me – some Filipino spaghetti, pancit noodles, savory chicken or lumpia. The women were mothers to any child that was born within their group. A baby came into the world, and they would swirl around the child and mother, fussing, cooing, and making baby faces – taking on the care of the newborn to give 'mother' a rest. The women, like Jane carried their ages well. One woman who kept to herself, smiling privately much of the time, told me that she had ten children under the care of her own mother back home, and to whom she was sending money each month. I thought she was joking, and her friend sitting next to her said, *"It's true."* There was the perky young mother who regularly cleaned my office and was glad to see me when she came; she took every opportunity to talk about her little son in the Philippines that she was desperately missing. She had been on her job in the Kingdom since he was one, now his seventh birthday was coming up. When she asked me for advice on whether to stay and work or go home to him, I supported her in making up her mind to let the job go and return to her son. That was something she wanted to do all along, she just needed a nudge of encouragement. It was a scary move for her to consider – leaving a secure job. But she got clear, because she was no longer coming to clean my office a few months later.

Then there was Juliet, who was my first masseuse, not a mother, but a symbolic 'mom' among the women. Juliet's day job was maintenance. In her fifties, she was an elder among the Filipino women and their lively center. With so much energy to spare she gave massages on the side, and to put some more money into her purse. I called her the *punisher*. Juliet would get me down on the floor and work her powerful hands into my body, turning me into a piece of putty – it hurt, but I knew I needed it and took it. On the comforter on the floor, she could better deliver the pounding and the pain! As she gave hard therapeutic treatment to my stubbornly taut and stressed muscles, I got to know her. She asked me to help her find her a husband, and that was not in jest. I told her I would try and believed that I could; she had big plans for the 'lucky guy'. However, Juliet's jubilant and fearless personality changed in a matter of weeks, as if overnight, following a sudden stroke. Thereafter, seeing her in the university halls was a sorrowful sight - her body movements were small and limited, her once strong right arm was now limp; she seldom spoke to me or anyone else with her lips, but with her eyes - eking out a smile when we said "*Hello*" to her. She became silent and distant and could be seen peering at everything and everyone from a corner or leaning against the wall off to the side in the bustling campus hallways. Juliet continued to work in less physically demanding maintenance functions - dusting and mopping floors. Each day, the Filipino women reserved a seat for her on the bus close to the exit door so that she could get on and off easily; and she was still sending half of her earnings back home to family.

There was so much more that could be said and told, for there was always a lot going on within the Filipino community. But I thought to stop here. The stalwart spirit that the Filipino women and men applied towards their own cause blessed the Kingdom. One hand scratched the other's back and vice versa; such was the way in the Kingdom of Saudi Arabia – with each one who was willing and able, making his and her own best way. Last I learned, due to continuing economic reverberations in the Kingdom, a majority of the Filipino women and men working there were being repatriated back to the Philippines because their work contracts in Saudi were not being renewed. In Jane's case, with no clear path for a job in her home country, she ended a twelve-year tenure in KSA. And I send her a text now and then.

39
The Sad Prophets

To proselytize was not a Muslim folkway. Perhaps that was why the store merchant would not accept my compliment on his 'goodness' when he told me that he kept his prices low to keep his customers happy and many. When he said that I naturally responded with: "You are a good man", to which he retorted, "No! I am not a good man!" Not really getting his point and thinking that he was being pious and polite, I said it again, to which he repeated in earnest: "No, I am not a good man" – looking me steely in the eyes. Perhaps I was being presumptuous and exalting him beyond his level of comfort and reason. Extending such words to another was not uncommon in the Arab culture, and I had a sense about him and said what I said to add strength and volume to my appreciation for his thoughtfulness when making my purchase.

I understood and respected that there was only one Prophet in Islam: Muhammad. And there have forever been people who came forth with things on their minds that they were compelled to share. Sometimes their words were useful, sometimes not; and sometimes their words were heard and heeded, and sometimes not. I thought that the latter was why I called the two gentlemen I met on that day in Bahrain the 'sad prophets'. They were Muslim men, not trying to bring me into their religious faith, nor claiming to speak for God; but, on the chance that someone would 'listen', they could not refrain from blurting out a set of beliefs and principles fit for our times.

While in Bahrain, shopping with my son, Julian-Sebastian, who was visiting me from Europe, we entered the merchant's store to look at Turkish lamps. I had grown to really like and prefer the Turkish lighting apparatuses and the pleasing glows they emitted. Those lamps proliferated in the old souk in many shops which lined the narrow streets, presenting me with a lot of choices; but I was on a deep search for one with crimson red tones. His was the fifth shop in my quest, and I was getting tired of all the walking around in the heat. That would be our last stop, I confirmed to myself. He asked, and I told him what I was looking for. I observed the big man as he poked around on shelves behind the counter, and eventually stepped onto a scant ladder also behind the counter - going up into an attic through a very small opening in the ceiling, disappearing for a while. The shop was quite small, with barely enough room to hold three to five customers at a time - who had to walk single file down the slim aisles – which no less, were packed with collectibles, trinkets, scarves, incense and burners, Turkish lamps, statuettes. He returned, stepping carefully back down the ladder with several lamps for me to inspect. He flipped off all the lights in the shop to make sure that the glow from each one he sampled would be luminous and perhaps to my liking. I easily chose the one with the mellow crimson glimmer. It was perfect, exactly what I had in mind. I asked him the price and was even more pleased that his cost was well below that of the other merchants' stores I'd gone to. He said he just wanted a happy customer. *"You are a good man."* Again, thinking that by saying so, it would cap off my satisfaction with the purchase. *"No! I am not a good man!"*

His name was Islam, ironically. He was tall in his long spotless white tunic – a bald, chocolate brown Sudanese man, clean shaven with angular facial features. He wrapped the purchased lamp in newspapers with giant hands, and there was no smile as he continued to retort the denial of his 'goodness'. "Why do you say that?" I asked him. He said: "I am not a good man, and we are not good people. We are not good for this world. We are the bad people who cannot do the right things and destroying things in the world." The words began to pour from Islam's mouth, and it seemed, from his depths. And He said more. "We have men who should lead us. But they are the biggest destroyers. When they should speak to a man to have him go the right way, they shoot him instead. And Allah sees this. We cannot hide from the gaze of Allah. We have not done anything to help this world. But we take and destroy. We take and destroy. We don't care about things or each other, the animals, the water, the land. We think about and do the wrong things. We are all bad." The world that Islam saw was a heavy weight on his weary eyes.

"Thank you for sharing this with me Islam." I said. "No, do not thank me. Just share the message with others. To let them see." Islam commanded, looking at me defiantly.

Islam told us that Prince Charles and his wife, Camilla visited his shop a year ago. He proudly produced photos of their visit showing the couple posing in the cramped aisles of his shop. When Camilla asked him to join them in a photo, he chose not to be in a picture with them. He did not explain to my son and me why he declined their invitation. And we did not ask. I found Islam

The Sad Prophets

intriguing and hoped and planned to visit him again. I felt his eyes on us, care-filled and in sorrow, as we left his shop.

On the taxi ride back to our hotel we met Mahmoud, our driver, and the very next man we encountered after leaving Islam's shop. I do not recall how the conversation got started but he echoed the words of Islam. *Was that our day for prophets or did my son and I just tap in an alternate reality – as in the Twilight Zone?* I had taken countless taxis in the Middle East, and those were unusual coincidences. I wondered about that. Mahmoud was Saudi, an energized man with matured good looks, and alert with questions: "Where are you from? Where do you work?" He wanted to know if we were married and had children; what we thought of the Middle East, etc. We could not answer his questions fast enough and then he broke out with his 'inspired words'. He proclaimed as if talking to himself: "We are too lost now with the technology. It is not that the technology is bad; it is how we use it. And it is taking us to the wrong places. We are lost to our traditions. There was a time when a plate given to a neighbor filled with food would be returned with food on the plate. Now the plate never comes back. What do you do madam?" I responded: "I am a professor at the university." Mahmoud then says: "Well, I tell my young people to respect your teachers, for they would have been a prophet."

I made the trip to Bahrain across the lengthy causeway as a getaway to relax and have release from my routine in the Kingdom, and to spend quality recreational time with my son. I did not expect to be met with or rather, showered with such benign wisdom. It was not asked for, but certainly a takeaway from our day trip. I took the men's words into me. *Did those words come more easily and freely because they came from a distance across the bay?* That was something else for me to ponder. Back home in my villa in the Kingdom, I remembered Islam and Mahmoud. The crimson red Turkish lamp worked out nicely, now emitting an intimate glow from the corner where I placed it – a true 'Turkish delight' – tempting my thoughts back to both men and what they had to say. And I wondered about Islam, and Mahmoud - the sad prophets, who looked at the world with downcast eyes. They spoke a truth that went unheeded in a modern age. They saw peace and righteousness in slowing down – looking and going back and making our way as we did in the past with our hands and our own heads – doing the right things. True, technology made us capable but not smart; it connected us but did not bring us together. I could easily see what Islam and Mahmoud saw and what made them sad.

Handy technological miracles had people so caught up in 'capturing' that they forfeited the moment to 'feel' and 'be' in their experiences. Yes, the young adults all over the world were technologically savvy – ever so preoccupied on their devices while they lacked basic life skills. The grip of technology was universally extensive and seductive. I'd seen entire families sitting side-by-side – with mother, father and children dug into their cell phones – more focused on that device than each another. With me, my entire day was thrown off when the internet was down. My computer and cell phones were indispensable and legitimate lifelines in Saudi that I simply could and would not do without - yes, I owned two phones for good measure. The Kingdom's highly complex and controlled networks and communications systems bolstered my wherewithal on the management of my personal technological devices, to keep those up-to-date, stable, and reliable in order to stay connected and to maintain access to information and entertainment. And I was certain that that was the same for countless others, Saudis, ex-pats, and foreigners, alike. True, wisdom and 'real love' took a back seat to speed, fluff, consuming and fear. True again, the world was mean, and corruption had risen to the highest ranks in government, politics, business, and religion. Absolutely - the planet was plundered, with plastic filling the oceans, lining the streets, and floating through the air. Social rights riots and protests were at new heights and reach. There was always more bad news than good. And with regard to how the world would keep turning with change, technology and apathy steering us, indeed, that train had left the station a long time ago.

The proliferation of hard and software technologies was needed to help us keep up with ourselves. But really?! Because it was sketchy to try to discern what was leading who between the technology and us, and who or what was setting that pace. It was just the nature of our racy 'pop culture' times. And we were all in with both our hands and feet. In our man-made 'Edens' wisdom was not esteemed as a useful 'tool'; it did not come at a cost in a world where things must have a price. People were more inclined to reach for the tangible and put money that could be spent towards a good meal or an upgrade to their latest device - something they could handle in their hands - that made their lives work. After all, the adult toys that we created performed so many useful tasks and were utterly meant to serve and take care of us, and they made us happy. So, who was listening to the modern-day warnings of the sad prophets - who were prophetically correct in what they perceived and spoke of – that we, as humanity, may not be evolving as we should? Who was listening to those men over forty and younger than sixty, driving a taxi and running a tiny storefront shop - those stoic melancholics, who were speaking into the rushing wind?

Incidentally, days before my son and I made the weekend trip to Bahrain my next-door neighbor rang my doorbell and presented us with a large platter of food. It was an assortment of savory Egyptian dishes prepared by Magda, his sister. The food was delicious, eaten quickly, and much appreciated. So, after returning from Bahrain, and remembering Mahmoud, I decided to heed the 'rightness' of his words about receiving a plate of food. I hoped that in some way in the subtle energetic sphere that my doing so might lessen his sadness, and that his words would have some impact and 'stay' in the world. Simply put, I was giving life to and spreading the energy of his 'wise words'. I filled the empty platter with fresh fruits and eagerly returned it to Magda and her brother. Could not wait to do it! In fact, it was something that I had thought to do anyway from an earlier time and was now more inspired! Magda's brother, Mohammad called me later to say: "Thank you, BUT you do not have to do this for us. We make food for you. We do this for you because you are alone. Please, when food comes from us, do not feel that you have to return the plate with food. This is not necessary." What would Mahmoud have said to Mohammad in that situation? I was sure that some wisdom would apply to that.

Were the sad prophets also wise? I guessed so. It was prudent not to mistake prophecy for wisdom, which were two different things. Prophecy foretold the future, whereas wisdom attempted to shed light on a matter; one mirrored the other. In Mohammad's case, maybe some old wisdom traditions had morphed into fresh ones. For sure, it was long held that in the act of giving one did not seek nor accept anything in return; and now: Those who had more 'should', not 'could', give to those who had less; and that there were good people who gave and good people who received. I listened. And yet, something more was there to note about the two men. Given the state of the world, some 'one' had to hold the space to bear witness and keep us all on alert of where we were falling short, which granted us a rejoinder of what was possible, better. We needed that – a need that was the one 'win' that those sad prophets could reap. What Islam had to say was profound. In his mind's eye he was not a good man to be a member of the human race as it stood today. There was plenty of time. And I still believed that Islam was a good man.

40
"Say, Bismillah!"

I witnessed in rapt fascination as the male Saudi clerk behind the counter said just under his breath, *"Bismillah"* and began to pour the golden oud from a sizable decanter into the tiny round opening of a one-inch, half-ounce bottle, determined not to spill a drop. That distinctive oud fragrance was preciously pricey. And he did not waste any of it – looking pleased in smug satisfaction as he closed and wrapped the little bottle and sanguinely presented it to me. That mild formality did not strike me as much as it did when I saw it performed again, weeks later as a Pakistani serviceman was about to take on the repair of my broken refrigerator. Before proceeding, he also uttered, ever so quietly: *"Bismillah."* That time I asked him, "What does that mean, and why did you say it before starting to fix my refrigerator?" It was a small question to a big answer.

In later months, the word, and the ritual of 'Bismillah' became more intriguing and personal to me. I knew that most medical and oral procedures required needles. Indeed, it was a universal practice and something to expect at most visits to the doctor or medical specialists. But I detested needles and had for as long as it was possible to remember. With age, I grew more brave when encountering a needle that sought me out, realizing that it was a necessary aid to my health and wellbeing – a slight shift in perspective. But I still winced a lot when a needle came near my arms and wrists. I have small veins which I supposed also didn't like needles, because they hid and were hard for the nurses and practitioners to locate - requiring several pricks and poking around, and making receiving the needle, whether to draw blood or for other medical procedures quite messy and grueling – even tortuous for me. That happened all the time, and I was always too glad to get the 'smiley face' sticker from the attendant when the ordeal was over.

On the day, I went into the medical clinic for my regular colonoscopy. I liked the Muslim internist and felt confident in the upcoming procedure. I had conducted prior research on him, as I would do any doctor – in Saudi or the US. It was chilly in the surgery room, and the blanket provided by the nurse felt good on me lying prone on the slender operating table. Yet, I was not quite ready for the necessary elongated, sharp, shiny, stainless steel anesthesia needle; seeing my angst, the male anesthesiologist came to my side and whispered into my ear: "Say Bismillah." And: "After this, tell us if this was done better here than in the US." He then proceeded to prepare the 'giant' needle and IV for my wrist. I said "Bismillah." It took just one stick, the vein was there, and I was out like a light. I woke up long after the procedure was done, and all was well in the world.

'Bismillah' was not just a beautiful one-word prayer that felt nice to hear and say, it was supernatural – it had power, it was potent, and covered a lot of ground. Following my observed and personal experiences I adopted the word into my way of life - saying Bismillah became a constant practice for me. The word was 'free', I did not have to be a Muslim to make it my own, for the anesthesiologist proved that point. The word, when voiced with a *'genuine'* intention and state of mind was the threshold one crossed to be in league with the Divine; and its connotations were broad. I would say *"Bismillah"* to drum up my confidence, strength, or some unseen force of aid to meet a task or a situation that I knew would be arduous, unpleasant, or testing. It could have been something I did not look forward to or did not wish to undertake. Bismillah was a declaration – it was gratitude for a wish to be granted – a favor to come. That was where much of its power lied, in the gratitude expressed before the receiving. When I said *"Bismillah"* I did so with the foregone conclusion that the task or situation before me was not bigger than me, nor would it overcome me; and if it was daunting to get through and mistakes were made, I would survive that intact; and I didn't think that the results I got were imagined. Saying 'Bismillah' was a shield, a helping hand, sometimes, a magic wand. I would say *"Bismillah"* when rising in the morning to face a hectic day, before going into a meeting, when boarding a plane, or when about to grade a mass of papers. I said it sometimes when sitting down at my computer to dive into the tasks for the day and before checking the mail. Saying and owning it made me more aware of its prevalence throughout the culture.

In the Arabic culture, saying 'Bismillah' was the incipient act to receive a blessing. It literally meant: *"In the name of God"* or *"Allah"*, and it conjured the hand of God – whose presence was accessed anywhere, anytime, and in the heart of any person. The Saudi culture was replete with situations where the heavenly word was spoken. The faithful said it before taking a bite at dinner, before starting a car, sitting down to write a letter, or pouring oud into bottles. Saying 'Bismillah' was a requirement in the prep of 'halal' foods - the foods that were permissible to eat in Islam such as goat, beef, and chicken. The 'Bismillah' intonation was institutionalized in the wholesale slaughter industry. The animals had to be killed in a proper and respectful way. Prior to the slaughter the person overseeing the operations and machines must invoke the name of Allah upon the animal by reciting *"Bismillah, Allah Akbar"* or at the very least, to say *"Bismillah."* That was done in acknowledgement, expectation, and thanks of animal life which sustained human life, and with a 'quality' of nourishment. A Bismillah was held for a child's initiation into Islam. The iconic airline for the Kingdom, Saudia Airlines did not take off before evoking a 'Bismillah' prayer through videos and over the loudspeaker on each flight for all passengers and attendants to hear and know. I observed bus drivers whispering *"Bismillah"* before starting their driving routes. Beginning an ardent task upon the recital of the word Bismillah was believed not only to bring a blessing but also protection. Like the Lord's Prayer or crossing oneself in the Christian faith, 'Bismillah' was a summons for Divine attendance and intervention where it was sincerely needed. And according to the Islamic texts: *"Satan could find nowhere to spend the night and no dinner if a person had mentioned the name of God in the form of the 'Bismillah' before entering his own house."*

It was universally recognized that words indeed had energy and carried a force - certain words more than others. Bismillah was one such word. So, when the anesthesiologist told me to say it – as if he knew intuitively that I would understand, it was an easy thing to do, with no questions or hesitation. I knew within my right self that the utterance was good for me and highly favored. The 'saying of the word' eased the fear and anxiety I felt and revealed its truth when the first needle prick struck my vein. The Saudi ritual rich culture did not cease to raise my eyebrows, and to amaze and delight me. The taut reverence for the sacred - the layered undergirding of spirituality and mystical rivers upon which life flowed was ever present in the desert on the far side of the world. And yes, the surgery procedure and subsequent ones in Saudi went as well as they could and did in the US. But that was another story.

41
The Jinn

With my feet firmly on the ground now in KSA, I sensed that there was a strong mystical undercurrent in Saudi Muslim culture. Most religions of the world had some basis in mysticism, or were spawned from it, that much I knew. I was learning some things and wanted to know more yet found it a stretch to access information, either by asking Saudi folks about mysticism or researching its precepts within the predominant culture. That did not stop me due to my bent towards the unspoken, unseen, untouched, and unheard – the elusive subjective aspects of life; I left that door wide open for any information and insights to come to me on the subject, and it did.

A recently graduated student came to my office one day and presented me with an unusual gift. It was a clear glass vase adorned with white flowers and containing salt. She told me that it was an item of protection in her culture and should be placed in an area of my home where I spent much of my time. She explained that it was always best to keep my strong wishes and plans close to me; and that there were always negative energies around that could interrupt and prevent a person from getting what they hoped for and really wanted. The totem from the young woman to me was meant to ward off bad spirits and other people's envy and interfering thoughts. Her visit, words, and gift, were fitting and no doubt, piqued my intent and need to dive deeper into Arabic mysticism, particularly in the Muslim faith. I approached my good friend, Haifa, and told her about the gift of the glass vase from the young lady and all that she said while giving it, which may have made it easier, maybe compelling for Haifa to tell me something more about Muslim mystical beliefs as they related to the gift I received. She told me about the jinn. She had no hesitance to tell me all that she knew from her understanding about the mystical aspects in the faith regarding the jinn and she strongly suggested that I consult the Qur'an and other Muslim texts for more factual information. I did that.

Here is what I learned. The jinn had held a significant space and foothold in Arabic culture for almost as long as the culture itself. They were alternate disembodied entities taken very seriously in the culture and were substantially referenced in the Qur'an. One was not a true Muslim if they did not have a belief and faith in the existence of the jinn; and that was saying a lot for the second largest religion in the world. The jinn were spirits that dwelled in a parallel realm next to our own as humans, who could flit back and forth between their realm and ours to influence the human experience. They had long been a source of inspiration and fear, having a shadowy duality, and whatever triggered them was a mystery. The jinn could help or harm and could also possess people; they could be pious and unconcerned with humans; and they could really screw things up for people and took delight in punishing humans for any injury done to them, whether it was intentional or not; for they were not entirely friendly, and their motivations fluctuated. Muslims believed that the jinn had an eerie advantage in the world and could even control the elements. The jinn who they saw as having cured diseases and mental illness and who inspired poets, soothsayers and pre-Islamic philosophers had also been known to ruin relations between couples.

The jinn could be anywhere; we did not see them, but the jinn saw us. Islamic folklore held that desert travelers, nomads and settlers sought refuge in seemingly uninhabited spaces which were controlled by jinn; and if they wished to stay in that place, they needed the permission of the jinn – if not, the jinn would send trouble to them. Whereas the jinn possessed certain powers, they were not superior to humans, and they did not have the full power to overwhelm humans or force them to behave in any particular way. The jinn did eavesdrop on people's activities, and could give suggestions and inspire evil, they could even beguile and make evil attractive. And although people could access the jinn to do their bidding, the jinn were not supposed to interfere with human affairs. Yet, because of their 'mystery' and 'self-rule', there was nothing to prevent that from happening. The only human who could fully control the jinn was Solomon, who could see and speak to them, which was known to be 'Solomon's miracle'. Like Solomon, but not to his same degree, persons who knew magical procedures could exploit or defray the jinn, as with the vase with the flowers and salt given to me.

From that point of learning, a logical part of continuing to make my way in the Kingdom's culture and society was acknowledging the reality of the jinn. One interesting footnote that Haifa shared with me was that Muslims were careful not to pitch water randomly about, as it might strike a jinn standing nearby. That act could incite the jinn to direct mischief towards that person. I

The Jinn

believed that; Haifa's salient advice heightened my awareness and cautioned my actions, particularly, when it came to the cats.

There were multitudes of feral cats running rampant in the Saudi coastal city streets; in fact, more cats than dogs could be seen loose and idling about, especially throughout the compound where I resided. There were dozens of cats crouching and slinking along the sidewalks and in the alleys between the villas - living out of the trash dumpsters. I mean, those were unsightly, smelly, dingy, scrawny, mangy, watery-eyed creatures, the kind that one would not want to touch or go near – to steer clear of catching some disease. There were browns, calicos, and blacks - cats so filthy that the accumulated dirt on the white cats turned them gray. On top of that, the cats were pests who bred ferociously - multiplying their numbers at a rapid pace. One time when arriving home, there was a female and her fresh litter of five kittens camped right at my doorstep. They had to be removed. A few hard-core feline lovers left food outside for the cats, making the situation worse. Occasionally, a sanitation agency sent a truck to collect the cats when people complained when their numbers and presence became unbearable. But the cats never failed to come back and their numbers too.

Adult cats could be heard on the road and in the gangways near my villa day and night, which drove me nuts; and more so when my sleep was disturbed in the small hours of the night by their incessant whining, yelping, fighting, and mating cries. Having had enough of that I would pounce out of bed, throw on my housecoat, fill a pot of water, and rush outside with no shoes on to where the cats were hanging out – *'never mind the cold asphalt'*; in a surprise move, I'd quickly dash the water from the pot onto the annoying cats. The cats could not react fast enough to miss being splashed by the water; and straight away they got the message to cease their activities in that vicinity. Then, I'd go back inside, drop back into bed and peacefully to sleep – undisturbed for the remainder of the night and into early dawn. However, the cats would return the next week or so with their nocturnal antics, and so would I. I'd be right back out there in my housecoat, in my bare feet, in the street, with my big pot of water to drench and shock them out of sight.

But after Haifa told me about the perils of throwing water around and the jinn, I became duly mindful about my routine with the cats. I did not stop it, I needed my sleep, but I gave potent thought to the possibility that it might not be just the cats that I was distressing with the water. Bottom line - I had found a sure-fire way to disperse the cats in an instant and free myself from their noises for a while; I definitely was not about to give that up. And those outlaw cats had absolutely no case worth defending. So, I reached into my little bag of Muslim wisdom that I had lately acquired to summon a blessing to 'have my back' in my water slinging. I would now say *"Bismillah"* before hurling the water onto the silly cats. I took Haifa's warning to heart, and the 'Bismillah' invocation was done in all seriousness to shield me from any possibly angered jinn. Doing so felt like tossing salt over my shoulder or knocking on wood. I said the word aloud each time before I raised my pot and did my thing. I thought it worked.

Afterwards, I laughed at the whole comical spectacle and myself. It was hysterical. When the water hit half a dozen cats hightailed it and made haste - lurching off, scampering, and scattering every which way away from me while looking back in alarm, their eyes wide and gleaming against the dark, as if to see just how far away they were from me and my pot. I fired off a curse word or two at them as they fled to make sure they knew that I was *"taking no shit"* - a point that was perhaps also aimed at a broader unrelated target. Well, by then I learned that one sometimes had to devise one's own amusements in the Kingdom. Maybe the unseen jinn hovering off to the side might have found it funny too, and that may have been my reprieve from its animus.

For centuries, cultures of people believed in the two worlds of the waking and the sleeping; of the objective and the subjective; in the world of humans and the world of spirits. However, people largely did not accept the reality that our lives were more impacted by things that were not apparent to our senses of sight, smell, hearing and touch. The Qur'an spoke on that universal hallmark as it cited: *Many people of the modern times are involved in the misunderstanding that the jinn are not real but are only a figment of the ancient superstitions and myths. They have not formed this opinion on the basis that they have known all the realities and truths of the universe and have thus discovered that the jinn do not exist. They cannot claim to possess any such knowledge either. But they have assumed without reasons and proof that nothing exists in the universe except what they can see, whereas the sphere of human perceptions as against the vastness of the great universe is not even comparable to a drop of water as against the ocean. Here, the person who thinks that what he does not perceive, does not exist, and what exists must necessarily be perceived, in fact, provides a proof of the narrowness of his own mind. With this mode of thought, not to speak of the jinn, man cannot even accept and acknowledge any* *reality which he cannot directly experience and observe, and he cannot even admit the existence of God, to say nothing of admitting to any other unseen reality.**

The Qur'an frequently mentioned the jinn and humankind in a manner which indicated that they were two separate creations having two separate existences. Humankind was an apparent entity that was created out of clay and the jinn were a concealed creation out of smokeless fire. In Islamic ideology the jinn were an invisible entity which roamed the earth before the first man. The jinn entities were believed to have human needs such as eating, drinking, procreation and dying, but were stronger than man in some ways. The jinn had their own relationship with Allah, and worshiped Allah. They were subjected to God's (Allah's) judgment and held to the same laws governing obedience and disobediences, as was man. And whatever the plan that the Divine had for creating the jinn, it was not known, nor was it comprehensible.

The term 'genie' was derived from the word 'jinn', which referred to a guardian spirit of people; and so it was in western folklore that some genies were good, and some were bad – as were angels and demons. In Muslim belief the reality of the jinn came with a little twist to it. Like other religions, in Islam the jinn were spirits that lived among us; they cooperated and even dis-operated in our lives. But contrary to western religious beliefs in angels and demons, the jinn could be a combination of both; and did not exist expressly to do good or evil, they just were. The jinn functioned in a grayer area than in Christian faith and behaved more like humans than angels and demons. That quality of the jinn mirrored that of human nature to a degree, in that humans may not be predisposed to be either good or evil but had the propensity for good and evil. How us humans evoked either capacity was largely situational – as with the jinn. Staying in the light and virtue for humans required self-consciousness, betterment and will, and which was universally a desirable state of 'being' and a human motivation. Yet, there was no known answer for what moved the jinn to be good or evil – or if that mattered to the jinn. According to the Qur'an, it was enough and more important to believe that they existed among humans, not try to figure them out, but to know their power and to mind one's own behavior while being distantly respectful of the jinn.

Perhaps, the jinn were another way that the Divine kept humans in check. Arabs and Saudis went about their lives with the certainty of the existence of the jinn living side by side with them, just as they did with their fellow human beings. For the Arab, the jinn were as real as the sun and moon and as close as kin. The awareness of the jinn and their ever presence was imbedded in the waking consciousness of the Arab; in what they said, thought and did, the Arab was aware that that parallel entity was there with them and that it was also 'aware'. Understanding the delicate balance between the joys and trials in a life kept the Arab prudent so as not to tempt or trouble an idle or mischievous jinn such as tossing water about, which was just one common behavioral safeguard. Precautions should be taken when openly talking about matters of importance, or which reflected one's innermost yearnings because a jinn might be listening; and if influenced by evil it could interfere with one's plans, hopes, and dreams. That explained to me the pattern of reticence from Muslim people I knew when the conversations might have turned to discussing the object of their desires and what they hoped and wished for, or their specific plans - anything that they were striving for or actively working on. Not only was secrecy a natural part of the culture of Saudi for the sake of modesty, loyalty, or fear of reprisals, but it was most likely to guard against a potentially interfering jinn. In that mystical landscape, an astute Muslim could not and should not look to an 'angel' for divine assistance or guidance through life, but only to Allah.

The jinn was another name for a recurring phenomenon in the sublime human experience. Humanity's co-existence with spirits in western and eastern cultures elegantly suggested the mystery, diversity and the hope that abounded in the universe - that we had company. It was not just us. And it was not just about us. I kept the vase of the white flowers and salt in my 'room' in my home that the young Saudi lady gave me, whose name incidentally, was also Hayfa, with a different spelling. It was one of my most precious possessions and a token from the treasure chest of mystical knowledge I gained in the Kingdom. I cherished it in gratitude that a person whom I softly knew felt that my protection and safety in the grand scheme of things was important.

*Excerpts were taken from the Qur'an.

42
Runners

Runners were discontented professionals who literally ran away from Saudi Arabia – usually ex-pats. They were dissatisfied to an extreme with their jobs and/or the Kingdom and took off without giving official notice. They breached their contracts, and some, according to how long they'd been in the Kingdom abandoned sizable amounts of money by running away. But that did not matter to them. Some hastily and scornfully left as if as an act of revenge, to make a point, while some were more methodical and strategic in making their clandestine exits. So why didn't runners go the proper route to negotiate a break from their contracts up front? That was because most did not trust that they would be paid their due by leaving before their contracts ended and there would be punitive repercussions – which were known to be quite hefty. Any business organization that employed or contracted with a foreigner either a migrant or professional ex-pat was called a 'sponsor'. Contracts were firm and difficult if not impossible to renegotiate once they were agreed to and signed at the onset of one's work assignment in the Kingdom. That was the case with most business sponsors. Stiff monetary penalties were imposed for 'breach of contract' that could put a serious dent in a person's pocket and financial plans.

Most contracts for professional ex-pats covered a two-year period and could be renewed after the two years were completed. Contractual concessions and exceptions to 'breaches' could best be earned after several years of service, or under emergency circumstances. Monetary bonuses accrued with each year of service; the standard was to award half the person's monthly salary to the 'pot' for each year of service. However, that money in the 'pot' could only be received upon the completion of the two-year cycle, not before. Those who would run realized within their first months and year on the job that they were egregiously unhappy and could not stay for the duration of the contract period; they likewise chose to run and avoid penalties and not lose the pay that was immediately due to them. The reasoning was that if a person was going to 'run' they'd better make up their mind and do it in the first year and lose nothing; the longer they stayed on the job the more money accumulated in the pot, thus the more they would lose. With that being clear, larger numbers of people ran in the first year, and fewer after being on their jobs in the Kingdom for several years and longer. Those latter runners just stopped caring about the money.

The prospect that there would be runners among us coupled with the fact that it really did happen, destabilized collegial relationships – which was off-putting. One day a colleague and I would have a friendly exchange of words, or they might be in his or her office, in the classroom, or administrating, and the next day they were gone. Poof! No one was at the desk, they did not show up to teach their class, and their villa was emptied of their personal belongings; instead what was left in their absence were a lot of questions. No one clearly knew when or where the person went, as his or her departure came as a total surprise with no clues. They were just gone and not heard from again. Chapter closed. Some ran but wanted to have the last word, so they left a variety of messages to show their disappointments and reasons for leaving. They vented on perfectly time-released email blasts for all to read and know, accusing their sponsors of this and that. Some left behind unpaid loans from Saudi banks and fellow colleagues; laptops and equipment provided by the sponsors were not returned, business files vanished. They were direct and outright in making their cases and points upon departing.

A lot of ex-pats, including myself talked about running; I contemplated escaping unannounced in my first year. Faculty and administrators had get-togethers that inevitably turned into bitching and moaning sessions dominated by some who *'would not be happy for being sad'*. Over cold drinks and finger food, people were visibly upset and fussed and laid out their detailed exit strategies while others said nothing as they regarded the complainers with a distant knowing calm on their faces – a kind of 'been there, said that' look. Few were satisfied with how things were going, and no one was jumping for joy. Initially, I was in with the complainers and had a mouthful to add. It felt good and somewhat of a relief to be validated and confirmed in the company of like-minded people. A few years later, I'd have something different to say to anyone who asked – that my life in the Kingdom was not easy and far from perfect, but I was having a pretty cool experience – a bit short of astounding.

Where continuing to live and work in the Kingdom was unbearable, running, in many ex-pats' minds was the only option. They did not want to risk having their bank accounts frozen, their national IDs confiscated, freedom of movement and computer access blocked, documents sequestered, or just being openly stigmatized as outcasts, those who went against the system. Saudi Arabia required an 'exit visa' when one completed his and her contractual assignment and was leaving their position and station in the Kingdom for good, as it were. When exiting, one needed official permission to get past check stations at the Saudi airports. Official permission to exit was also clearance that a person was leaving with no debts or unfinished business, no offenses to be rectified etc. Moreover, in Saudi, all travel for everyone was monitored, it could be detected when anyone entered or left the Kingdom, down to the date and time and destination – information that sponsors could access. So instead of dealing up front with the red tape and possibly being denied clearance, some people just packed up and quietly left, in a sideways manner, when they were not happy and saw no workable future for themselves in the Kingdom. Subsequently, runners were banned and could not reenter KSA for an undeterminable number of years.

I observed two categories of runners: active and passive. Active runners did so in real time, at any time; they suddenly exited the Kingdom, steeling away without permission and unannounced via circuitous routes; the passive runners took their usual yearly summer breaks to go to their home countries, giving the impression that they would return as expected, but they never came back to Saudi Arabia – most runners took that route. Classic passive-aggressive. Come the beginning of the next fall semester, there was a surprise shortfall of people who did not return from their vacations. That deficit of faculty sent the fall class schedules into a tailspin, and new hires were needed, quick. However, runners in both cases made sure that they stayed just long enough and up to the day when they collected and cashed their last paychecks.

Those that I knew who ran were decent people. I liked and respected them – even with their quirks. I missed them. Their absences altered the social atmosphere and the feel of things a bit for me. There was the tall, sinewy Greek professor who brought a lot of attention to himself on his high exploits in academia and the books he authored – who left after throwing a tantrum at a meeting with senior management; there was the American guy I never met but knew about who included me on his scathing email blast to top management when he departed – he was really pissed off. There was the dapper British fellow who was fairly new, he spoke very little and just observed what was going on around him and with other people much of the time; he was one of few men on the bus sometimes, who was suddenly no longer there.

There was my good friend Dr. Vera. Caucasian. She was miserable almost from the day she took on her post as professor, despite her high salary. She cried on the transport bus more than once at the end of her long day at the office – spilling it out with tears on how awful she felt about her job and being in the Kingdom. She was beginning to see that she did not belong there and could not understand what made her decide to take the job and move to KSA in the first place. She missed being home in the states for the holidays. The social restrictions were too much for her. She was a social butterfly and lively bird who liked, maybe needed to move around free and easy, wearing fashionable clothes and accessories. She craved activity. She wanted to get up and go when she wanted – taking the train to Riyadh on a whim - just because, hunting for odds and ends in the shopping malls at night, frequent getaways to Bahrain, and she eagerly hosted some of those 'complaining' parties. Management and leadership at the university were bothersome for her whom she saw as unethical and underhanded. *"The playing field was not fair"*, she would say – *"too much inequity"*, *"women were treated poorly"*; and she could not adjust her standards to work within a system that was trying to *"modernize at too slow a pace"*, particularly where women's rights were concerned. She viewed the Saudi customary phrase of 'In sha'Allah' as *"an overriding excuse for all that was wrong in the Kingdom."* Dr. Vera was in her mid-fifties, never married and wanted a husband before she got too old and while she still had her looks and figure. Throughout her adult life, the job always came first, but not anymore. I noted how my friend grew increasingly bitter in the ensuing weeks and months.

Eventually, five months into her first year, Dr. Vera confided only to me her plan to 'run', weeping inconsolably. There were too many eyes and ears around that could confound her plans and expose her prematurely. Dr. Vera was a cagy woman, and discreet and organized in making her getaway. In her enthusiasm when she first came, she overcommitted and accumulated a lot of things on her frequent shopping binges – buying collectables and gifts for family and friends back home, and household items, paintings, decorations, and furnishings to make her Saudi villa elegant and homey; she even shipped a trunk full of her books to Saudi in her early days there. Now it was a daunting task for her to sort through and manage all that stuff – to decide what items she should keep, could do without, sell, or pack and ship back to the US. She ended up giving a lot of things away. And all of her actions had to be done quietly so as not to draw attention or raise questions. I thought that I was a good listener and support for her. She needed a reliable witness – so I became that.

It saddened me that she was leaving, and I even felt a little jealous that she was about to fly into the wind away from her troubles, which was what I too wanted to do, as I was also in my first contractual year, and feeling the pain. But I was on a different timetable and trajectory than she and had my own reasons. "Is there anything you want from my things that I can give you Dr. Elizabeth?" Easy question for me. Says I: "I would like to have your black abaya – the one that you wore most often." Snap! She said she would be happy to give me that abaya – the one I coveted each time she wore it; I liked the way it hung on her. She had a similar body type to mine, and I thought that her abaya would solve my abaya problem after so many unsuccessful attempts at finding a right one. And it did. It fit me just right, at least as best as could be and under the circumstances; and it served as a perfect memento from my unhappy comrade.

On the night before she left the Kingdom, Dr. Vera had her driver load her suitcases into his car to store overnight. When he'd come to pick her up the following evening she would not want anyone to suspect that she was leaving her villa to go to the airport – leaving with just her purse would make that unlikely. Earlier that week she had cleared her computer and office. She timed her date of departure for the day after payday, when she would collect and cash her check and close out her account with the bank. She took the transport bus to the university as usual on the morning of her departure – her plane flight was to be later that evening. On that morning on the bus, I observed my friend, Dr. Vera as she was taking a long quiet last look at the faces of those with whom she had shared that daily ride so many times – saying *'goodbye'* in her own way, in her mind – for there was no way they could know what she was about to do. She would visit with me one last time later that day, and to bequeath to me her abaya; I would wear it practically every day after that.

That evening Dr. Vera would leave the Kingdom via taxi to the Bahrain airport where she would fly out. Visas and IDs were less scrutinized there than at the Saudi airports. Dr. Vera's secret exit from the Kingdom was swift, clean, and quiet. My eyes lingered on her back, with a sinking feeling inside me as she walked away from my villa after saying our goodbyes – watched her leaving, perhaps going closer towards a promise. I felt forlorn, left behind and knew that I would not see her again. Dr. Vera and I had a special connection that I was beginning to count on. In the wake of her departure, she submitted a lengthy treatise to senior management with suggestions on how to lead an ethical business organization and university. She circulated that document to a select few people, including myself.

Then there was Dr. Greenfield – a brilliant, eloquent, middle-aged African American man who had clearly paid some serious dues during his 'illustrious' academic career and who ventured to Saudi with an impressive portfolio. Practically, from day one, he was not pleased with the reality he met on the ground once in Saudi Arabia, which he found jarring and unacceptable. Dr. Greenfield was a passive runner who did not return from his first year vacation break – no forenotice, reasons or explanation – just another 'poof'. But before he departed for summer break and while in the Kingdom, he made a lot of noise, publicly voicing his disappointments and spewing his brand of vitriol. It seemed that his brief experience in KSA altered his personality. He regularly called me on the phone, and more often stopped me in the halls in the 'green zone' with a rich tirade, going on about all that was making him mad – sweating and besides himself, all in a hissy-fit, looking like he was about to blow his top. Because he was new, I tried to coach and advise him to be cool. But he was on a roll and began to make a display of himself, thumbing his nose, as it were, at the university policies, the students and even the Saudi culture. Although he became targeted as a malcontent and troublemaker, he did not care. He was taking on the system single-handedly. Like Don Quixote, he really believed that he could make the 'leviathan' budge.

And my dear friend, Dr. Bonita, an Islander woman, she was also a passive runner. She often complained to me and forecasted that one day I would look out of my office window just in time to see her climbing over that high fence in the distant desert, in her bright yellow abaya – *"Leaving this place."* We had a good laugh about that, but there was a hard truth in that prediction. I did not see her climbing over the high fence, she just did not return from her upcoming summer break and was not heard from again. Her being there in the Kingdom added a dimension to my experiences which was no longer there.

When anyone 'ran' either actively or passively, it interrupted the flow of work at the university, but not for long, because there was always a 'next' person to take over their jobs. As long as people were carping or grumbling but staying in their jobs, nothing moved - nothing changed. Neither, the Kingdom, nor the university would adjust to any disgruntled ex-pat's expectations. As people left the Kingdom as runners, it made me wonder why them and not me.

I had my frustrations, which lessened as I got better at understanding and managing them. One of my colleagues imparted some sober advice to those who would listen: *"No matter how bad you feel or how much you hurt and want to go, be certain that you have a financial situation firmly in place before leaving."* He'd been trying to leave his position for many years, a good man. But every person who lent counsel to the 'disenchanted' did not necessarily have the best intentions; there were some curious characters in the mix who played a nasty game with the most agitated and vulnerable, and naïve would-be runners. Some people who wanted to run sought moral support to help them take that leap, and those 'bad actors' sped to their aid, so to speak. I called them 'phony' runners who also vigorously complained about what was wrong and justified anyone else's need for a quick exit. They spoke the loudest and attracted other potential runners to their camp. Those phony runners deliberately pumped others up to 'get hot' and run – got them fired up to just 'get the heck out of Dodge' - proclaiming that they would be leaving too, and right behind them, giving them false comfort with their 'head start'. They knew that misery loved company and they played that to the hilt with unsuspecting people who had sketchy exit plans. 'Phony runners' had no designs to leave their jobs; and instead got some perverse amusement or pleasure from seeing others twist in the wind with pangs of loss and regret for having given up their best and only option for a secured salary and paycheck, and all too easily and too soon.

From their secure perches, the phony runners eyed some who were taking the plunge and crashing, which might have made them feel even safer in their own discontent. Some runners had little or nothing to go to when they left, or their plans fell through on the other side, and they desperately tried to get their jobs back in KSA. They would email and call in vain to try to return to the Kingdom; they realized that the person who encouraged them to leave, saying that they were *"gonna leave too"* had stayed behind and were carrying on with their jobs and affairs. Only then would it dawn on the ones who ran that they had been duped. But, really, by whom? The phony runners were long-time survivors and knew how to hang in there. Well, by then, I'd seen how the Kingdom brought out the best and the worst in people. *What a shame.* I thought to myself, and found it instructive how people got called out of themselves – even jerked out. I also knew how close I might have come to making that same misstep.

Into my first year I had an overwhelming urge to run. However, with legacy, reputation, and my level of responsibility to faculty and thousands of students staring me in the face I discarded that idea. I knew I had it in me to stay the course for the two years. So instead, I decided to honor and ride out my two-year contract commitment and not renew when it was completed. But lo to my surprise, not only did I get over the initial two-year hump but stayed through to five years, renewing twice in the process.

That which was most obvious did not really represent the truth of a matter. In my Saudi residential compound, someone had a rooster in a back patio area that was close and within earshot of my villa. I could hear that rooster crow throughout the day; and came to know that the rooster crowed not because morning was coming; the rooster crowed because it was bright outside – hours after the sun had met the sky. And that was a different thing. As it related to runners, that was my theory: The reasons why people ran were not as clear as they thought and expressed. As a rule, whatever the factors were that pushed those who were 'fed up' to and out the door, they ran because they were chasing an ideal. In the Kingdom they were caught up in a whirlwind: It was the heat, it was culture shock and the bewildering student learning culture; it was the social restrictions and the absences of luxuries and necessities they were accustomed to having and which some could not live without; perhaps it was not comprehending the Bedouin mind and how things were done in the Kingdom; it was the low status and treatment of women; it was money and contractual misunderstandings and beating one's head up against a rigid reactive institution that was still in its adolescence; and it was about themselves.

Although there was a 'real and present' strain and discomfort that drove runners out of the Kingdom, they were disenchanted with something in the places from whence they originated, which was why they came to KSA; they were going back and forth – from the frying pan into the fire, as it were. There were those who had 'running' on their minds day and night, and yet, were judicious and held onto their jobs; after weighing the pros and cons, most stayed and spoke of running no more. And there were those who were 'cock sure' and yanked about by their urges to flee when those urges to bolt might have needed to simmer down and maybe taper off. Sometimes running away was not the best thing to do. We were all looking for a situation that would make us feel satisfied, whether it was in the Kingdom or in our home countries.

If we could not find what we were searching for in our home countries, we thought we would in Saudi Arabia. But that was an ideal that could not be geographically pinpointed. And as long as people searched for that ideal, they would feel insecure. Perspective was key; I coached myself on that, which was a part of what kept me still. Where some had an appetite for intrigue, others had the capacity for endurance. What they had in common, and which was the real 'enemy' was the voice of discontent that whispered to them and kept them unhappy wherever they were. That voice would not allow some to adjust nor others to understand. The reasons and answers were not about *where* people were situated, but in *who* they were. *Wherever you go, there YOU are.* That adage spelled it out perfectly. It was not only places that made us happy or unhappy.

Not saying that runners were bad, but *'a bad man is a good man's teacher'*. To that end, someone had to take the dare to make the point for all to witness. Because where would we be without risk? One thing I credited to the runners was that they gave us pause to think about the quality of our lives – of how crucial that was and that we owed that to ourselves - for those who stayed, for those who fled, even for those phony ones. Running was the one 'affirmative action' a person could take that proclaimed that: *'I am alive and as long as I have feet, legs, and my will, I will seek a way to live on my terms'*. Having been in the Kingdom many years, my good friend Dr. Bonita's choice was not willy-nilly; she knew exactly what she was running towards and was more than ready to go when she left the way she did, although, without a word of goodbye.

But I would say goodbye. Even though I had my frustrations, trials, and discomforts in the Kingdom, it was a truly rare and fascinating experience. It enhanced me, it expanded me and kept me connected to the wider world; it helped me to grow and to become stronger, in new ways. The days dragged on as the weeks flew by. But I stayed, and that bore fruit, and now I have stories to tell, that need to be told. By slowing down, waiting, and meeting the culture where it was, a person could gain what they needed to be not only financially, but personally sustained. My exit from the Kingdom was done in broad daylight with a lot of people watching, giving me farewell presents, taking me to dinner, and finding it hard to see me go; it came with my final paychecks being formally handed to me with the full complement of accumulated yearly bonuses, plus a stipend to pay the cost to ship my belongings back to the US. The door was left wide open for me to return. The Kingdom had its grip on me and would not let go. No, I did not run away. A big chunk of me was still there.

43
Whatever Happened to Dr. Bonita?

Some connections between us ladies did not come easy in the 'planet of the women'. Ours came with an instant liking and trust of one another, Dr. Bonita, and me. It was a friendship that bloomed quickly and helped to anchor me in those initial years in the Kingdom, and her too, while she was there. It was partly on the candidness of her words that I decided to go to Saudi Arabia to work in response to the job offer. *"Just make sure that your reasons to come here are strong"*, she told me in our first and only Skype conversation. As it turned out, the reasons for which she exited the Kingdom the way she did, years later, must have been strong also. My first and good friend in KSA, Dr. Bonita would become an enigma to me. And in the course of our friendship, then and 'then', I would learn some important lessons.

When I got the 'ask' to go to Saudi Arabia to take on the contract position, I thought that it would be naturally prudent to do in-depth research on the lay of the land; to get a feel for what I was getting myself into. A contact person there set me up with a Skype call to a woman who was working there and could be helpful. I did not like or did a lot of Skype because it added pounds to me, and the transmissions were often not clear. But the need to know as much as possible about the Kingdom outweighed my vanity, so we set it up.

Dr. Bonita came onto the Skype screen, which was going in and out; she was clothed in black - her head covered with a hijab, her body with the abaya. Her face showed more concern than doubt, but there was some wisdom in the background. With her being a woman of color, I thought that I would get the real scoop and answers to my questions, no matter how discouraging those might be.

I did not carefully plan or think through the questions I would ask, for I simply did not know what to ask – just wanted to glean some sense from her that might move my decision forward to go to KSA or not. She did not offer much, but rather submitted to any questions I surfaced in our talk, which seemed appropriate. I thought that she was being careful so as not to give me false hopes or to set my expectations too high about coming to Saudi Arabia. With a piercing stare, she emphasized dryly and more than once: "Just make sure that your reasons to come here are strong." She would add: "And you need to know that there is nothing to do here, only work. That is all that is here." I'm thinking as I listened to her: *"If that is all she has to tell me; surely, if what she is sharing is the long and the short of it, then the decision is made. I'm going."* Economics was one of my reasons; I was getting behind the 8-Ball financially and needed to buoy myself up in that area fast and to keep my career on track. I was also up for the adventure and a few other reasons. I did not divulge the entirety of my motives to Dr. Bonita but kept that information to myself for the present time – such prudence would turn out to be a tendency which would intensify and become a useful tool once my job appointment began in the Kingdom. Dr. Bonita learned my reasons later, after I hit the ground and met her face-to-face in Saudi, and after we had become close friends and confidants. The position I took on as Chair of the College of Business Administration made me her superior, with her reporting to me. She was a senior member of my faculty team of all-women on the female campus. We easily formed a balanced professional and personal relationship. Our positions did not get in the way of that. Had she not already been in the Kingdom, it would have been a tad trickier for me to acclimate in those first months.

 Dr. Bonita was an easy six feet tall; she was not fat, but a full handsome woman, and she carried that well. When she walked, she glided. She spoke in a distinctive baritone voice, laced with the dulcet lilt of her island accent - it was like hearing a song. She never rushed her words, nor her steps across the floor, room, or through the corridors. She took her time when she looked at you. Her very presence was comforting, as she was even, and solid like a rock, it seemed, having a way of making people feel assured and sane in the crazy restricted lives they led. Although an American ex-pat, she daily dressed in the traditional abaya attire, opting not to expose her hair which was covered with the hijab or scarfs. And she was known for her 'signature' loud jewelry. Her office was a hub for students and faculty who went there for talk, an ear, or some form of sustenance, helping themselves to the sweets that were a mainstay on her desk. The female Saudi students gravitated to her warmth where they felt safe and supported. She had the quality of being so present with the many young ladies who invaded her office on the spur of the moment.

Dr. Bonita She was giving and gifted many things to me effortlessly – once taking off her dazzling necklace that I admired and handing it over to me, insisting that I have it simply because I liked it. *"It would look better on you anyway."* She'd say. She could be so straight-faced funny with the stories she told, and that was such a good thing. I grew to love her, and she me. We'd go through a whole lot of trouble to secure a forbidden little bottle of vodka for our Barbican/vodka cocktails that we'd slowly sip over a long talking session in our villas at night. We talked on end about many things: Our work, a little gossip here and there about the zany campus life and its people, laughing until our bellies ached; then complaining while weirdly honoring our maddening, eclectic lives as single women in a foreign land - sharing notes about our journeys, the high points, and the lows - going into detail about the pleasures of food, travel, wine and men, and the things that mature women only tell each other. It was natural to disclose our private selves and intimate feelings on just about anything, I mean the nitty-gritty of what we could barely think or say to ourselves, yet we poured that out in our tete-a-tetes, as if out of necessity.

Often those lengthy talking sessions did not wait until off-time and were spent in our campus offices. No problem. I was running things and made room for 'woman talk' during work hours as much as was warranted with all my staff. But my friendship with Dr. Bonita did not begin at 8 am or end at 4 pm, nor was it perfect. We'd dress up and go to students' weddings or to other outings; and check in with each other regularly to make sure that things were OK - witnessing one another going up and down with decisions we had to make alone. And there were a few times that we fell into misunderstandings and argued when the pressures got to us, but very soon, we'd cry ourselves back into one another's graces. Our friendship of four years covered a lot of ground. It seemed as though we had a bonafide connection, and I could not understand nor comprehend how or why it ended so unceremoniously.

It really threw me for a loop when she just suddenly up and left the Kingdom without a word, to anyone – not even me. There was a disconnect between the woman who possessed so many fine qualities and the person who abruptly went away from us and became another runner. I could not say that she did not give forewarning and that I did not see the signs of her deepening discontent - of which I was all too familiar. She warned me that she would disappear from the Kingdom one day, and we would bet against one another on who would be gone first – *"I'll leave before you!"* *"Uh uh! I'll be out of here waaay before you honey!"* It was a fun exchange, but we were dead serious about leaving all the same. I did not know that something so intense was going on inside her that caused her to vanish without a word, a trace nor a response to inquiries via phone or emails. And it hurt.

There was something about the 'life' in the Kingdom that could drive a person to the edges. Our relationship was so alive up to the months before she 'turned' and left. I recall her expressing increasingly her weariness; that she was tired of working, getting worn down by the students and their neediness, who were taking too much of her energy; that having a relationship and marriage was becoming all-important as she was getting older - any single middle-aged woman's sweet dream. She lamented that she was wasting precious years working in *"this place"*, having her life so limited and stunted. She hated her villa and loved being close to the water. Chasing after and possessing quantities of money was losing its significance, and when she made her 'escape' she vowed that she would find a way to live on very little, while having a better 'quality of life', which was her new imperative. She would say to me, more than once, twice, or thrice, that one day I would look out of my office window and see her scaling the high walls on her way *"out of here and going home."* I was listening to her all the time, I heard her, and understood every word and agreed and urged that she keep a strong grip on what was essential to her life.

Dr. Bonita was saying less and less, then nothing. She became withdrawn and aloof in those weeks leading up to her unforeseen departure. Her slow distancing was not only felt by me, but by a community of professionals and students who knew and had grown attached to her. Seeing her slipping away I offered to cook us dinner and suggested movie nights in our villas, which she declined; we hardly visited as we did before. Her silence was blaring. I was surprised and caught off guard when she called out to me one day with*:* "*Dr. Elizabeth!"* from the far end of the corridor between our offices. I immediately walked over and hugged her, expecting that we might have an exchange – that she would say something – more. She did not have anything to say, she just saw me and called me over to her. That was it. I did not understand, but accepted that, and still tried to connect with whatever was going on inside that was drawing her away and inward. But could not. *Was she ill, did she break?*

Although it crossed my mind, I did not indulge the thought for a minute that she had pretended to be so present with our friendship those four years. That was something one could not fake. If so, she had been really, really, good!

But I didn't think so, and why would she? We had no falling out - nothing I had done untoward to her that I could think of; we'd stumble through and flesh out those things. Something happened, something snapped. Those were my thoughts over and over – going nowhere – getting no answers, like the cryptic Skype interview. After she left, days, weeks and months passed with no word, no reply to mine or other people's texts, no one answering the phone. I would slowly ease into letting that go and accept that good people would come and go in my life and there was nothing I could do about it. The Kingdom was emptier for me, remaining there for another year after Dr. Bonita was gone. She won the bet.

But my lost friend found me in dreams in those few months following her unwelcome absence - vivid, poignant dreams that I clearly recalled – the kind that beat into my mind. Oddly, they came on three consecutive nights. The dreams 'informed' me that the connection we had was real and something to celebrate and which deserved to be remembered while smiling. The dreams refreshed my understanding of how people were more complex than we could possibly know. Relationships did not belong to us. All we had was the moment with the people we met, knew, and loved; and it was important to let go when the time came. There were no regrets or bad karma when we knew that well; and accepting the wisdom that what we could control was to meet another person in good stead in our journeys and to give each encounter our best.

* * *

Dream 1: Dr. Bonita appeared with her sister. They were hugging one another and happy together. She was looking at me, directly smiling saying no words but communicating to me: *"This is not about you. I have no answers – it just is what it is. There was no other way for me to do what I had to do. And I know that you are big enough to understand that."* The impression I got from the dream was that she was content and where she wanted to be – perhaps with her family.

Dream 2: I ventured deep inside the Moroccan medina and through the souk searching for a place to rest. I was ambling in and out of places, when suddenly I saw Dr. Bonita leaving her apartment. I hid from sight. And then entered her apartment, not sure why. I went into her bathroom looking through her things for a clue to know what happened to her and why she left. Then I felt the need to lie down, so I did. She came in and found me there.

I said to her: *"I don't understand and want to understand why you left me hanging with no word about why you left. We had been through a lot together and got each other through some difficult times. Why did you leave like that with just a zero? I love you and I know that you love me."* As I spoke, behind Dr. Bonita's back I saw a thin blond woman come out of another room in the apartment. Saying nothing. Diverting her eyes. There was something sneaky about how she was doing that. Then Dr. Bonita began to haul off to try to strike me, with a vacant look, and her face like a mask. I reached up and held back her arm. Then she tried to strike me with her other hand. I held that one back too. Then I said again, *"I love you and know that you love me too."* I then left the apartment. It was so tight in there and closing in on me. I exited on those last words to her, not seeing the thin sneer evolve on her face behind me.

That dream seemed to say that there were just some things I was not meant to know – that did not require my understanding. I got the meaning that it was time for me to release her and myself from the past and any idea of even remotely salvaging our friendship, at least in this lifetime.

Dream 3: There were several people and me idling around in an automobile junkyard. Dr. Bonita entered the scene and handed me a heavy bag. I looked inside to see that there was just a handful of grapes which did not justify why the bag was so heavy; it didn't add up. Then I saw my brother who was deceased in real life, come on the scene. He looked marvelous and I was shocked and elated to see him so alive. Then he was gone. Grief overcame me and I wanted to just get in my car and go home. But Dr. Bonita found some old car parts that were the color of dusty rose – a shade that I favored. She put them all together to make a car that ran and offered to drive us both to Texas. I accepted and abandoned my plan to go home alone and got into the car with her.

From that dream I gathered that what we had as friends was not wasted or lost and would remain alive and nurture us in some way, even if just in spirit. Perhaps, she was there in the dream still being a friend by helping to assuage my real-life grieving on my brother's recent passing, which hit me hard. The bag held the weight of good things that could not be seen but had significance. And that interpretation of the dream was putting it simply. I had no further dreams about Dr. Bonita in my remaining time in the Kingdom.

Dreams were windows to our deepest beliefs, thoughts, and intentions. Dreams were wellsprings of useful information and could be arenas where matters left undone in waking life were processed and finished and sometimes rendered to help us understand and navigate our lives. Noted psychologist Carl Jung saw dreams as *"Highly valuable and a way of knowing what was really going on."* It seemed that Dr. Bonita and I were in a different relational landscape now. Our rich closeness could not help but to seep through into dreams. The friendship had its day in real time and then closure in a dreamscape. For me, the dreams eased a trifle and filled a little of the blank space in our aborted friendship, which I felt had something to do with the 'trying' Saudi life, the sand, and the heat. Human connections struggled against, and many could not transcend the stresses, strains, and fluctuations of that life; and no matter how close people came, few relationships could withstand or resist the pull of life that took them in different directions, wherever they might be on earth. That dynamic was a natural part of life - a linear thing that could not be negotiated or stopped.

Dr. Bonita's caprice and leave-taking brought the vagaries of attachments to others into fuller view for me. Her absconding chided me on the wisdom to let go; and primed me for the goodbyes and more partings that were coming – that did come. I knew that relationships were laboratories in which we learned life lessons. I knew that the relationships we held dear were transitory; and many whom we hoped would stay in our lives were merely passing through. I was getting better at being okay with that. I was getting better at accepting that which was hard to know, which lie just below the surface in people and situations – in the crevices that harbored the deepest pains and sadness and stories that could not be told. I knew that with time, some things were just not that important anymore. But what remained so, and that I could say with beating heart, was that I loved her as much as any woman could love a friend.

Part Five

TOMORROW IS TODAY

UNDER THE ABAYA

44
God Save the Kingdom!

I became embroiled in a fierce argument with a long time and very dear friend a few weeks before I departed to Saudi Arabia to take on my contract work assignment. I was privileged to have shared a uniquely smooth friendship for over thirty years with him, where there was hardly a harsh word exchanged between us. Fighting about Saudi Arabia was our first serious rift. Bob was a tall, genteel Swedish man who was easily prosperous, in business, assets and in spirit; he was resolute and balanced – a total Libra. I called him, and he was a 'perfect gentleman'. He was many years older than me – not a father figure, but a mature man who took a keen interest in my life and how I was going about it. I appreciated that and him. The matter that sparked our intense quarrel was something he said to me totally out of the blue about going to Saudi Arabia. He supported my decision and reasons to go but felt the need to impose high-handed warnings and instructions to me about exhibiting *'proper behavior'* once I was there. I never experienced him to be so upset about anything having to do with me. I did not like it and fought back against his words and his tone. Voices were raised and emotional with his repeating that I should make sure that I did not *"go over there and cross anybody and get into trouble"* or at worst, *"harmed."* Of course, he was talking from what he thought he 'knew' about the human rights problems and dominant 'oppressive' masculine culture of Saudi Arabia, and how it would not tolerate and might even quash an independent, willful, and self-possessed woman like me.

Bob knew me well. And he felt that it was inevitable that my nature would clash with Saudi culture. I could forgive him for his concern, and I knew that he was speaking from a deep love that had grown over many years – and in essence he saw it fit to try to protect me from myself. Already, people close to me had been casting doubt and raising questions about my decision to go to Saudi Arabia. I suppose that Bob's high-pitched caution was a tipping point for me. I resisted that from my gut. I wanted him to understand, and to trust that I was a lot more than independent, outspoken, and strong - I also had good common sense, prudence, and wisdom – and was dismayed that in his 'panic' he did not remember that. I stubbornly refused to instill that 'panic' vibe into my consciousness and take it into Saudi Arabia with me. In fact, I knew that it would hurt more than help me and perhaps even become self-fulfilling. I wanted him to back off and accept that I did not see anything to be afraid of. We locked horns and argued back and forth for days, with him insisting vehemently that I did not really know what I was getting into and should be extra careful to control myself. I simply would not say: *'Okay Bob, I'll be good and behave'*, which was an assurance I felt he wanted from me, and instead said to him: "Let us agree to disagree." And that was that.

We were still the most loving of friends. Much later in my reflections, while on the ground in the Kingdom it struck me how Saudi Arabia could ignite such disquiet in someone even from so far away, like Bob, who had never been there. Two years hence, Bob was pleased and relieved to see that nothing bad happened to me and I did not cause any trouble for myself - he even liked the idea that I was going to renew my contract for another two years. I like to think that Bob learned a lot more about me and perhaps, about the nature of things, as I did. Bob's initial concern was not far off base, but it was not the whole story.

Change would start to brew after I was in Saudi Arabia and into my third year there. It would thicken and be ramped up, thereafter. The life I was living there was already intriguing and got more interesting. Things were happening and women were rising and becoming essential to the Kingdom's sustainability and progressiveness. A new time was at hand with openings for women that began during the reign of King Abdullah and were continuing with the nation's transition to the incoming King Salman, and the Saudi Vision 2030, launched in 2016. It was said that when you lift the women, you lift the country, and you lift humanity. That was beginning to ring loud, true, and clear throughout the Kingdom.

Still, Saudi Arabia had the long-standing, rare distinction among nations of having multitudes of women fleeing to escape poor women's rights. Women fled not so much from poverty, economic strife, or political persecution as refugees from other countries tended to do, but to have a different and more fulfilling experience as a woman. They escaped from what they'd undergone as an aged-old repression of women that did not fit with modern times. I knew women on both sides of the fence – those who fled the Kingdom and made their home in the US and those who remained loyal to their country - who were poised, watchful, and anticipating better and brighter days ahead for the women of the Kingdom, and ready to do their part to make it so.

During the five years, I made regular return trips home to the US taking annual summer breaks from my contracted work in the Kingdom. Folks back home were curious to know how I could possibly spend so much time and 'survive' in Saudi Arabia as a foreign, 'strong independent' woman. It seemed unfathomable to some who assumed that I was 'compromising' myself in some way to do so. None of that was true, I was not surviving or compromising. In fact, I was beginning to thrive there on many levels. I was an outsider looking in, and notwithstanding having to wear the mandated abaya, as a US ex-pat, I was exempt from the hard customs that limited and controlled women such as Sharia and the male guardianship laws. Interestingly enough, I easily passed as a native Saudi woman until I spoke, revealing my western accent.

While on my US home ground during those sojourns I met Saudi women who were self-declared 'escapees' from the Kingdom; and they had much to say, up to a point. They told me why they left KSA, but they would not disclose any details on how they made that journey across the great sands and ocean. Those were young Saudi women, perky, pretty, and full of dreams which they felt could be better realized in other countries. Legions of women were taking circuitous routes out of Saudi Arabia to find new homes in the US or Canada, mostly. Those women severed themselves - leaving their Arabic homeland to take refuge in western sanctuary countries; they were forsaking ties with their families if not for an indefinite period then certainly, permanently. They knew that they could never go back. And that was a reality that they were willing to face. They broke out of KSA and were received and became 'situated' in other countries with the help of an already existing network of people, some were westerners, and some were expatriated Saudis. The women's new sanctuary 'families' set them up with housing, jobs, and other necessities to establish a new, albeit a low-key life far away from the Kingdom.

One young woman I met in California told me how she found a way to work around the 'male guardianship' rule which she believed was a kind of 'legislative blockade' to also prevent women from running away from the Kingdom. She got her father's permission in Saudi Arabia to come to the United States on a visitor's visa to attend university; she subsequently left the university; she did not say if she graduated or not. But she would not have been able to leave Saudi without her father's permission, which was her driving goal.

When I asked where she was living and what she was now doing - essentially, how did she get economically established in the US, she succinctly declined to give any such details. All she said was that she was *"Supported by a lot of people."* She stressed that saying more would put her and those who helped her at the risk of being identified and persecuted by the Saudi government which had 'reach' even from such a long distance and after she had made her 'escape' years ago. Putting my own experience in the Kingdom up against hers, I felt that she really did not have to divulge any specific information to me about her networks and resources. Women were exiting the Kingdom through a modern day 'Underground Railroad'. The women did not say much of anything about how that happened or the nature of the support they received in their 'sanctuary' countries. They demanded anonymity; and I knew that even the names they gave may not be their real ones, first and last. Yet, with emphasis, they reported *why* they left.

One professed that she wrote a book about her transition out of her life in the Kingdom to the United States – a book she said would go unpublished for fear that she would be tracked. She volunteered her reasons to me, saying that Saudi was too much like a black hole, full of secrets. She said that not only were women the victims of restrictions on their lives, but so were the men. She said that people saw and experienced inequities in a 'duo standard' in the Kingdom, wherein some privileges were allowed for upper class people and not for everybody else who must live by the strict rules – even religious ones. She said that many men did not like seeing the women's lives stifled under all the inequalities for them, which also had a negative impact on men's lives. She went on to say that average Saudi men and women did not say anything about the unequal standards for fear of being punished and they went along and accepted things as they were. "There were too many secrets, too many things that people could not do, too much unfairness and too much fear." She said to me. So, she told herself that it was *"enough"* that "I came here to be free. And there are too many Saudi girls like me who are escaping in droves by deception." With so many women leaving Saudi Arabia she felt that her country was losing female power. When I mentioned that things appeared to be changing and opening for women in the Kingdom, she replied: "Change was happening too slowly", pointing to the 'male guardianship' laws that remained firmly in place. That young woman's sentiments were echoed by other Saudi women 'escapees' I would later meet on my home turf in the US.

The 'male guardianship' system or law was at the core of the suppression of women's rights, which mandated that every woman must have a male to oversee key matters in her life, usually from birth to death. In that system women must have a man's permission – a father, husband, brother and in some cases, a son for such things as traveling and getting a passport, getting a job, getting an education, marriage and more recently, driving a car. The 'male guardianship' system no doubt, spawned other tenets of women's oppression and gave it strength. It was general knowledge, especially among women that that system remained the strongest impediment to women's rights in the Kingdom; and given all of the recent changes with the Vision 2030, nothing would fundamentally erase women's legalized suppression until the 'male guardianship' system was eliminated. So, even with the new vision, women continued to take flight from the Kingdom to have basic rights, and to the tune of approximately one thousand per year; and that number was even higher due to unreported cases of women who fled, whose families did not want to bring shame upon the family and kept quiet about it. In addition to basic female liberties, women ran away because of domestic violence, which was fettered by laws that unilaterally favored men, and they left because of other forms of discrimination in healthcare, divorce, child custody and inheritance.

Although it seemed that way, the situation concerning women was not so black and white. I also saw that a lot of women were not complaining. In the mix there were: The discontented women who were entirely 'done' with the Kingdom and bolted; as well, there were those who were loyal to the Kingdom as 'soldiers' to usher in the unprecedented vision – they could even be advocates and agitators for change; and there were the staunch traditionalists who wanted to keep the old ways.

The exodus of woman from Saudi Arabia had been drawing a lot of international attention and criticism, and to a degree, it overshadowed the reality and the stories of the women who remained steadfast in their faith in the Kingdom, particularly in a time of epic change and transformation. Just as there was a constant stream of women fleeing Saudi there were hundreds of thousands more who wanted to be a part of their 'forward moving' homeland. They too, had dreams and their whole lives ahead of them. There were those Saudi women who went abroad by the thousands, on visas to western countries to get a higher education and returned to directly apply that education to enrich their country. I spent time with many of those women - who were doggedly loyal and not necessarily plain and neat about it. Many were passionate and spoke truth to power, realizing with a fury how distinguished, progressive, and bright their country could be. Their protests were made known – I stood a hair's breadth from their outbursts. In fact, the young lady who was arrested for boldly trying to drive a car into Saudi Arabia before women's driving was legal was a university student. It drew global attention but was also a controversial news story in the Kingdom.

Personally, I walked a fine line between the two sides - finding my right and as Bob might say, 'safe' place on the ground. I wound up somewhat in the middle, more in allegiance with the loyalist women, who stepped up to help the Kingdom change and to come in their direction. I was no stranger to their struggles for I too, had to navigate overt sexism and systemic inequalities as a woman to function in KSA; and there were situations that I simply had to turn away from and let go for my highest good. I was not about to be David going up against Goliath in a foreign land. But I never allowed anything to cross my threshold of self-respect. I should say here that the climate towards women was not much different than the racial one that I endured all my life in the US, which tempered and prepared me for Saudi Arabia.

Choosing the high road, I immersed myself into the Saudi culture, unlike many of my ex-pat compatriots. I found the culture and the present day shifts fascinating and energizing, and which welcomed my participation as a western woman – not to impose western values, but to assist and lend my energy to the cause of elevating Saudi women who were already self-determined. I marked how prodigious those women were in their intelligence, their tenacity and how they collectively were a paragon of female power. I was a helping hand for them to fashion and establish their own way to be liberated and self-guided, not only through education, but through motivation, personal unfolding and mastery, problem-solving and business acumen. I was even making headway to produce an inspirational film that would profile outstanding Saudi women – an idea that could not fly in the social climate at that time. *'God save the Kingdom'* was the clarion call and unspoken battle cry amid women's bitter flights from the Kingdom and the urgent need to harvest the power of those who would stay and play a major role to move their country forward. I jumped in with both feet, and I did not step on any toes, ruffle any feathers, or upset the cart at all.

Indelible changes were occurring in the Kingdom that were triggered by: Fluctuations in the global markets that were lessening dependence on Saudi oil; by growing restlessness among the majority population consisting of younger adults; and by rising pressures to address women's rights, among other things. Change was pushing the Kingdom to rethink and modify how it brought in money and made profits. And women power loomed large on the horizon because of the jobs they could fill and the businesses they could develop and lead that could financially strengthen the Kingdom. The Saudi Vision 2030, sponsored by the Crown Prince, Bin Salman endorsed the goals for the Kingdom to be a main-streamed, progressive, and relevant nation. The promise of change was made evident on the faces of women - young, mature, and old, and even the men. Getting an education had more meaning and advantages for women. There was a job and a career at the end of a degree program rather than the traditional singular option of getting married, having children, and passively watching the world go by. Women could now actively participate. *Educate the women and you grow the country*. The women knew that.

I was in good company with women who were alive with awareness and were doing something with that awareness. They were maximizing every inch forward that they could in a climate that was still a bit schizoid about women's advancements. It was not prudent to move too fast given the slow machinery of traditional mindsets that would allow just so much; but move they must, to get a toehold into a widening door. Yes, I was helping to stir the pot and cheering them on. Women moving and growing away from being persons that people looked at but did not see was good medicine for the Kingdom. The women who crossed my path better expressed that sentiment in their own words:

Sara: "As a result of this vision, shop's unemployment rates among Saudi women have decreased and there are more women working everywhere. Shops and supermarkets have Saudi women working, where before those positions were held by men, even in women's clothing and abaya shops, men held those positions. Now with the new vision, if shops do not have women working, the government will close the shop and store until these employ women."

Hussah: "I'm the kind of person who has 'infinity dreams' and now I can be what I want to be."

Zara: "One of my friends faces many obstacles to get to do what she wants to do; she faces many arguments with her family, relatives and the society itself. Thanks to vision 2030, it gave her the right determination into pursuing her dream of becoming an artist and expressing her art to not only the nation but to the whole world. This vision has opened people's eyes in so many ways."

Baneer: "Men nowadays can never look down on women of this nation because this vision has allowed them to be treated as equal."

Asma: "The way the Saudi vision persuades people into believing that they can accomplish more than they think has helped or, should I say, has impacted me into creating a better vision of myself. I am motivated and confident of getting a well and profound job."

Rafah: "I now feel I can dream."

Nouf: "I saw lots of changes especially in my family. For example, before 5 years ago, my father strongly disagreed with the driving women and now he is totally agreed with that, and he has supported me to driving. My father gets out of all the hard, traditional reasons that have affected our lives. Moreover, my friends have a new level of thinking."

Dalal: "The community gets rid of preventing men from mixing with women because this is their right, and what happened in the past is wrong. All these changes have created great differences that will help establish the new Saudi state and its progress."

It was interesting how one could hardly speak or write about Saudi Arabia without using the word 'new' as change was romping through the land, even me.

In its sovereign way, the Kingdom did want to embrace the world and to be embraced in kind. Government laws and legislations had power, and that was no different with the Saudi Vision 2030; it was 'the new Saudi Arabia' captured in a stunning mandate for a change. It would seek to 'revise' the rules, traditions, and even the mindsets within the Kingdom – a green light allowing something untried and promising, and long awaited to enter the consciousness and ways of life in the Kingdom. In fact, it was nothing short of a command to do so. And it was received and acquiesced to by most. With their eyes on the future, men and women believed that the Vision might be the one thing to stem the tide of women fleeing the Kingdom and give rise to multitudes who would stand behind it.

Contrary to the positive changes for women that were occurring, there were those who were wedded to and wanted to keep the old traditions in place – a stance which showed the diversity of values among Saudi women. As well, there were those men and women who feared that the Crown Prince's novel vision would steer the country towards an extreme direction and cause it to lose its identity. I personally did not believe that would happen. If anything, I thought the Kingdom would be more progressively dynamic in its 'becoming', perhaps surpassing the societal norms of some western countries – achieving a total 'about face' while blending the old with a contemporary idea. I thought so because I had been in the Kingdom long enough and done enough to know that Saudi Arabia, despite how it was perceived and portrayed in the world had a great old soul as an Arabian culture rooted in ancient traditions, wisdom, and heart – that forever lived in its people.

Scholars, theologians, educators, businesspeople, and laypersons have lamented through the centuries that the world would have far fewer problems, schisms, and suffering if it were less ruled by men. From time immemorial humankind's idea of God was male. In our modern day and era, many and more were asking: *"Why did Jesus, appear only to a woman after he resurrected?"* And in a more forward inquiry: *"Why can't God be a woman?"* As the Kingdom evolved, taking cues from the times and its people, and turning women loose, perhaps in that act of saving itself it just might instruct the world that was ever watching on that very point. And from my bird's-eye view, I could easily see that in the Kingdom, the future was 'female'.

45
Change and the Crown Prince

There were many kingdoms still existing in the world such as Norway, the Netherlands, Sweden, Denmark and Vatican City. Saudi Arabia was one of five kingdoms that was an absolute monarchy ruled by a king who was the supreme authority across the land. He was not subject, bound or restricted by any laws, legislature, or customs. There was no 'rule of law' in the country, only that of the King who was not elected but inherited the throne. The Kingdom of Saudi Arabia was established in 1932 by the 6'9" King Abdulaziz Abdul Rahman Al Saud known as Ibn Saud by the West and who gave the incipient surname which fathered the country. Saudi Arabia had its flourishing roots in the earliest civilizations of the Arabian Peninsula. From about 500AD to 1000AD the Peninsula was a historic trade center between Arabia and the Roman/Asian empires; it was the birthplace of Islam which endured as the country's foremost religion. Nomadic Bedouin life dominated the immense and barren deserts of Saudi Arabia for centuries, and Bedouins were the country's majority population for the first half of the 20th century. As the Kingdom grew and life diversified among nomads, villagers, and townspeople, so did the necessity for change.

The essential process for all existence and civilizations through the ages was change, and thick nomadic and Islamic traditions of the Kingdom were not exempt from that imperative. The simple Bedouin lifestyle of herding and agriculture gave way to modern economies more dependent on commercial oil production, which began in 1938 - and continuing well into the 21st century. A later shift set in, pushing the beleaguered present-day Kingdom to transition and to tap and develop other resources for revenues. As such, the Kingdom with a rapidly growing population approaching 36 million, and with a land mass 4.6 times smaller than the United States, but ages older as an Arabic culture, was thrust into a global sea of high-stakes change.

There was a *boon time* to be in the Kingdom up to 2018-2019, and during my last contract years. The Kingdom's economy relied, primarily on oil profits, and secondarily from trade in major commodities such as natural gas, iron ore, copper, gold, and wheat. There was cash overflow and a plethora of job and money-making opportunities. Billions upon billions of dollars were pouring into the Kingdom each day, coming from eastern and western countries, including the US, pulling for Saudi's precious, plentiful, and affordable 'black gold'. At the center of that prosperity on steroids was Saudi Aramco, which ballooned to be the largest and richest corporation in the world – a juggernaut, taking in well over a billion dollars per day, which gave a boost to the Saudi society and economy. Saudis who wanted jobs were readily employed largely in cushy positions, in which they were paid well and enjoyed relaxed working norms. Citizens' lives were supplemented by easy government stipends and college scholarships, cheap energy, utilities, and water. There were no taxes. Social services and amenities were gratuitously provided to any citizen who wanted those. Societal life in that regard was a utopia for the average Saudi who did not have to worry about working hard or keeping a steady job because the country had so much and would provide. They were blessed and privileged to be citizens of a country that was so wealthy and taking care of its people in that abundance. Prior to and during King Abdullah's reign from 2005-2015, the Kingdom was a powerful magnet for professionals from the East and West and migrant laborers who came in droves to partake in the bonanza.

From past generations leading up, also to 2018-2019, the Kingdom relied heavily on foreigners to bring their professional expertise and labor in diverse fields; that trend began during the early days of the discovery and production of oil, which steadily intensified in the ensuing scores and decades. Saudi Arabia was benefiting from the high-level skills of easterners and westerners and was willing to pay a steep price for that. Western professionals especially, were making enormous tax-free salaries, which they otherwise could not acquire in their own countries. They were easily accessing an outgrowth of 'oil production generated' jobs and contracted work, much of which 'comfortable' and so-called, 'spoiled' Saudis could not or would not do. Overall, a lot of money was being made for Saudis and ex-pats – with expats dominating most professional jobs including teaching, which were disproportionately filled by ex-pats, and when education was high on the list of the Kingdom's priorities. The cheap labor of migrants out of India, Pakistan, the Philippines, Africa, and other Asian countries who filled primarily low-skilled jobs added substantially to the Kingdom's riches. And then in time, during 2016-2019, it all hit a big wall. In its unmitigated exorbitance the Kingdom had not been proactive to recognize and react timely to troubling undercurrents both within and outside the country. The sledgehammer of 'excess' came crashing down on the Kingdom's long era of unbridled prosperity and whacked everything from left to right - altering a cozy work/life system for millions of Saudis and foreigners, alike. It was also during that time that a new regime was in place under King Salman following the death of King Abdullah in 2015. King Salman would hand much of the reins of power to the Crown Prince bin Salman, who brought with him a new vision for the Kingdom: The Saudi Vision 2030. He would be known as the 'Change Prince' in many circles. With his entre as the Kingdom's leader change would be apparent - from the impetus for a young woman to reflect deeply about herself, to a decree that placed women at the helms of moving cars – from the laying down of sidewalks to encourage more walking outside in the open for leisure and health to the disbanding of the religious police.

A perfect storm was occurring in the Kingdom during those years. The easy days were gone; days got hard, then very different. The influx of money from oil began to diminish as the world and mostly western countries were less and less dependent on the Kingdom's oil. That slowed down the trek of foreign nationals into KSA who were now exiting the Kingdom by the hundreds of thousands per year. The lure of Saudi Arabia's riches was waning for ex-pats also because the easy access to exorbitant salaries and plum jobs was decreasing as sweeping economic changes were clearly seen ahead. Change was making the Kingdom less attractive and no longer a 'best bet' for mostly westerners to come there to fill their coffers. Moreover, the tons of money that ex-pats made throughout the years never cycled back to enrich the Kingdom but perpetually flowed outside; that was exacerbated by long entrenched laws that restricted foreigners from making investments in property or to establish their own businesses in the Kingdom, unless with a Saudi majority co-owner. Thus, the gross reduction in oil sales, and the exodus of foreign nationals who made no reinvestments in the country did not help and were resulting in problematic deficits. The Kingdom needed to quickly diversify its sources of revenue to leverage the presently ailing economy, which would include taxation. The decline of foreign labor and internal pressures made it a priority to increase employment for its people which called for large scale education and training. Change was afoot and it was forcing the Kingdom to switch gears on its own steam. Call it evolution, transformation or survival, the Kingdom had to react swiftly and acutely. It was clear to me that the bottom line was that the Kingdom was reclaiming itself - its most solid option. It was a dramatic process for me to witness – the country making a 'sea change' from having its long run of prosperity to tightening the belt in order to reckon with the times and an emergent vision.

The complexities of change was a multi-headed dragon. It uprooted, upset, and delighted a mixed bag of people. The Saudi Vision 2030 was gaining momentum to meet the 'demand' for change, driven by and large by economic forces, which was utmost on people's minds; it articulated the specific ways that the Kingdom would regroup and refashion itself. The Vision was the official recipe for change, fully sponsored by the Kingdom's new 'de-facto' ruler, Crown Prince Mohammed Bin Salman. Reforms on women's rights would ride on the coattails of the Vision. Some said that the changes were too much, too fast and that citizens in general were not ready. That sentiment came from Saudis and ex-pats, alike. Indeed, the changes were not perfect, nor meant to be, and they were certainly not devised to meet western standards. They were relevant to the needs of a nation trying to come into its own. For me, being there amid the changes, witnessing and feeling the 'before, during, and after' effects; and participating in the Kingdom's time of profound modernistic transformation was an honor and a privilege.

I stepped into Saudi Arabia at a propitious time when King Abdullah was in power; it was also the tail end of the Kingdom's heyday. People were 'fat and happy', so to speak. Work was plentiful and the Kingdom was 'reeling in the dough' and 'rolling in cash'. Everything fit. Abdullah was considered a 'good king.' During his reign the *'mighty door'* was opened that raised the quality of education for women. Came a point when I began to witness more of a gradual easing of the 'legacy oppression' of women as more *'doors'* were beginning to open. For instance, women were still required to wear the traditional abaya while in public and had to succumb to the 'male guardianship' rule; women were not permitted to drive, and the professional job market was not readily accommodating them. On the other hand, it was highly speculated that the law preventing women from driving might be changing. During that spell more and more young women were entering universities that welcomed and put them on an educational footing equal to men. Scholarships were delved out to anyone, the majority being women, who wanted to go to university. That money was provided with no strings attached by the government. Education was the one widening avenue for women that triggered an upsurge and a steady stream of them pursuing college degrees. That generated even more pathways such as job internships – expanding the 'playing-field' for women – having a 'Trojan Horse' effect in the social climate and on the economy. The genie, being the 'will' of women, was out of the bottle.

The difference between the outgoing, King Abdullah and incoming King Salman reigns was apparent; the new reign of Salman was more influenced by the changing dynamics in the oil industry as glut had carried the country thus far; social murmurings on the ground would also play a part in shaping his rule. In the ensuing years after King Abdullah's death Saudi's economy began to twitter and falter, and the government needed to cut back on excesses. The door to women's education would remain open. However, some things were taken away. Scholarships declined drastically. Taxes were imposed for the first time on all purchased goods. Job benefits in the public and private sectors were cut back; contract fringe benefits for ex-pats were significantly scaled down. Thusly, stripped of the job benefits and perks they had grown accustomed to, expats left the Kingdom - many with the families they had transplanted to KSA. And Jobs were unilaterally taken away from ex-pats and given to Saudis under the new Saudization laws.

Although jobs were increasingly available as ex-pats were vacating them due to loss of benefits and from Saudization, it was still a competitive market because of the high numbers of university graduated males and females, and who would need to meet employers' standards for professionalism and work ethics – standards that were more stringent in order for companies to stay efficient and productive in a vacillating economy. I surmised that vacated jobs and Saudization would offset a growing inactivity among people under 35 years of age who represented approximately seventy percent of KSA's population. That statistic alone intensified the pressures to modernize within the global community and markets. As well, female students began to grow impatient with the slow pace of change that would better their lives with opportunities and complained openly. They could accept that change was happening and that it was slow, and pushed for 'more' anyway. Again, the genie had been let out of the bottle, and was not about to go back in there - not now, especially with the Saudi Vision 2030 that rushed in on the authority of the new Crown Prince. And this is where I am going to back up a bit to fill in a few more details:

King Salman ascended to the throne of Saudi Arabia on his 81st birthday, in 2015 upon the death of his brother King Abdullah. Shortly thereafter, the King handed the reins of power over to his son, the Crown Prince Mohammed Bin Salman, popularly known as MBS. The new Crown Prince was young, handsome, charismatic, and a complex visionary leader. Taking on that rule in his thirties, he could easily relate to the growing young adult population who again, were presently the majority of the citizenry. And that may have been something that history and fate dictated that he had to do. From my view, the tall order for the paradigm shift that the Kingdom needed, practically landed in his lap. The 'Arab springs' that happened in Tunisia, Egypt and Libya which began in 2010 were driven by the massive populations of unemployed and frustrated young adults, especially men, who saw their countries slipping away from them and the country leaders as non-responsive to their needs. They saw no life or gains for themselves and revolted. Many said that the same scenario was now staring the Kingdom of Saudi Arabia squarely in the face.

Prior to 1979 Saudi Arabia did not have many of the cultural restrictions that were put into place thereafter, and which characterized its modern-day society. Women did not have to wear the abaya, alcohol was allowed, there were movie theaters and men and women mixed freely, etc. The Iranian revolution from 1978-79 generated a stir in the Saudi 'imagination', which saw the country at the risk of having the same kinds of revolts – things were too loose and there were too many freedoms akin to western values that were perceived by Arab traditionalists as shallow and dangerous, and which could tempt and give free reign to a similar revolt. Therefore, the Kingdom's leaders saw fit to curb the lifestyles of people to eliminate distractions and that certain threat; to maintain civic control and social decorum. An edict established that all women must wear the traditional (black) abaya; movie houses, drugs and alcohol were banned; and the separate cultures of men and women became institutionalized, required, and entrenched. The Mutaween became a fixture to enforce social controls. The irony was that the social controls put in place back then had to be reconsidered and loosened in the present day for the same reasons – to hold the country together. It could either implode or modernize.

Saudization and Taxation

The Kingdom was losing money after a long period of unfettered profits from oil; it was beginning to dip into and deplete its reserves of billions of dollars to keep the economy afloat. Saudization and taxation were some answers to the Kingdom's declining revenues, which again, was happening for several reasons, some were: 1. With other countries' reduced dependency on oil and turning to alternative sources, the Kingdom's revenues from its principal product were declining; and a new constant and reliable source of revenue was mandatory; 2. Billions of dollars earned by ex-pats was not being cycled back into the Kingdom; too much money was leaving the country. And along with that, having so many of its professional jobs taken by non-Saudis was now an unaffordable liability; 3. Economic levity was needed where Saudi citizens were falling short. Saudization was like the equal opportunity legislation in the US, but on steroids. The newly instituted 'sales tax' law was akin to that which started in the US in 1821. Saudization and new taxation were widespread and happening fast.

Saudization was a full-spectrum countrywide overhaul, and an urgent economic intervention. Saudization was 'taking the country back' to become more self-sufficient. It was set up to quell rising unemployment, especially among Saudi young adults, and set up out of the need to increase and retain dollars in the Kingdom. It secured entire job sectors for Saudi citizens, requiring that certain positions be held exclusively by Saudis. And there were stiff penalties if the new employment quotas were not met by business organizations. It first mandated that all Human Resources (HR) positions be assigned to Saudis, whereas before, those positions were mostly held by ex-pats. No less than immediately it seemed, that all HR jobs were declared to be the privilege and exclusive right of Saudi citizens. Gradually, the law of Saudization was rolled out in phases and confiscated professional jobs in various other sectors – handing them over to Saudi citizens, including engineering and accounting.

In smaller markets Saudis were deemed to be the only merchants allowed to sell gold and silver – precious metals being one of the Kingdom's key commodities. The hundreds if not thousands of jewelry shops that lined the downtown streets, alleyways, and souks throughout the Kingdom, and that had been typically run by Turks, Indians or Pakistanis were either closed or taken over by Saudi merchants. I could now enter my regular jewelry shops and each time find behind the counters highly preened and pleasant Saudi men dressed in the traditional regalia of white thobes, checkered shemaghs and oqals. One of my favorite Turkish merchants who in the past sold me jewelry was now downscaled, selling low cost and 'a dime a dozen' artifacts and trinkets – not allowed to sell fine jewelry anymore. But he kept some left-over pieces of fine jewelry from before, hidden behind his counter; and because he liked me and I had been a good customer in the past, he took those out to show me. All while he was showing me the jewelry he was anxiously peering out of his store window to make sure that no one saw him do that. If he were caught, he knew that his small shop would be shut down. He had come to rely on jewelry sales for higher profits and was now predicting that his small business might not last another year, and he would have to leave Saudi and return to his home country. His, like all such shops were required to have a Saudi sponsor and majority co-owner, even prior to Saudization. With the complete Saudization of jewelry shops came the takeover of electronics stores and it went on, like dominos.

Taxation was another economic strategy to bring steady money into the Kingdom. Ex-pats and Saudis alike were reeling from the advent of Value-Added Taxation (VAT), which was a first time five percent surcharge on all purchased goods – up from zero percent and which was inevitably going to rise.

How did Saudization and taxation impact me personally? First, the western model of education was still preferred in Saudi Arabia, as were western business norms and standards. My position as an educator and someone who was actively contributing to women's learning and advancing in the academic and business sectors was not threatened. In fact, it was predicted that it would take KSA approximately forty years to shift to having teaching and professorial positions held mostly by Saudis – overturning the current ninety-five percent ratio, which was dominated by ex-pats. That may or may not have been a fair and accurate assessment depending on how swiftly adjustments were being made in the Kingdom's academic arena. I was already seeing signs of how that shift was happening with special training and apprenticeships set up to develop and produce teachers from the pool of Saudi college graduates. And that was good; I wrote recommendations and referred several young women for first level college teaching positions. Moreover, western oriented universities were now required under Saudization to hire Saudis as teachers and professors, whereas prior to Saudization they preferred and exclusively recruited people who held advanced degrees from European, Canadian and US universities.

Secondly, going from paying zero to five percent taxes overnight on anything I purchased was a shock to my purse, but I got used to it. Realistically, I could appreciate its necessity.

The Saudi Vision 2030

The National Transformation Program, known as Saudi Vision 2030 was launched in 2016 with the full backing and endorsement of the Crown Prince. The landmark Vision laid out targets that the Kingdom would focus on for the coming years and were threefold: To modernize Saudi Arabia to be 1. A Vibrant Society, 2. A Thriving Economy, and 3. An Ambitious Nation. By and large, the Vison was launched to redirect the Kingdom away from oil as its primary commodity and towards alternative sources of revenue to boost the economy, and to become more competitive in the world economy. In that process job opportunities would be generated, and entrepreneurial development would be made available to the rising numbers of young adults, both to motivate them and to improve their quality of life; that could also go a long way towards abating idleness and frustrations that could otherwise, ignite resistance and revolution.

The Vision 2030 garnered changes in the Kingdom in most every aspect of Saudi life. One specific change in addition to the Vision was quite pivotal. What were once shushed conversations and then escalating talk that the Crown Prince was going to allow women to drive, actually became a reality. He gave that decree in 2017. The law stating that women could drive went into effect almost year later in the summer of 2018.

Woven into the Vision 2030 was the call for women's upward mobility - that they should, could, and would play a larger role in developing the Saudi economy, and that women would be in the workforce alongside men. Women were now occupying retail jobs that were formerly long held exclusively by men – even women's apparel shops. Women were being appointed to medium to high leadership positions and cabinet seats in ministries and governance councils; the 'male guardianship' law was softening to allow women to travel and move around in the world without the permission of a man. In essence, the Saudi woman was gaining some ground on making basic decisions about her own life without requiring the 'OK' or signature of a man, be it a husband, father, uncle, or brother. And publicly, more Saudi women began to break away from the standard black to increasingly wearing abayas of many colors. Prior to the Vision Saudis traveled extensively to neighboring countries such as Qatar, Bahrain, or the UAE (Dubai) for entertainment – again, taking much money out that could otherwise remain within to enrich the Kingdom; now entertainment and tourism were new values and priorities, respectively; venues for movie theaters, concerts, festivals, and live shows would be allowed, even public dancing. Written into the Vision was the goal that the Kingdom's citizens be healthier by increasing their exercise and recreation; that edict with other changes in the Kingdom generated increased opportunities for men and women and boys and girls to publicly mix. That was taking a wide departure from the traditional separate cultures of women and men in the Kingdom. Over time, the awkwardness from the unfamiliarity of one sex to another could be eased and perhaps even the fear and discomfort with women in the culture. Volunteerism was a top agenda item in the Saudi Vision 2030; tapping into the 'altruistic' potential of Saudi citizens was aligned and intrinsic to Islamic religious principles. In that regard, women were eager and the largest group gravitating to volunteer work. The Kingdom sanctioned those opportunities for women that helped them gain experience, advance their skills and power up their resumes as a volunteer. Volunteerism at a heightened level, no doubt helped to fortify the Kingdom. There were fewer restrictions for foreigners to obtain visas to enter KSA; and there were even discussions on the table that the limited availability of alcohol might be allowed, and that the unilateral mandated prayer time shutdowns for businesses might be lessened. More extraordinarily, the Crown Prince dealt a resounding blow to the religious police – the 'Mutaween' – disbanding them outright. With that, a sigh of relief could be heard from Saudis and ex-pats, alike. The Vision energized the Kingdom; and its people wrapped themselves around it and their Prince. In him, young adults saw someone who connected with them.

Saudi Citizens' Relationship with the Crown Prince

The citizens of Saudi Arabia awarded full credit to the Crown Prince bin Salman for the positive changes taking place in the Kingdom. That was not because the Saudi Vision 2030 was happening under his watch, but because he was the embodiment and advocate for the change they wanted and needed. Despite the global noise and swirling controversies surrounding the Crown Prince at that time, there was little to no talk about that in the circles I moved in within the Kingdom, other than how he was *changing things and making life better* for its citizens. And that was the story that dominated the news and headlines, if not the conscience of the nation. The Crown Prince's 'change' was something most people, young, older, and elder welcomed and hungered for.

The promise to become a part of the twenty-first century was a dream coming to pass – to modernize and no longer be looked down upon as a third world developing nation. It was a matter of national pride.

Saudis revered their Prince. Their desire for change, hence, the broad upgrades for the Kingdom that it promised and delivered outweighed any controversy or stain on his leadership. Discussions containing the Crown Prince's very name were upbeat. Among Saudis, there was high praise and respect in speaking anything about him, emphasizing the 'good' that was so apparent. Young Saudi women who were initially impatient now appreciated the change as *fast and positive* with one of my students proclaiming aloud: *"Comes a vision that is freeing women from sitting in their homes and living the life of past generations."* There was a perfect confidence and faith in what the Crown Prince represented, and in his economically driven Vision 2030.

The Saudis' relationship and loyalty to the Crown Prince was not my business. And those who came to be my friends were still my friends. Outside my conversations among ex-pats, no Saudi person I knew volunteered any comments that were political or not related to the positive changes that the Crown Prince was instituting. I conversed with the Saudi man and woman about the Crown Prince only in the light of change, letting them dictate where they wished that conversation to go. It was easy to do that. Whatever sentiments they might have other than that were private, shielded, and sensitive – and not worth discussing for them. I perceived that there was a tribal consciousness in force, having to do with a 'oneness' of mind and loyalty to the group identity as 'Saudi'. Indeed, the Crown Prince embodied the 'ideal change'. And for the Saudi people to regard or treat that any other way was to deny themselves. For them, he was a 'savior', and outsiders simply could not understand nor touch that! I could only and realistically bear witness to how they were so lifted – especially, the womenfolk; and that was information worth knowing.

* * *

As I considered the upheavals in the Kingdom, and how I was also contributing to and experiencing them I knew that paradoxically mammon, not virtue was behind the greatest tragedies and triumphs in civilizations. Wars were waged because of it, even holy wars. The US system of slavery was about economics, which was the same reason for it to end. Money was at the root of the persecution of the Jewish people, as was the Pilgrims' flight from England and the so-called discovery of America by Columbus. Mammon pushed major progressive and paradigm shifts and transformations of human societies and drove a nation's race towards modernization. Now, it was Saudi Arabia's turn, and even there, money was the key driver behind its transformation – one that was flirting, big time, with modernization. I saw within the culture that there were heavy feelings and deep concerns for how the Kingdom was judged and besmirched by the outside world. It was a sensitive, delicate pain for many – from the Uber driver to the students, to their parents, and the businessman – to my friends. They voiced that clearly to me. They did not want the world to look down upon them, to disdain them and point the finger. They knew that their culture might be harsh and hard to understand, BUT the people within it were not. They were tribal first and would carry that identity ad infinitum. And if modernizing the Kingdom meant fortifying the economy, putting more people to work, and retaining money in the Kingdom, the question was: *Can tribalism be balanced with the spirit of modernization that was knocking at the door?* That was a thing that could not be readily known. It would be a marvel to see what new 'thing' might emerge as the Kingdom moved in that direction. Perhaps with that, the Kingdom would dazzle and show the world a thing or two – that it was not about 'either/or', but maybe 'both/and'. I personally wished not to see the Kingdom and its people lose their soul in the process of working that out.

So, there I was, a single western woman smack-dab in the middle of the combustion of change in what was perceived as the most repressive culture on the planet. I did not take my presence there for granted, nor a person, nor any situation; but kept earning my way to 'see', to know and experience all that I could and came there for – to try to keep my wits about me on what I learned and taught myself. Asking questions, open mind, open heart. I was touched and it was compelling to have compassion for the women and the men of Saudi Arabia. In my way, I understood and respected the process of renewal for the people and how they were meeting it. The Crown Prince proclaimed it, now the people had to do it. The call for and its force promised that more upheavals were coming in the land. When I spoke about the Vision with my senior female students, I asked them all just one important question: "In what ways are you adapting your behavior and lifestyle to help make the Vision a reality? Because is it nothing without your effort." Most of them had a clear and ready answer.

46
"Woman, Drive!!"

Now that women could legally drive in the Kingdom, twelve-year-old Hessa prissily said to her father, Yusef: *"Daddy, when I get a little older I really want a Lamborghini!"* That was not too far-fetched; her dad did drive a Bentley after all, and he knew that Hessa was serious.

Before the long awaited and whispered about 'Women Can Drive' royal decree which came in September of 2017, the women were already secretly driving cars in the Kingdom – years before, that I knew about. Young, college-aged Saudi women especially, would not be denied having what they wanted, including hamburgers. They bragged about their nightly driving exploits. One told me that she had a craving for a hamburger when there was no man around in the house to take her out for one. And she did not want to go through the trouble of calling on a driver to take her out for her burger. The second family car was parked in the driveway and the keys were in sight, so she took them and drove herself to the Burger King several miles away. "How did you manage to be in a car driving around like that?" I asked her. She told me that driving at night shielded her identity. "It's dark at night and no one is paying attention to who is behind the wheel nor can see me easily." She said that no one saw her get into the car; and when she arrived at the fast-food outlet she slid over to the passenger's side when exiting the car and walked to the 'Female Entrance' of the restaurant to make her order. With burger in hand, she then reentered the car on the passenger's side and slid back over to the driver's side, then drove away from the Burger King. Doing the Drive-thru was clearly not an option. She performed that same routine by exiting on the passenger's side upon returning home, after she noiselessly parked the car, of course. "It was simple, like arithmetic!" She proclaimed excitedly.

Being legally allowed to drive was a giant step forward for Saudi women. The restriction to drive in their country was the one thing that utterly separated them from other women of the world. The fact that it was unlawful for women to drive in the modern world was hard to accept for many Saudi women; and it was the big elephant in the room during changing times in the Kingdom. It had to be addressed. Erasing the ban on women driving was the epicenter where fundamental change had to begin and could begin. Women driving in Saudi Arabia would be a breakthrough event that would certainly open doors for more advances by women in the country. The same technological, social, economic, and business evolutions that were accelerating in the world were also impacting life in the Kingdom, compelling it to adjust ancient traditions and culture. The futures of seventy percent of the majority of people under 35 years old would require that. Surely, there would be arguments in the streets and scuffles and conflicts, maybe more accidents. But that was to be expected from what people told me. Women's gains had typically met with resistance, most recently in the past decade when women were allowed to get a college education with curriculums in the same fields as men.

 The right to drive was the best thing that could happen for most women, in sync with their dreams, goals and ambitions. But it also came with some disruptions and inconveniences for a lot of other women. Not all women were happy about, nor welcomed the new freedom to drive. Traditionalist believers saw it as eroding religious values, which deemed women and men's traditional roles as absolute and inviolate. And where something was gained, something was taken away, such as privileges particular to women that they enjoyed in the 'pre-driving' era. That included not being required to work as hard as men to support a family; also being taken care of and pampered – of having things easily come to them due to their limited mobility. For instance, women were customarily the first to be serviced and given immediate priority over men, even in a room full of people waiting their turn at the front counter. I should know, that happened to me several times, and I really did not mind it at all! Moreover, under traditions that relegated women to the home, they had a lifestyle in which drivers dutifully ran errands for them and/or drove them around; they could relax in the car while the men did all the driving, sparing them from the fuss of having to deal with frantic traffic and car stuff. From that prerogative significant numbers of women were of the mind that women need not drive, for *'Why drive when you can be driven'*.

 Essentially, some saw the advent of new liberties that would and did come on the wings of 'women driving cars' as threats to having the idyllic lives they had before. In that life, a woman could indulge her 'womanly frailties' – wherein, she was seen and treated as needing and entitled to layers of support, of being tended to, winning favors and considerations. In that life 'she' did not view the 'suppression' of women's rights with as much ire as other 'freedom seeking' women. That was all passing now, and their new prerogatives would in time exempt women as a collective group from those luxuries and female privileges. With rights and mobility, more would be expected from women; they would be no different than any other western woman. *Yuck!* was what many Kingdom women thought about that.

Incidentally, the advent of women driving was a benefit to men and the family. When women could not drive it imposed a further burden on the men in the households who had to be regularly on-call and alter their schedules to accommodate women who needed to get around. The cost of having a regular driver for the family or woman took up a significant part of the budget which was a growing factor of concern to family breadwinners - usually men; that was compounded by reductions in wage increase percentages and job benefits brought on by the changing economy The Crown Prince's decree that women could drive customarily required permissions from male guardians that they actually 'would' drive. And from the numbers of women applying for licenses as soon as the decree went into effect, it was clear that most Saudi men readily granted their approvals and 'say so', most likely, because it was an improvement in their quality of life just the same. Those grown women who had no fathers, husbands, or other male guardians to make that decision for them were self-empowered to 'cash in', so to speak, and determine for themselves that they could and would drive.

A car was analogous to the human body. It was a vehicle to get a person from one place to a destination. It was mobility and freedom, and it was hard to do life in modern days without it. With cars as an extension of their bodies now under their control, the women of Saudi Arabia could exhale and be on the same independent footing as other women of the world. I thought that that was essential to my Saudi students and friends, and when it finally came to be that women could drive in KSA, I expected that it would be 'hallelujah time'. But it was a quiet advent. The faces of young Saudi ladies were modestly triumphant and signaled that 'driving' was still just a beginning. There was no loud screaming or exaltations, but a silent 'approval' of a thing done well and about time! That was among the women I knew and encountered. They were inwardly surveying, expecting, and waiting for more, because even that momentous development in women's rights was not enough. My students who were taking to the wheel would say: *"With every 3 steps forward, we might be taking 1 step back."* But for most, the difference was worth it and worth taking those 3 steps forward.

The very first time I saw a woman drive a car in Saudi was like the remote viewing of a vivid dream. It was Ghida. Ghida, was one of those blond women who was born on the land but not Saudi. For years and months, I saw as she exited the university building after work. I watched her tall and statuesque figure, with movie star looks gracefully pile into the bus with everyone else. Now, I observed as she glided past the women's transport bus over to her own compact black car. So much more befitting for her. And I marveled as she made it a point, to direct one of the male bus drivers nearby to make sure that he left enough room for her to back out next time, and not nick her car by parking too close. It was an intriguing segment of the overall debut of women's new freedoms, and with Ghida, how hers came with voice and attitude.

My older Saudi female friends informed me that Saudi women had long been exercising their independence, largely because they had no choice not to do so. Life in remote desert hamlets was demanding and required more than one set of (men's) hands. Women chipped in heartily to make life work. Women were driving the cars available when they needed to travel far to trade or fetch things the family needed. And that was not criticized or stopped. Comparatively, women driving cars in the more congregated urban areas would naturally draw attention and consternation and fly in the face of the social norms. My friends told me that the groundswell and fanfare of late, about women being legally allowed to drive was good and important. But it made official something that women were already doing behind the scenes, albeit, undetected and in much smaller and isolated numbers. From the urban college student who stole away in the family sedan for a burger in the night, to the desert-dwelling wife and mother taking the old hooptie to run her chores - in her heart, the Saudi woman always knew that she was free.

One month into the new era of women drivers, I requested a taxi through Careem, which was the Saudi version of Uber and Lyft. I'd been using that service for over a year as an alternative to my regular Pakistani and Indian freelance male drivers. That time, it was surprising and delightful to see that my assigned driver was a young Saudi woman. That was a *righteous first,* I had to acknowledge within myself. Her name was Asma, and in our excitement of meeting each other in that car, we easily dove into a hardy conversation. She worked in sales and drove for Careem, part time. She was fun to talk with and it struck me how her fingernails which were painted a glossy black matched her black abaya and hijab. I could still see her hands, after I exited the car, arriving home. When Asma was not animatedly waiving her long slender hands about gesturing as she spoke on what she was doing with her fresh liberties, the hands were tightly clutching the steering wheel as she navigated the vehicle through the streets. Her words and hands told the story for a lot of women – feeling free while holding on. She said to me: "Now that I met my first goals to have two jobs and drive a car, I will apply to university. It's crazy on the road here, and I am scared to drive, but I like to keep busy." Still reflecting on Asma long afterwards, kept me smiling. Pleased also with the thought of the hard working, multi-tasking, survivalist, desert hamlet dwelling Saudi women that my friends proudly spoke of. Give the woman the wheel and she would take us all anywhere we wished to go.

47
"Now Go Collect Your Driver's License."

Almost a year after the Crown Prince bin Salman made the decree that women could drive, the machinery kicked in to facilitate the order throughout the Kingdom. The granting of the permission to drive was simple, implementing the mechanisms to make that happen was not. A whole new system had to be worked out and set up to accommodate the coming army of women who wanted to get behind the wheel. Any new system for women would have to exist independently and parallel to the one already in place for men. There was, indeed, a lot to do. Following the decree of September 27, 2017, the new law went into effect on June 24, 2018. It took that long for systems to be put into place including brand new legislative, structural and technological protocols to get millions of women registered, certified to drive, trained, and then tested. Most women had to be trained as first-time drivers. Those preparations, however thorough they were, could not address the traditional mindsets of many.

In those incipient months after the law went into effect I could count on one hand the number of women I saw driving. Women were slow to approach and go through the process it took to be able to legally drive a car. There were stories that women were being cautious to avoid resistance and retaliation and attacks from Islamic hardliners - both men and women who were opposed to women driving. There was an incident, wherein an irate man set a woman's car on fire and stood by watching it burn. She was not in it, of course. He waited until she got out of the car that she so proudly drove and neatly parked. In time, resistance to women driving would take care of itself.

I noticed that more ex-pat women were among the first in line to get their existing western licenses certified in the Kingdom; and once their licenses were 'Saudi certified' it took no time for them to find out where to buy, lease and rent cars. Understandably, the process was often disorganized and continuously changing to improve itself; it involved a complex web of approvals, tests, and digital technologies to navigate. The company buses which had for many years shuttled primarily women to and from their jobs at the university were now becoming less occupied as women took their new places at the controls of their own cars or rode along with those women who had cars. While riding through the streets, whether I was on the bus or not, and still counting the women that were driving alongside, I saw that number starting to multiply by the day.

Us women, both Saudi and ex-pats were elated with the new dimension that was added to our lives. It was the talk. We could now come and go as we pleased. We could jump into the car and drive to the market when we ran out of butter, eggs, or milk, or when we just wanted a late-night bite to eat; and we would not have to tarry at all, to wait or pay a driver. Life had just gotten a lot easier. We gained some power over ourselves.

For a while, I put off engaging the arduous process of getting certified with a Saudi driver's license. I had been consumed with work, and I wanted to wait for the certification and testing apparatuses for women to become more congruent, organized and streamlined, and hopefully user-friendly. The idea of me driving in the Kingdom dearly appealed to me. It would be a token of the time I spent in KSA, and of being a part of that groundbreaking history – of being in the mix of the 'driving' issue for women, pun intended, as it burst forth from staunch prohibition to a vital right, feeling something like a miracle. No doubt, even though I was not Saudi, it was simply a thing I could not deny myself as a woman, period. It was a matter of being in solidarity with the women of the Kingdom with whom I was sharing the same experiences. I knew how it was to have to rely on a driver to take me everywhere and for every little thing. As part of my contract, I was given a modest monthly stipend to pay for drivers. That money was spent fast, mostly on drivers and was gobbled up by other things that would come up in the meantime. Thus, there was a constant flow of cash leaving my wallet, going into the hands of drivers.

I wrestled with the thought of what to do when I ran out of eggs, or butter, pasta, or if it were a treat I wanted from the store like ice cream or going for take-out food. Each time I had to decide whether it was worth the 50-60 riyals ($13-16 US dollars) I would pay a driver to take me the short distances there and back for such a small item – not to mention the time to wait for him to arrive to pick me up – both ways. It was not cost or time effective. It forced me into an elaborate system of food management. I froze a lot of foodstuffs such as vegetables, butter, onions, bread, and milk to keep them from spoiling – thus, extending the time before I would need more; and I froze pre-made meals

"Now Go Collect Your Driver's License."

to reduce having to daily prepare dishes using fresh vegetables. I kept an ongoing stringent itemized list of what I needed from the store – so that when I did pay the 50-100 riyals to go grocery shopping it would be more worth my while – as I would have gotten every item I could possibly need in that trip. And I made sure that I got enough of whatever I needed to last until the next time I had to shop. But I was still going to the store to shop every 1-2 weeks. All of that took effort, and it went on for years - all due to the restrictions of movement placed on women. And that was not just limited to food.

There were also the occasions of getting out of my villa for recreation and visiting. That also cost for drivers. If I had several errands to run or places to go during the day, I would pay the driver for every destination and then to take me back home. It added up. Going to Bahrain was a feat if one were to pay 250-350 ($67-93 dollars) riyals each way across the 15-mile causeway to and from Bahrain where 'a lot of fun' was guaranteed. Going there was not simply a 'sally' out of KSA, but a big commitment of money and time – as it took hours to ride from the Kingdom and enter Bahrain. To avoid the hassle of dealing with costly drivers for every move we made single women, like me, just stayed put most of the time. And now we could drive. Us ladies had our own cars at our disposal. We could get licenses, we could borrow, rent, lease, and buy vehicles and move around as much as we chose.

Anyone who wanted to drive was required to have a Saudi Driver's License; and that license could *only* be issued after taking and passing a driving test in KSA. That rule applied even when a person was certtified to drive in another country and had been driving a long time. Therefore, starting from scratch, my initiation to driving in the Kingdom happened like this:

The pathway to obtain a license was evolving and somewhat of a moving target that one had to nail down. It was a process that required resolve, patience, and determination, as it was entirely new and set up especially for women. Not certain how to go about it, I eavesdropped on much of the chatter among the women talking about the 'process' and how they were going about getting their licenses – that was on the company bus on the way to our offices in the morning and again at the end of the workday, taking us home. Kathy was full of advice for women on the bus. She was the ex-pat who schooled herself and seemed to know the most and even succeeded in obtaining her license in record time; she was the one I needed to approach for guidance on the step-by-step process. So, I tip-toed into the fray.

First was to establish an online Absher account. That was the national database for every person in the Kingdom - Saudis, ex-pats, and foreigners, especially those who were working, and residents. All had to register their identity and vital information with the government. That central platform recorded, validated, and qualified a person for multiple services and privileges within the Kingdom. A person could not do anything that involved legislation or commerce without being registered in the Absher system. It was also through the Absher portal that male guardians such as husbands and fathers would grant formal permissions for women in their families to do certain things such as traveling and driving. Once registering with Absher, I was to have my US driver's license verified as active and in good standing and translated into Arabic for issuance of a Saudi license. That part was tricky, and Kathy walked me through how to proceed with getting the translation.

I contacted the most recommended translation agency - for there were many and some were not well organized or legitimate. They instructed me to scan and send them my US driver's license. Once they received and verified the scan, they translated the US license and issued one in Arabic which was to be ready for me to pick up the following day. The cost was 60 riyals ($16). That next day, I scheduled my driver, Ajmal to take me to the neighboring town of Dammam, where the agency was located; but it was closed that day, and I also went to the wrong office. I misinterpreted what the agency representative on the phone told me were their open hours and address – no information was online, and it was a language thing. On my second trip there the next day, I did not know that the tiny office was tucked away inside a building off the main street, and no one answered when I tried to call; I left for home again empty handed. Oh boy! That was my bad. By now, the back and forth and wasted trips was costing me hundreds of riyals and too much time, as the 'mysterious' translation office in Dammam was roughly 25 miles away from my home – a lot farther than the trip to the store.

There was always something to be learned from such mishaps. I knew and accepted that rather than pulling my hair out and pointing a finger. Seemed I was moving a little too fast and had to slow down and pay closer attention to what I was doing. Finally, a day later, with the official Arabic version of my US driver's license in hand, I felt the adrenalin rush of extreme accomplishment! And I was approaching the finish line of driving in Saudi Arabia as a woman. The next step was to have the official translated US driver's license uploaded onto Absher. The document itself was quite impressive and attractive, suitable for framing. Uploading took several attempts but it got done. Now I was to go to the medical clinic to get blood and eye tests – and those results too, would be uploaded onto, you guessed it, Absher. I made the appointment with my primary doctor to request the documents authorizing the blood and eye tests.

Taking time off from work, I called my driver to take me to the clinic, which was also where I had all my regular medical care done along with local Saudis. Now I was in the clinic waiting area among the ex-pat and Saudi families with their nannies tending to the children running around while mothers were with their doctors. The elderly, the middle-aged and younger men in their perfectly starched white thobes, seated away from the women shrouded in dense black abayas, and hijabs were all there too, waiting for the petit and formal Filipino nurses to call their names to enter the doctors' offices. There was Arabic coffee and dates available for the taking on a little caddy near the Reception desk. English was spoken there. However, one needed to know the routine on how to get things done in the all-in-one clinic system with reception, billing, primary doctors, specialists, eye doctors, dentists, lab-work, surgeries, and insurance happening under one roof. My name was called.

Doctor's authorization was now done. Next step was to pay for the tests at the intake desk in the main lobby. The clinic had a special rate of 189 riyals ($50) for the tests. I paid, got the receipt, and proceeded to the lab for the blood test – and waited for the results. I then proceeded to the optometrist's office to present my documents and receipt authorizing me to take the eye test. The test was super easy, with the jumbo alphabet letters so 'in my face,' I could not miss. That took 30 seconds, really. With passing blood and eye tests, I was good to go! I then went to the special area set up expressly for uploading documents onto Absher within the clinic. After uploading the test results, I immediately received a text on my phone saying that the upload was *successful*, and I would *be notified within a few days when to schedule my driving test and where to go*. There was no contact information.

The driving tests for women were scheduled weeks and months out, and once the date was set it was hard to change. After that series of steps in the process it dawned on me that women's driving was an emergent and solid source of revenue for the Kingdom, from the registrations and clinic fees, and the sales, leasing and rental of cars – taxed under the new Value Added Tax law. Not to mention that with increased and ease of mobility, women would do a lot more shopping and be stronger consumers, paying more taxes. It was brilliant. And the system was improving day by day to make it easier for women to get *certified*, *tested*, documents *uploaded*, and into a car.

I waited for the text message that would tell me when to schedule my driving test and where to go. Days went by, weeks went by, and I heard nothing. *"Are they that busy"?* I thought. Eventually, after almost a month, I learned that I was not going to be contacted by the system on when/where to schedule my driving test but had to pursue that on my own. No worries. Now I doubled back to Kathy for advice. I figured out with her help that my blood and eye tests were now in the Absher system, but I needed to circumvent the system at that point and upload my translated US license directly to a certain government portal and through which I could be scheduled for the driving test. Now I had a date and choice of where to schedule the test: Dammam again, 25 miles away or Al Hassa – even farther, about 50 miles. Of course, I choose Dammam to save my time and money. Driving tests were still being booked more than a month out due to the high demand from women. The system was jammed, which was probably why I never received the 'text' from Absher.

I missed my scheduled driving test date due to a family crisis – I had to travel back to the US. When I returned to KSA I tried in vain to rebook a new date on the government portal. So, I decided to just go to the place where I was initially told the test would be given. I went there early, taking the morning and eventually, the whole day off from work – going there on a whim with my Saudi ID, my 'impressive' translated US driver's license and blood and eye test results in hand. As it turned out, it was the wrong place – it was the driving center for men – and boy did I get a lot of stares there. It was confusing as there were only men coming and going and who were clearly perplexed about my presence there. I spotted and approached an official-looking man to ask him where I should go. He told me. By then, my driver who dropped me off there had already gone so I had to call for another from Careem. He came right away and took me to a plain building where he said the Women's Driving Authority (WDA) should be. The building had no distinctive markings designating it as such. The landmark was there, that the official at the men's center told me about - a quaint little hotel *"next to the WDA"*. I knew that I was near the right place, and walked around, circling the building several times looking for an entrance; I eventually asked a nearby security guard where to go. He pointed me to a nondescript door at the back of the building. The place seemed to be

"Now Go Collect Your Driver's License."

an old warehouse that had been converted to the WDA and its parking lot was restructured into a small makeshift driving test area. All that mattered was that I was there. I went inside.

The security guard who pointed me to the right door advised me to just tell them inside that I missed my appointment for the driving test and wanted to take the test that day. He also asked me not to tell the people inside that he gave me that advice. And even as he chose to be anonymous, I surely noticed that he came into the center after I entered to make sure that the men behind the check-in counters *took care of me*, which they did. I was called up almost immediately from the rows of people seated, waiting their turn. *How did they know?* I wondered. I produced my information and documents in preparation for the driving test that would take place right away, outside in the testing area in the converted parking lot.

Once my documents were approved and recorded by the busy male clerks at the counter, I was directed to go out into the parking lot and wait in a one-story shack-like structure adjacent to the driving test area. Inside there was space enough for a few chairs and several women were standing at the one window looking onto the driving test area. They had a bird's eye view of the woman who was presently taking her test. I joined them. I was fourth in the queue to be tested and had to pee in the strongest way and paused to think about it. I did not want to take the test with that pressure tugging at me. I wanted to be totally at ease and unperturbed and knew that I had short minutes before my turn came for the test. So, I went into the tiny restroom to relieve my bladder.

In the tight stall there was a porcelain-lined hole in the floor over which a woman would squat – no tissue; instead, there was a hand-held water spray hose hanging on a fixture to the wall next to it. That was the custom, which was held as a cleaner and fresher way to use the bathroom with the body not touching the toilet seat and using water. But up to then, I immediately declined that 'way' every time, as most women's restrooms in KSA had a full-seated toilet as an option – but not in that 'shack'. And I had to decide, quick, because I did not want to miss my turn at the driving test and go through all that again. I thought on it a mere second, then heard my voice lowly saying: "I will do this." I bit the bullet, hoisted my abaya skirt, squatted, let loose, and sprayed – resolving in my mind that if I was going Saudi all the way today to get a driver's license, I might as well get into the fullest spirit of it.

Back inside the shack room I saw that the number of women waiting was fewer – down to two. From the window we could see everything. Outside, a uniformed Saudi man was 'manning' a small booth and from there directed the women driving around the wide circle taking their tests. There was no doubt that he was the authority over that last phase of our driving fates. He directed the women when to start up the car and begin to drive it. He noted if they observed the Stop and Yield signs situated about the wide circle, and he told them when and how to park the car. He directed them to drive the circle again and back the car into another parking space – which was the hardest part. The driving director did not sit in the car beside the women to avoid proximity – keeping with Saudi norms. The driving circle area was compact enough for him to maneuver and direct the women and be heard and seen by them. The woman who was first in the queue breezed through the series of exercises, but not the one after her and just before me. When it was her turn to take the test, she anxiously left the waiting room, walked to, and got in the 'test' car, but she immediately, got out of the car and raced back inside the shack with tears welling up in her eyes. With more of us waiting in the little room now, us women took her in, understanding that she was just nervous and needed more time to gather her confidence. The man outside was waiting. After a few minutes of encouragement from us she went back out to the car, got in, started the engine and she nailed the test to our cheers: "You go girl!!!"

Then came my turn. And I was surprised that I was also nervous, after having driven for more than 30 years, and had been the owner of 5 cars! I really felt that I could fail that test! Something, anything could go wrong, and then what? I said *"Bismillah"*, got into the test car and took the directions from the fine-looking Saudi man. Within five minutes I was relieved to be done with the last part of backing into the parking space after making the last drive around the circle. I stopped the car at the booth where the young driving director made an input on his electronic note pad, which was instantly forwarded to the central desk inside the non-descript building, and he said to me with a matter-of-fact grin: "Now go and collect your driver's license." I had come such a long way and time for those easy words. And it seemed to be his pleasure to say them to me.

Back inside the WDA building I went to the issuance counter for the final act of receiving my license. It seemed anticlimactic and rested on a simple choice: Did I want the license for 2 years, 5 years or 10 years. I chose the 2-year

"Now Go Collect Your Driver's License."

option as I was in my last year and on my way back to the US after living in KSA for the past 5 years. Within minutes, my Saudi driver's license was in my hand. I exchanged proud glances with the Saudi woman standing close by who also had just been granted her official license. We congratulated one another, sharing our prized moments and relief. I knew and I thought she did too, that going through that labyrinth of a process to obtain it was just as indispensable as the license itself.

A serendipitous aura overtook me. With my newly issued Saudi driver's license in my possession I studied my feet while strolling away from the Women's Driving Authority, finding them interesting right then - walking me to the quaint little hotel nearby. Those feet worked hard for me all those and these years in the Kingdom and had taken me a long way - from pounding the hot streets and sidewalk pavements to very soon working the foot pedal of a car. At the hotel I would use its wi-fi to call a Careem driver to take me home, as mine had just expired. And a glittering thought came to me that was new: I would rent a car for the coming weekend! I would drive for hours far and wide, and not care if I got lost.

48
Riding in the Car with the 'Girls' – Things That Got Said

Riding in the car driven by a woman in the Kingdom was an epic event for me when it happened for the first time. Like the improbable come to pass - a hardened, protracted foe waving the white flag to end a raging war, an alien from another planet landing in one's backyard, Moses parting the Red Sea, and so on. The cultural norms of the Kingdom had customarily forced women together and now with a miraculous turn of events - into a moving car with only themselves. I'd secured my Saudi driver's license by then and had driven rented cars and found the experience thrilling when I knew what it meant not being allowed to drive before and entitled to do so now.

Dr. Jolene was one of the first women that I knew to buy a car. Said she was *"So tired of taking that bus and twice as fed up with its drivers"* who never drove the way she thought they should. She bought a used silver SUV – the biggest SUV she could find – it was wide, deep with two sets of rear seats, and it sat almost a foot higher from the pavement than the average car or SUV. A bit of a clunker, it needed frequent repairs, but it never failed us on our rides. I asked her why she got such a big car and she said that the price was right, the size was convenient, and she did not care to be dominated on the roads with all those men. Needless, to say, the vehicle was a 'good-time' bubble for us girls to and from work. And she never accepted money from us when we offered to chip in for gas. Once inside Dr. Jolene's full-sized SUV we were the 'girls', riding high off the ground, the bunch of us middle-aged ex-pats, all Caucasian, except me, getting out of our offices for the day and weekend - transformed and frisky; us being in the vehicle with 'just us' brought that on. We were not stifled or reserved, as we tended to be with males around and controlling the car; we became a collective entity, indulging wise, good old-fashioned girl talk – a thing that could not happen that way inside in our offices behind company walls.

As the last hours of the workday ticked by, us women filed out of our offices and trekked down the stairs and out of the building. Company transport buses were there idling outside in the roundabout, scheduled to depart at 4:00

and 4:15 pm to take women home, to their respective residential compounds. Whenever I exited the building and saw Dr. Jolene's silver SUV I knew that a car ride home was assured. Whenever she saw me, she waved me over. *"Come on in sweetie"*, she would say, having no problem hauling the lot of us home. She would drop each of us off at our door in our respective compounds and be more than willing to pick us up in the morning to shuttle us back to work. Sometimes my choice to ride with her depended on who else was inside the vehicle. I treasured my privacy and had grown selfish with it – a safeguard, which preserved my quality of life in the Kingdom. But I also knew that Dr. Jolene liked having me in her car, and wanted me there, regardless of who else was also riding along. And I really got a kick out of taking a ride while a woman was driving. So, most days, especially in the afternoons I climbed inside to join in with the diverse personalities of the women who were there much of the time – the usual suspects. We'd be all too happy to be done with work for another day and closer to Thursday when the weekend started, or maybe it was already Thursday, and we were more 'up' about that. It was interesting that we women hardly had a direct conversation with one another during the course of the day, or for that matter, we did not really hang out with each other outside of Dr. Jolene's means of transportation.

On a day, because I was out of the office building early, I got to ride shotgun next to Dr. Jolene; and watched as the other work-weary women exited the building and gathered inside the car minutes afterwards. There was Sondra, Dr. Jolene's best friend. I could swear that they were sisters – with the same body type, voice timbre, and way of speaking with the same southern drawl, and plump girlish prettiness in their mature faces. I liked seeing them together because they looked so satisfied with one another as friends. There was Suzannah, a plain looking, studious Brit - our sometimes tactical 'go to' person for how to navigate this and that automated system or process; there was Sherry, a perky, buxom, blond from Arkansas, and plenty smart too. Dr. Marva, a tall, dark-haired, matter-of-fact, Latina would sometimes join us.

Once everyone was seated inside, Dr. Jolene began the unhurried drive home, which would take about 10 minutes longer than the bus – *"Driving all over tarnation"*, I would think to myself. She preferred to take her time getting us to and from the office, driving at the required miles per hour and taking the roads less trafficked and that had fewer speed bumps – circumnavigating with a lot of turns and going off the highway, up and down un-named streets and through alleyways. She said that the too many speed bumps on the regular roads upset her equilibrium. None of us really cared how long the 'tour' going home took, because we were in our bubble in that 'light truck'. Riding in the 'car' when the day was done was the best time; and we were not whistling Dixie once we climbed inside Dr. Jolene's 'big ole' SUV at that ripe time of the day. Us girls said what was on our minds, often choice items we had been holding on to all day and waiting for that minute to spew forth and come out with it, talking over each other to get it said, and off our chests. We did our ultra-necessary venting, which was juicy, stirring and sometimes naughty – getting our 'jabs' in. For me, it was an entirely different bunch of women from the 'womb room', which had its merits.

Nothing or no one was exempt. We yacked about anything and everybody that we could squeeze into that 50-minute time period it took to travel to our compounds. *'If you are going to talk about others, you'd better assume that words will also be said about you'*. That was an unspoken code operative in that arena. I understood before I started to ride with the 'girls' that *'you've gotta have some mustard in you to partake in this company of women'*. Heck, I suspected that I was the subject of some of their banter when I was not on a particular ride with them or as soon as I stepped out of the vehicle at my stop. No matter, it was not important and just part of the ritual, which was more felt than we cared to explain. They might have said something about what they heard about me in the rumor mill – which was incessantly churning. I could not imagine them making up stuff about me like the saucy tales spun by the gossip queens – nothing malicious that would be slanderous or injurious to me, but maybe some little tidbit to exaggerate what was already true about me, just to fill the space and keep the talk and jabber going.

When and if I was not there they might have said something like: 'That Dr. Elizabeth, she is hard to figure out. You know she has a boyfriend – wonder who he is. Says she is leaving the Kingdom soon, been here a while, wonder what she is going to do then? Said something about becoming a *woman of leisure,* wonder how she is going to make that deal,' etc. They probably had more questions than answers, and no concrete facts or affirmations about me. I never gave them much to work with, anyway. I also operated by my own code, which was *'what other people said about me behind my back was none of my business'*. But they were still the 'girls' to me and I was a part of them when I was with them. There was nothing more to it. That was just the nature of that kind of 'carrying on' when nobody but us girls in that car was looking or listening. Like gas, the 'women yacking in the car ritual' had to fuel itself. It did us all good. Kept us sane. And we were lighter, anyway, once we exited Dr. Jolene's SUV, relieved and even better informed.

In our work environment, it was often what a person did not know that could unexpectedly, bite her in the butt. Hopping in Dr. Jolene's car to go home instead of taking the company bus was not so much eventful for me as it was worth it and opportune to be in touch with women 'in the know' - who carried a wealth of information that would otherwise not be had; and with the extra incentive of finding any excuse to let the howling laughter come in. I had my good share of laughs. Some of us would not have as much fun for the entire coming weekend as we did in that SUV riding home. Fact was that none of us 'girls' was in an awful hurry to get there. Often, weekends were bland, or otherwise sprinkled with tedious or trifling busy work. In that car enclosure things came to life; and it was 'tell all'. And we knew about it all, speaking in terms of the 'facts'; if we were not sure of something, one of us volunteered to get the real scoop and brought it back to us. We knew who was showing up at the office drunk and about to get fired, who was sleeping with whom, who was taking bribes from students, who was leaving the Kingdom either voluntarily, being kicked out, or had run away from it all in the night. We'd touch upon a number of subjects in rapid succession, to get it all in, said and done.

Dr. Jolene: "Dr. Emil, that Greek they hired just a month ago left the Kingdom. They paid him a lot of money, but he still took off."

Sondra: "I heard he got into a shouting match with one of the old guards and that was it for him. The writing was on the wall. Easy come, easy go." And Dr. Jolene: "Yeah, and easy go, easy come."

"I am not a blond bimbo! Been there, done that!" Sherry blurted out as she launched into her rant of having had a bad day with a male administrator who was a bit too controlling for her blood. She went on: "He's trying to tell me how to do my job that I am fully trained and well educated for, much more than him. We went back and forth on that silly issue of assessing problem students. I challenged him on some key points and said that he was wrong. Actually, I caught him in a contradiction that clearly showed he did not know what he was talking about. It was written all over his face. But instead of admitting to his error, he told me 'You can't say that', and I said right back to him, 'Well, I did just say that!'" Sherry continued with colorful descriptions of that singular male. She got a fast round of applause from us all.

"How are you Suzannah. Its been a while?" Sondra asked. "I got married recently." Suzannah replies. Sondra: "What! How, to whom, where did you two meet?" Suzannah: "I met him on OK Cupid. We dated six weeks and then we decided to get married. He's Turkish."

Me: "Good for you girl."

Dr. Marva: "Professor Louisa moved her husband here from the UK. He couldn't find a job there after looking for a long time. Now she's the happy breadwinner. He's there waiting for her at home with the door held wide open when she arrives from work. And that's every day that I know about. Mmmm."

I held back and did not tell the girls about my male companion of the past two years, which they probably already knew a little about. Did not want to open that up for the gossip, which would surely be added to when I was not around. I just congratulated Suzannah and stayed quiet on the subject.

"You know there are more men to women in the whole Middle East. Women can have their pickings." Says Sherry. And Suzannah replied: "True that's good to know. Not easy to meet a man here though with the separations and restrictions and all that. Online is a good option. You just have to focus." Sondra added: "I'm not interested anymore. Men are more trouble than they are worth."

Sondra focusing back on Sherry: "He's afraid of you. They all are."

Dr. Marva chimed in: "We must have some huge balls to say the things we did at that meeting yesterday with those men. Them asking us what we thought needed to be done to end the gap between the male and female campuses. And then you, Dr. Elizabeth said they should turn off that tape recorder before you made your controversial comments."

Dr. Jolene: "What do you think that was all about Dr. Elizabeth?"

Me: "They don't care what we have to say. They are not listening to what we have to say, they are just feeling us out to see who we are and what we think – who is who, and who is trouble for them, and who is safe that they can work with. It's a power and control thing." We all agreed to that.

"But at least I delivered my message to them whether they want to embrace and hear it or not. If they want to grow their own daughters and women as leaders in the Kingdom then they need to start with supporting and valuing female leadership at the university in our present roles." That was also coming from me.

Dr. Marva: "Well, we've got our own rules girls, strictly taken from the Saudi woman's playbook on dealing with the man. One: Never do more than you can. Two: Always have a specialty that only you can do. And three: Never do something that he can do!"

Suzannah: "You said it girl." "Works for me!" Says Sherry.

Now we moved on to sharing our experiences in the work culture and certain 'characters'. "There are fewer people who can be trusted and who are progressive here. And some are just downright criminals, one in particular." Said Dr. Jolene.

Dr. Marva: "Oh yes, I think I heard a baby crying in his villa."

Dr. Jolene: "Really?" Marva: "I know the cries of a baby when I hear it, and it ain't one of those cats that are taking over the compound." "Wonder why he might be concealing his having a baby if he just got married." That came from me.

Sondra: "I don't think he would conceal that. In fact, he would brag about it, not keep it a secret. He would want to make sure that everybody knew how virile he is." Hysterical laughter.

Dr. Marva: "Maybe it was someone visiting with a baby then."

Dr. Jolene: "Well, anyway, that one is so corrupt. It's all over the internet. But they keep him around. He can't go anywhere else because he is a criminal. And it's out there. Everybody knows. They are all in that gang. Does not matter how incompetent or corrupt they are, as long as they are male, and can speak Arabic and I have been here long enough to know that."

Dr. Marva: "We must remember that we are in a work culture that says, 'Hey this is awesome, so let's NOT do it'." Laughter.

Sondra: "They do things differently here for sure. There is a different way of understanding and how things get decided. There is no oversight, no rhyme or reason. What worked yesterday is done in a different way the next day. Rules seem to be made up as they go along. And you never really know where you stand."

"This place is crazy, and we are all crazy to be here, but I have to say, that with what I am experiencing here I would be so bored if I had to leave and go back home to the states now. It's crazy, but it's interesting! Not a dull moment in a given day. There is always something to happen to amuse and to amaze me. There would have to be a compelling reason for me to go back home. My life back home would be a long bore compared to how it is here with how this country is run and how people do things here. And I've seen and experienced some pretty wild stuff!" Said Sherry. Here, we were mostly in agreement.

Sondra exclaimed in frustration: "I want to leave so bad, but I need to work two more years. I have people close to me depending on me in the states for support, to send them money."

I said, to lighten things up: "So, Dr. Jolene is sho' nuff driving this car!" "It's so freeing. Better than that dammed bus." She responded. Then we all got quiet and sank into the ride a bit, in our thoughts before the next words would come. We gazed at the cars going by outside the windows.

And then from Dr. Marva: "Hey ladies, listen to this. How many western gals can say that they were on the ground floor of a primal breakthrough for women in this world? We can!!! We witnessed before, during and 'afta'. We were here!!!" With that declaration we all let out the loudest screams - slapping high-fives in agreement.

One could say that women were always close in the Kingdom. But the freedom to drive brought us closer. It generated new forums and opportunities for us to get together; gave us more things to do and more that we were able to do, all of which made us stronger and more independent. Driving and mobility enabled us to take care of each other more; it freed up men who would no longer need to split their time shuttling their women folk and other family members around – especially those men who could not afford it or did not trust the regular taxi drivers with their 'women'. With our minds no longer obsessed with 'women not driving' KSA citizens and us ex-pats could focus our energies more on other evolutions within the Kingdom. Women got involved more, especially with volunteering, we bought more things that paid taxes into the Kingdom's struggling economy. Riding in the car with the girls, I beheld the changing pattern of drivers in the other cars on the roads and highways, which was showing many more women behind the wheel. They'd be covered in hijabs and niqabs or wearing lipstick and dressed up hair. In the open environment, I saw the increasing rainbow colors of abayas as acceptable alternatives to the predominant black – adding a new complexion to a growing parade of women walking along the streets. Indeed, changes could be seen and lived outside the car and felt within it too.

No one was turned away from a ride home if there was room inside that SUV and when we were going to the same compounds at the end of the day. That was because Dr. Jolene, with her sweet face and her cheerful disposition had a heart as big as Texas, which was where she was from. On one occasion a different woman joined in for the ride home. That was a woman who was known for her nefarious dealings that hurt people, she was not trusted, even by most of us 'girls'. Maybe she missed the regular bus or maybe she just wanted to nosy in on our 'fun' or better yet, was drawn to us in some subconscious way from a desire for our upbeat energy. She was not totally aware of how much she was disliked and perhaps assumed that it was okay to hop in with us. Funny, it might have just been a few days earlier that we spent the whole time in our bubble dissecting her disowned rage and the ugly things she had done or was up to, as if she thought that nobody knew. She was either oblivious to her issues or arrogantly presumptive that she was 'all that'.

In her prudence, Dr. Jolene knew that to refuse 'that woman' a ride would make us fresh targets for her mischief - in full view. And we did not need that. Her presence brought a heavy weight and lowered the energy inside the car. So, in our unspoken agreement among us 'girls' we made the conversation light and banal, to make her feel included since she was already there. We shifted gears to focus on a common scandal we knew and could all speak freely about. But we kept our guard and general talk on the surface so as not to give that so disliked, uptight, evil-doing, interloping woman anything to use against us. As soon as she got dropped off at her stop, we'd get back to our usual 'riveting' banter and bring the energy to where it was supposed to be for that short time left before we also reached our stops. We were all thinking it, but not saying it. No need to comment about the shady woman who was just in our midst, it had all been said before. And she was a long way from being one of us.

Dr. Jolene was most times calm and careful behind the wheel – bright red nail polish on toes peeking out from sandals as her tiny foot gingerly pressed down on the gas pedal. She could be feisty too, laying on the horn to get those 'crazy men' drivers out of her way. She would yield when necessary and let them pass but was full on ready to hurl southern curses at them if they came too close to her slow-moving SUV, which was usually the biggest vehicle on the scene. It was Thursday, and we all would be back in there come Sunday, the beginning of the next week. "You all let me know if you wanna go grocery shopping with me at Carre Four tomorrow morning, I'll come by and pick ya up. OK!?" Said Dr. Jolene.

49
Noura's Muhammad

Most Muslim mothers and fathers named their firstborn or at least one of their sons Muhammad; and a daughter's second name was traditionally that of her father, which would most often be Muhammad. In perpetuity, Muhammad had been and continued to rise as a most favored name for Muslim children around the world, and especially among Sunnis. It was a name that had several variations including Mohammed, Mohammad, Mohamed, Muhamad, Mahmet and Mahomet. Some said that the popularity of the name in the Muslim community was because there was little variety in boy Muslim names compared to non-Muslim names. That may or may not have been the case, however, the prevailing reason was that it was a venerated name among Muslims given to a newborn child as an act of devotion honoring the Prophet Muhammad, the Founder of Islam. Additionally, Muslim names customarily alluded to the highest virtues that one could possess and were thus, given to children at birth in hopes that those virtues would be reflected in their lives. That reasoning was verified when I asked people I knew to tell me about the meaning behind their names, and Muhammad in all of its variations meant *"One who is praised."* I found that to be a beautiful thing.

Noura's Muhammad was an integrated man. I felt that about him because I'd been in his company and observed him enough times to come to that appreciation. He stood out in my eyes from among the men I'd met and known, and not only in the Middle East. While men represented sun, and women, moon in Arabic culture, Noura's Muhammad was both sun and moon, in my mind's eye, having made his way in the world of men with his heart rich from a genuine love of women.

I spent a lot of time in Noura's home over the course of several years partaking in frequent invitations for casual dinners and gatherings where we played bongos, got down to hip hop jams and told stories over Arabic coffee and splendid deserts. There were mostly women attending, with Noura and her two sisters, their mother, family relatives and friends, and myself. There we were, every few months or so, sequestered in their mini mansion of a home behind a large ornate iron gate off a secluded street, all too glad to be in one another's company.

Muhammad, the family patriarch, it seemed would intuitively make his appearance just as us women got all settled in with each other in our 'womb room', as I called it. We'd sit softly on cushioned seats, in the glow of discreetly appointed Arabesque lamps. Muhammad would emerge from his separate sitting room in the home and enter the women's setting, tall and lean in his pristine white thobe, his salt & pepper hair cropped close to his head, and beard neatly trimmed as if for the occasion of greeting and welcoming us into in his home - a handsome man with an easy likable face. He'd sit and chat with us for a little while, not saying much, but just enough to familiarize himself with who was there and to make them feel at home and comfortable – passing a special glance and nod my way, that was always reserved for me, a regular guest in his home. After a few moments of small talk, Muhammad rose from his seat to say that he hoped we would enjoy the chicken shorba soup he prepared for our meal, and he left us women to ourselves. It was easy to tell from the way the family lived that Muhammad was well off. How he made his living in the past was not something I was anxious to know about. He may have been a different man in his past who might have overhauled some long-held convictions, as humans were tasked to do at some time in their sojourns on earth. But I was simply moved by the man he was in that moment, gracing our time, with him enjoying his wife and his daughters and the company they kept.

Daughters needed their fathers in an utterly special way. Father was their 'first man', who affirmed their womanhood. A father's love, great care and approval instilled the daughter with the safety and confidence to make her fullest expression as a well-rounded woman in the world. Muhammad had no sons, but three gorgeous, voluptuous daughters who blossomed and thrived under his fathering. They were dressed well, ate well, were well-educated with impressive jobs, well-traveled and loved up and supported to the brim. They were decent women, all three, self-possessed and busy in their lives. Their father gave them the nurture and space inside and out that they needed to be fully alive and themselves; and there was nothing they could conceive that they could not do or become. His love for them was so transparent. I could tell up close and from a mile away, so to speak, that they were his real treasures as was his wife. I saw how it filled him to love his women and how he lived, it seemed, to cherish them. And for Muhammad to love the women in his life so entirely, he had to intrinsically love and honor the feminine part of himself.

The sad and joyful stories that I saw unfold in the Saudi Kingdom were no more joyful than sad in the lives of men and women. Some stories, no matter how tragic, had to be told. And perhaps in the telling it would lessen the sorrow felt by the persons that certain things happened to. At best, the telling energetically shone a beam on a matter that should no longer take refuge in the shadows - making less darkness in the world and more illumination. Yasmin's was one of those stories, and she had a very different Muhammad.

Yasmin started coming to my office in my first year in KSA and made regular visits ever since. She was a young Saudi woman blossoming into life wanting a friend, but really in need of some mothering and fathering. Her mother left the family when Yasmin was a tender-aged girl, leaving her in the care of a physically and emotionally absentee father, an older brother who unerringly followed his father's lead and a brooding uncle.

We celebrated Yasmin's 20th birthday in my office with silliness, dancing and shaking our bottoms, with balloons everywhere, slapping high fives and closing our eyes in playful Star Trek 'mind syncs', and taking selfies. I saw her growing stronger, smarter, wise, and lovelier while meeting the challenges of any young, feisty, and spirited woman growing up in the Kingdom. And she was quite mature for her years.

Yasmin would spot me in the corridors and race up to me for a hug or pop into my office to talk, and for a hug, to show me pictures, to sit, to take candy from the treat jar on my desk, and more hugs before she left for her classes. She was dabbling at becoming a vegan and was curious about the western world, while at the same time she was deeply devoted to her country, religion, and prayer. She told me how she lived under a strict curfew in her home life and with restraints that went beyond the usual for other young ladies her age; she told me of her loneliness and isolation and how she danced alone in her room at night or otherwise took in a lot of Netflix.

Cheerfulness and impishness masked the depression that was building up inside Yasmin. She came to tell me that she started seeing a therapist who prescribed anti-depressants. The family men who were her guardians did not understand Yasmin and from what I knew, they were wary of her rare spirit. They acted in unison, on all matters of Yasmin's life, deciding what she could and could not do, disapproving her dreams and ambitions and plans other than what they saw fit for her - stifling and blocking her at every turn. And those were her words. Muhammad, her father may not have been in the home on a regular basis, as he was preoccupied with other women, but his authority was ever present. One year Yasmin was offered a membership in a prestigious international organization for college women. She worked hard to compete and achieve that. Yasmin made us in the university community proud with that recognition of her brilliance and promise. And yet, with that prize she was ordered to decline to accept the opportunity by her father, brother, and uncle. Their reasons were obscure but from what she told me as painful, as it was for her to say and bare, they all thought that she was not ready for the 'limelight' that that recognition would bring and that it would spoil her life; or she would certainly do something in that window of exposure that would embarrass the family.

I witnessed Yasmin as she turned 20, 21 and 22 with her depression and anxiety deepening – something for which she blamed herself. She was having careless accidents and physically hurting herself, caused by the distractions from being so depressed, she said. She soon, thereafter, told me of the growing cancer in her young body that had to be cut out again and again. I saw the cancer as being brought on by toxic stuck energy in her body stemming from her constant state of worry, sadness, and resentment of being under siege. Her exuberant energy that should be expressed in the world was instead, stagnant, spoiled, and turning in on her. In my wisdom, in addition to the cancer that befell Yasmin, I identified the other culprit at work: *'fear of the feminine'*.

The light within Yasmin, it seemed was blinding to her caretakers who were moved to tamp it down. That light was now becoming dimmed from her trials, but not for long. Time passed, and she still came for hugs. I nudged and at times demanded that she keep telling me her dreams and wants and goals as she used to do, with her haplessly admitting that she had none anymore. I expressed to Yasmin that her light was too fierce for defeat, and it would flicker to bright again and guide her back to her dreams. She was a true fighter and continued to come see me, to talk or just sit with her, and always for the hugs. It would take years, but she got through it and was becoming herself again, leaving the cancer behind.

Yasmin's experience may not be much different from any other young woman growing up in a world that struggled to understand, trust, and uplift the feminine. I'd seen that played out in many ways in other cultures, including my own. Living in Saudi Arabia brought that entire issue front and center for me - from all time, past, present and future. It was more than ever, hard to ignore as an essential part of the 'story' and the 'stories'.

Fear of the feminine had become a collective strain lasting through the ages, and part of what was hindering humanity's evolution. That legacy, that pattern, that ailment of humanity was not just 'peculiar' to the Middle East, Islamic cultures, Arabic men or just men. It was an individual and collective dynamic that was neither exclusive to men nor women. It was the alienation from the *divine feminine*, which was within every man and woman. That disconnect was at the root of much of the pain and suffering in the world and in personal lives. I supposed that was why I became so intrigued with how the Saudi women collectively exemplified the epitome of female qualities in a repressed culture, and with how men such as Noura's Muhammad respected and honored that.

It was complicated. Men's and even women's strain against the 'feminine' may have been taught, expected of them, or instilled from a hurtful experience with a mother figure or a slight from an important female in their past – a 'dislike' spawned from their legacy with women. People were psychologically predisposed that way; in some it was a blind spot, and in others a very conscious and wholesale indictment of the female species that was usually acted out on the women close to them or in general. Personally, much of the time I could ascertain how a man would treat me based on his relationships with the other women in his life – his sisters, his daughters, and especially his mother. It was an easy tell, a quintessential 'woman' thing. It also seemed to me that a man was at his best and more prone to be happy when his genuine love of women arose from his deep embrace of the feminine parts of himself. That was impossible to fake; and that principle applied to a woman, just as well in her relation to the masculine and the feminine within 'her-self'. I realized that the general antagonism directed towards women was not so much about the literal physicality or gender of 'female' but about the subtle qualities of the 'feminine' such as humility, collaboration, intuition, empathy, receptivity, vulnerability, etc. – qualities that people collectively believed had no relevance, value or push in a world long driven by hardy masculine values. That strain against 'HER', nonetheless, caused pain, upset, unhappy relationships and endings, and broken people. And whether individual or collective, it was an aberration of the human spirit.

The 'fear of the feminine', which had been so cogently studied and pondered was chalked up to the human malady to fear that which could not be understood - a tendency akin mostly to men. We lived with that verdict, and not well enough. The female could be a complexity, but not any more than the male. It was a complexity of a different kind, nonetheless, still feared and resisted. If we searched back far enough in time we would know that that was not always the case and far removed from the troubadours of the Middle Ages who aspired towards 'good' through 'love of woman,' and whereas during that time the meaning of the French word for love was 'feminine'.

Iconic minds such as Carl Jung, Abraham Maslow and Stanislaw Grof maintained that people, both individually and collectively, needed to recognize the inherent masculine and feminine aspects within everyone. Those men were original contributors of knowledge in that area. Jung stated: *"As a rule, a man needs the opposite of his actual condition to force him to find his place in the middle."* And: *"The undeniability of the one (masculine) must be matched by the compelling power of the other (feminine)."* Our feminine nature embodied vital universal energies, and our masculine nature expressed that in the world. Both had a role to play in a life. In essence, what helped us to evolve as individuals and as a humanity was to achieve a balance between the masculine and feminine forces. Individually, that balance was reached when both of those forces were integrated and involved in how we lived and how we reflected them through our gender identities as male or female. That brought us into harmony with ourselves. It was a process referred to in classical Christian mysticism as 'the path to the Sophia' – Sophia meaning 'wisdom' and the feminine aspect of God. Through self-reflection, awareness, and acceptance of our inner duality, the 'Sophia' state of being was achieved. Here, the phrase: *'As above, so below'* could be turned around to say *'As below, so above'* because peoples' individual 'evolutions' fostered humanity's evolution.

For every man who insulted, denigrated, or put the brakes on a woman, because she was a woman, there was one who celebrated and honored women. Saudi men championed women's advancement as much as women, working right alongside them in the Kingdom. I went to KSA with not just my eyes open, but also my mind and heart, and allowed myself to behold the wonders in the Arabian desert, thus capturing a stark view of what was going on between women and men. I knew about the restrictive lives of women in the Kingdom, even had that kind of life myself living and working there. I was aware that woman-hating and abuse were keenly associated with Arab men in the Kingdom. The oppression of women had certainly cast a thick dark cloud over them. But I also knew that not all men in the US were gun-wielding cowboys; nor was every white southerner a racist. People knew that, although America's legacy of slavery, racism, and the conquests of peoples and nation states had long drawn heightened global attention and rebuke.

I met a lot of Muhammads, both from Yasmin's and Noura's worlds. I saw that Noura's Muhammad was not the exception, but part of a multitude of men in the Kingdom of Saudi Arabia whom one from the outside might want to examine a little closer to appreciate. Noura's Muhammads were many and everywhere in men named Faisal, Ahmad, Khalid, Ibrahim, Fayed, Omar, Maged, Malik, Abdullah, Ali, and so on – men who could really see and allow the feminine 'her' fullest breadth and bloom. As to the meaning of the name Muhammad, praise can be afforded to those men, women, and nations as they aspired to reach that male to female equilibrium and even bliss. And it thrilled me to think of how that might play out in the Kingdom now that the long pent-up energies of women were flowing throughout the land.

The women who were rising in the Kingdom and in the world with the new vision and transformations would do so anyway; but they would do so a lot easier on the shoulders of the Muhammad's of women like Noura. And they would, perhaps model and teach sons and daughters how remarkable they could be when they felt good about both the girl and boy within them.

In Closing

Many moons have passed since my time of life under the abaya. Yet, much of what I experienced and witnessed seems so alive. Aspects of that life still informs, impresses upon, and feeds me. In sharing these forty-nine episodes I'd like to think that there is enough here that you might take away and perhaps make your own, wherever you are in your journey.

Blessings,
Dr. Elizabeth

About the Author

Dr. Elizabeth D. Taylor spent her entire career advancing the learning, development, and betterment of peoples in the world as a professor and leader at universities, as a business owner, visionary personal growth leader, media producer and author. She is the Founder and President of Wisdom To Go. She was a professor at universities in the US and abroad teaching a variety of subjects in business management and organizational development. As a guest lecturer, speaker, seminar leader, executive coach and dialogue specialist, Dr. Taylor worked with corporate leaders and staff on leadership, organizational  effectiveness and transformation, diversity, women's empowerment, conflict management, human resources management, life skills, visioning and complex problem-solving. She was invited to conduct 'reconciliation' dialogues in South Africa by the SA Minister of Education at the end of apartheid.

Dr. Taylor was a nationally syndicated radio talk show host, discussing topics of the day concerning personal and spiritual growth and development needs. In her research and quest for ever-expanding knowledge, Dr. Taylor engaged indigenous communities abroad focusing on personal growth and evolution, spirituality and native wisdoms in Central America, South America, Europe, Asia, Hawaii, Africa, the Caribbean and Middle East. Dr. Taylor most recently spent over five years in the Middle East as a university professor also involved with an inter-nation campaign for the education and advancement of Saudi women - acting as consultant and liaison between universities and corporations in the Kingdom.

Dr. Taylor holds a Ph.D. from the Union Institute & University in Organizational Psychology and Leadership, and a Master of Science from University of San Francisco in Human Behavior and Organizational Development. She is a specialist in Jungian depth psychology, metaphysics and mysticism, classical theories of human growth, and behavioral sciences. She is an award-winning author with several books under her wings, including, ***Straight Up! Teens' Guide to Taking Charge of Their Lives,*** for which Dr. Taylor received the American Library Award. ***Formula 9: Fortified Conscious Living for Modern Generations*** was launched in 2017 as a university textbook. From its success among college students, it is now on the scene as a commercial resource for larger audiences. ***Under the Abaya*** is a colorful telling of Dr. Taylor's 5-year immersion into the Kingdom of Saudi Arabia, and during its seminal period of transformation.

www.ingramcontent.com/pod-product-compliance
Lightning Source LLC
Chambersburg PA
CBHW020416010526
44118CB00010B/278